Wendy Doniger O'Flaherty

DREAMS ILLUSION and other REALITIES

The University of Chicago Press *Chicago and London*

Wendy Doniger O'Flaherty is Professor of History of Religions and Indian Studies in the Divinity School, the Department of South Asian Languages and Civilizations, the Committee on Social Thought, and the College at the University of Chicago. Among her previous publications are *Asceticism and Eroticism in the Mythology of Śiva*; *Hindu Myths: A Sourcebook Translated from the Sanskrit*; *The Origins of Evil in Hindu Mythology*; *The Rig Veda: An Anthology*; and *Women, Androgynes, and Other Mythical Beasts*.

The University of Chicago Press, Chicago 60637
The University of Chicago Press, Ltd., London

Printed in the United States of America

93 92 91 90 89 88 87 86 85 6 5 4 3 2

LIBRARY OF CONGRESS CATALOGING IN PUBLICATION DATA
O'Flaherty, Wendy Doniger.
Dreams, illusion, and other realities.

Includes tales from the "Yogavāsiṣṭha."
Bibliography: p.
Includes indexes.
1. Dreams. 2. Mythology, Indic. 3. Yogavāsiṣṭharāmāyaṇa. 4. Yoga—Early works to 1800. I. Yogavāsiṣṭharāmāyaṇa. II. Title.
BF1078.0'45 1984 111 83-17944
ISBN 0-226-61854-4

for David Grene

Contents

Illustrations

Guide to Pronunciation and Terminology

Sanskrit vowels are pronounced very much like Italian vowels, with the exception of the short *a*, which is pronounced like the *u* in the English word "but"; long *ā* is pronounced like the *a* in "father."

As for the consonants, a reasonable approximation will be obtained by pronouncing *c* as in "church," *j* as in "jungle," *ṣ* as in "shun," *s* as in "sun," and *ś* as something halfway between the other two *s*'s. The aspirated consonants should be pronounced distinctly: *bh* as in "cab horse," *dh* as in "madhouse," *gh* as in "doghouse," *ph* as in "top hat," and *th* as in "goatherd." *ṛ* is a vowel, pronounced midway between "ri" as in "rivet" and "er" as in "mother."

I have tried to be consistent in substituting English words for the various Sanskrit terms for different kinds of mental error. "Delusion" translates *moha*; "illusion" is *māyā*; and "mistake" is *bhrama* or *vibhrama* or *bhrānti*. I have called *pratibhāsa* "reflected image," *pramāṇa* "proof of knowledge" or "way of knowing" or "authority," *saṃvid* "conscious perception," *pratyakṣa* "direct perception" or "first-hand experience" or "before one's own eyes," and *vāsanā* "karmic memory trace." I have also tried to distinguish between the various castes of demons: Asuras (demons), Rākṣasas (ogres), Piśācas (ghouls or flesh-eating ogres), Vetālas (vampires), Pretas (ghosts), and Bhūtas (ghosts or has-beens). I have not tried to distinguish between the various castes of Untouchables but have used the word "Untouchable" to translate several different Sanskrit terms for people beyond the Aryan pale—Caṇḍālas, Pulkasas (or Pukkasas, or Puṣkasas), Śvapacas (Dog-cookers), Bhūtas (Spooks), and Kirāṭas (hunters).

The translations are all my own unless otherwise attributed, but they are often summaries of long texts rather than complete translations; I have added nothing, but I have left a lot out. In condensations of European texts, as in translations from the Sanskrit, something of the flavor of the original is inevitably lost, but I hope that the structure and some of the meanings still come through.

Acknowledgments

The ideas in this book first began to take shape at a symposium, organized jointly by the journal *Daedalus* and Emory University, which met in Atlanta on October 23–27, 1979; the papers read there were subsequently published as the Summer, 1980, issue of *Daedalus*. I am grateful not only to Stephen Graubard (editor of *Daedalus*) and James Laney (president of Emory) but to all of the other contributors to that symposium (particularly to Judith Shklar, Karl H. Pribram, James Boon, Stanley Cavell, Stephen Jay Gould, and Leon Cooper) for generating such fertile excitement in me and, indeed, in all who were present. The continued research for the book was made possible by a grant from the National Endowment for the Humanities, for the summer of 1980, and the John Simon Guggenheim Memorial Foundation, for 1980–81. A preliminary report on my researches formed the substance of the Sir George Birdwood Memorial Lecture of the Royal Society of Arts, delivered in London on May 20, 1980; the Royal Society of Arts also generously contributed to my expenses in obtaining the plates to illustrate that essay (which was published, under the title "Illusion and Reality in the *Yogavāsiṣṭha*," in the *Journal of the Royal Society of Arts*, January 1981: 104–23) and to illustrate this book. Preliminary versions of scattered parts of the book have been published as articles in *Daedalus* ("Inside and Outside the Mouth of God," Spring, 1980, pp. 93–125, and "The Dream Narrative and the Indian Doctrine of Illusion," Summer, 1982, pp. 93–113); in *Quadrant: The Journal of the C. G. Jung Foundation for Analytical Psychology* ("The Scientific Proof of Mythical Experience," Spring, 1981, pp. 46–65); in *Parabola* ("Hard and Soft Reality: The Indian Myth of the Shared Dream," Spring, 1982, pp. 55–65); and, in German, as "Der wissenschaftliche Beweis mythischer Erfahrung," pp. 430–56 of *Der Wissenschaftler und das Irrational*, edited by Hans Peter Duerr (Frankfurt: Syndikat, 1982).

I am grateful to the librarians of the Chester Beatty Library in Dublin for the great trouble they took in enabling me to use their manuscript of the *Yogavāsiṣṭha* on several occasions and for allowing me to reproduce several illustrations from it in this book. It was also most helpful to me to be able to present parts of the work in progress in the form of lectures, first at the American Museum of Natural History in New York, under the joint sponsorship of the C. G. Jung Foundation and the Museum, on March 22, 1981; then as the Foerster Lecture on the Immortality of the Soul, at the University of California at Berkeley, on March 9, 1982; then as the Mead-Swing Lectures at Oberlin College, March 22–25, 1982; as the Otis Lectures at Wheaton College, October 25–27, 1982; as the invited lecture at the South Asian Conference of the University of Wisconsin at Madison, on November 5, 1982; at a panel of the American Academy of Religion meeting in New York on December 21, 1982, organized by Jack Hawley and chaired by Edward C. Dimock; as the Snuggs Lectures at the University of Tulsa, March 14–16, 1983; and, finally, as a course of lectures at the University of Chicago in the spring quarter, 1983.

The Joint Committee on South Asia of the American Council of Learned Societies and the Social Science Research Council awarded me a generous grant to pursue my studies of the relationship between mythology and science, of which I was able to spend only a small fraction (to take Thomas Kuhn and Leonard Nash to lunch). David White made the Index of Names and Terms.

I am grateful to Allen Thrasher, A. K. Ramanujan, Arnaldo Momigliano, James Boon, Sir Ernst Gombrich, Richard F. Gombrich, Sudhir Kakar, David Shulman, Susan Wadley, Gail Hinich, William K. Mahony, John Castelein, and Dorothy Stein for detailed and sensitive responses to the first draft; to Jacob Arlow and Martin Stein for discussions about the relationship between psychoanalysis and mythology; to Leonard Nash, Stephen Toulmin, Thomas Kuhn, David Szanton, and Clifford Geertz for discussions on religion and science; to Anthony C. Yu for help with the Chinese sources; to Ed Hamlin for help with the *Lankāvatārasūtra*; to David Shulman for help with the Tamil sources; and to John Strong for the Kunāla legend. I am beholden to several of my students for permission to quote from their unpublished essays and translations: Gail Hinich, David White, Philip Lutgendorf, Paula Richman, Sean Dwan, June McDaniel, and Stephen Gabel.

This book is dedicated to David Grene, who first inspired me to search out the *Yogavāsiṣṭha* in Dublin, who read every word of every draft, who cheered me on when I hesitated to rush in where classicists and philosophers feared to tread, who chastised me for sloppy thinking and breathless writing, who manfully (but in vain) wrestled with the temptation to tell me what Plato had said about each point raised by the Indian tradition, and, above all, who kept urging me to say what I really thought, myself, about all of this.

Derrycark, Belturbet, Ireland
July 14, 1983

DREAMS ILLUSION and other REALITIES

Introduction: Transformation and Contradiction

This is a book about myths, dreams, and illusion. It is about the ways in which they are alike, the ways in which they are different, and what each teaches us about reality. Transformations of one sort or another are at the heart of myths; Ovid called his great compendium of Greek and Roman mythology *Metamorphoses*. Transformations are particularly characteristic of the great Hindu myths, and here they may appear to take different forms: sometimes they are regarded as actual changes in the physical nature of the world, sometimes as illusions, sometimes as dreams, sometimes as temporary magic changes in the physical nature of the world, sometimes as the unveiling of another level of reality. If the storyteller sets out to tell a tale of illusion, various transformations may seem to take place, in waking life or in dreams, but in the end we cannot tell whether anything has happened or not. If the storyteller sets out to tell a tale of dreams, he may relate events that seem to be physically unreal but turn out, at last, to be real. If he sets out to tell a tale of magic, he may describe some physical transformation that a magician or a god actually caused to take place. And if he sets out to tell a tale of revelation, he may describe events that peel back the physical veil to reveal another, more mystical, reality that was always there but not recognized.

These stories tend to blend into one another; a story that starts out as a tale of magic, or even explicitly announces (as many do) that it is going to be a tale of magic, may be transformed into a tale of illusion. Sometimes it is only the genre of the story, marked by the presence of certain motifs conventionally associated with one sort of transformation or another, that lets us know whether the story is intended to depict a dream or a magic show. These interactions and interchanges are not the result of simple borrowing, back and forth, between related themes. One sort of transformation often becomes transformed, as it were, into another sort of transformation in mid-story because one of the points of the story is to demonstrate how difficult it is to tell one sort of transformation from another.

The tales of dreams suggest, for instance, that dreaming and waking partake of the same reality, which is both spiritual and physical (chapter one). That they do so is the point of the myths of shared dreams (chapter two). The tales of illusion go on to suggest that we cannot tell whether we are awake or asleep during our experience of many sorts of transformation, nor can we judge which half of the dream/waking experience is more real. This is the point of the myths of the mouth of God (chapter three). And the tales of magic may be given a twist at the end to show that the enchanted man, or the dreamer, cannot be certain that he has awakened from the last of a series of dreams within dreams. This is the point of the myths of the receding frame (chapter four). Finally, the dreamer who believes that he is in the last frame of his own dream may still be forced to consider the possibility that he is part of someone else's dream. This is the point of the myths of the dreamer dreamt (chapter five).

The stories in this book are themselves examples of yet another kind of transformation, the transformation of human experience into words and images through narrative. Both dreams and myths draw their vocabularies from certain intense moments in actual human experience, but it is art that transforms those moments, bringing them from the private realm of the dream into the public realm of the myth. Moreover, our awareness of the experience of art allows us to perceive ourselves as we become aware of the experience of life; art allows us to watch ourselves having the illusion of life (chapter six).

One of the most intense mythic experiences is the experience of events that make us question our certainty about what is real and what is not. From the Indian point of view, the basic condition of human experience is the condition of illusion (chapter three). When we glimpse the power of illusion in waking life, we may resist it or misunderstand it; but when the barriers of rational thought are lowered during sleep, we dream about illusion—that is, we dream about things that turn out to be different from what they seemed to be, about things that seem to be transformed, back and forth, from one shape into another (chapters one and two). When we wake, we may subject these insights to various forms of tests, attempting thus to establish some relationship between the reality of the dream and the reality of waking life (chapter four). But whatever the results of these tests, we find ourselves ultimately facing an ontological cul-de-sac that renders the tests meaningless and requires a leap of faith if we are to guess what is real and what is not (chapter five). This leap is an imaginative, artistic act of creation and discovery (chapter six).

Each chapter turns on its own set of narrative subthemes, though these often spill over into other chapters. These themes include dream transformation—the adventure of the hero who flies or rides to the woman in the other world (chapter two); illusory transformation—change of sex or the creation of a double self or double world (chapter three); social transformation—the dramatic change in status of the king or Brahmin who becomes an Untouchable (chapter four); ontological transformation—rebirth as another person or an animal (chapter five); and artistic transformation—metaphor and simile (chapter six).

All of these themes occur throughout the range of classical Indian texts, and chapters one, two, and three will provide the classical Indian treatment of them, beginning with the earliest recorded text (the *Ṛg Veda*) and continuing through the medieval Sanskrit Purāṇas into contemporary folktales. But in chapters four and five (and at scattered moments in other chapters as well) I will concentrate on one particular Sanskrit text, the *Yogavāsiṣṭha*, composed in Kashmir sometime between the ninth and twelfth centuries A.D. (Appendix Three provides a list of the stories from the *Yogavāsiṣṭha* that are cited in this book.)

Although all of my main texts are Indian, my arguments rest on a comparison of Indian and non-Indian (primarily ancient Greek and twentieth-century European) approaches to dreams and illusion, and this often involves the citing of non-Indian texts and arguments. Many Western parallels occurred to me as I wrote this book; others will, I am sure, occur to each reader. But I made a strenuous effort to leave most of them out of this final version, in order to highlight the Indian texts. I have had recourse to the Western texts that I have used, not in the hope of saying anything about them that has not been said before by scholars better versed in the Western tradition than I am, but as an aid to understanding the ideas expressed in the Indian texts. It is, in any case, impossible for us to ignore our own assumptions and preconceptions when we read foreign texts, and only by examining those assumptions, to see what it is that makes us find the Indian texts so puzzling, can we hope to understand why some Indians did *not* find them puzzling, while others did.

The inclusion of these Western texts thus serves a kind of psychological or epistemological purpose: it helps us to understand how we understand the Indian texts. But it is meant to serve an ontological purpose as well: to help us understand the actual problem set by the Indian texts. For our understanding of the Indian ideas is greatly enhanced when we reflect on the insights provided by some of our own sages who have thought long and deep about these same problems.

Rather than muddy the waters by mixing together the Indian and non-Indian theories on every minor point, I have grouped the Western theories together at the end of each of the first five chapters, giving by far the greater weight to the Indian texts, which are lesser known by most people and better known by me. But I would encourage the Western reader to keep both approaches in mind simultaneously as much as possible, one hovering in the wings while the other occupies center stage, and to allow each one to come forth when it has something to say, like the little man and the little woman balanced on an old-fashioned weather-house barometer. It is artificial to go on separating the two approaches forever; I have treated both traditions, Indian and Western, together in the introduction and conclusion, in the final section of chapter six, and from time to time throughout the entire book. Yet, though the two approaches to many of the same problems are, I think, mutually illuminating, they are never truly comparable; for even when the content seems superficially the same, the different cultural contexts often show us that the apparent congruences are the same answers to different questions—and are therefore not the same answers at all.

The reader should also be warned that I have mingled not merely Indian and Western arguments and Indian and Western stories but stories and arguments themselves. I have made a general attempt to separate texts from arguments in chapters one through four, but in chapter five they are formally combined, and in fact there are arguments that link stories throughout the book. In this I am imitating the tradition about which I am writing; that is, the form of my book mirrors its content. Unconsciously, I found myself swinging between text and commentary, as the *Yogavāsiṣṭha* itself does (see chapter four), and as, in fact, all Purāṇas do. This book may therefore be read as a kind of American academic Purāṇa, leading the reader from one story into another and another and another, with commentary provided as necessary. Moreover, like the Purāṇas, I have felt free to borrow from any tradition that seems relevant to the point, using not only classics from other countries but folk traditions, limericks, and children's books. That the classics are not only Indian ones does not, I think, nullify the Purāṇic nature of this book, for a Western audience would react to these classics as an Indian audience would react to the Indian classics usually cited in Purāṇas; the effect is thus comparable (though, again, not the same).

But a Western audience may perhaps have more trouble in following the pattern of thought in a Purāṇic text (like this book) than an Indian audience would have. Mine is not a tightly structured argument; it is an argument, I hope, but one that feels free to digress and switch back on itself, to wander into bywaters before flowing on to its next stopping point. Because this is a book that tells stories within stories, the reader may think it is all over when one story ends—but it is not over; each final point turns out to be merely the halfway mark of another final point, which is in itself . . . , and so forth. By way of apology and exhortation, I say, Have courage; all the points are meant to be points, and the book *does* end.

I have already admitted one thing that this book does not intend to do: it does not intend to give anything like a complete (or even balanced) view of the Western approaches to the problems raised by dreams and illusion. There are many other things that it does not attempt to do. Historians should not expect a steady chronological development; though a few points are traced through their history where that history seems relevant to their final form, most of the time I have drawn on any text that serves my purpose at a given moment. Anthropologists should not expect a thick description; such data are rarely available for the periods in which most of my texts were composed and are seldom relevant to the arguments I wish to make. This is a book about the history of ideas; it is not a history of social forms or customs. In chapter four (pp. 158–60) I will defend this principle of selection and interpretation at some length. Here I will simply say that my procedure can be defended on the basis of its sympathy with the procedure of the texts with which I am dealing, texts that steadfastly deny us any possible access to the sort of material that anthropologists and historians might hope for, because the Indian authors do not regard such information as relevant to the problem of dreams and illusion. I take quite seriously the conventions of genre and the multiple voices and viewpoints of illusioning illusion, and from this vantage I attempt to ask certain questions of Indian as well as non-Indian stories and theories. The free-wheeling form that results from this process was, I think, well characterized by the reader of an early draft of this book, who described it as "an intricate compilation of texts that sets both Hindu and Buddhist themes into mutual plays of illusioning—kings' views of monks' views of Harijans' views of women's views of men's views of hedonist views of asceticism's view of Vedic views of philosophic views of inverse views of all these views viewed from outside and inside and before and after in foreshadowings and flashbacks of lives now and then and ultimately or cyclically extinguished . . . and all that."[1] This is a spiraling rather than a linear approach, and it will, I fear, exasperate the sorts of people who like to be able to make outlines of the structure of an argument.

I have used as wide a range of theoretical tools in the interspersed analyses as I have used genres in the texts themselves. Because each chapter takes up a different facet of the problem of reality and illusion, I use different hermeneutical tools, both Indian and Western, at different points. Though each is particularly relevant to a single chapter, they blend into one another, just as the themes themselves do, and they may make brief reappearances in chapters other than those in which they make their principal contributions. In chapter one, I draw on Plato, Freud, Piaget, and several contemporary anthropologists in order to analyze the Indian approach to dreams. In chapter two I have recourse to the Jungian concept of the archetypes. In chapter three I make use of classical Indian philology and Western epistemology to analyze the theory of illusion. Chapter four involves the philosophy of science, particularly the writings of Sir Karl Popper, Thomas Kuhn, and Michael Polanyi. To come to terms with the paradox of the dreamer dreamt, in chapter five, I have found certain Western logical paradoxes useful, particularly as reformulated by Douglas Hofstadter. And finally, in chapter six, I have relied on Sir Ernst Gombrich to illuminate the use of illusion in art.

This is the moment when I ought to produce, like a rabbit out of a hat, a working definition of reality. I cannot do this; the whole book is my rabbit. The man in the street (in India and in the West) has hunches about reality, and he vaguely supports these by resting on various authorities he does not really understand. Because of this rather wobbly ontological base, he is always trying to gather some sort of positive evidence to support his hunches, and, if you push him hard, he will fall back on ad hoc definitions in order to defend his primitive beliefs. The stories in this book press on the raw ontological nerve in that way; they show us what we have believed but not defined. Indeed, some of these beliefs cannot be defined; as Isadora Duncan is said to have remarked, when asked what one of her dances meant, "If I could tell you, I would not have to dance it."

When we speak of reality, we are usually referring to a cluster of assumptions. We do not have a set of precise definitions of reality in our heads—indeed, we usually do not bother to define reality at all—but we somehow assume (usually with good reason) that we all agree on what we mean. In general, we mean that reality is what we value, what we care about. But often we mean something far more specific, more debatable, less relative than this. Some of us mean that reality is what is solid; others mean that reality is what is *not* solid. We tend to assume that our way of thinking is simply an expression of common sense, the most obvious way of understanding and manipulating the everyday world. But since common sense carries with it an implicit definition of reality, to define reality in terms of common sense is to commit a tautology. Common sense, as Einstein once remarked, is what we are taught by the age of six; that is, common sense is an attribute of culture, not of nature, a part of myth rather than a part of reality. As scientists and artists become more adventurous in restructuring their reality, common sense is thrust unceremoniously into a dusty old attic, along with the astrolabes and the perpetual-motion machines. As Clifford Geertz has shown, common sense is a highly variable cultural construct, involving massive a priori judgments;[2] yet each culture thinks that it not only knows what common sense is but knows how common sense differs from other ways of viewing the world—ways that may be, but are not necessarily, mystical or magical.

In the West common sense is often treated as if it were the same as the scientific point of view, but it is not. Reality is not a problem for physicists, except in the most trivial realm of accuracy of measurement; their stable sense of what is real is taken for granted long before they reach for a slide rule.[3] Common sense is any world-view that is assumed a priori. Scientists have one—or, rather, several; nonscientists have others; and mystics have theirs. (The Hindus, as we shall see in chapter four, admit from the start that common sense is not an authoritative source of knowledge.) Newtonian (and Freudian) ideas have certainly helped to construct our common sense, but most of us do not usually read or indeed use Newton (or Freud) in our daily, common-sense lives. Our common-sense view of reality is so deeply embedded in us that it is unlikely that any single definition would satisfy us or would meet with general acceptance.

There are two basic lines of common sense in the West, one derived from Plato and the Christian tradition, the other derived from Hume and Locke and scientific empiricism. These two world-views are so dramatically opposed that it is remarkable that our culture has been able to hold them in suspension for as long as it has. It makes no sense, therefore, to speak of a "Western" view without specifying whether we have in mind Plato or Hume. Yet we *do* speak of "the West," just as we speak of an "Indian" view, and some limited purpose is served by such generalizations. In selecting "Western" texts to contrast with my (equally selected) "Indian" texts, I have chosen those that provide the most dramatic (and often the most extreme) antithesis within each culture. This may give a misleading impression of the schizophrenia of Western ontology; it may also provide a more striking contrast with the Indian point of view than might have appeared had I chosen texts from other, perhaps more recondite, Western traditions. But one of my central concerns is to show the contrast between what *most* people think and what philosophers think, not only in the West but in India, and another is to show the contrast between what most people think in India and what most people think in the West. To make such contrasts, one is necessarily led to concentrate on the famous Western credos. To have dealt more fairly with the Western tradition in all of its complexity would have weighed this book far too heavily away from the Indian materials that are its primary *raison d'être*.

It is useful to distinguish, however tentatively, between the two major Western approaches to the problem of reality. Most people think that reality is physical, public, external, and somehow "hard," and they think that what is not real is mental, private, internal, and somehow "soft" (chapter three).[4] The terms hard and soft are also used to distinguish people who accept this distinction (hard thinkers) from those who feel that *all* phenomena (physical or mental, public or private, external or internal) are equally hard and soft (soft thinkers). Hard thinkers think that you should always define, sharply, at the start, what you think and that you should always continue to think it; soft thinkers feel that you can play it by ear and shift your definitions as your understanding grows. Hard thinkers think that you cannot believe two contradictory things at once; soft thinkers think that you can. These definitions are self-referential: soft thinkers do not think that they, or hard thinkers, exist as a separate category; hard thinkers think that they do. In the light of my attitude to the terms "hard" and "soft," I would be called a soft thinker by people who think that there is such a thing as a soft thinker as opposed to a hard thinker—a distinction that I would challenge, as a soft thinker should, though I used it myself only a few paragraphs back. The metaphysical implications of such a circular definition, spiraling in upon itself, will be discussed in chapter five, in the analysis of the dreamer dreamt. But within both the Indian and the Western traditions we will encounter thinkers that hard thinkers would define as hard and thinkers that hard thinkers would define as soft.

"Hard" and "soft" are lamentably gross terms for dealing with the complexities of ontology. The assumption implicit in their use—the fond hope that reality can be pinned down so simply—is so full of holes that one could drive a carriage and pair through it. In the course of this book, the inadequacy of hard and soft as basic terms will become increasingly apparent, and once we have used them to scramble up, untidily, to a spot from which there is a good metaphysical view, we will kick them out from under us, ungratefully. Still, it is not easy to replace them with other, more satisfactory, terms. This is so because the conceptual dichotomy that they represent—and that will be represented, in turn, by any similar pair of contrasting terms—is itself at fault.

How is it that the myths in which these categories are blurred seem to violate common sense, and why is it that people have attempted to apply hard scientific criteria to phenomena that they themselves have defined as soft? This is the question that will be asked in chapter four. Here the problem of common sense—that is, the conflict between common sense and other primitive beliefs—comes into sharper focus as it conflicts with both soft phenomena (the experience of dreams) and hard criteria (the standards of scientific falsifiability). At this point, the argument runs aground on the problem of contradiction. I have just now maintained that hard thinkers think that you cannot believe two contradictory things at once, while soft thinkers think that you can. We owe to Plato our belief that it is impossible at one time to hold contradictory opinions about the same thing; many Indian texts, by contrast, would argue that, if two ideas clash, both may be true.[5]

Sir Ernst Gombrich has formulated several questions that are highly relevant to our present inquiries:

> Do all cultures make the same radical distinction between "appearance" and "reality" which ours has inherited from Plato? Are their hierarchies the same? In other words, do they necessarily accept the demand that contradictions must be ironed out and that all perceptions that clash with beliefs must force us either to change our views of the "objective world" or declare the perception to have been a subjective experience—an illusion? Even in our rationalist culture we don't often live up to this logical precept. We try to evade it, especially when our emotions are involved.[6]

Many Indian texts are troubled by contradiction; their attitude in this may seem to us Platonic. And all of them distinguish, at least nominally, between appearance and reality. But they do *not* ultimately iron out the contradictions; they alter their definitions of reality in order to let the contradictions survive intact.

For we find, often side by side in the same Indian text (such as many of the myths in this book), two basically contradictory views of the world. These views interact in ways that cannot be entirely contained within the categories of hard and soft. The first is the world-view preserved in the *Ṛg Veda* (c. 1200 B.C.) as well as in many Purāṇas and vernacular devotional texts from the medieval period and even in present-day India. This world-view holds that worldly life (*saṃsāra*) is real and good; to be born, to eat, to make love, and to work are real experiences that one values and hopes to go on experiencing as long as possible, even in as many rebirths as possible. The *Kauṣītaki Upaniṣad*[7] suggests that a man who has died travels to the moon as a way-station in the round of rebirth; there he may ask to be engendered by a man in a woman, or else he may proceed to a world from which there is no rebirth. Though this passage is apparently unique in the Upaniṣads, the idea that, given a choice, one might choose rebirth rather than *mokṣa* (release) is characteristic of much of later Hinduism. Purāṇic Hinduism rejects *mokṣa* implicitly, for Hindus in their private *pūjās* and in their temple worship ask the gods not for *mokṣa* but for health, children, and, sometimes, rebirth as another, better, human being. The Hinduism of *bhakti* (devotion) rejects *mokṣa* explicitly, often mocking the ascetics, who have become stuck in this inferior religious goal instead of progressing to the higher goal of eternal life in the heaven of the loving god. The commitment to the goal of *saṃsāra* is thus both ancient and still widespread in India. In this view, death and dreams are also real, an essential part of living and waking experience. To a limited extent, this might be seen as a hard view of reality. Against this we might set the world-view that first appears in the Upaniṣads (c. 700 B.C.) and continues throughout Indian tradition to this day; it, too, is found in the Purāṇas and the devotional texts, as well as in the *Yogavāsiṣṭha*. This view holds that birth, sex, and marriage are not good and that the wise man seeks release (*mokṣa*) from them and from the whole vortex of worldly life (*saṃsāra*). Both views *believe* in both *mokṣa* and *saṃsāra* as true facts of human life, but they *value* them differently; *mokṣa* is what is real for one, while *saṃsāra* is what is real for the other—real in the sense of valued, and hence true.

But the *mokṣa* school is Janus-faced in its turn, for it exists in two significantly different forms. One, which we might characterize as soft, is the school of extreme idealism; it maintains that everything that we think of as real (our lives) or unreal (our dreams) is in fact illusion—equally real and unreal. Yet something else *is* real, and that something is Godhead (*brahman*).[8] (The very softest view of all, denying the reality even of Godhead, is limited to a few esoteric Buddhist and Hindu schools, to which I will refer only in passing.) The second significant form of the *mokṣa* view, a kind of modified idealism (or modified realism) or hard-soft school, argues that there *is* something real in the world but that we constantly mistake it for something that is unreal. Moreover, since it is often impossible to know when we are making this mistake, it is impossible to know precisely what *is* real. This is, I think, the dominant Indian view, but it often appears interwoven with more realistic (*saṃsāra*-slanted) or more idealistic (*mokṣa*-slanted or Buddhist-influenced) views.

We have seen that there are at least two major kinds of common sense in the West—Platonic and empiricist—and that we usually feel constrained to choose one or the other. Both are indeed still strong in our culture, and because of their strength we continue to see them engage in serious combat. We see it when our legal system (materialist) steps in between Christian Scientist parents and their child, whose life may be threatened by the parents' confidence that God (spirit) will cure the body as well as the soul. We see it in the passionate, though still confused, arguments about creationism versus Darwin. In India, too, there are two modes of common sense: common sense A (*saṃsāra*-linked, and materialistic) and common sense B (*mokṣa*-linked, and idealistic). But Indians are often able to hold both kinds of common sense in their heads at once and to reconcile both kinds with their perceptions of their lives. In the West only a gaggle of professional metaphysicians or fanatics will have enough genuine familiarity with such ideas to be able to internalize them and act on them instinctively, but Indian children learn about metaphysics as Western children learn about sex, on the street.

In order to illustrate these ideas, I have selected the myths in this book out of thousands of stories in Indian texts. I chose them because I think they are deeply important to Indian culture but also because they are full of meaning for us. True, one could have made a different selection to illustrate other facets of Indian thought; it is notoriously simple to prove *anything* with citations from the great compendia of Indian texts, so rich is their pluralism. But I would argue that the themes in this book are truly central, and in support of this contention I would point to the great number and variety of the tellings and retellings of the myths about them. I have collected here only a fraction of these subspecies; most of the myths in this book are paradigms for many others.

The various Indian approaches to the problem of reality are woven in and out of a tradition that spans three thousand years and reached its climax in the masterpiece of Indian philosophical narrative, the *Yogavāsiṣṭha*. My goal is to set that text in its cultural context and to listen to what it tells us about illusion, dreams, and myths.

1 The Interpretation of Dreams

The Western assumption that dreams are softer (more subjective, false, private, transient, and illusory) than the hard facts of waking life (which we think of as objective, true, public, permanent, and real) is an assumption that is not shared by Indian texts devoted to the meaning of dreams. Indian medicine and philosophy do not recognize the distinction between two aspects of dream analysis that is made by Roger Caillois, who speaks of "two types of problems concerning dreams that have always puzzled men's minds." The first is the meaning of the images inside the dream; the second is "the degree of reality that one may attribute to the dream," which depends on our understanding of the relationship between dreaming and waking.[1]

The two aspects of dreams merge from the very start in India, since one word (*svapna*, etymologically related to the Greek *hypnos*) designates both the *content* of dreaming—i.e., the images in the dream, the actual dream that one "sees"—and the *form* of dreaming—the process of sleeping (including the process of dreaming), which involves the relationship between the dream and the waking world. The first is what we would regard as the soft or subjective aspect of the dream, visible only to the dreamer; the second we think of as the objective or hard aspect of the dream, visible to other observers. The first is what we examine on the psychoanalyst's soft couch; the second we analyze with the hardware of the sleep laboratory.

Indian Texts

Dreams in Vedic and Medical Texts

The earliest Indian reference to dreams, in the *Ṛg Veda* (c. 1200 B.C.), describes a nightmare, but it leaves ambiguous the question whether what is feared is merely the experience of the dream (the process of having a bad dream) or the content of the dream (the events in the dream and the implication that it will come true): "If someone I have met or a friend has spoken of danger to me in a dream to frighten me, or if a thief should waylay us, or a wolf—protect us from that." Are the thief and the wolf part of the dream, too, or part of a contrasting reality? A different sort of ambiguity is posed by the waking dream, which is mentioned in the *Ṛg Veda* as an evil that one wishes to visit on one's enemies.[2] Yet another Ṛg Vedic verse tells of an incubus who bewitches a sleeping woman in her dream. He shades off into the actual person who rapes the woman, either by transforming himself when she is awake or by manipulating her mind when she is bewitched by the demonic powers of illusion:

> The one who by changing into your brother, or your husband, or your lover lies with you, who wishes to kill your offspring—we will drive him away from here. The one who bewitches you with dream or darkness and lies with you—we will drive him away from here.[3]

These scattered references reveal an assumed link not only between the worlds of dream and magic but between the worlds of dream and reality. They also give us an indication of what the ancient Indians thought people dreamed about: a friend warning of danger, a thief's attack, a wolf, or being raped by someone who assumes an illusory form. These motifs recur in later Indian dream books and myths about dreams.

By the time of the Upaniṣads (c. 700 B.C.), the question of the reality of dreams was approached in a more systematic way. These texts speak of four states of being: waking, dreaming, dreamless sleep (all natural states), and the supernatural, transcendent fourth state, the identity with Godhead.[4] Later Indian texts concentrated much of their attention on the first and fourth levels, waking and Godhead, and on the ways in which waking is a distorted image of Godhead. Dreamless sleep and dreaming are the intermediate steps: dreamless sleep gives us a glimpse of the true *brahman*, the divine mind that does not create; dreaming sleep gives us a glimpse of the god (Viṣṇu or Rudra) who creates us by dreaming us into existence.

Other Upaniṣads add certain significant details to the outline of the four states. Waking, one knows what is outside and is common to all men; dreaming, one knows what is inside, and one enjoys what is private.[5] The private, internal nature of dreams is emphasized: "When he goes to sleep, these worlds are his. . . . Taking his senses with him, he moves around wherever he wishes inside his own body."[6] The fact that the dream exists only inside the body of the dreamer does not, however, imply that it is unreal, as such a dichotomy (inside vs. outside, private vs. public) might imply in Western thinking. The fourth state, which is called the Self (*ātman*), is the one in which one knows neither inside nor outside; but the dreamer in the second state, it is often said, knows both of these. The third state, deep, dreamless sleep, may also have the creative qualities that are usually associated with dreaming (the second state): in deep sleep, the sleeper constructs (*minoti*) this whole world and becomes its doomsday (*apīti*).[7] The dream of a universe created and destroyed is a theme that we will often encounter in Indian texts.

The question of the reality of the dream world is taken up in discussions of dreams as projections. The verb *sṛj*, used to express projection, means literally to "emit" (as semen, or words), and it frequently occurs in stories about the process of creation (*sarga*, from *sṛj*) in which the Creator emits the entire universe from himself the way a spider emits a web:[8]

> A man has two conditions: in this world and in the world beyond. But there is also a twilight juncture: the condition of sleep [or dream, *svapna*]. In this twilight juncture one sees both of the other conditions, this world and the other world. . . . When someone falls asleep, he takes the stuff of the entire world, and he himself takes it apart, and he himself builds it up, and by his own bright light he dreams. . . . There are no chariots there, no harnessings, no roads; but he emits chariots, harnessings, and roads. There are no joys, happinesses, or delights there; but he emits joys, happinesses, and delights. There are no ponds, lotus pools, or flowing streams there, but he emits ponds, lotus pools, and flowing streams. For he is the Maker [Kartṛ].[9]

This text has not yet reached the extreme idealism of certain later schools (particularly Mahāyāna Buddhism) that suggest that *all* perception is the result of projection; rather, in one particular liminal state the dreamer is able to understand the relationship between the two worlds, both of them equally real and unreal. The dreamer takes apart the elements of the outside world and, like a *bricoleur*, rebuilds them into an inside world of dreams, without affecting their reality status. The text does not pass judgment on the substantiality of the elements out of which the external world is built and the internal world is rebuilt; the same verb is used, here and throughout Indian literature, to denote one's perception of both worlds: one "sees" (*dṛś*) the world just as one "sees" a dream. Moreover, the same verb (*sṛj*) that encompasses the concepts of seminal emission (making people), creation (making worlds), speaking (making words), imagining (making ideas), and dreaming (making images) is also used for the simple physical process by which a turtle "emits" (i.e., stretches forth) its limbs, and this is one reason why God is often visualized as a turtle.

In the Upaniṣadic view, the nature of the content of dreams—the subjective reality of dreams—is closely related to the problem of the status, or objective reality, of dreams. The texts tell us the sorts of things that people dream about: "The dreamer, like a god, makes many forms for himself, sometimes enjoying pleasure with women, sometimes laughing, and even seeing things that terrify him. . . . People seem to be killing him, overpowering him, stripping his clothes from him; he seems to be falling into a hole, to be experiencing unpleasant things, to weep."[10] The pupil to whom this doctrine is expounded (Indra, the king of the gods) comes to realize that, because such violent things could not happen to the transcendent Self, the self that one sees in dreams cannot be truly identical with that transcendent Self or Godhead. The nature of dream experiences—their emotion and instability—is taken here as evidence of the inadequacy of dreams as witnesses of reality. Many later philosophers, including Śankara, continued to argue that dreams are less real than waking experience, though the unreality of dreams was taken as a clue to the fact that waking experience, too, is less real than Godhead.

The four Upaniṣadic stages of being also suggest a technique of realization, a means of approaching enlightenment. For if one understands that one is, in fact, dreaming when one thinks that one is awake, one can begin to move toward the true awakening that is enlightenment—the fourth stage. Thus, it is argued in the *Yogavāsiṣṭha*, when we take the material universe to be the ultimate reality, we make a mistake comparable to the mistake someone makes when he thinks he sees his head cut off in a dream,[11] a traditional image in Indian dream books. The metaphor of the dream is further developed:

> When someone dreams while he is awake, as when one sees two moons or a mirage of water, that is called a waking dream. And when someone throws off such a dream, he reasons, "I saw this just for a short time, and so it is not true." Though one may have great confidence in the object that is experienced when one is asleep, as soon as sleep is over one realizes that it was a dream.[12]

These texts argue that what we call waking life is truly a kind of dream, from which we will awaken only at death. The minor mistakes that we make in confusing waking, dreaming, and dreamless sleep are a clue to the entirely different nature of Godhead, which is not really in the same series at all.

Many of these Upaniṣadic concepts persist even in present-day Indian medicine as practiced by the Āyurvedic physicians, or *vaids*:

> The *vaids* maintain that the widely held belief that we are in the waking state ("consciousness") during the daytime is delusionary. In fact, even while awake, dreaming is the predominant psychic activity. Here they seem to be pre-empting Jung's important insight that we continually dream but that consciousness while waking makes such a noise that we do not "hear" the dream.[13]

Indian dream theory not only blurs the line between dreaming and waking but emphasizes the importance of dreaming as a kind of mediator between two relatively rare extremes—waking and dreamless sleep. In fact, the Upaniṣadic fourth stage, added to the triad, is the whole point of the original analysis; called simply *turīya*, "the fourth," it is, in a sense, "the first three all in all,"[14] the true state toward which the other three point. And since all four stages are regarded as progressive approaches toward what is most real (Godhead), some Indian philosophers assume that dreaming is more "real" than waking. In dreams one sees both the real (*sat*) and the unreal (*asat*),[15] and this liminal nature of dreams is the key to the material power they possess in later Indian texts. The content of the dream is explicitly related to the objective world: "If during rites done for a wish one sees a woman in his dreams, he should know that he has seen success in this dream vision."[16] The particular significance of the woman in the dream is also highly relevant to later Indian dream analysts.

The significance of the content of the dream was the subject of the sixty-eighth appendix of the *Atharva Veda*, composed in the sixth century A.D. This text organized dreams with reference to the objective, waking world—for example, according to the physical temperament of the dreamer (fiery, watery, or windy), the time of night the dream took place, and so forth—but it was primarily concerned with the subjective symbolism of dreams or, rather, with the objective results of subjective contents. This is also apparent from the fact that the chapter on the interpretation of dreams is immediately adjacent to the chapter on the interpretation of omens or portents; that is, the things that happen inside people have the same weight as the things that happen outside them and are to be interpreted within the same symbolic system.

The first chapter of this text describes the dreams that people of particular temperaments will have. The fiery (choleric) man will see in his dreams tawny skies and the earth and trees all dried up, great forest fires and parched clothes, limbs covered with blood and a river of blood, gods burning things up, and comets and lightning that burn the sky. Tortured by heat and longing to be cool, he will plunge into forest ponds and drink. Mocked by women, he will pine away and become exhausted. These are the symbols (*lakṣaṇe*) by which the dreams of fiery people are to be recognized. The dreamer in this text creates an entire world, with planets and trees and everything else; and it is a world marked by his own inner heat. By contrast, watery (phlegmatic) people construct cool rivers in their dreams—rivers covered with snow—and clear skies and moons and swans; the women in their dreams are washed with fine water and wear fine clothes. Windy (bilious) men see flocks of birds and wild animals wandering about in distress, staggering and running and falling from heights, in lands where the mountains are whipped by the wind; the stars and the planets are dark, and the orbits of the sun and moon are shattered.[17]

On the simplest level (the level of primary interest to the Indian medical texts), dreams reflect the psychosomatic condition of the dreamer; for example, when a particular bodily sense is disturbed, the dreamer will dream of the objects of that sense.[18] But there are other causes of dreams, as well, for it is said that dreams that are not conditioned by one's temperament are sent from the gods.[19] The text does not expand on this laconic remark, but it goes on to describe the effects that will result from dreaming specific dreams—or rather, perhaps, from *knowing* that one has dreamt specific dreams. For it is clearly stated: If one sees a string of dreams but does not remember them, these dreams will not bear fruit.[20] So, too, if a man has an auspicious dream and wakes up at that moment, it will bring him luck.[21] This may imply that it is the dreamer's awareness of the dream that brings about its results. The dream is the beginning of a chain of causes, not the result of such a chain or a mere reflection of an event that was always fated to happen and has simply been revealed to the dreamer through his dream (as other Indian texts imply). These two ideas—that dreams reflect reality and that they bring about reality—remain closely intertwined in Indian texts on the interpretation of dreams. Is it always necessary for the dreamer to be conscious not only of his dream but of its hidden meaning in order for it to come true? This is a question that remains highly problematic for the Indian authors. For one might believe that the dream was sent by the gods, or by one's own unconscious mind, or by someone else, but the agent who would carry out the events in the dream might not necessarily be the same as the sender of the dream, and this agent might work with or without the knowledge of the dreamer.

Chapter two of the *Atharva Veda*'s appendix sixty-eight is devoted to the symbolism of dreams. Good luck is said to come to anyone who experiences any of a series of what we would certainly classify as nightmares:

> Whoever, in a dream, has his head cut off or sees a bloody chariot will become a general or have a long life or get a lot of money. If his ear is cut off, he will have knowledge; his hand cut off, he will get a son; his arms, wealth; his chest or penis, supreme happiness. . . . If he dreams that his limbs are smeared with poison and blood, he will obtain pleasure; if his body is on fire, he will obtain the earth. . . . If, in a dream, a flat-nosed, dark, naked monk urinates, there will be rain; if one dreams that one gives birth to a female boar or female buffalo or female elephant or female bird, there will be an abundance of food. If someone dreams that his bed, chairs, houses, and cities fall into decay, that foretells prosperity.[22]

Thus, apparently, even an unpleasant dream is regarded by Indian tradition as a good omen, presaging the fulfillment of a wish. But if these are auspicious dreams, one may ask, what would an ominous nightmare be like? Dreams of bad omen are for the most part as unpleasant as the so-called good dreams. Indeed, it is hard to generalize about the characteristics of good versus bad dreams in Indian theory. A systematic (not necessarily structural) analysis of the lists, along the lines of Mary Douglas's analysis of Leviticus, might tell us much about India, but probably not much more about dreams. Since "good" and "bad" are not trustworthy labels to stick onto any reality, it is necessary to interpret the dream images in their cultural context. Words like "auspicious" and "inauspicious" (*śubha, aśubha*) imply things that we do and do not want to have happen to us, but we may be wrong either in wanting or not wanting them. For someone committed to the world of *saṃsāra*, for example, the death of a son is the worst thing that can happen; for someone seeking *mokṣa*, the death of a son may be the first move on the path to enlightenment. Thus a dream of the death of a son may be a good dream or a bad dream, depending on the point of view not (as in depth psychology) of the individual dreamer but rather the point of view of the author of the particular textbook on dreams. In the text just cited, the dreamer—a man—gives birth to various female animals, and it is a good dream. For a man to dream of giving birth is not regarded as an unnatural nightmare, in part because many mythological males give birth in India,[23] and in part because this text assumes that all dreamers are male and therefore that any dream—even a dream of parturition, in itself a natural and positive image—may retain its positive symbolism when applied to a man. The combination of natural symbols, cultural restrictions, and values of the author of the text determines whether a particular dream will be interpreted as portending good or evil for the dreamer. The authors of the Hindu medical textbooks on dreams are primarily *saṃsāra*-oriented; the Buddhist and philosophical texts are primarily *mokṣa*-oriented. To an impressive degree, they agree on what people do dream about, but they often differ about whether the dream portends good or evil. The Epics and Purāṇas draw on both traditions of dream interpretation according to the tastes of the author and the situation of the dreamer in the story.

To return to the *Atharva Veda*, let us take up the other side of the story and look at part of a list of dreams portending what one does not want to happen:

> Whoever dreams that he is smeared with oil, or that he enters his mother or enters a blazing fire, or falls from the peak of a mountain, or plunges into wells of mud or drowns in water, or uproots a tree, or has sexual intercourse with a female ape or in the mouth of a maiden, or vomits blood from his throat, or is bound by ropes—he will die. A dream of singing, dancing, laughing, or celebrating a

> marriage, with joy and rejoicing, is a sight portending evil pleasure or disaster.[24]

The dreamer's awareness of certain bad dreams, culturally defined as portending evil, is expected to produce bad results in his life.

By an extension that has fascinating implications for later Indian theories of dreams and myths about dreams, it is also said that the dreamer can dream the dreams of other people; that is, he can have dreams that symbolize the future events that will happen not to him but to his family, particularly to his son or his wife:

> If a man sees [in his dreams] objects cut into pieces—teeth, or an arm, or a head—these will cause the destruction of his brother, father, or son. If a man sees shattered two bolted doors and a bed and a doorpost, his wife will be destroyed. If he sees a lizard or a jackal or a yellow man mount [his wife's] bed, his wife will be raped. If a man kills a white, yellow, and red serpent in a dream or cuts off the head of a black serpent, his son will be destroyed. If a man dreams that a bald man or a man wearing brown or white or red garments mounts his wife, she will be attacked by diseases. The same will happen if a man dreams that she is mounted by a dog or a serpent or a lizard or a snake or a porcupine or a crocodile or a wild dog or a tiger or a leopard or a serpent with a monstrous hood.[25]

The sexual symbolism of much of this dream content is quite evident, but this apparently natural or universal or, in Jung's terms, archetypal symbolism (the serpents and violated bedrooms, the bestiality and physical mutilation) is combined throughout with symbols that have a primarily cultural or specific or manifestational weight: the man in red garments suggests both the ascetic's ochre robe (anathema to the *saṃsāric* author of this text) and the robe of the condemned criminal in ancient India, and the particular colors of the sinister serpent also have cultural meanings. Moreover, unlike the Buddhist texts and Hindu Epics and Purāṇas, which, as we shall see, described the dreams of women and also depicted women as skillful interpreters of dreams, the medical texts defined a woman as a person whose own dreams were of no significance. Because of this, the woman's husband had to dream for her; the woman was never the author or subject of a dream, but she was frequently the object of her husband's dreams. Indeed, she was often dreamt about by her *future* husband, a phenomenon that has reverberations in the story literature. The husband may dream this sort of dream about his future wife:

> If a man sees a lute marked with a cobra's tooth, he will get a woman. If he sees birds soaring over lotus ponds, or if he mounts

an elephant in rut in his dream, he will take away another man's wife. If he is bound by iron fetters, he will get a virgin.[26]

This passage supplies a transition between the one in which the man dreams his own dreams and the one in which he dreams for his wife; here he dreams *of* his wife.

Many of these symbols recur in Indian stories about dreams. One of them in particular is basic to the myths of dreams, illusion, and rebirth: "A man who dreams that his relatives weep pitifully over him will become satisfied; a man who dreams that he is dead will obtain long life."[27] In keeping with the basic view that dreams about sorrow or pain may portend or bring happiness or pleasure, the dream of death is a dream of life. But in the *mokṣic* context, the vision of oneself as a corpse, being mourned by others, forms a basic metaphor, as we will see.

Thus Indian dreams may have a material effect not only on the dreamer but on those close to him—his wife, children, parents, and others. This makes more sense in the South Asian context than it does in the West, because in India the self is by no means so clearly limited to the individual as it is for us. That is, the individual feels himself to be a physical as well as mental part of other people, to partake in what McKim Marriott has called the "coded substance" of other members of his family and his caste. He is responsible for the sins of his parents; he can amass good karma and transfer it to others; he must pay for the mistakes committed by his own previous incarnations. And, beyond the social level, he is linked not only to those intimate partners in his life but to all people through the matrix of reality (*brahman*), which is the substance of which all souls are made. Given these strong invisible bonds, it is not surprising that Indian dreamers can dream for other people or that their dreams can affect the lives of other people.

Later ritual texts added more details to this basic approach to the interpretation of dreams. Men possessed by certain goblins (Vināyakas) will see water in their dreams or people with shaven heads, camels, pigs, donkeys, Untouchables (Caṇḍālas), and so forth. They will also dream that they walk on air, or they will have impure dreams.[28] The dream of flying is here linked with the sexual dream, a link that we will encounter again in the myths of dreams. These goblins will also cause a man to think, when he walks on a path, "Someone is following me from behind."[29] The dream of danger is thus tied to the paranoid experience of danger in waking life.

The medieval medical texts greatly elaborate on the symbolism of dreams. As befits a profession devoted primarily to the diagnosis of disease, their emphasis is on violent dreams that presage violent realities. Someone may dream that a black woman wearing red garments, laughing, with disheveled hair, grabs him and ties him up and drags him toward the South; or that ghosts or monks seize and embrace him; or that men who have deformed faces and the feet of dogs smell him all over; or that he is naked but for a red garland on his head; or that a bamboo, lotus, or palm tree grows out of his chest; or that a fish swallows him; or that he enters his own mother; or that he falls from the top of a mountain or into a deep, dark pit; or that he is carried off by a swift stream; or that his head is shaven; or that crows overpower him and tie him up . . . . The list goes on and on, and it is all ominous: the man will be destroyed.[30]

Some dreams have more specific diagnoses. A man who dreams that his teeth fall out will die. Dreaming of friendship with a dog means that the dreamer will become feverish; with a monkey, consumptive; with a demon, insane; with ghosts, amnesiac.[31] Some of these motifs are picked up by the Indian mythology of dreams: the black woman with red garments is the Untouchable woman, the succubus who seduces the dreaming king; the fish that swallows the dreamer is the vehicle of transformation and rebirth. Other motifs, like the man who dreams that he enters his own mother or falls from a great height or falls into a deep pit or has intercourse with animals or feels his teeth fall out, occur in the *Atharva Veda* and are familiar to us also from our own dreams or from Freud's summaries of widespread dreams.

But the statement that a man who dreams of intimacy with ghosts will lose his memory makes a different kind of sense, for it implies that a dream of a ghost, a figure from the past, will harm one's mental control over the past. The relationship between ghosts, memory, and dreams is used to explain certain bad dreams: ghosts (*pretas*) get into your head when you are asleep. Whenever one dreams that one sees the death of one's wife, friend, son, father, or husband, it is the fault of the ghost; for these ghosts change their forms into that of an elephant, horse, or bull, and they appear to their sons, wives, and relatives.[32] Here, long before Freud, is the hypothesis that animals in dreams represent close relatives; and "ghosts" is not a bad way of describing the figures from the past who haunt our dreams and force us to imagine the deaths of those we both love and hate. The ghosts, whose reality status is somewhat vague, nevertheless mediate between two sets of entirely real people: the dreamer and his dead relative or wife. Ghosts are also implicated in the dreamer's attempts to avert the effects of bad dreams: "If one has a sinister dream, he should not relate it to anyone, but should pass three nights in the temple to honor the ghosts. He will then be delivered from the bad dream."[33] The remark that *not telling* the dream is a part of the process of making it unreal is surely significant, and it is reinforced by another passage in the same text: "Just as a dream that reflects one's true nature may be forgotten and come to naught, even so the things that we see and think in broad daylight may have no effect."[34] The text implies that the dream that is not remembered, and therefore is not told, will not have the effect it might have had were it remembered and told; and in this, the text states, dreams are no different from the mental perceptions of waking life.

The question of the distinction between dreams and waking life leads us back, out of the territory of the symbolism of the content of dreams, to the question of the boundaries between dreams and other mental processes or between various kinds of dreams. We have already encountered the Upaniṣadic fourfold classification (waking, dreaming, dreamless sleep, and the experience of the ultimately real) and the *Atharva Veda*'s threefold classification (according to the three humors of the body), with its supplementary categories of dreams sent by the gods and dreams caused by the excitation of one sense or another. A Buddhist treatise, *The Questions of King Milinda*, adds to the threefold categorization by humors three more: dreams influenced by a god, dreams arising out of past experience, and prophetic dreams. The first two of this supplementary triad correspond to the two supplementary categories of the *Atharva Veda*, and the third corresponds to the bulk of dreams that follow in that text, dreams that are portents.

Similarly, the medical text attributed to Caraka divides dreams into several categories: dreams that reflect what has been seen in waking life (*dṛṣṭa*), dreams that reflect what has been heard in waking life (*śruta*), dreams that reflect what has been experienced (*anubhūta*), dreams that foretell the future (*bhāvika*), and dreams that reflect the disturbance of a particular bodily humor (*doṣaja*). The first three categories would seem to reflect observations somewhat akin to our own; these categories, however, must be understood in contrast to other classifications, such as that of the Jains, who divided dreams into those that reflect things that have been seen (*dṛṣṭa*), dreams that reflect things that have not been seen (*adṛṣṭa*), and those "inscrutably seen" or "both seen and unseen" (*avyakta-dṛṣṭa*).[35] Indeed, these latter two areas are also covered by Caraka in his two final categories: dreams that dramatize individual fantasies (i.e., things unseen), though perhaps based on memory data (*kalpita*); and dreams that are wish-fulfillments, gratifying desires that could not be gratified in the waking state (*prārthita*).[36] These seven categories of Caraka thus cover waking experience, somatic impulses, imagination, and the influence of the supernatural.

The category of things "unseen" (*adṛṣṭa*) takes on a new meaning when it appears in another taxonomy of dreams. In certain philosophical schools, *adṛṣṭa* is "a euphemism, meaning in effect a condition which the philosopher cannot otherwise explain, but which develops later into a fairly sophisticated theory of the unconscious energies of the self."[37] According to the Vaiśeṣika philosopher Praśastapāda, *adṛṣṭa* causes one of the three kinds of dreams, the kind in which "we dream of things completely unknown in waking life." These *adṛṣṭa* dreams are dreams of omens; good ones come out of *dharma* (dreams in which the dreamer rides on an elephant or gets an umbrella) and bad ones from *adharma* (dreams in which the dreamer is rubbed with oil or rides on a camel). This category seems to correspond to Caraka's *bhāvika* (future-foretelling) and to the *Atharva Veda*'s category of dreams sent by the gods or to the larger, unspecified category of dreams of portent. The second category of Vaiśeṣika dreams is that of dreams due to the strength of the karmic memory traces (as when we dream of things we have thought about hard when we were awake); this corresponds to Caraka's categories of things seen and heard and experienced. The final Vaiśeṣika category is the most basic one; this is the category of dreams due to the *doṣas* or humors of the body; for example, a man may dream of flying when wind predominates in his body.[38] It is surprisingly hard-headed of this text to give a purely physiological source for the dream upon which the greatest metaphysical and literary energy has been expended in India: the dream of flying.

The most elaborate classification of dreams that I know of appears in a Tibetan Mahāyāna text called "The Meeting of the Father and the Son."[39] In this text the threefold classification according to humors is replaced by the threefold classification according to the three "poisons" (also designated by the word for the humors, *doṣa*): lust, hatred (or anger), and delusion (*kāma*, *krodha*, and *moha*). This triad forms just one axis of the system, however; the other, perhaps based on the Hindu category of dreams arising from the excitation of a particular sense organ, consists of the five sense organs plus the sixth sense, imagination. The resulting grid is shown in figure 1.

The first general point to be made about figure 1 is the evidence it shows of the close attention that Buddhists—particularly Tibetan Buddhists—paid to dreams, an observation that is supported by many Buddhist myths, as we will soon see. Second, we might note the emphasis on emotions as the source of dreams, a factor that we will find essential to our understanding of the Hindu mythology of dreams. It is also significant that imagination and delusion appear as factors in the generation of dreams. Finally, the content of the dreams is strikingly similar to the content of the standard dreams listed in the Hindu sources, though there are different emphases and some new items (such as the loss of the sense of smell or taste or understanding). The familiar items are the vision of sexual pleasure, the vision of a corpse (though here it is the corpse of a parent, not of a child or the self), the eating of good and bad food, a flood that sweeps everything away, the smell of a putrid corpse, and the attack of demons. The important Tibetan category of objects magically created by a magician frequently appears in Hindu myths about dreams, though it is not included in the older Hindu texts on the interpretation of dreams.

Sense Organ	Lust	Hatred	Delusion
Sight	Sees his sexual play with the belle of the land	Sees himself fighting with an enemy	Sees himself set upon by a demon (*ḥdre*), and being confused with fear
Hearing	Hears the singing and instrumental music of the belle of the land	Hears lamentation upon mother's or father's death or upon loss of any pleasant thing	Hears something said but is unable to understand the meaning of the words
Smelling	Is anointing his body with sandalwood or other perfumed substance	Smells the clinging odor of the carcass of dog, man, or snake	Feels that he has lost his sense of smell
Tasting	Hungry, he eats to satiation very savory food	Ravenous, he resorts to eating the seeds of pumpkin gourds and other (disagreeable) seeds	Feels that he has lost his sense of taste
Touching	Embraces the waist of the belle of the land	On his lap is a blazing copper slab	Feels that he has lost his physical sense organ (touch)
Imagining (the sixth sense)	Dreams that he enjoys the 5 sense objects magically produced by a magician	Along with attendants and retinue, he is carried away by a flood	Feels that he is much inebriated by wine

Figure 1. A Tibetan Map of Dreams

This chart, which appeared originally in slightly different form in Alex Wayman's article "Significance of Dreams in India and Tibet" in *History of Religions* 7 (1967): 5, is reproduced here by permission of *History of Religions*, © 1967 by The University of Chicago.

The manipulation of the dream itself through magic techniques was also a subject of great interest to Buddhists, particularly in Tibet.[40] Tibetan influence spread quickly to Kashmir, where the study of dreams took a new turn in India, leading to a technique by which the dreamer could make the object of his dream materialize when he woke up. This special Tibetan yogic technique was to be employed at the junction of waking and sleeping, the liminal moment of dangerous transition between the two worlds.[41] The accomplished yogin is able, at that particular moment, to evoke the desired dream, the dream that becomes real, because he has power not only over the dream but over the objects or people perceived in the dream. The *Tantrāloka* explains how this comes about: The master and disciple sleep near the sacrificial fire during the initiation; since they have the same consciousness, they have the same dream.[42] In this way, the dreamer could actively, purposely, dream a subjective dream that was shared by his teacher and that created an objective, material thing that had not previously existed except in his mind.

Dreams in the *Rāmāyaṇa*: Sītā and Bharata

The Hindu Epics and Purāṇas incorporated into their narratives many of the traditional dreams analyzed in the philosophical and medical texts. In Vālmīki's Sanskrit *Rāmāyaṇa*, when Sītā has been stolen by the demon Rāvaṇa and is being held captive on the island of Lankā, Rāvaṇa gives her this ultimatum: if she refuses to share his bed, he will have her cooked and will eat her for breakfast.[43] The story continues:

> Sītā lamented, saying that she could not go on living without Rāma. She said that she would never deign to touch Rāvaṇa with her left foot, let alone submit to his lust. "Rāvaṇa will pay for this," she insisted; "Lankā will soon be destroyed. But since I have been abandoned by Rāma and am in the power of the evil Rāvaṇa, I will kill myself."
>
> The ogresses threatened Sītā, saying, "Today the demons will eat your flesh," but one old ogress, named Trijaṭā, said to them, "Eat me, but do not eat Sītā. For last night I saw a terrible dream that made my hair stand on end, foretelling the destruction of the demons and the victory of Sītā's husband. I saw Rāma coming in a chariot made of ivory, drawn by a hundred horses, and Sītā, wearing white garments, reunited with him. And I saw Rāvaṇa fallen from his chariot, lying on the earth, being dragged about by a woman, and he was wearing dark garments and his head was shaven bald. And then I saw him in a chariot drawn by asses, wearing red garlands and red ointments, driving south into a lake of mud, while a seductive woman dressed in red garments, a dark woman, whose body was smeared with mud, was dragging him southwards to the region of the king of death. And Lankā had fallen into the ocean, and all the demons, wearing red garments, had fallen into a lake of cow dung. So do not revile or threaten Sītā, but console her, or Rāma will never spare you. Such is the dream that I had about Sītā. She will be released from her sufferings and get her beloved husband back again, and then, I think, all the suffering she has undergone will be as insubstantial as a shadow. I see, in her, portents of

the victory of Rāma and the defeat of Rāvaṇa: her left eye is twitching and the hair on her left arm is standing on end, for no apparent cause."

But when Sītā heard the unpleasant speech of Rāvaṇa, she trembled and resolved to kill herself; she took the ribbon from her hair and said, "I will hang myself with this cord and reach the home of the god of death." Just then, however, she saw many portents: her left eye twitched, her left arm trembled, and her left thigh quivered. These portents enlightened her, for they foretold that she would soon get what she wanted. Her sorrow vanished, her fever was assuaged, and her languor was dispelled.[44]

Trijaṭā's dream rings true in at least two ways. First, the symbolism clearly corresponds to the events in the life of Rāvaṇa, who is to be destroyed by a woman (Sītā) for whom he lusts, dragged down into the mud and condemned to death at the hands of the woman's husband. Second, the symbolism of Trijaṭā's dream contains traditionally accepted Indian images of evil portents: the red garments, the bald head, the asses dragging the chariot, and so forth. Trijaṭā also correctly glosses the physical signs that appear on Sītā's body. Yet her dream has no bearing on Sītā's state of mind, perhaps because Sītā does not know about it (it is not clear from this text whether Sītā is still present when Trijaṭā tells the other demon women about her dream).

When this episode is retold in the Tamil *Rāmāyaṇa* of Kampaṉ, it is explicitly stated that Trijaṭā does in fact tell her dream to Sītā. Indeed, the ogress tells Sītā why she is revealing the dream to her, and her reason is a most significant one: knowing that Sītā is in despair and is even beginning to worry that Rāma will blame her for all his troubles and will not bother to rescue her, Trijaṭā has pity on Sītā and says to her, "Because you cannot sleep, you have had no dreams. Listen, then, to what *I* have dreamt, which will certainly come to pass."[45] This statement is built on several assumptions that might not be as obvious to a Western reader as they are to an Indian reader. In the Sanskrit *Rāmāyaṇa*, in a passage that we are about to look at, Sītā does complain that she cannot sleep and therefore cannot dream. Trijaṭā therefore has the dream for Sītā, just as men often have dreams for their wives (whose dreams would not have been recorded or analyzed) and lovers often dream for each other. Here, in the Tamil *Rāmāyaṇa*, the ogress dreams on behalf of her prisoner, while in the Sanskrit version the ogress recognizes the external portents on Sītā's body; since dreams and portents are closely linked, the Tamil simply substitutes for the somatic portents in the Sanskrit text the internal portents of the dream. Trijaṭā in the Tamil text sees into Sītā's mind as well as into her body. The dream is basically the same in both texts (Rāvaṇa is in a chariot pulled by asses, and so forth), but in the

Tamil text it is Sītā's dream even though it is dreamt by Trijaṭā and then "reported" to Sītā.

In the Sanskrit *Rāmāyaṇa*, by contrast, Sītā ignores the entire episode and simply responds to the earlier threats of Rāvaṇa. But Sītā does respect the evidence of portents that she experiences in her own body: she is convinced by the trembling of her eye and arm and thigh, the very signs that Trijaṭā had seen. To this extent, Sītā and Trijaṭā may be said to have shared the dream of the good omens, though they did not know that they shared it. This is a situation that we will examine more precisely in chapter two.

It would appear that Sītā is a practical lady who believes in traditional omens when she can feel them herself. Her hard-headedness continues to prevail in the following encounter. Rāma has sent the monkey Hanuman to Sītā; but when Sītā sees Hanuman, she is thrown into an agony of confusion:

> "Today I have seen a grotesque dream, the dream of a monkey, that is condemned by the textbooks [on the interpretation of dreams]. I hope nothing bad has happened to Rāma or his brother Lakṣmaṇa or my father the king. But this cannot be a dream, for I am so tortured by sorrow and misery that I cannot sleep. . . . I have been thinking constantly of nothing but Rāma all day today, obsessed by the mental image of him alone, and that is why I have seen and heard these things. This is just wishful thinking—but, nevertheless, I wonder about it, for this monkey speaks to me and has a clearly visible form. I hope the news that he has brought to me will turn out to be true, and not false."[46]

When Hanuman continues to approach her, Sītā speaks to him to test his reality. She compares this incident with her previous encounter with a false and destructive illusion: her abduction to Lankā took place when the demon Rāvaṇa took the magical form of a wandering monk, fooling Sītā and luring her away from safety. With this in mind, Sītā is suspicious of Hanuman, and she says to him,

> "What if you are a form of Rāvaṇa himself, the master of illusion, once more engaging in magic illusion to make me suffer? It was Rāvaṇa who concealed his true form and took the form of a wandering monk when I saw him in the forest. But if you are truly a messenger from Rāma, welcome to you, best of monkeys; and I will ask you to tell me about Rāma. I have been held captive for so long that I find great happiness in a dream. If I saw Rāma and Lakṣmaṇa even in a dream, I would not despair; even a dream can be exhilarating. But I don't think this can be a dream, for if you see a monkey in a dream it is an omen of nothing good, but something good has happened to me. This could be a delusion in my mind, or

> some disturbance caused by indigestion, or madness, or a mental distortion, or a mirage. But it is *not* madness or delusion, for I am in my right mind, and I see both myself and this monkey."[47]

As she wavers in this way, Sītā is inclined to believe that Hanuman must be a demon after all, but then he describes Rāma in great physical and psychological detail and narrates all the events of the *Rāmāyaṇa* up to that point. Sītā now rejoices and realizes that Hanuman is in fact "truly a monkey" and that it is "not otherwise."[48]

In her semihysteria, Sītā has ricocheted back and forth between doubt and blind faith. Her cynicism made her think that she was being duped once again by a demon or that she was simply losing her mind and projecting her wishes onto the empty air. Yet she was confident that she had *not* lost her mind, and she rationalized this inner conviction by a sophisticated argument based on scholarly tradition (a very orthodox thing to do, as we shall see in chapter four): she accepted the traditional dream-book judgment that a dream of monkeys results in unhappiness (she had already remarked that the dream of a monkey was condemned by the texts of the dream books); then, since she was in fact happy, she argued that she could not have dreamt of a monkey. Moreover, this appeal to learned authority is now supported by yet another "text": the story of Rāma, the very *Rāmāyaṇa* in which she herself is appearing as a character. By listening to her own story, she convinces herself not only that she is real but that Hanuman, the narrator of her story, is real. This spilling-over of the story into the frame of the narrative is a technique that is basic to the Vālmīki *Rāmāyaṇa*. For example, Vālmīki himself appears as a character in the story, as a sage who raises the two sons of Rāma and Sītā and teaches them the *Rāmāyaṇa*, and, when the boys recite this story to Rāma, he recognizes them as his true sons,[49] even as Sītā recognizes Hanuman as a "true monkey" when he tells her the story.

The *Rāmāyaṇa* also recounts the dream seen by Bharata, Rāma's brother, during the night preceding the day on which messengers will arrive to tell him to usurp the throne that would rightfully descend to Rāma, the elder son:

> On the very night before the messengers arrived in the city, Bharata saw a most unpleasant dream, and at dawn he was deeply upset. He said to his friends, "In a dream I saw my father dirty and with disheveled hair, falling from the peak of a mountain into a lake of cow dung. I saw him swimming in that lake of cow dung, and drinking oil from his cupped hand, and laughing over and over. Head downward, he kept eating rice with sesamum, and his whole body was smeared with oil, and he plunged down right into the oil. And in my dream I saw the ocean dried up, and the moon falling to the earth; I saw the earth split open, and all the trees dried up, and

> the mountains shattered and smoking. And I saw my father the king dressed in black garments and seated on a throne made of black iron, while lascivious women, dressed in black and yellow, laughed at him. And his body was adorned with red garlands and smeared with red ointments as he was heading south in a chariot drawn by donkeys. This is what I saw during that terrifying night. Either Rāma or Lakṣmaṇa or the king or I will die. For whenever a man dreams that someone travels in a chariot drawn by a donkey, soon the smoke will be arising from his funeral pyre. That is why I am so sad. My throat is dry, and I cannot steady my mind. I somehow despise myself, though I do not see any cause for this. But when I recall that evil dream, which contains many images and cannot be puzzled out, a great fear grasps my heart and will not let go; for I keep thinking about the king, who appeared to me in an unthinkable form."[50]

Some of the images in this dream arise directly out of the story that is being told: the king is indeed about to "fall" and to die (to head south, to the land of the dead), and he is being mocked by a lustful woman (the queen, who has made him crown Bharata in place of Rāma). Other images are validated by the traditional dream books, as Bharata himself recognizes. In particular, the images point to fiery or choleric people (as they are characterized by the *Atharva Veda*), a personality type appropriate to a king. Moreover, as in the *Atharva Veda*, Bharata dreams not only for himself but for others—his father and his brother; for his brother is about to be exiled, and his father is about to die. Bharata thinks that he does not understand his dream or understand the form in which he saw his father, but he *does* glimpse the meaning of it; for he despises himself, and this is not, as he claims, for no apparent cause, for he is about to consent, albeit unwillingly, to his brother's exile, and this will break his father's heart.

Dreams in the *Mahābhārata*: Karṇa and Kārtavīrya

The other great Sanskrit epic, the *Mahābhārata*, presents a set of contrasting dreams on the eve of a great battle: nightmares in those who are about to be defeated, auspicious dreams in those who are about to conquer. These dreams are then paired with good and bad omens observed in the two camps, for the *Mahābhārata*, like the dream books and the *Rāmāyaṇa* (in which Trijaṭā's dream is linked with Sītā's omens), treats the two phenomena together. Karṇa tells Kṛṣṇa why he believes the Pāṇḍavas (Kṛṣṇa's faction) will win the battle and the Kurus (on whose side Karṇa is fighting) will lose:

> Many horrible dreams are being seen by the Kurus, and many terrible signs and gruesome omens, predicting victory for the Pāṇ-

ḍavas. Meteors are falling from the sky, and there are hurricanes and earthquakes. The elephants are trumpeting, and horses are shedding tears and refusing food and water. Horses, elephants, and men are eating little, yet they are shitting prodigiously; wise men say that that is a sign of defeat. They say that, by contrast, the mounts of the Pāṇḍavas are quite happy and that wild animals are circling their camp to the right, a good sign, while all the wild animals are circling the Kurus' camp to the left. Peacocks, wild geese, and cranes follow the Pāṇḍavas, while vultures, crows, kites, vampires, jackals, and swarms of mosquitoes follow the Kurus. For them, too, the god has sent a rain of flesh and blood, and a magic city in the sky hovers nearby, shining in its walls, moats, ramparts, and gates.

And I had a dream in which I saw the Pāṇḍavas climb to a palace with a thousand pillars. All of them wore white turbans and white robes. And in my dream I saw you, Kṛṣṇa, drape entrails around the earth, which was awash with blood, and I saw the Pāṇḍava Yudhiṣṭhira climb a pile of bones and joyously eat rice and butter from a golden bowl. And I saw him swallow the earth that you had given to him; clearly he will take over the earth. The Pāṇḍavas were mounted on men, and they were wearing white robes and turbans and carrying white umbrellas, while we Kurus were wearing red turbans and were riding in a cart drawn by a camel, traveling to the South.[51]

This passage, which I have greatly condensed, adds to the traditional list of portents a few original ones, but it tells a fairly straightforward dream, the meaning of which is clear to the dreamer. Animals loom large in both the omens and the dreams, as do directions (left and South being inauspicious) and colors (red being inauspicious, white auspicious). The inauspiciousness of the magic city in the sky, which we will encounter again in chapter six, adds delusions to omens and dreams as a third category of portents.

The medieval Hindu Purāṇas, with their baroque style and insatiable appetite for detail, outdo both the philosophical and medical texts in the lurid features of their dream analyses. The traditional lists of good and bad omens and dreams are built into stories that then go on to demonstrate the consequences of these dreams in the lives of the dreamers. One myth of this type takes the traditional episode that we have just seen in the *Mahābhārata*—the description of good dreams and omens for one side on the eve of battle, bad dreams and omens on the other—and breaks it into two separate scenes. First we are told of the dreams of the hero, Paraśurāma, to whom the gods have sent happy dreams of good omen, which include the following visions:

At the end of the night, Paraśurāma saw sweet dreams that he had not thought of with his mind. He saw himself mounted on an ele-

> phant, a horse, a mountain, a balcony, a bull, and a flowering tree; he saw himself weeping and being eaten by worms; his whole body was smeared with urine and shit and covered with lard and pus; he was playing the lute; . . . he saw himself eating many kinds of delicious food; he saw himself terrified, being eaten by a leech, a scorpion, a fish, and a snake and running away from them. Then he saw that he had entered the orbit of the sun and moon; he was looking at a woman who had a husband and a son. . . . Adorned with jewels and clad in celestial garments, in his dream he lay with a forbidden woman [*agamyāgamanam*]. He watched a dancing girl and a whore, and he drank blood and wine; and in his dream his whole body was covered with blood. He ate the flesh of yellow birds and men. Suddenly he was bound with chains, and his body was wounded with a knife. When he had seen this, he woke at dawn, thrilled with joy because of the dream, for he knew that he would surely conquer his enemy.[52]

One would hardly call this a sweet dream, even if one took into consideration the many pleasant images that I have omitted from my condensed selection. But it is a good dream in the sense that many of its images, however violently painful as natural symbols, are sanctioned by Indian tradition as formal or cultural indications of good luck. Moreover, Paraśurāma knows that the dream did not come from his own mind; from this we may infer that it was an unseen (*adṛṣṭa*) dream, sent to him from the gods. Thus, even an unpleasant dream is regarded by this tradition, as it was by Freud, as a kind of wish-fulfillment; but where Freud regarded the dream itself as the fulfillment, Indian dream theory regarded the dream as the omen of an event that would fulfill the wish.

But if Paraśurāma's dream was a good dream—the dream of the victorious hero—what, one wonders, were the villain's nightmares like? The text tells us:

> King Kārtavīrya told his wife that morning, "My dear, listen to the dream I had. The earth was covered with ashes and red China roses; there was no moon or sun in the sky, and the sky was sunset red. I was riding on a donkey, wearing red garments and iron ornaments, playing and laughing in a pile of cremated ashes. I saw a widow whose nose had been cut off; she was dancing and laughing coarsely; her hair was all disheveled, and she wore red garments. Then I saw a funeral pyre with a corpse on it but no fire, just a lot of ashes; and there was a rain of ashes, and a rain of blood, and a rain of fire. . . . I thought, 'A pot full of water has fallen from my hand and shattered,' and then I saw that the moon had fallen from the sky, and I saw that the sun had fallen from the sky to the earth. And then I saw a terrifying naked man with a hideous body and a gaping mouth coming toward me. A twelve-year-old girl, wearing fine clothes and jewels, was going out of my house in a fury, and

> you were saying, 'My king, give me permission to leave; I am going from your house to the forest.' This is what I saw in the night. And an angry Brahmin cursed me, and so did an ascetic, and also my guru. And I saw painted dolls dancing on the wall. And I saw dancers and singers at a joyous marriage. . . . A naked widow with disheveled hair, dark-skinned and wearing dark clothes, was embracing me. A barber was shaving my head and beard and cutting my nails. Dried-up trees and headless ghosts were whirling about in the wind, and garlands of skulls, terrible to see, were whirling about in the wind. Ghosts with disheveled hair, vomiting fire, kept terrifying me. And I saw a naked man wandering on the earth with his head down and his feet up."[53]

This dream seems more genuinely dreamlike than the dream of Paraśurāma, though not necessarily more sinister. The traditionally bad features (the widow, the upside-down man, and the cremation ground) are followed by strangely surreal sequences: a pot breaks in Kārtavīrya's hand and becomes the moon in the sky; a young girl rushes from his house in distress, and his wife leaves in dignified sorrow. Unlike Paraśurāma, Kārtavīrya makes no judgment about the portent of his dream, but his wife reacts immediately:

> When the queen heard what the king had said, her heart burned in anguish, and she wept and stammered as she said, "Don't fight Paraśurāma. You think you are a hero because you conquered the evil Rāvaṇa. But he was conquered by his own evil, not by you. Good men [*santas*] know that the material world [*saṃsāra*] is like a dream." She tried in vain to dissuade him from entering the battle, but he argued that one could not overcome time, destiny, and the will of the gods. "I know for certain," he concluded, "that he is going to kill me, for I know the whole future."
>
> The queen then committed suicide in the arms of her husband. He performed her funeral rites, consigned her body to the fire, and went to the battlefield. On the way he saw many omens: a weeping naked woman with her nose cut off and disheveled hair; a widow in dark clothing; a bawd, diseased and unchaste in mouth and womb; and a man-chasing witch who had no husband or son. Then he saw a funeral pyre, a burnt corpse, ashes . . . a broken jar . . . a blind man, a deaf man, an Untouchable [a Pulkasa], a man whose penis had been cut off, a man drunk on wine, a man vomiting blood, a buffalo, a donkey, urine, shit, phlegm. . . . Though the king was disturbed at these sights, he went forth to battle, where Paraśurāma killed him.[54]

Not only do the sights that the doomed Kārtavīrya sees resemble his own dream (corroborating and supporting the omens in that dream); they also supply the mirror image of Paraśurāma's "good" dream: where

Paraśurāma saw a woman with a husband and son, Kārtavīrya sees a widow and a woman who has no husband or son. Thus this text comes to terms with both of the classical dream problems at once: it interprets the dream, and it establishes a definite positive link between dreams and reality.

Buddhist Dreams: Kunāla and the Wicked Queen

The Buddhists, as we have seen, devoted much attention to the interpretation of dreams; they were also concerned with the problem of the relationship between waking and dreaming. The question of the reality or nonreality of dreams was treated at length both by the Sarvāstivādins (Buddhist realists, whose name reflects their doctrine that "Everything exists") and by the traditional Theravādins. A Buddhist tale of dreams is clearly in the same Indian tradition as many of the Hindu tales of dreams:

> The Emperor Aśoka had a handsome son with beautiful eyes; he called the boy Kunāla. One day a Buddhist monk predicted that Kunāla's eyes would soon be destroyed, and from that time forth the boy devoted himself to Buddhist teachings. Tiṣyarakṣitā, Aśoka's chief queen, fell in love with Kunāla, but he rejected her and called her "Mother." Aśoka sent Kunāla to Takṣaśilā on an embassy; on the way, a Brahmin fortuneteller foretold that the prince would lose his eyes.
>
> It happened that Aśoka became very ill. Tiṣyarakṣitā commanded the doctors to send her a man suffering from the same disease; she had him killed, slit open his belly, and examined the stomach. She found a worm there, to which she fed various substances until she discovered that it died when she fed it onions. She then fed onions to Aśoka, who recovered from his illness. In gratitude, he granted her her wish that she would rule as king for seven days. During this period she composed a letter, in Aśoka's name, telling the people of Takṣaśilā to put out Kunāla's eyes.
>
> Now, when Aśoka wanted something to be accomplished quickly, he always sealed the orders with his teeth. Therefore, that night, Tiṣyarakṣitā went to Aśoka, thinking that she would get him to bite the seal on the letter with his teeth. But something startled the king, and he woke up and reported that he had had a nightmare: "I saw two vultures trying to pluck out Kunāla's eyes." A second time she tried, and this time he dreamed that Kunāla was entering the city with a beard and long hair and long nails. The third time, Tiṣyarakṣitā managed to get the letter sealed with Aśoka's teeth, and he did not awaken, but he dreamed that his teeth were falling out. In the morning, the queen sent the letter to Takṣaśilā, and Aśoka asked his soothsayers to interpret his dreams. They said that

anyone who dreamed such dreams would see the destruction of his son's eyes, and the death of his son.

The people of Takṣaśilā obeyed the commands in the letter, though they did not want to, and had Kunāla's eyes put out. Kunāla returned to Aśoka's palace but was not recognized by the guards. He began to sing a song, telling how his eyes had been ripped out and how he had then attained a vision of the truth. Aśoka recognized the sound of the voice and the song as Kunāla's, but his servants said it was just a blind beggar. Then Aśoka said, "In a dream, long ago, I saw certain signs; there can be no doubt now, Kunāla's eyes have been destroyed." Aśoka sent for him and at first did not recognize him; but when the boy said, "I am Kunāla," Aśoka fainted. Revived by water splashed in his face, he embraced his son and wept. When he learned that Tiṣyarakṣitā had had Kunāla blinded, Aśoka raged with anger and said, "I'll tear out her eyes, and then I think I'll rip open her body with sharp rakes, impale her alive on a spit, cut off her nose with a saw, work on her tongue with a razor, and fill her with poison and beat her." Though Kunāla begged Aśoka to forgive the queen, he threw her into a lacquer house, where she was burnt to death.[55]

Hard and soft attitudes to the dream, and to reality in general, are combined in this tale. The hard attitude may be seen in the queen's highly empirical and scientific approach to her husband's illness (which she cures not out of love but rather out of fear that, if Aśoka dies, Kunāla will become king and will have her killed) and in the text's implication that the king's dreams were the direct result of physiological stimulus: he dreamed that his teeth were falling out because the queen had touched his teeth while he slept. Superimposed on this materialistic model, however, is a far softer approach: the dream of teeth falling out symbolizes impending death or mutilation. In this case, the loss of teeth is explicitly equated with blinding, the punishment inflicted on the stepson who rejects his stepmother's advances (even as Oedipus was blinded for succumbing to his mother). The soft approach to the dream may also be seen in the value set on the dream as a predictive device; in its equation with other, nondream, predictions (by Buddhist monks and Hindu soothsayers); and in the fact that it is Aśoka's belief in his dream that allows him to recognize his son, despite the son's violently altered physical appearance. The truth of the dream is set against the falseness of waking life on several levels. On the level of the plot, it is set against the false queen (who says, "Long live Kunāla" when the king tells her his first two nightmares). On the philosophical level, the metaphor of the dream is absorbed into the larger metaphor of the seeing eye that is blind to the illusion of the world; Kunāla is grateful to the queen, he says, for by having him blinded she has enabled him to obtain true sight.

The actual glossing of Aśoka's dream by the soothsayers is an essential part of his enlightenment, though he is not completely convinced until the dream comes true; for him, a hard proof is necessary before he believes. In this he is dramatically contrasted with his son, who believes the first prediction by the Buddhist monk; this contrast is maintained even at the end of the story, where the compassionate Kunāla forgives and blesses the queen, while the passionate Aśoka takes a sadistic revenge upon her.

The interpretation of dreams to enlighten a king is a recurrent Buddhist motif. In a Kashmiri text that contains many dream adventures, a Buddhist monk interprets a king's dream in order to convert him.[56] Doubtless, these stories reflect actual Buddhist practice, for other sources corroborate the tradition that Buddhists converted many Indian kings by a combination of public debate, private counseling, medical ministrations (at which the Buddhists surpassed the Hindus, who were restricted by considerations of caste and pollution), and a kind of primitive psychoanalysis: "Always by means of this subtle sleep that owes nothing to experience, the king discovers, little by little, all the faults that stayed hidden at the bottom of his unconscious."[57]

Dreams are closely integrated into the hagiography of the Buddha. Gautama himself had several highly significant dreams before his enlightenment, and these were corroborated by the dreams of his father and his wife on the night before his departure from the palace.[58] The wife of the great Buddhist king, Vessantara, had a dream that her husband interpreted for her just as Tiṣyarakṣitā interpreted the dreams of King Aśoka.[59] We will examine these Buddhist stories more closely in chapter four. But it would be wrong to suppose that the "psychoanalytic aspect of the dream" was more particularly Buddhist than Hindu,[60] for it is evident from the sources that we have barely skimmed that such stories are part of the nondenominational, pan-Indian science of the interpretation of dreams.

Western Arguments

Pindar and Plato

Our Western attitude to dreams is largely derived from traditions inherited from the Greeks (especially Plato) and from the psychoanalysts (especially Freud). Let us turn to them now, in part to use them as a touchstone against which we may understand the contrasting Indian view, in part to make us aware of the way our assumptions color our reception of the Indian texts, and in part to come to a better general understanding of the meaning of dreams by recalling what a few of our own greatest thinkers have understood about them.

A striking instance of the ambiguity in the Greek attitude to dreams appears in Pindar's tale of the taming of the winged horse Pegasus by Bellerophon:

> [Bellerophon] suffered greatly beside the stream in his longing to yoke Pegasus, the son of the snake-girded Gorgon, until the maiden Pallas brought him a bridle with a golden band. Suddenly the dream became a waking experience [*hupar*]. She said, "Are you sleeping, king, son of Aeolus? Come, take this charm for the horse, and sacrifice a white bull to the Father, the Tamer [Poseidon]." This is what the maiden with the black shield seemed to say to him as he slept in the darkness. He leapt to his feet and seized the marvel [*teras*] that lay beside him, and joyfully he went to find the seer of that land, the son of Coiranus. He showed him all that had happened, how he had lain down at night on the altar of the Goddess, as the seer had bid him do, and how she herself, the daughter of Zeus who hurls the thunderbolt, had given him the golden thing to tame the mind [of the horse]. And the seer ordered him to obey the dream as quickly as he could.[61]

Pindar's tale begins with the formulaic dream: Bellerophon sleeps at the altar precisely in order to dream, and Athena addresses him with the words that identify her as a creature in his dream: she chides him for sleeping and wakes him up, as various figures in Homer chide and wake the dreamers to whom they appear. Yet, right *before* Athena speaks these words that identify her as a dream, Pindar tells us that she is *not* a dream; and he uses the traditional formula from Homer to express this, too: the dream is not a dream (*onar*) but a waking experience (*hupar*). This phrase is used in Homer sometimes within a dream and sometimes after a dream. In either case, it functions as a commentary, redefining what we thought was a dream and telling us that it was not, in fact, a dream. But Pindar tells us that Athena brought Bellerophon a bridle in a dream and that then the dream became a nondream; she spoke to him (in a dream, as her words indicate) and gave him not a dream bridle but a real, "waking," bridle. And when he woke up, though he regarded the bridle as a marvel (since it was the materialization of a dream image), he held it in his hand and used it. It is significant, I think, that the power of this dream bridle—like the power of all bridles—is not primarily physical but mental; the bridle tames not the body of the horse but the *mind* of the horse. Athena gives Bellerophon the mental power to tame the horse, and so she gives him a magic bridle. The bridle is all the more appropriate for taming Pegasus because Pegasus himself is a dream figure; he is the winged horse who carries the hero into his dream in many myths of this genre, the magic creature who allows the hero to fly to the woman in the dream world. In the myth of Bellerophon, by contrast, the dream horse comes into the hero's real life and enables him to fly into battle with nightmare women—the Amazons and the fire-breathing Chimaera, whom Pindar goes on to tell us about in the next lines of the ode. The distinction between dreaming and waking is still there—Pindar uses it as the pivot of the entire episode—but the traditional elements of the dream adventure are redistributed in new ways along the continuum.

Bellerophon's dream embodies a paradox that troubled the minds of Greek philosophers and inspired a more systematic investigation. Greek "common sense" is well expressed by Heraclitus' famous dictum: "For the waking there is one and the same [literally: common] cosmos, but of the sleeping, each turns away to his own [cosmos, when dreaming]."[62] Indian common sense also asserted that, while dreaming was private, the waking state was "common to all men" (*vaiśvānara*).[63] But in India, as we shall see, there is more than one kind of common sense. The Greeks, too, speak with many voices. Plato provided several challenges to Heraclitus, and it is wise to treat them severally.

In the *Theaetetus*, Plato challenges the idea that there is no permanent reality apart from our mental constructions of it. When Theaetetus agrees that people who are crazy or dreaming are *wrong* when they think they are gods or when they imagine, in their sleep, that they have wings and are flying, Socrates asks, "What proof could you give if anyone should ask us now, at the present moment, whether we are asleep and our thoughts are a dream, or whether we are awake and talking with each other in a waking condition?"[64] Theaetetus then admits that the very conversation they are having could just be something that they were imagining in their sleep, just as people can imagine, in a dream, that they are telling their dreams. "So you see," concludes Socrates, "it is even open to dispute whether we are awake or in a dream." Thus we can never *prove* that we are not dreaming. The wise man, however, will never assume that he is truly awake.

When we turn to the *Republic*, we find several different approaches to dreams. First, Plato implies (*contra* Heraclitus) that everyone in the world is actually asleep, with the exception of a few philosophers, who are awake. The man who does not believe that there is such a thing as absolute beauty is dreaming even when he is physically awake, since he believes that something that is merely a likeness of something else is actually the thing itself; the man who does not make such a mistake is awake.[65] So, too, the people who have gone out of and then back into the cave (the mouth of God, in the Indian metaphor) will "rule in a state of waking [*hupar*], not in a dream, as most cities are now ruled, by men who fight shadows."[66] Finally, Plato points out that the beginning of true wakefulness comes only when we realize that we are in fact dreaming; the Heraclitean opposition between actual public waking and illusory private dreaming has thus been replaced by an opposition between illusory public dreaming and actual private awareness of dreaming. A person who is still trapped in the first category, unable to distinguish the idea of the good, is "taken in by dreams and slumbering out his present life; before waking up here, he goes to Hades and finally falls asleep there."[67] The alternative to this state is not the state of being fully awake, which Socrates does not claim for himself, but merely the state of not being "taken in by dreams"—of being aware that, like everyone else, one is dreaming.

One of the qualities of dreaming that made Plato mistrust it was its association, in his opinion, with the lower animal instincts and emotions. (This attitude was by no means shared by all Greeks, but it was Plato who set the fashion, and so it is with him that we must come to terms.) The belief that dreams arise out of powerful and dangerous emotions is, as we will see in chapter five, characteristic of the Indian viewpoint (as it is of Freud's). The *locus classicus* for this argument is the beginning of Book IX of the *Republic*:

> There are superfluous desires . . . that are awakened during sleep, when the rest of the soul, the rational and gentle and dominant part, is asleep; but the part that is like a wild beast and untamed, full of food and wine, leaps up and throws off sleep and tries to get out and satisfy itself. Then he will dare to do anything at all, since he is set free from all shame and reason. He will not shrink from copulating with his mother (as he imagines that he does), or with any other human or god or wild beast, and he will not hesitate to commit a polluting murder, and there is nothing he will not eat.[68]

The crimes that the sleeping soul commits—or, rather, *thinks* that it commits (Plato is explicit on this point)—include incest, union with a god, bestiality, murder, and the eating of forbidden food (which, in the Greek context, may well indicate cannibalism). (In Indian myths about dreams, all of these sins, but cannibalism in particular, are committed by the dreamer. We will see this in the tale of Triśanku in chapter three and in the myths of Lavaṇa and Gādhi in chapter four.) Plato then goes on to argue that when a man is drunk, or crazy, or in the thrall of erotic passion, he becomes like a tyrant; sleep releases the lawless desires that dwell in all of us, even those who seem to be most moderate.

> [The tyrant], being under the tyrannical sway of lust, becomes, always and waking, what he has been rarely and in dreams, and he will hold back from no terrible murder nor from any kind of food or deed. But the lust that holds tyrannical rule within him, and lives in all anarchy and lawlessness, being itself *his* monarch, will lead him who possesses it, like a polity, into every sort of outrage.[69]

It is not really necessary for us to know whether we are dreaming or waking, since the god will not deceive us with illusions either in waking or in dreaming.[70] This last point is in notable contrast with the predominant Indian attitude, but, in almost everything else in the *Republic*, Plato is thinking along lines remarkably parallel to those that were being developed in India at this time. The congruence between the two philosophies emerges even more clearly when we look at the myth that Plato used (found or invented) to illustrate his doctrine—to express what, as he himself admitted, was impossible to express in argument.[71]

The great Platonic myth of dreaming and dying is the story of Er:

> Once upon a time, the warrior Er was killed in battle; but after twelve days, when they laid his corpse on the pyre, he came back to life and told what he had seen there [in the other world]. He said that his soul went out of his body and journeyed, with many others, to a place where they were judged, and they cast lots and chose the next life that they would have, as animals or humans, out of the great variety of lives represented in the lots. Yet the choice was both laughable and amazing, since most people chose according to the habits of their former life. The soul that had been Orpheus chose to be a swan, because he so hated the race of women—at whose hands he had met his death—that he did not want to be conceived and born of them. And Er saw a swan changing into the life he chose as a man. When all the souls had chosen their lots, they went to the Plain of Oblivion and drank from the River of Forgetfulness, and then they all fell asleep. In the middle of the night, they were suddenly carried to their births. Er himself did not drink the water. He did not know how he returned to his body, but suddenly he opened his eyes at dawn and saw himself lying on the pyre.[72]

The memory of former births forces the souls to go on perpetuating their flawed lives; yet that memory is erased before the new life can begin. Er's unique achievement is in witnessing the process of rebirth without drinking of the River of Forgetfulness; he is the one traveler who returns from the undiscovered country of death. The problem of memory in rebirth is, as we shall see in chapter five, central to the Indian myths of transmigration; and the swan, who appears at the very start of the list of reborn souls, is an Indian symbol of both memory and transmigration.[73] In Plato's version of this myth, Er is always on the outside looking in. He does not experience the rebirths, as the characters in the Indian stories do, but merely sees them and tells about them. Where the Indian hero becomes all the different lives, Er just sees them scattered about, to be experienced by a number of different people.[74] The whole long passage is set, rather awkwardly, in indirect discourse; each scene is what Plato says that Socrates says that Er says that people said to him in the other world. This nesting of levels of discourse is also, as we shall see, an Indian trick; yet here it serves to remind us constantly that all of this is happening only in Er's mind. The text does not explicitly say that Er is dreaming, but at the end he opens his eyes at dawn. Moreover, all the other people inside Er's dream fall asleep when they drink the waters of forgetfulness and are reborn; Er, by contrast, does not drink the waters, and he wakes up. He is the man who is not "taken in" by the dream—not even when he is inside the dream. He is, therefore, he man who wakes up and the man who does not die—who actually comes back to life after dying. For in Greece, as in India, Death and Sleep are brothers.

Freud on the Reality of Dreams

The relationship between the realities of dreaming and waking was a problem that troubled the man who wrote the dream book for our era, Sigmund Freud:

> Dreams, as everyone knows, may be confused, unintelligible, or positively nonsensical; what they say may contradict all that we know of reality; and we behave in them like insane people, since, so long as we are dreaming, we attribute objective reality to the contents of the dream.[75]

Yet Freud did try to establish what he regarded as scientific ways in which dreams might be distinguished from reality. Clues to the distinction were provided by the dream work of distortion, condensation, and so forth, and by the nonlogical ways in which dreams ignore rules of time and space. Freud also argued that, even while people dream, they are (*pace* Theaetetus) always aware of the fact that they are dreaming. Not only are they aware of the existence of outside reality, but their primary purpose in dreaming is in fact to keep that reality at a distance. "I am driven to conclude that *throughout* our whole sleeping state we know just as certainly that we are dreaming as *we know that we are sleeping*,"[76] Freud remarked, and he used this hypothesis to explain the recurrent dream motif in which the dreamer, within the dream, tells himself that he is dreaming:

> "Let the dream go on"—such was his motive—"or I shall have to wake up." In every other dream, just as in this one, the wish to sleep lends its support to the unconscious wish. . . . That same wish must, however, play an equal part in allowing the occurrence of all other dreams, though it may only be from *within* that they threaten to shake the subject out of his sleep. In some cases, when a dream carries things too far, the preconscious says to consciousness: "Never mind! go on sleeping! after all, it's only a dream."[77]

The judgment "It's only a dream" is made when the dreamer is threatened "from within" by something that would otherwise wake him up. This same assertion ("It's only a dream") is the basic theme and metaphor of the Indian myths of illusion, in which *all* of life is only a dream. It is significant that in this key dream, on which Freud chose to hang his theory, the thought that the dreamer wishes to deny, the reality that he (wrongly) insists on regarding as "just a dream," is the fact that his young son is dead. The dreaming father is sleeping beside the coffin of the child. The death of a son is, as we will see, the trigger that awakens many Indian dreamers from their dreams. It is regarded throughout the literature of dreams (a literature of which Freud is certainly a part, as he himself maintains when he discusses his forebears) as a basic experience of reality, of the suffering that characterizes reality and removes illusion—the very illusion of which it is also a part.

Freud has more to say about the judgment "This is only a dream":

> Here we have a genuine piece of criticism of the dream, such as might be made in waking life. Quite frequently, too, it is actually a prelude to waking up; and still more frequently it has been preceded by some distressed feeling which is set at rest by the recognition that the state is one of dreaming. When the thought "This is only a dream" occurs during a dream, it is aimed at reducing the importance of what has just been experienced, and at making it possible to tolerate what is to follow. . . . In my view, the contemptuous critical judgment, "It's only a dream," appears in a dream when the censorship, which is never quite asleep, feels that it has been taken unawares by a dream which has already been allowed through. It is too late to suppress it, and accordingly the censorship uses these words to meet the anxiety of the distressing feelings aroused by it. The phrase is an example of *esprit d'escalier* on the part of the psychical censorship.[78]

This censored material that slips through is the most important part of the dream; it is the part of the dream that is *real* in Freud's terms:

> The intention [of that part of a dream that is described in the dream as "dreamt"] is to detract from the importance of what is "dreamt" in the dream, to rob it of its reality. What is dreamt in a dream after waking from the "dream within a dream" is what the dream-wish seeks to put in the place of an obliterated reality. It is safe to suppose, therefore, that what has been "dreamt" in the dream is a representation of the reality, the true recollection, while the continuation of the dream, on the contrary, merely represents what the dreamer wishes. . . . If a particular event is inserted into a dream as a dream by the dream-work itself, this implies the most decided confirmation of the reality of the event—the strongest *affirmation* of it.[79]

One could hardly be more emphatic about the reality of the dream within a dream, but of course one has to know precisely what Freud means by "reality" in this context. There is one rather decisive bit of evidence on this point: Freud repeats the phrase "to rob it of its reality" in a parallel passage that refers to *really* real reality. When discussing the influence of somatic factors on dreams (dreaming that you are under water when your feet really get wet in bed), he remarks: "The currently active sensation is woven into a dream *in order to rob it* [the sensation] *of reality*."[80] Thus, in keeping with the argument that one dreams in order to stay asleep, the dreamer incorporates the *actual* physical sensation into the dream (in a disguised form) in order that he may ignore its reality and not wake up. "It is only a dream," he says to himself; "my feet aren't really wet." But of course they *are*, really, wet.

The relationship between the dreamer's physical need to remain asleep and his need to dream has recently been reinforced by sleep-laboratory results. In describing what is referred to as "paradoxical sleep," so named because the dreamer is physically least active when he is oneirically most active, William Dement refers to a powerful inhibitory influence that paralyzes the sleeper: "It is this paralysis that enables us to have vivid dreams and yet remain asleep." Otherwise, as he points out, "the sleeper would quite literally leap out of his bed."[81] That is, because the dreamer thinks that his dream is *real*, he would take real physical action appropriate to the dream situation. Instead, the dream paralyzes him, channeling his energies from physical to psychic activity. In order to dream, and to experience his dreams fully, the dreamer makes use of some inhibitory device, as Odysseus did when he had his sailors tie him to the mast so that he alone would not have to pour wax in his ears and miss the song of the sirens. A mental equivalent of this physical inhibitory device is embodied in the dreamer's remark to himself, "This is only a dream."

In dreams, the props of common sense—which are false props, but which the dreamer relies on when he is awake—fall away from him, and then (as Plato warned) *anything* can happen. That is where the terrors of solipsism overtake the dreamer, and that is why he reintroduces common sense into his dream. This common sense takes the form of banal detail or of the explicit statement "This is just a dream."

This clue to moments when the dream tries to avoid reality—the clue of framing the dream as a dream—is one that we may now recognize in literature and science as well as in the texts of psychoanalysis and theology. Indeed, it is precisely because we are so familiar with the theme of dream bracketing as a literary device that we are able to employ it when we are (apparently) awake. When Ebeneezer Scrooge encounters the Ghost of Marley, the Ghost observes that Scrooge does not believe in him, and he asks Scrooge what evidence of his (the Ghost's) reality he would have beyond that of his senses, and why he doubts his senses. Scrooge replies, "A slight disorder of the stomach makes them cheats. You may be an undigested bit of beef, a blot of mustard, a crumb of cheese, a fragment of an underdone potato."[82] In other words, Scrooge is accusing Marley's Ghost of being a somatic dream.

But what is the reality status of the *non*somatic factors that are "robbed of their reality" by being bracketed as dreams within dreams? They, too, are absolutely real, on two distinct levels. To the extent that the latent content can be deduced from the manifest content, the latent content is real in the very hardest sense of the word; it represents the dreamer's true feelings and, often, true experiences and facts (such as the fact that the dreamer's son was dead). The affect is entirely real. Thus Freud cites Stricker's remark that "Dreams do not consist solely of illusion. If, for instance, one is afraid of robbers in a dream, the robbers, it is true, are imaginary—but the fear is real."[83] This distinction between manifest content (the robbers) and latent content (the fear) is made in the *Yogavāsiṣṭha à propos* a typical Freudian dream: "The universe is like a dream of sexual intercourse with a woman; for by the imagination of something unreal we experience real emotion."[84] This is, as we will see, the source of the ambiguity of the physical evidence of semen after an orgasmic dream. So, too, Ramakrishna argued, "It is not easy to get rid of illusion. It lingers even after the attainment of knowledge. A man dreamt of a tiger. Then he woke up and his dream vanished. But his heart continued to palpitate."[85] In Indian terms, we mistake (*bhrama*) the real thing (the emotion, or the latent content) for the unreal (the object of the emotions, or the manifest content). But the dichotomy between latent and manifest is yet another Western construct along the hard-soft spectrum. As we shall soon see, Indians do not regard as latent what we regard as latent (which is mainly, but not entirely, sex); whether they have something *else* that is latent is a problem that we will later approach.

In commenting on the real fear of unreal tigers, Freud remarks that "*affects* in dreams cannot be judged in the same way as the remainder of their content; and we are faced by the problem of what part of the psychical processes occurring in dreams is to be regarded as real, that is to say, has a claim to be classed among the psychical processes of waking life."[86] Freud glosses as psychically real the latent content of the dream while denying any status of reality to the manifest content, despite the fact that the manifest content often incorporates real, and trivially real, events.

Near the end of his study of dreams, Freud writes,

> The unconscious is the true psychical reality [*die reale Psychische*]; in its innermost nature it is as much unknown to us as the reality of

> the external world, and it is as incompletely presented by the data of consciousness as is the external world by the communications of our sense organs.[87]

In this remarkable passage, the rapprochement between mental and external reality comes about not so much through a hardening of mental reality (a granting of the status of reality to the affective content of dreams) as by a softening of external reality, accomplished in much the way as Indian philosophy and certain modern philosophies of science soften external reality: by saying that we cannot know the external world. Here, again, there would be no conflict between truth claims in most situations: the manifest content is true in its way, the latent content is true in its way, and it is unnecessary to construct a hierarchy of realities between them. The evidence of semen after an orgasmic dream is ambiguous because it is proof not only of the latent content (the emotion of sexual passion) but also of the manifest content (the experience of a *real* orgasm, as real as those *really* wet feet). The dream adventure of making love to a woman in the other world (see chapter two) is thus a record of the dream that most vividly straddles the line between reality and illusion.

If the affect is real, it follows that we are lying when we say, of the crux of the dream, "This is just a dream." Yet the affect is not *really* real, according to Freud. Though the dream is in a sense a wish-fulfillment, it is not a *real* wish-fulfillment but rather the fantasy of a fulfilled wish. The degree to which that fantasy is in itself a satisfaction of the wish is evaluated somewhat differently in Freud's discussions of reality-testing and dreams. Toward dreams, as we have seen, Freud is fairly soft; he grants dreams a psychic reality on a par with objective reality. When he turns to reality-testing, however, Freud is considerably harder: he posits an early stage at which "wishing ended in hallucinating" but "satisfaction does not follow; the need persists":

> An internal cathexis could only have the same value as an external one if it were maintained unceasingly, as in fact occurs in hallucinatory psychoses and hunger phantasies, which exhaust their whole psychical activity in clinging to the object of their wish. In order to arrive at a more efficient expenditure of psychical force, [it is necessary to] seek out other paths which lead eventually to the desired perceptual identity being established from the direction of the external world.[88]

Only a madman, in other words, is satisfied *merely* to dream of what he wants. Referring to the experience of a man who dreamt that he had conquered Bohemia, Freud cites Hans Sachs's remark, that "The only peculiarity of the case was that the dreamer with whom we are here concerned was not content with the fulfillment of his wish in a *dream*, but knew how to achieve it in *reality*."[89] The dreamer happened to be Bismarck; one could hardly imagine a "harder" dreamer.

Freud's Bismarck is reminiscent of Plato's tyrant, the man who actually does what all the rest of us merely dream of doing; and Freud may have had Plato in mind. Yet the fact that some people can make their dreams come true lends no objective reality to the dreams themselves; on the contrary, it merely serves to highlight the sharp demarcation between dreams that do not come true and realities that do come true.

Freud may be seen as straddling the two ends of the Western hard-soft spectrum: he is hard in his definition of reality (in contrast to what he regarded as the incorrect perception of reality held by madmen), but he is soft in his appreciation of the effects that fantasy has on the experience of reality. For by defining mental products as "psychically real" (in contrast with the judgment of "nonsense" that had prevailed in the previous century), he softened the concept of reality, though he remained hard in insisting that "psychically real" phenomena are different from "objectively real" phenomena.[90]

Freud rejected, on several counts and on several occasions, the tendency to smudge out the line between subjective and objective reality. In this, as in much else, he was explicit in his debt to Plato. His argument turns on a passage that we have cited from the *Republic*, dealing with the unrepressed desires of the tyrant. Freud somewhat misrepresents this argument ("the virtuous man is content to *dream* what a wicked man really *does*") and then goes on to ask: If a man dreams of assassinating a tyrant, is he guilty of treason? The answer is somewhat hedged:

> I think it is best, therefore, to acquit dreams. Whether we are to attribute *reality* to unconscious wishes, I cannot say. . . . If we look at unconscious wishes reduced to their most fundamental and truest shape, we shall have to conclude, no doubt, that *psychical* reality is a particular form of existence not to be confused with *material* reality.[91]

It is interesting to note that in the first edition of the *Traumdeutung*, published in 1909, Freud took a much softer line on this point, merely suggesting that "Psychical reality too has more than one form of existence." By 1914 he had distinguished psychical reality from "factual reality," and finally, in 1919, he further hardened this concept to "material reality."

Thus, though "psychic reality" is not as real as "material reality" to Freud, it is still real enough to give the lie to the statement "It's only a dream" when we insert such a phrase into the core of the dream within the dream. But what of the corresponding critical judgment, "This is all perfectly real," which also occurs in dreams, either in a literal statement or in the realism of the events depicted in the dream? Is this also a lie? To all intents and purposes, Freud's answer is in the affirmative: dreams are also lying when they insist on their reality:

> It by no means rarely happens that innocent and unimportant actions of the previous day are repeated in a dream: such, for instance, as packing a trunk, preparing food in a kitchen, and so on. What the dreamer is himself stressing in dreams of this kind is not, however, the content of the memory but the fact of its being "real": "I really *did* do all that yesterday." . . . "I dreamt," she said, "of what I really did yesterday: I filled a small trunk so full of books that I had difficulty in shutting it and I dreamt just what really happened." In this instance the narrator herself laid the chief emphasis on the agreement between the dream and reality.[92]

According to Freud, the dreamer affirms the reality of the dream both in her explicit statement and in the care with which she incorporates realistic details. The inclusion of trivia serves not only to supply the building blocks of the *bricolage* of the myth but, especially with the explicit emphasis that "This is real," to convince the dreamer of the reality of the *unimportant* part of the dream—i.e., the manifest content. The lie comes in the censor's efforts to convince the dreamer that these trivial, banal events are what the dream is *really* about, to fool the dreamer into taking the manifest content at its face value. Trivia in myths serve a similar function, though here the details frame rather than disguise the latent content, which is far more prominent in myths than it is in dreams.

The lie implicit in these judgments is not a lie about the literal truth of the experience. The literal truth is, in any case, irrelevant, for in a dream one might just as well say, "I am really flying," which turns out *not* to correspond to the events of the previous day, as to say, "I am really packing a trunk," which turns out to correspond to those events. The problem may be implicit in the unresolved judgment on the reality of the trivial manifest content: am I in fact packing a trunk, or am I dreaming of packing a trunk? But this question does not usually arise—until one wakes up and breaks out of the frame of the dream. When, however, the dream work has done a more thorough job of distortion and the dream is dominated by scenes that we usually describe as "dreamlike"—fantastic, in violation of normal laws of causation, capricious in concepts of time and space, and so forth—the judgment that "This is real" might be expected to provoke resistance. Indeed, why do we not wake up immediately from all "dreamlike" dreams? And why, while we are still dreaming, do we insist on telling ourselves that these are not dreams?

We have already noted that our common sense seems to abandon us when we dream. William Dement stated the case more strongly when he asserted that people who mistake dreams for reality are hallucinating.

But the force of this assertion is somewhat muted by the implication that *all* of us may hallucinate in this way.

> Because the dreams of REM [rapid-eye-movement] sleep are "real" to the dreamer, and because the human memory must sort and process an incredible amount of information, it is not unusual for a person who is presumably sane to "remember" some dream detail as if it were fact. When this happens, we search the past and ask ourselves, "Did it really happen, or was it just a dream?" . . . It is no problem to label as "dreaming" any incongruity that has appeared in a dream. If I had dreamed of seeing a purple kangaroo in the lecture room, I would scarcely have remembered it as "fact." But our more prosaic dreams may overlap reality far more often than we know. Maybe a dream detail is being recalled when we say, "I *distinctly remember* putting that letter in my desk drawer, and now it isn't there!" . . . Sanity depends upon a reliable memory.[93]

In this way, the sense of the reality of the dream may persist, through memory, and spill over into our waking life even after we emerge from the dream frame. Dement assumes that this is a sign of madness; the Indians do not. He also assumes that only those details that do not violate our common sense will insinuate themselves into our later memory of what was real; this, too, is an assumption that the Indians do not share with us.

In the West, it is assumed that anyone who believes that his dreams are materially real must be out of his mind. It will have been noted that this thought similarly occurs to the Indian dreamers in the myths but that it is not the final judgment of Indian tradition. How basic is it to Western thought? Madness, like dreaming, may be regarded with a hard view (which would maintain that madness differs from sanity in clearly definable ways) or a softer view (which is uneasy with such sharp differentiations). We have seen both the hardness and the softness of Plato and Freud in dealing with the relationship between madness and dreams. For the hard Freud, according to Stephan Beyer, "the imagination functions only to produce private images. . . . A schizophrenic, it is felt, creates a reality, much as does the yogin, but it is a personal reality of terror and exclusion, unshared and therefore imaginary."[94] And we can hear echoes of the hard Plato in Dement's remarks on dreams and mental illness:

> Hughlings Jackson, the great neurologist, said, "Find out about dreams and you will find out about insanity." The essence of dreaming is that we see, hear, smell, touch, and taste things that are not really there. If we were awake, the dream would be called an hallucination. Probably anyone who hallucinates is in some way insane,

> and all the more so if he believes in the reality of his hallucinations. . . . Dreams *are* madness and represent a kind of safety valve by which all of us can be quietly and safely mad every night of our lives. . . . [Research experiments in which the subjects are deprived of REM sleep] have attempted to break down the barrier that prevents this nocturnal madness from entering into wakefulness.[95]

One factor that condemns the dreamer to madness, in the Western view, is his inability to subject his dreams to scientific tests or to corroboration by other people. This is a problem to which we will return in the context of Indian tales about shared dreams (chapter two) and tested dreams (chapter four). Freud took up this problem, and cited Strumpell's formulation of it:

> In the state of sleep, [the mind] lacks the criterion which alone makes it possible to distinguish between sense-perception arising from without and from within. It is unable to submit its dream-images to the only tests which could prove their objective reality. . . . It is in error because it is unable to apply the law of causality to the content of its dreams.[96]

Yet, precisely because we fear that we are going mad when we believe our dreams, we attempt to apply scientific laws to the contents of our dreams; we reintroduce common sense into our dreams. Sir Ernst Gombrich remarks on this phenomenon:

> Sometimes a phantom of critical reason snakes into our dreams to perplex us. I remember being puzzled in a dream by the discovery that I could walk in the air, and deciding to test whether I was dreaming. . . . I clearly saw the actual brickwork [on the roofs of the buildings I was flying over] and was convinced that my experience must be real.[97]

Thus even fantastic dreams can be made to pass explicit reality tests. But the fact that such tests actually fail (Gombrich was *not* flying) even when they seem to succeed arises from the confusion regarding precisely what level of the dream is being tested. We *can* apply scientific laws to the contents of dreams, *pace* Freud, but not to the process of the dream—to the question of whether or not it is a dream, of whether or not we are awake. We may interject proofs into any of the layers inside the dream, where each dream is framed by yet another dream, but not into the outermost layer, where the only frame is what the dreamer regards as waking life. We will return to this question of receding frames in chapter four.

But how is it that we are able to outwit our own common sense so shamelessly? Why do our dreams seem real to us even when they are filled with impossible contradictions? This is the question with which we began our discussion of the critical judgment "This is not a dream," and it is one for which we found no simple solution. One possible answer comes from William Dement's sleep-research laboratory:

> We were able to account for the heightened sense of reality in dreams by hypothesizing that the brain is doing in the REM [rapid-eye-movement] state essentially the same thing it does in the waking state; a sensory input is being elaborated. In other words, the dream world is "real" precisely because there is no detectable difference in brain activity.[98]

Even when distortions occur that indicate the presence of magic or illusion, the brain processes these distortions in the same way that it processes waking experiences. (A similar hypothesis has been formulated to explain the phenomenon of *déjà vu*: the part of the brain that normally expresses memory accidentally produces a signal at the same time as another part of the brain actually processes a new experience; hence the new experience is felt to be both remembered and lived for the first time, in a kind of mental double exposure.) In the Indian view, this simply means that the brain processes mental projections, magically wrought visions, and mystical experiences sent by the gods in the same way that it processes waking-life experiences. This is one of the basic teachings of the Indian theory of illusion.

For all of these various reasons, it is simply not possible to be sure at any moment whether one is dreaming or awake. Through the use of everyday detail, as well as through the explicit statement "This is not a dream," the dreamer produces a smoke screen that gives the impression that common sense is at play when in fact it is not. Gombrich's anecdote of the brickwork on the roofs demonstrates how it is possible to trivialize even flying. These same trivia are invoked in the *Theaetetus*: if one dreams of something as ordinary as a conversation with Socrates, it is impossible to tell whether or not it is a dream.

Freud noted, on several occasions, the difficulty that we have in making critical judgments within dreams and the necessity of making them outside of dreams:

> [In dreams] we appear not to *think* but to *experience*; that is to say, we attach complete belief to the hallucinations. Not until we wake up does the critical comment arise that we have not experienced anything but have merely been thinking in a peculiar way, or in other words dreaming. It is this characteristic that distinguishes true dreams from day-dreaming, which is never confused with reality.[99]

Here Freud seems to be saying, like Socrates in the *Theaetetus*, that we can never tell the dream from the reality until we wake up. This is a contradiction of his hypothesis that we always know when we are sleeping and dreaming. That hypothesis indeed applies better to what he calls "day-dreaming" and we have come to call "lucid dreams" than it does to the true dreams that constitute his major data. For in most of the passages dealing with this problem, Freud seems to insist that we cannot in fact tell whether we are dreaming or waking. Within the dream, even the distortions produced by the dream work do not convince us that we are dreaming; only when we wake up do we recognize that they are distortions of reality.

Freud speaks of "Dreams from which we do not awaken—for instance, some in which we dream that we are dreaming,"[100] and he cites, with evident approval, Delboeuf's analysis of this phenomenon:

> We believe in the reality of dream-images, he says, because in our sleep we have no other impressions with which to compare them, because we are detached from the external world. But the reason why we believe in the truth of these hallucinations is not because it is impossible to put them to the test *within* the dream. A dream can seem to offer such tests: it can let us touch the roses that we see—and yet we are dreaming. In Delboeuf's opinion there is only one valid criterion of whether we are dreaming or awake, and that is the purely empirical one of the fact of waking up. I conclude that everything I experienced between falling asleep and waking up was illusory, when, on awaking, I find that I am lying undressed in bed. During sleep I took the dream-images as real owing to my mental habit (which cannot be put to sleep) of assuming the existence of an external world with which I contrast my own ego.[101]

We have encountered a similar argument in the *Theaetetus*, in Gombrich's brickwork, and in Dement's comparison of the mental processes of waking moments and REM moments: the mind behaves in the same way when awake and when dreaming. The Western mind cannot "put to sleep" its assumption that there is a sharp demarcation between the ego and the external world; it goes on thinking that the external world is real even when it is the external world of a dream. Only in retrospect can we tell the difference between the real external world and the unreal external world; the real one is the one that is still there when we wake up.

It is worth spelling out the implications of this impasse. It is possible to verify the hypothesis that we are dreaming: we can verify it by waking up. The corollary of this assertion, or rather another way of putting the same fact, is the statement that it is possible to falsify the hypothesis that we are awake: we can falsify it by waking up. But the opposite is not true. It is not possible to falsify the hypothesis that we are dreaming or to verify the hypothesis that we are awake. We will return to this quandary when we take up the problem of scientific testing in chapter four.[102]

In understanding the ways in which Hindus regard some things as "realer" than Freud would have, we may use Jung as a mediator. I once suggested that Freud would have made a great Tantric guru;[103] in response to this, David Shulman has remarked that, "If Freud, in his former birth, wrote the *Linga Purāṇa* [the "Phallus-Mythbook," a Sanskrit text relating many of the myths of Śiva], Jung must have written the *Yogavāsiṣṭha*."[104] In his psychological commentary on the *Tibetan Book of the Dead*, Jung raises the question of the resistance of modern Western thought to the possible reality of mind-created things. He argues that the fear of subjectivity leads us to deny reality to the psyche. Though Jung himself did not go so far as to give the status of reality to thoughts, he did point out the largely cultural basis of our assumption that this status is impossible to justify. In his essays on "synchronicity,"[105] Jung suggested that there might be ways of explaining certain events without invoking such hypotheses as causality and that there might be other realities besides objective reality. In challenging the Western "uncritical assumption that everything psychological is subjective and personal," Jung argues, "Now whether a thing is 'given' subjectively or objectively, the fact remains that it *is*."[106] In this view, although it is indeed possible (and necessary) to distinguish between the inner reality and the outer reality, it is *not* necessary (or, indeed, possible) to value the one above the other.

It struck a Western observer as strange that "The Indian patient says, 'The god told me' without needing to add '. . . in a dream' to prove his sanity; the dream's psychological reality is taken for granted."[107] But embedded in this comment is the assumption that Indians regard the dream as a legitimate source of information but that they would *not* regard a conversation with a god as an equally legitimate source. The "psychological reality" of the dream legitimizes the message from the god, in this view. But one might just as easily say that it is the "psychological reality" of the god, in India, that legitimizes the dream. Indeed, both the dream and the god partake of an inner reality that is "taken for granted" in India; each substantiates the reality of the other.

The Dreams of Post-Freudians and Children

How people come to distinguish between inner and outer realities is a problem that has occupied the attention of child psychologists and anthropologists for many decades. In the rather primitive perception of many early anthropologists, it was assumed that children, savages, and madmen were alike in their inability to distinguish internal perceptions from external perceptions; all of them took their dreams to be real. In recent years, although both anthropologists and psychologists have come to modify their views somewhat, there is still a general underlying assumption that normal people must move from understanding dreams as real and external to understanding them as unreal and internal. In this view, our Indian mystics, together with children, savages, and madmen, have not yet seen the light.

Jean Piaget is the man with whom these basic approaches to child development are most closely associated. According to many oversimplified reductions of Piaget's views, the early behavior of children suggests that they cannot tell fact from fiction or their own person from another. As Michael Polanyi summarizes this view, "They live in a world of their own making, which they believe to be shared by everybody else. This stage of infancy has been called 'autistic' by Bleuler and 'ego-centric' by Piaget; but the blurred distinction between self and non-self, which underlies the child's state of mind here, might as well be described as 'selfless.'"[108] Polanyi's use of the term "selfless" for the "ego-centric" child is a sign that he sympathizes with the child's refusal to draw the line between "self" and "world." Similarly, it is the express goal of Buddhism (and some forms of Hinduism) to teach people to dissolve the borderlines between themselves and the outside world, to erase the sense of self. Are the Buddhists therefore fixated at any early stage, like children or savages or madmen, or have they moved from that stage, perhaps *through* the stage that Piaget would regard as normal or adult, to a stage that superficially resembles the first stage but is in fact far more subtle and profound?

A recent study by Richard Shweder and Robert LeVine challenges the Piagetians on precisely this ground.[109] Their essay is a response to a study by Lawrence Kohlberg,[110] who had argued that children in all cultures learn, step by step, that their dreams are not real and external (as they had originally thought) but are, rather, unreal and internal (as they all come to realize). Challenging this conclusion on several grounds (some of which are not germane to my purposes here), Shweder and LeVine raise several points so relevant as to merit detailed summary and quotation.

Kohlberg had demonstrated that American, Canadian, Swiss, and Formosan children all arrive at the consensus "that the events in their dreams are internally-located and inherently private 'appearances' (instances of 'mental imagining')."[111] The original childhood understanding of dream events persists, according to Piaget, "in defiance of personal circumstances, experiences, and overheard conversations."[112] This "original" understanding is of the dream as external, and it arises "spontaneously." Yet, somehow, all children eventually discard this understanding and arrive at the belief that dreams are internal.

Kohlberg and Shweder and LeVine use three main attributes against which they measure the child's understanding of dreams: reality (unreal vs. real [i.e., seeming vs. being]); visibility (private or public); and locality (inside or outside the dreamer's body).[113] These are among the criteria on the "hard-soft" spectrum that typifies Western thinking on this and related subjects; all (including real/unreal) are the child's own judgments. Shweder then expands Kohlberg's analysis to spell out what Kohlberg regards as the only four logical ways of describing experience:

1. as external perceptions (real, publicly accessible, and externally located)
2. as mirages (unreal, publicly accessible, and externally located)
3. as hallucinations (unreal, privately accessible, externally located)
4. as fantasies (unreal, privately accessible, internally located).[114]

But Shweder goes on to point out that the four "illogical" ways of describing one's experiences do, in fact, refer to known human experiences:

1. internal perceptions: real, publicly accessible, internally located —such as intrasomatic events during surgery
2. internal sensations: real, privately accessible, internally located —such as a pain in one's stomach
3. private perceptions: real, privately accessible, externally located —such as perception of auditory stimuli
4. shared fantasies: unreal, publicly accessible, internally located.

Of category 4 Shweder remarks, "No one can deny on logical grounds the possibility of the existence of a species whose fantasies were pictorially displayed on a small screen located just behind the retina and visible through the pupil from the outside (an internal screen which rapid eye movements during dreaming seem to suggest is imagined by our sensory apparatus)." This final category is also exemplified by the shared dream or, rather, as we will see, by the *myth* of the shared dream —the universal dream of the shared dream.[115]

But Shweder and LeVine go on to supplement the Kohlberg data with new data of their own, derived from a study of Hausa children. This is their basic finding:

> Initially, Hausa children believe the events in their dreams to be real occurrences, potentially capable of public perception, which take place outside their bodies (i.e., external perceptions). Although they come to believe the events in their dreams to be unreal appearances, located inside their bodies, to which only they have potential perceptual access (i.e., fantasies), there is no single transitional route to this ultimate childhood understanding. Betwixt their initial "realism" and subsequent "subjectivism," one set of children come to believe that dream-events are real, potentially visible experiences which happen inside their bodies (i.e., internal perceptions); another set of children believe the dream-events are

> unreal appearances which are invisible to others but have locations outside the body (i.e., hallucinations).[116]

That is, midway in their development, the children change their minds about *either* the reality *or* the externality of the dream events but not both; dreams are viewed either as mirages or as internal perceptions and, still later, either as hallucinations or as internal sensations; in the end, all of the children believe that dreams are fantasies. Shweder and LeVine speculate on some of the factors that would make a child change one rather than the other of his beliefs, always in response to disconfirming data presented by waking experience and highly influenced by the culture's interpretation of those data.

This study raises several fascinating and important questions:

> How are we to interpret the agreement between six year old Hausa children and four year old American children that the events in their dreams are external perceptions (real, capable of public perception, and externally located)? . . . How [is it] that lacking, for example, the distinction between real and unreal, young children should understand dream experiences as characteristically *any* one pole of an absent distinction, and why, given that they do respond so characteristically, [is it] *that* one pole and not the other that is preferred? Either young children understand their dream experiences *and* everyday waking perceptions to be neither real nor unreal (which tells us very little about how they do understand them but is at least consistent with the notion of "lacking a distinction") or, as we think more likely, they distinguish by some criteria the real and unreal but have no good reasons to view dream-events as anything but real.[117]

This final suggestion fits very well with the mainstream Indian attitude toward dreams and similar phenomena: there *is* a distinction between the real and the unreal—there *must* be—but children place dreams on the "realer" end of the spectrum. Why should children have chosen to locate their dreams nearer to the real than to the unreal pole? Once again, Shweder and LeVine have a simple but entirely convincing suggestion:

> All knowledge available to the organism, whether preadapted in the evolutionary history of the species or the cultural history of the group, or postadapted in the life-history of the individual, begins with external perception. There may well be a preparation of *Homo sapiens* to understand experiences as external perceptions until such an understanding is shown to be deficient.[118]

In our evolutionary beginnings, therefore, the tendency would have been to respond to dreams as real rather than not to respond. For if one is not sure whether one is confronted with a saber-toothed tiger or simply with the image of a saber-toothed tiger, the people who run away, fast, while juggling the ontological possibilities, will in the long run outlive those who stand still and doubt their senses. In a pinch, it pays to regard reality as the fail-safe position. Even when dreams are the phenomena in question, they, too, will be taken for real. Yet, at all times and in all places, children have learned from experience when to respond to dreams and when not to respond to dreams; this, too, is selective behavior. If there is such a thing as universal common sense, it is common sense to regard a dream—to regard *everything*—as real until it is proven guilty of unreality. Yet the schools of Indian philosophy that carry idealism to the extreme attempt to reverse this inbred assumption, to take unreality as the fail-safe position.

All children come to abandon the common sense that regards all phenomena as real; they come to arrive spontaneously at the definition of dreams as fantasies on the basis of "certain universal facts about waking experience, that is, untutored in the entailments of adult dream concepts and the subtleties of their application to everyday experience."[119] Shweder and LeVine demonstrate that children get from A to B by a number of different routes of reasoning and experience, largely tempered by cultural conditions, rather than by a single, inevitable route, as Kohlberg had claimed. But what happens to the children *after* they get to B, after they have all come to agree that dreams are (mere) fantasies? The usual Western assumption is that, once they have seen the light, the children do not revert to their infantile misperceptions. Yet it is well known that among many non-Western peoples—the People of the Dreaming in Australia, certain Brazilian tribes,[120] the Hausa, and, of course, the Hindus and Buddhists—adults have developed elaborate theories in which dream events are regarded as real, visible, and external. Hopi children, for instance, regard the masked figures in their ceremonies as real. When they grow up, there comes a moment when these figures are literally unmasked; the children learn that these "gods" are just men dressed up, like fathers in Santa Claus suits. But then the children are taught, at great length, to understand how it is that the masked dancers are, in fact, entirely real in a very different sense.

We must assume that the adult Hausa (and Hindus) go *beyond* the "subjectivism" at which they all arrive at one point (the view that dreams are unreal, inside, and private). This is the realm of "adult dream concepts and the subtleties of their application to everyday experience" to which Shweder and LeVine refer. Shweder expands on the implications of these findings in the course of a rebuttal of Hallpike:

> Hallpike claims that, with the exception of an occasional "highly intelligent informant," primitives are pre-operational in their think-

> ing and hence not "capable of recognizing the subjective basis of dreams . . ." (p. 419). What a remarkable claim. . . . By the time they are 10 years old, [Hausa children] believe dreams are mere "fantasies," unreal and internally located. Any Hausa 10 year old is capable of arriving at this belief (presumably) on his own. Later, however, as adults, Hausa children change their minds. Adult theory tells them that their 10-year-old understanding of dreams (which, of course, is *our* adult understanding of dreams) was inadequate—that dreams are a type of "vision" giving access to an external, objective numinous realm of the soul and its wanderings. Hausa are not only capable of a "subjectivist" view of dreams. They entertain that viewpoint as ten year olds, and reject it![121]

The people who develop an "objectivist" view of dreams often continue to hold this view in preference to the common-sense view that is maintained both by the Westerners with whom they come into contact and by certain sectors of their own society. As the Australian People of the Dreaming described the encounter of the two cultures, "The people of the dream watched the people of the clock come out of the sea and strike their flagstaff firmly into the sand."[122] If you *know* that the land is made of sand, you do not waste time and pride planting the banner of the clock in it.

Thus, though children relinquish their initial view of the reality of dreams in the face of cumulative waking evidence to the contrary, they may go on to rebuild a theory of dreams as external perceptions, not in ignorance of the facts of waking experience but somehow in spite of them, not in the absence of the ability to reason scientifically but in defiance of that ability.[123] This is the level of speculation on which our Indian myths are set. Though these myths may share some of the freshness and imaginative freedom that characterize the thoughts of children, they are not at all naïve, any more than the sketches of Picasso are naïve, like the children's drawings they superficially resemble.

Our myths are made out of the dreams of childhood recollected by adults, the way poetry is made (according to Wordsworth) from "emotion recollected in tranquillity." Myths are not made by children. Nor do most cultures push their myths into a closet, as we do, and give them that inverse X-rating: "Only for children."[124] Children often have the fantasy that they can make the things that they think of become real. Indian yogins claim to have a similar ability. Although one might perhaps see the child's early longing, secretly cherished over the years, as one of the driving factors behind the yogin's will to achieve this power, the resemblance stops there. The yogin has developed an elaborate ontology, over and beyond the common sense of his culture, that brings him to a point of view quite different from that of the child; he doubles back in a spiral, not a simple circle. True, there is much written in Hindu and Buddhist texts about clearing the mind of the debris that the culture has cluttered it with over the years, so that it can revert to the translucent directness of the child's point of view; but to this directness there has been added a complex and profound theory of reality.

There are several ways in which the Tantric image of God resembles and does not resemble the child's "transitional object," described by Winnicott.[125] Where the child, in playing, uses the transitional object to move from internal reality to external reality—to redefine his dreams—the Indian Tantrics use the image of God to move in the other direction, to move from material objects to the greater reality of *brahman*. In both cases, the transitional object—the teddy bear, or the image of God—is ultimately discarded; it is the ladder that one kicks away when one has climbed to the right place. But the child has climbed to a place where the teddy is replaced by a *real* bear, while the yogin has climbed to one where there are no bears at all. The glass that child psychologists would regard as half full is one that the Indian sage would regard as half empty (*śūnya*).

On a common-sense level, Indians are perfectly capable of dismissing dreams. When the psychoanalyst G. M. Carstairs said to one of his informants in Rajasthan, "You may have heard that I'm very interested in hearing about people's dreams," he received the curt reply, "Those are all imaginary things, dreams."[126] Yet many Indians are willing to deal with dreams on a shared, public level.

The Indian myths of dreaming dissolve the line between waking and dreaming reality by dissolving the distinction between a shared waking world and a lonely dreaming world, or they make it possible to drag back across the still acknowledged border between the worlds those dreams that enrich and deepen the reality of the waking world. The philosophical goal of many of these myths is to dissolve the line, but the secret agenda of many of them is to understand the reality of life through the insights that come from dreams.

Do Indians enrich their waking life with the latent or the manifest content of their dreams? How literally do they take their dreams? Questions of this sort force us to reconsider the nature of the Indian spectrum. Latent and manifest content are very close indeed in India. Or, rather, they are very close in Indian myths. Myths always tend to highlight the latent content of dreams, but never more so than in India, where, for instance, castration is often symbolized by the removal of the male organ rather than by blinding or beheading (which also occur).[127] One is tempted to speculate that the latent content of these dreams and myths is, therefore, not sexual. Is it, perhaps, theological? Is sex a euphemism for God? Is the ease with which Indians blend the real and unreal (in our terms) a cause or a result of the ease with which they blend the latent and manifest levels of their dreams? All that one can say is that they *do* both of these things more than we do and that they manage to go on doing them when they grow up, as we generally do not.

Paul Feyerabend has suggested that adults can and, indeed, must retain the ability to experience major conceptual changes of the sort that Piaget has said occur only in childhood:

> Now is it reasonable to expect that conceptual and perceptual changes of this kind occur in childhood only? Should we welcome the fact, if it is a fact, that an adult is stuck with a stable perceptual world and an accompanying stable conceptual system, which he can modify in many ways but whose general outlines have forever become immobilized? Or is it not more realistic to assume that fundamental changes, entailing incommensurability, are still possible and that they should be encouraged lest we remain forever excluded from what might be a higher stage of knowledge and consciousness? [128]

One knows of many dramatic examples of such fundamental changes occurring in adulthood: religious conversion, falling in love. The Indian myths suggest other changes even more dramatic and no less basic. They describe moments when adults, suddenly confronted with dreams that behave in ways they had not thought possible, are, like children, converted to an entirely new perception of reality.

2 Myths about Dreams

Indian Texts

In one type of romantic adventure the hero flies, or rides on a white horse, to another world, where he meets a princess. This romantic adventure becomes an explicit dream adventure when the hero finds his princess after falling asleep or when he visits her magically every night. Implicitly, however, one might regard all "other worlds" as dream worlds and all romantic adventures as paradigms of the dream of sexual adventure. In these ways, the romantic adventure and the dream adventure often overlap; one such combination results in the myth of the shared dream.

In some versions of the romantic adventure, the hero succeeds in rescuing the dream princess and bringing her back to his own world; the Sleeping Beauty is such a story, and the Brothers Grimm collected many others, in which everyone lives happily ever after. In other versions, however, the hero fails to keep his princess in the real world; the Swan Maiden (as in the ballet *Swan Lake*) is such a story,[1] and many more are preserved in the Greek myths, which usually do not have happy endings. We might view these two variants as representative of two attitudes to the reality of the dream world: the first regards it as a real world, from which one can bring back the princess and keep her, just as Bellerophon kept his bridle; the other regards the dream girl as a mere figment of the imagination, which fades when one wakes up, as the tiger faded from Ramakrishna's dream. In other words, if the prince regards his experience in the other world as a real experience, he brings back his princess; if he regards it as a dream, he does not bring her back.

The Shared Dream

In India, however, these two themes are combined, since there is no impermeable boundary between dream and reality. Here the hero acknowledges that his dream was "just" a dream—but he still succeeds in bringing back his princess. Indeed, when he finds her, he may find that she has been dreaming of him; the Sleeping Beauty may well have been also a Dreaming Beauty, dreaming that her prince would come to awaken her with a kiss.

The story of the dream adventure may itself be subdivided into two variants. In the first, a man dreams of a woman he has never seen, searches for her, finds her, and marries her. This tale, probably originating in India, was carried to Ireland, Russia, medieval Greece, France, and Germany; Chaucer ridicules it in the tale of Sir Topas, who dreams that he is to marry the queen of fairyland and wanders off to search for her. The motif, which Stith Thompson calls "Future husband (wife) revealed in dream," otherwise known as D 1812.3.9,[2] is also related to "Youth makes statue of a girl and seeks a girl like the statue" (T 11.2.1.1). This is a popular romantic theme, with an Indo-European distribution pattern.

But the second version of the story is, to my present knowledge, the special achievement of India and of the lands with which India had direct contact. This is the theme of two lovers, unknown to each other, who dream of each other and subsequently find each other in waking life. The broader form of the motif, "Love through dreams" (T 11.3), which corresponds to our first version, occurs widely and is even identifiable as an entire Tale Type (516): "Falling in love with a person seen in a dream." But the more specific inflection, our second version, "Lovers meet in their dreams" (T 11.3.1), is attested only in Indian folklore.[3]

One of the simplest as well as one of the earliest examples of this second version is a Persian story that occurs in both the *Shahnamah* and the *Zend Avesta*; thus it is part of a literature that dates back to the Indo-Iranian period, in which India and Persia shared many major literary and religious themes:

> Zairivairi . . . was the handsomest man of his time, just as Odatis, the daughter of King Omartes, was the most beautiful woman among the Iranians. They saw each other in a dream and fell in love. The princess was invited to a great feast at which she had to make her choice and throw a goblet to the young noble who pleased her. When she failed to see Zairivairi, she left the room in tears; but then she saw a man in Scythian attire at the door of the palace, and she recognized the hero of her dreams. It was Zairivairi.[4]

The woman in the dream must defend her private sense of reality against great social pressure, must hang on to her vision for a long time before, finally, she is supported by physical evidence that others can see—here, the appearance of the dream prince himself, in the flesh at last, to tell her that he, too, had dreamed of them together.

Vikramāditya Finds Malayavatī

A far more elaborate story of a shared dream is the myth of Vikramāditya and Malayavatī:

> A painter copied an image of a girl from a traveler's book. King Vikramāditya saw the picture and fell in love with the girl. That night he dreamed that he was making love to the girl, but suddenly the watchman woke him up. The king banished the watchman in a rage; he was convinced that the girl existed, though he despaired of finding her. He told his friend about his dream: "I crossed the sea and entered a beautiful city full of armed maidens who rushed at me, shouting, 'Kill him! Kill him!' Then a Buddhist nun took me to her house and said, 'This is a man-hating princess named Malayavatī; she makes her maidens kill any man she sees.' The princess entered the nun's house with her maidens, and I put on woman's clothing and came out to see her: she was the princess I had seen in the picture. As soon as she saw me, she forgot her hatred of men and was overpowered by desire, even though I had the form of a woman. She took me back to her palace, where we played marriage games with her maidens; and when we had been married, that night we entered the bridal chamber. I told her who I was and revealed myself and embraced her, and she lost all modesty as I began to make love with her. As we were passionately united, that cursed watchman woke me up. Now that I have seen Malayavatī in a picture and in a dream, I cannot live without her."
>
> The king's friend, realizing that this was a true dream, told the king to draw a map of the city on a piece of cloth. He showed it to everyone, until one day a poet came from afar and told this tale: "In the city of Malaya, the king's daughter, Malayavatī, hated men until she saw in a dream a certain man in a Buddhist house, and in her dream she brought him to her palace and married him and entered the bridal chamber with him. But just as she was making love with him in bed, she was awakened at dawn by her chambermaid. She fired the maid and vowed that she herself would die if she did not find that man in six months, of which five have now passed." When the poet had told this tale, with all of its striking agreement and similarity, the king rejoiced in his certainty and set out for the city.
>
> He found it just as the princess was about to enter the fire. When she saw him, she said, "This was my dream bridegroom," and when Vikramāditya saw his beloved with his own eyes [*sākṣāt*], just as she had been in the picture and in his dream, he regarded it as a marvelous favor from the gods, and he took her back with him to his own city.[5]

What makes the story particularly striking is the mass of detail, "with all of its striking agreement and similarity" between the dream of Vikramāditya and the dream of Malayavatī. The two dreams weave together traditional elements from Indian romantic literature (the Buddhist nun as a go-between), Indian myths of illusion (the king's change of sex, which in this story is merely a masquerade), and Indo-European folklore (the man-hating princess, the ice maiden—Turandot—who is melted by the ardor of the king). These themes correspond so precisely in the two dreams, and there are, in addition, so many identical small arbitrary facts (such as the proper names), that mere coincidence is out of the question.

King Vikramāditya is certain that his dream is real, and it is the dream, not the portrait of the princess, that convinces each of them of the other's existence. For the dream has many details that the picture lacked, and the princess, who had only the dream and no picture, believed it just as firmly as Vikramāditya did. The story thus takes the conventional motif of the lovers who fall in love as a result of seeing each other's portraits and brings it to another level of meaning. The king has yet another picture, the map, drawn *after* the dream, to back up his faith, and these two pieces of evidence supply physical corroborations for other people (the friend, the poet), who might otherwise have doubted the reality of the dream. Since Vikramāditya knows how to draw, he is able to turn his mental image into a physical object even before he finds the girl: he draws a map of his dream world.

A series of versions of another myth of this type demonstrates some of the ways in which the storytellers continually juggled the details relating to the physical verification of the shared dream. At first the emphasis is on the physical reality of the dream lover; then it shifts to his mental reality, then to the physical proof of that mental reality, and finally to the philosophical implications of that proof. Although this development is not strictly a chronological one, since some of the more subtle details appear in texts that are apparently older than those that contain simpler accounts, it is perhaps best to begin with the less elaborate versions of the myth and add details as they build up, bearing in mind that we are dealing with a fluid oral tradition that may be rather misleadingly and arbitrarily fixed in written texts from time to time.

The myth is the story of Uṣā and Aniruddha, and it is told in several Sanskrit texts. It is retold often, in part because it is an integral part of the much-loved saga of Kṛṣṇa (for Aniruddha is the son of Kṛṣṇa's son Pradyumna, whom we will encounter in chapter three in a tale of magical doubles), and in part because it is the kind of story that Hindus like to tell, a story about dreams that come true. It is useful to regard this tale together with the story of Vikramāditya and Malayavatī, because it presents a kind of mirror-image of that myth. Vikramāditya's story is told from his point of view, and the woman is depicted as bloodthirsty and causelessly violent toward him; but Uṣā's story is told from the woman's point of view, and the hero's entrance into her bedroom is seen, in some versions, as a bloody and violent rape.

The Rape of Uṣā

The simplest (though not the oldest) variant tells the story in considerable detail:

> The demon Bāṇa had a daughter, Uṣā, who, though a virgin, dreamed that she made love with a man she had never seen or heard of before. But when, on waking, she failed to see him, she cried out, "Where are you, darling?" She felt confused and then, in the midst of her friends, embarrassed. She told her friend Citralekhā about her dream, and Citralekhā said, "If he exists in the triple world, I will bring to you the man who stole your heart; point him out." Then Citralekhā drew pictures of all the gods, demons, human beings, and other creatures in the universe. When Uṣā saw the picture of Aniruddha, she lowered her head in embarrassment, smiled, and said, "That's the one! That's the one!" Citralekhā, who had yogic powers, recognized Aniruddha and flew through the air to get him; she brought him, asleep, to Uṣā, who rejoiced to see him. He awoke, and they made love in her room until Aniruddha lost count of the days. When she lost her virginity, the servants noticed this by means of signs that were hard to conceal, and they told her father, the king, "Your majesty, we have noticed behavior on the part of your daughter that is defiling the family; the virgin has been violated by men." When the king heard this, he hastened to the girl's room, where he saw Aniruddha playing dice with her. Furious, Bāṇa bound Aniruddha with serpent bonds, but Nārada reported Aniruddha's capture to Pradyumna and Kṛṣṇa. A great battle took place; Kṛṣṇa conquered Bāṇa and took Aniruddha and Uṣā back to his capital, at Dvārakā.[6]

Since Uṣā apparently lacks Vikramāditya's skill in draftsmanship, Citralekhā helps her. Citralekhā's name means "Sketcher of Pictures," and her art is a magic one: she draws a map of the universe in which Uṣā can pinpoint her man like a witness leafing through the pages of faces in the police rogue's gallery to identify a criminal. Uṣā believes in her dream from the very start; Citralekhā, however, is not entirely sure that the man exists until Uṣā is able to identify him as a man whom Citralekhā knows to exist. The element of physical corroboration reappears near the end of the story, when the physical signs of loss of virginity alert the harim guards and convince them, too, that Uṣā's dream man truly exists. It is significant, however, that this corroboration occurs only after Aniruddha himself has been transported to the harim. Thus Uṣā is convinced by the dream that Aniruddha exists; Citralekhā is convinced by the picture (even though it is a picture that she has drawn herself); and the guards are convinced by the signs "difficult to conceal": marks on Uṣā's body, perhaps—a common theme in Indian erotic poetry—or blood or semen on the bed—a common theme in myths of dream seductions.

The presence of semen in the bed of a *man* who has dreamt of a sexual adventure is a better-known example of the ambiguous physical evidence of the reality of a dream.[7] For an orgasmic dream or a wet dream is physically real; a real orgasm has taken place, inside and outside the body of the dreamer, and it seems at first to have happened more or less as it would have taken place had the dream partner been physically present. In another sense, however, the orgasmic dream is emotionally unreal; one has had a fantasy of an experience that cannot be entirely real without a partner. On waking, the dream reveals its unreality in the form of a heightened sense of loneliness. The orgasmic dream is in this sense the most solipsistic of illusory experiences. The semen is a biological fact, but it is proof only of the fantasy. Unlike other "things" that the hero brings back from the dream world, the semen cannot prove the physical existence of the person who caused it to be present in the dream—the lover from the other world. Like the dream itself, in Sanskrit philosophy, semen is "emitted" by the dreamer in one of the basic processes of illusory creation.

For a woman, blood replaces semen as evidence of a sexual dream. In the tale of Uṣā, the dream of Aniruddha leaves her with precisely this sort of ambiguous physical evidence. Being the daughter of a demon, Uṣā understands the ambiguity of magic; her father tries to capture her lover with magic ropes that are serpents, a reversal of the traditional metaphor of illusory perception: where we normally mistake ropes for serpents, demons *make* ropes out of serpents. These ropes then fall away, and in a later version of the myth they revert to their serpent nature and are destroyed by their natural enemy, the great Garuḍa bird on which Kṛṣṇa rides.[8] The magic is undone so that natural physical forces can triumph.

The physical evidence of the dream lover is strengthened in another version of the myth of Uṣā:

> One day when Śiva was making love with the Goddess Pārvatī, surrounded by hundreds of celestial nymphs, the best of the nymphs, named Citralekhā, took the form of the Goddess and charmed Śiva, and the Goddess laughed, and all the nymphs laughed. Now, Uṣā, the daughter of Bāṇa, saw Śiva making love with the Goddess, and right in front of Pārvatī she made a wish, thinking, "How fortunate are women who make love with their husbands." Pārvatī, knowing her mind, said to her, "Uṣā, you will soon make love with

your husband, just as I make love with Śiva." When she heard this, Uṣā worried and said in her heart, "*When* will I make love with my husband?" Then Pārvatī laughed and said, "Listen, Uṣā. On the twelfth night of the bright half of the month of Vaiśākha, a man will rape you in a dream, and he will be your husband."

Indeed, on the very night that the Goddess had spoken of, a man raped Uṣā in a dream, for he had been incited to this act by the Goddess. As he entered Uṣā, she screamed; smeared with blood, she wept and arose suddenly in the night, terrified. Then she said to her friend Citralekhā, "Now that I have been defiled in this way, what will I tell my father? I think it would be better for me to die now than to live." As she went on weeping, her friends all said to her, "Your *mind* has not been defiled. If a person breaks a vow of chastity in the course of a dream [or sleep, *svapna*], the vow is not broken. You have committed no sin. You are a chaste woman, and since this happened to you while you were asleep, no *dharma* has been violated."

Citralekhā said to Uṣā, "Uṣā, don't you remember what the Goddess promised you in Śiva's presence? So what are you crying about?" Then Uṣā remembered and was no longer sad, but she said, "If this man is to be my husband, how can we know him?" And Citralekhā said, "The man who stole sexual pleasure from you in your dream was someone whom you had never seen or heard of before. So how could we know him? That man who entered the harim and took you by force cannot be an ordinary [*prākṛta*] man, for not even the gods can enter this well-guarded citadel. You are lucky to have such a husband given to you by the Goddess. But now you must find out who his father is and what his name is."

Then the nymph Citralekhā sketched for seven nights, drawing all the gods and demons and demigods and serpents in the world of men, and she showed them all in order to Uṣā. Bewildered and deluded by lust, Uṣā saw Aniruddha; her eyes grew wide in amazement, and she said, "That is the thief who defiled me in my dream. I recognize him. What is his name?" Citralekhā told Uṣā that it was Aniruddha. She then flew to Aniruddha and found him in his harim, drinking wine and making love to all the women. For a moment she worried about how she could manage things, but then she wrapped him in darkness by her magic power, and he vanished from the midst of his women in the harim. She flew with him through the sky and brought him to Uṣā, who was amazed to see him.[9]

Citralekhā and Uṣā appear now not only in the main story but in a prelude that provides a frame for the actual event. After that prelude, they recall the Goddess's promise as one more piece of evidence supporting the reality of the dream. This text also includes a laconic but striking discussion of that reality. When Uṣā says that she has been ruined because she dreamed that she was raped, Citralekhā regards this as a physical fact. She comments on the man's extraordinary prowess in getting past the harim guards, which implies that she feels that he was physically there; she also insists, quite sensibly, that Uṣā find out what sort of family he comes from, so that she can begin to make suitable marriage arrangements. Yet that very statement—that the man must have been extraordinary to have gotten into the harim—could mean precisely the opposite: it could mean that no real flesh-and-blood man could have gotten in, that only a figment of Uṣā's imagination could have managed it. This same ambiguity characterizes the further discussion of the implications of the rape. The blood that appears on Uṣā's body after her dream is taken as a specific example of the "signs of intercourse" more vaguely mentioned in the first text as material proof of the reality of the event. Yet Uṣā's friends argue that a rape in a dream is not a real rape, not because it is not *physically* a rape, but rather because it is not *mentally* a rape. The ambiguity of the word *svapna* leaves undecided the question of whether the women are arguing that one is not responsible for the thoughts in one's dreams or that one is not responsible for the things that are physically done to one when one is asleep. Perhaps both implications are intended. In any case, according to this text Uṣā was raped during the dream, not during the later, physical visit of Aniruddha.

Aniruddha is not literally asleep when Citralekhā finds him, though his senses are muddled by wine and sex. One manuscript tradition inserts a suggestive variant at this point: when Citralekhā brings Aniruddha to Uṣā, he remarks, "I have never seen this place before, but often, in the night, I used to dream that I saw such a great city with its harim full of maidens. And now you have helped me to come to precisely this place."[10] This passage hints at the answer to a problem that hovers over the other variants of the tale. The story of Uṣā as we have it in these first texts is not literally a shared dream, for, though Aniruddha is asleep when Citralekhā finds him, he wakes up either right then or in Uṣā's presence, and it is not said that he was dreaming of Uṣā. However, the wider context of Indian stories in which heroes fly to demonic women in the other world suggests that we might regard the entire story as Aniruddha's dream of Uṣā's dream of him.

This hypothesis, which is supported by the passage in which Aniruddha expresses his sense of *déjà vu*, is vindicated by the final and most baroque of all the versions of the tale of Uṣā and Aniruddha. This text, considerably later than the others, certainly cannot be used to prove that the story was always meant to be a story of Aniruddha's dream, but it does show that at least one Hindu author felt that the story could be placed within that genre.

> Aniruddha was the son of Kāma [the god of erotic love] incarnate as Pradyumna. One day, as he was lying asleep on a bed covered

with flowers, he saw in a dream a young woman lying on a bed of flowers. Her face was lustful, and the wind blew her clothes aside to reveal that she was on fire between her legs. When Aniruddha saw her, his mind was churned by lust [*kāma*], and he said to her, "Are you a goddess or a nymph? Whose wife or daughter are you? Whom do you desire? I am Aniruddha the son of Kāma, in the prime of youth, full of lust and a past master at the erotic arts [*Kāma-śāstra*]. Let me make love to you; I am very good at it." But since she was a virgin, she was shy about making love. She looked at him out of the corner of her eye and said, "If you are so full of lust, why don't you get married? I am Uṣā, the daughter of Bāṇa. A woman is never independent; she is dependent on others. A whore may be independent, but not a good woman. A father gives away a woman to a suitable bridegroom; a maiden does not choose her own bridegroom. You and I are well suited. If you want me, ask Bāṇa for me—or ask Śiva or Pārvatī." And then the woman vanished, and the boy woke up, full of lust, obsessed with lust, though he realized that it had been a dream.

Aniruddha stopped eating and sleeping, and when Rati and the other wives of Kṛṣṇa told Kṛṣṇa about it, Kṛṣṇa laughed and said, "The daughter of Bāṇa once saw the loveplay of Śiva and Pārvatī and became disturbed by lust. Then the Goddess granted Uṣā's wish: she made Aniruddha see a dream that clouded his mind. Now I will cloud the mind of Bāṇa's daughter with a dream." And then Kṛṣṇa, who knows all forms of magic, made Uṣā see a dream. As she slept on a bed of flowers, she saw a handsome man in the prime of youth, and she fell in love with him and said to him, "Who are you, lover? Make love to me, for I am tortured with desire. I have just reached womanhood and am longing for my first taste of sex, and I am in love with you. Marry me by the Gandharva marriage ritual of mutual consent, the easiest of all eight forms of marriage." But he said, "I am the grandson of Kṛṣṇa and the son of Kāma. How can I take you, my darling, without the permission of those two?" And as he said this, he vanished. Overpowered by lust when she could no longer see her lover, Uṣā woke up and arose from her bed and wept.

When Uṣā stopped eating and sleeping, her friend Citralekhā told Bāṇa and his wife about Uṣā's condition. The queen wept, and Bāṇa fainted dead away. But when Śiva heard Citralekhā's report, he laughed, remembering the Goddess's boon and Kṛṣṇa's role in sending the dream, and he told Citralekhā to bring Aniruddha to Uṣā. Citralekhā went to Dvārakā to summon Aniruddha as he slept; she brought him in a chariot while he was still asleep. Then she awakened him, and by her magic and her yogic powers she brought him to Uṣā in the harim, though it was well guarded. She awakened Uṣā; and when Uṣā saw her husband, she rejoiced. He married her with the Gandharva ritual, and they made love for a long time. The son of Kāma was so full of lust [*kāma*] that he did

> not know night from day, and Uṣā fainted away at the very touch of the man.
>
> After a long time, the guards went to Bāṇa and said, "These are evil times. Citralekhā has served as the go-between and brought a handsome hero to Uṣā. Now your daughter Uṣā is pregnant; her body is marked by nails all over, and she makes love with her lover all the time." When Bāṇa heard this, he was ashamed and angry, and he determined to attack, despite Śiva's attempts to persuade him to let Uṣā marry Aniruddha. "For," Bāṇa replied, "the guard said, 'Your daughter is pregnant,' right in front of the whole assembly, and those words still burn like poison in my ears." The battle took place, and Kṛṣṇa brought Uṣā and Aniruddha back to Dvārakā.[11]

This story begins with Aniruddha's dream, to which Uṣā's dream is merely a response. Aniruddha dreams of himself as lustful and his bride as chaste; her dream is the opposite. When she quotes *Dharma-śāstra* to him in *his* dream, he quotes it right back to her in *her* dream. The dreams are thus not so much the same dream as reciprocal dreams, two different views of the same encounter. Aniruddha realizes explicitly that his dream was nothing but a dream, not a true encounter with a woman; the physical evidence is then provided not by the dream but by his physical reaction to the dream: he stops eating and sleeping (and hence, we may suppose, he does not dream any more). This evidence then causes the report of the dream; Aniruddha's mother tells Kṛṣṇa, just as the guards tell Bāṇa of Uṣā's dream in the other versions. In those versions there is physical evidence of intercourse. Here there is no such evidence, in either Aniruddha or Uṣā; but she too stops eating and sleeping, so they share their lovesick behavior. Citralekhā can carry the story to Bāṇa without betraying Uṣā, for evidently Citralekhā regards Uṣā's chastity as intact, as indeed it is: in this version, Uṣā and Aniruddha do not make love in their dreams; they merely express their love and their lust, and they argue within themselves, as well as with each other, about the measures they should take to make their dream come true.

The reason for their ambivalence is stated by Śiva when he tells the story: "When she saw the young man in her dream, Uṣā was full of desire but was restrained by her awe of *dharma*." Still, Bāṇa faints away at the knowledge of his daughter's *mental* state. (This is a reversal of the argument in our second text, where Uṣā's friends reassure her, when she was raped in a dream, that her mind is pure even if her body has been defiled.) But when Aniruddha finally reaches the harim and physically marries Uṣā, the guards report to Bāṇa as they do in the earlier versions, and this time they cite the ultimate in undeniable physical proof of intercourse: they say that Uṣā is pregnant. They also add that her body is marked by nails, making explicit what may have been implicit in the other texts that referred to "signs of intercourse" after Uṣā had *dreamed* of making love with Aniruddha and "signs hard to conceal" after she had actually made love with him. Though Uṣā has in fact married Aniruddha by the Gandharva ritual (an informal ceremony consisting of nothing but sexual consummation), Śiva suggests that she still might have a formal wedding to save the family honor, but Bāṇa will not hear of it. Thus Śiva moves inward from the outer frame (the curse-boon of Pārvatī) into the inner frame (the conversation with Bāṇa), even as Citralekhā and Uṣā move out of the inner frame into the outer frame in the second version. Śiva is aware of both sets of dreams, as is Kṛṣṇa, though the human lovers, once awakened by Citralekhā, do not care whether they are awake or dreaming. Where the other texts said that they lost count of the days, here they cannot even tell whether it is day or night.

The Brushwood Boy

Another example of an Indian tale of this genre appears in a short story called "The Brushwood Boy," written by Rudyard Kipling in 1898. I think I am justified in calling it Indian, both because Kipling knew Indian literature (and had an Indian nurse) and because it uses many Indian themes—in British transformation:

> A young boy dreamed all his life about a girl whom he met beside a pile of brushwood in a place called the City of Sleep; there, beside the Lily Lock of the Sea of Dreams, he rode with her along the Thirty-Mile Ride until a Policeman called Day awakened him. He grew up, and the girl in his dream became a woman with black hair that grew into a widow's peak. He joined the cavalry in India, played polo, and became a popular officer; but he never kissed a woman. He drew a map of the place in his dream ("I'm gettin' the hang of the geography of that place," he said to himself, as he shaved next morning), and kept it up to date, for he was a most methodical person.
>
> As he was travelling home by ship, an older woman whom he had met on the ship stole into his cabin and kissed him as he slept. That night, he dreamed that the girl by the Sea of Dreams kissed him, and as he woke up, "he could almost have sworn that the kiss was real." He returned to his parents' home in England, where he heard a girl singing a song about the Sea of Dreams, the City of Sleep, and the Policeman called Day. He came into the room and saw her—the black hair in the widow's peak, with that peculiar ripple over the right ear; there was also the small, well-cut mouth that had kissed him. But she did not recognize him.
>
> Then they went riding together, and after a wild gallop he told her of his dream, with details (such as the Thirty-Mile Ride) that she had not mentioned in her song. ("I know I didn't. I have never told a living soul.") She burst into tears and asked, "Am I mad?" and he replied, "Not unless I'm mad as well." Finally, as they con-

> tinued to compare details of the dream, she cried out, "Then you're the Boy—my Brushwood Boy, and I've known you all my life!" When she asked him what it meant, he said, "This! Perhaps when we die we may find out more, but it means this now." After he kissed her, he told her of the time he had kissed her before, in his dream; she told him that she had dreamt, that same night, that another woman had kissed him. But he denied ever having kissed anyone before, and they rode home happily together to be married.[12]

The thrilling gallop side by side is Kipling's version of the dream image of flying through the air with a female magician or on a winged horse; the woman who comes to the hero and kisses him in his sleep is the dangerous succubus, who threatens his careful chastity, while the innocent girl in England is the other aspect of the shadow woman in the other world, the princess who is his reward, not his temptation. Set against the unemotional banality of the life of the upper classes in Victorian England, the dreams are made out of that very same banality—dreams of quiet downs and well-bred ponies and a solid British bobby (the enemy who awakens them, as the watchman and the maid awaken Vikramāditya and Malayavatī). The only thing that makes the dream exciting is the fact that it is a shared dream, a shared map of an imaginary country (that this map becomes a real map when the dreamer is in India may well be an indication that Kipling was aware of the story's ancestry). Kipling's hero draws the map, as a good English officer would do, but then he shows it to no one; it remains a private document, like the dream itself, shutting him up in his solipsistic romance until, one assumes, he can show it to the girl. The girl is at first terrified when she realizes that her dream is a shared dream, and even the smug young officer expresses tentative intimations of another world.[13] As in other examples of this genre, the girl is less certain of the waking world—she does not recognize him as quickly as he recognizes her—and is more aware of the interpenetration of the two worlds: she knows that a *real* woman also kissed him on the night that he dreamt of kissing her, though he denies it.[14]

In Kipling's story (as in many Indo-European stories of the simpler version of the romantic adventure), the hero rides on a horse. In most of the Indian stories, the hero flies through the air to the woman in the other world. The image of the winged horse—Bellerophon's Pegasus again—provides a convenient synthesis of the two versions: the hero rides *and* flies. Riding is a perfectly realistic thing to do; flying is not. Yet, as we have seen, dreams (and stories) do not make a firm distinction between what is and what is not possible. Flying and riding may be, as Freud suggested, two closely related dream metaphors for sexual passion; in any case, they seem to serve an identical function in tales of sexual adventure.

Western Arguments
Shared Dreams and Archetypal Myths

What is the meaning of the shared dream? How can it happen that two people share the same dream? Why do people write stories about people who share the same dream? The answer to all of these questions begins, I think, in our recognition of the human terror of solipsism. The shared dream functions in India as a powerful symbol of unfathomable intimacy. When Queen Līlā converses with the goddess Sarasvatī, who has flown with her through the air to visit her husband (as Citralekhā brought Aniruddha to Uṣā), their conversation is said to be "like the conversation of people who have had the same wishes and dreams," and the modern commentary suggests that, "In the world, by the grace of god etc., two people sometimes have the same dream, like Uṣā and Aniruddha."[15] The commentator explains his point by citing a story, in traditional Indian fashion, and it is, I think, significant that he cites the story of Uṣā and Aniruddha as an example of a shared dream. He may be referring to the most baroque Hindu variant, in which Aniruddha's dream precedes Uṣā's, or to the underlying pattern that persists in atavistic details even in variants of the tale in which Aniruddha does not, in fact, reciprocate Uṣā's dream.

Roger Caillois has described the appeal of the shared dream:

> Nothing is more personal than a dream, nothing else so imprisons a person in irremediable solitude, nothing else is as stubbornly resistant to the possibility of being shared. In the world of reality everything is susceptible to universal test. The dream, on the other hand, is an adventure that only the dreamer himself has experienced and which only he can remember; it is a water-tight, impenetrable world which precludes the least chance of cross-checking. The temptation now arises to believe that two or more persons (or even a whole multitude) may at times have the same dream or have dreams that are parallel or complementary. The dreams would thus be corroborated, fitted together like the pieces of a puzzle and, by acquiring in this way the solidity and stability possessed by the perceptions of the waking world, would be verifiable like them and, even better, would create certain bonds between the dreamers—secret, narrow, restricted, and imperious bonds.[16]

The dream that becomes verifiable, passing scientific tests, is in some ways the opposite of the dream shared by only two people; the former becomes part of the accepted knowledge of the world, while the latter, by very virtue of being denied by all the rest of the world, is what links the two who share it. The dream of Vikramāditya and Malayavatī partakes of both aspects: at first, it is only their mutual love that binds the two dreamers, but when both of them make public their dreams, a general belief in the truth of the shared dream arises in the public at large. The dream of Kipling's lovers remains private forever, for they are English. At the other extreme, certain philosophical Indian texts that we will encounter in chapter five use the motif of the shared dream as the starting point from which to develop a variant of the argument of pure idealism: the world that we regard as public (shared) is in fact merely the manifestation of a single mental image, a private dream dreamed by God and shared by all of us. These texts thus invoke an outer frame that is soft—like the theological frame invoked, in a far weaker way, in the second version of the tale of Uṣā and Aniruddha—in order to harden the reality of the shared dream. The words of the god corroborate the images of the dream; one does not need a dream to corroborate the reality of the god.

The hypothesis that there may be dreams that are shared by a number of different people (the "multitude" of which Caillois speaks) underlies a phenomenon found throughout the world: the use of "dream books," that is, textbooks or codebooks that decipher the meanings of dreams, of which we have seen examples in the Hindu texts. The fact that generalizations of this sort can be made at all implies an awareness that certain themes and motifs recur in dreams recorded at different times and in different places. It also involves the implicit assumption that these dreams will in fact *be recorded*, that they will be *told*. This awareness also underlies our own depth psychologies' interest in the meaning and sharing of dreams. Though Freud and Jung differed considerably about whether the same dream, dreamed by two different people, had the same meaning (or was, in a deeper sense, the same dream at all), both admitted that there are, indeed, typical or perhaps even universal dreams and that these pose special problems of interpretation over and above the problem of relating the dream to the life of the specific dreamer.

These universal dreams, the stuff that dream books are made of, are shared in quite a different sense from the shared dreams of the Indian lovers. The universal or archetypal dreams are shared because different people have dreamt the same things and have told one another about it; the lovers' dreams are shared because different people have dreamt the same things and have dreamt *about each other*. This true reciprocity is further enhanced by a far greater amount of detail in the Indian stories than in the archetypal dreams. The universal dreams share a few basic motifs, which are explained either by universal human experiences or (in the Jungian system) by the inheritance of a few archetypal symbols arising out of those experiences.

Indian philosophy includes within its expansive bounds several concepts quite comfortably compatible with a theory of archetypes. The extreme form of Vedānta, which maintains that no physical matter is real, is particularly amenable to such an interpretation. For if there is a rope on the path, there is no need to invoke archetypes to explain why we might mistake it for a snake; a snake does look very much like a rope. But if there is no rope there, why should we *all* think of a snake? Because, perhaps, we are all born with archetypal images of snakes in our heads. Thus it is said that "similar sayings appear in the minds of many people."[17] Even more impressive is the *Yogavāsiṣṭha*'s assertion that men of great enterprise are able to contract together and do business by relying on pure chance and the power of the (collective) karmic memory traces in the mind of each one.[18] Apparently they all imagine the same contracts, the same lawyers, the same assets and liabilities, and agree on the imaginary price. Similarly, it is said that "Many men see the same dream; many little boys play the same game."[19] Mass hallucinations are also attested in the West: "Hallucinations can be socially determined, and there are cases of many people 'witnessing' together events which never occurred."[20] But such phenomena, which we regard as rare and aberrational, are easily accommodated by the basic Indian line of thought:

> There is no objective datum which forms the common ground for the illusory perception of all people. Just as when ten persons see in the darkness a rope and having the illusion of a snake there, run away, and agree in their individual perceptions that they have all seen the same snake, though each really had his own illusion and there was no snake at all, [just so do we constantly share in a common illusion of the universe].[21]

Ironically, this argument now renders superfluous and meaningless the search for consensual authority to corroborate the reality of the shared dream, since, even if two people agree, *both* can be wrong.

The *Rêve à Deux* in Psychoanalysis

When we contrast archetypal dreams with our Indian narratives of shared dreams, we see that what the lovers share are not, in fact, archetypes but manifestations; that is, what they share are not general symbols or even the learned symbols of their shared culture but, rather, a number of striking, cumulative, exact details. These shared dreams are not "parallel" or "complementary" dreams, for one lover sees the exact buildings, the exact clothes, hears the exact same words, and spends the exact same amount of time in the adventure as the other sees, hears, and experiences.

An explanation of this phenomenon was suggested by the psychoanalyst Jules Eisenbud, who interpreted what he called "a telepathic *rêve à deux*" dreamt by two of his patients. The first dreamt that she was walking in a heavy downpour and took shelter at the home of her neighbor; the second patient dreamt, on a subsequent night, that the first patient sought refuge in her home from a heavy downpour. It might well be argued that there is so little detail in the coincidence of the two dreams that they qualify only for the more general level of our theme, the basic sorts of things that people tend to dream about: rain, night, and being lost. But Eisenbud regarded it as a more striking phenomenon, a truly shared dream, and he tried to explain it:

> Once we admit the possibility of telepathic activity in dreams, we are no longer at liberty to assume that a given dream is exclusively the private concern of the dreamer who had it, since analysis is capable of demonstrating that one dream may be the vehicle for the latent material of two, three, or more individuals, or that two dreams are essentially one, existing separately only in the way that two intelligence agents may carry separately the complementary details of a plan which can be understood only when both sections are viewed together.[22]

The elements of this plan are broken down like the pieces of the puzzle that Caillois referred to. The separate bits of the broken message correspond to the separate versions of a myth that combine to make a statement that no single version of the myth can make.[23] For dreams, as for myths, there is a master plan. But whose plan is it? Since the analyst is the only one who can understand the two dreams, he is evidently the master spy, the double agent, the one who (through transference and countertransference) has mediated between the two dreamers, allowing them to dream of each other through him. In this way he provides the outer frame for their dreams, just as God provides such a frame for the Indian nested dreams. In medieval Indian theology, God is inside the dreamer in a way similar to the way that (in the myths) lovers are inside each other or that (in the psychoanalytic scenario) the analyst is inside the patient. God is the witness of all dreamers, and he is the dreamer of the universal dream, on the outside; but he participates erotically on the inside as well. He is an actor in the drama—a character in the dream—as well as the author—the analyst of the dream.

An even more explicit example of the role of the psychoanalyst as a medium for telepathic dreams—or as a god—comes from Géza Róheim, one of whose patients reported having dreamt the following dream:

> "I am still at home . . . and I am in time for next day's analysis. I have had a dream which I am going to tell the analyst. The dream was this: A white dove alights on a pink cloud. I see this, and the sky is blue. I come into analysis, enter the room, but the couch stands crosswise. You begin to talk instead of letting me talk, and

> you say, 'I dreamed that a white dove alights on a pink cloud. The sky was blue.' I am so happy."[24]

This is both a nested dream (a type that we will see in chapter five) and a dream about a shared dream. But the plot thickens when Róheim explains the analytic frame in which it occurred:

> The patient dreamed this the same night that I was thinking about the problem of telepathy, a subject I had never been interested in before. . . . It is obvious that she dreamed of having dreamed the same thing that I had, that is, *we have before us a telepathic dream on the subject of telepathy*.[25]

Thus the analyst provides the hard frame that enables the patient to make the dream real; he is the spiritual master who makes dreams come true.

But psychoanalysis takes advantage of yet another time-honored way of hardening dreams: by telling them. Like Roger Caillois, Charles Rycroft is aware of the great need that people have to tell their dreams to someone else, but he sees this need as doomed to inevitable frustration:

> While dreaming we appear to enter a world of our own . . . but we can share none of this with anyone else. We can, it is true, tell our dreams to someone else and, if we are lucky, his imaginative response to them may give us the illusion of a shared experience. But if the person we tell a dream to turns out to be a sceptic, we have no means of convincing him that we really did have the dream we have told him. If he asks for proof that we had that precise dream and no other one, that we have remembered it correctly, we cannot give it. We cannot ask the people who appeared in the dream to confirm our story. Unlike the events of everyday life, which can, in principle, be confirmed or otherwise by the laws of evidence, and unlike the events of our intimate personal relationships, which can be confirmed or otherwise by reference to the identical or reciprocal responses of the other, dream experiences have a peculiar privacy about them, which can only be partially and often only self-deceptively reduced by recounting them to others.[26]

Yet in the Indian stories, as we have seen, people do "ask the people who appeared in the dream to confirm" the reality of the dream, and in doing this they combine two things that in our society are, as Rycroft points out, separate: first, the "imaginative response" to the telling, which gives the mere "illusion of the shared experience"—a sharing on the most general level; and second, the offering of an "identical or reciprocal response," which may be given by someone with whom we are intimate. This is the force of the lovers' *rêve à deux*, for here the dream is told to the one person in the world close enough to be inside the dreamer, the one person who does not need to be told the dream in order to know it.

Telling and sharing the dream are what convince the individual dreamer that he is not mad, as he otherwise fears he may be. This may also be true of Tantric yogins, as viewed by the Hindu psychoanalyst Sudhir Kakar:

> The tantric imaginative reality is not the personal, imaginary reality of the psychotic. . . . The imaginative reality created by tantric exercises is both shared and public in the sense that it is based upon, guided and formed by the symbolic, iconic network of the tantric culture which the adept inhabits. In other words, if tantric visualizations are conscious dream creations, then they are dreams which have been dreamed by others.[27]

This is what happens when mystics unionize, as it were—when antisocial rebels form a society. Yet the experience that is captured by this group is, in a very basic sense, one that can never be described in words. This belief is expressed in a poem by a medieval Islamic poet:

> Different he is from us, different and unseen,
> and his story is different from all others.
> Like the dumb one who had a dream,
> who knows and understands and pines,
> because he cannot tell his tale.[28]

The mystic experience of the ultimately real is perceived as a private dream that cannot be told or shared and as a dream that many mystics have tried in vain to tell about and share. Indeed, this very frustration—the urgent need to tell something, stifled by a paralytic inability to utter a sound—is in itself an archetypal dream experience.

When we do succeed in telling the dream, we feel that we have made it something public rather than private. In chapter one we attempted to distinguish public or cultural dreams from private or universal dreams. Public or cultural dreams are dreams that people are told about in a particular society and that they are encouraged to dream; private dreams are the dreams that people create out of their individual lives, often invoking universal human experiences and symbols. (Private elements—the unique factors in each human life—and universal elements—those basic events and basic perceptions of events that are attested all over the world—together bracket cultural dreams, which are neither individual nor universal.) The actual symbols that occur in many of the Indian stories and dream books—the teeth falling out, the ride on horseback, the nightmare of being dismembered or beheaded or blinded, the vision of the death of oneself or someone one loves—are private dream symbols that people do dream about; we know them from our own dreams or from the writings of Freud. These private dreams are, in a sense, universal. But the glosses on these dreams are public, cultural: in India, the dream of teeth falling out means that your son will die, whereas an American analyst might gloss it as symbolic of the dreamer's own fear of impotence or as an expression of his hope of recovery: after all, when one lost one's baby teeth, they grew back.[29] And, as we have seen, universal and cultural dream images often appear side by side in a single text.

Myths are often made out of private dreams: "The core of the myth is a dream actually dreamt once upon a time by one person."[30] Dreams and myths alike draw their power from certain intense moments in actual human experience; but art transforms the private understanding of the dream into the public understanding of the myth. A myth is a private dream that has gone public. But dreams are also made out of myths,[31] for people tend to dream not only about their lives but also about the myths they have been taught. Dreams incorporate into personal fantasy elements of traditional, shared mythology. The distinction between cultural and personal dreams may be initially useful, but it runs aground because of the mutual feedback between dreams and myths: *a* gives rise to *b*, but *b* gives rise to *a*. This paradox, like our riddle of the chicken and the egg, is expressed in India as the mystery of the seed and the tree. Indeed, it is more properly a triangular cybernetic process, for it connects myth and dream, myth and reality, and dream and reality.

Normally, we share our myths and many of our waking experiences; communication across those points of the triangle is easy enough. But in the *rêve à deux* we communicate from dream to dream, directly. The shared dream of lovers may be seen as the result of a kind of intense heightening of the basic bond that joins all humans. It has been suggested that "everybody's unconscious perfectly understands everybody else's unconscious" and that telepathic dreams occur because, "when persons are bound together emotionally, the tie of love opens one unconscious to another."[32] In this view, the flint of love strikes a spark that jumps from one mind to another. The events described in the Indian stories could be explained, in a similar way, as transformative mental events. It has been further suggested that the power of this emotional magnet extends across time as well as space, that there is some substantial force that, though not yet manifest, is already pregnant with the future, even as a ghost lingers by the grave of the past. This force is drawn to us across time and space, flowing backward against the current of material time in a way that cannot be measured with hard instruments or accounted for by our present scientific knowledge. In this view, just as the ghosts of people whom we have loved in the past may haunt our dreams, so too the shadows of people whom we will love in the future may first fall across our lives in our dreams.

The medium through which such transmissions could take place is the human substratum that links the universal dreams one to another, a kind of dream ether, an all-pervading substance in which we all move as fish move through water. In Jungian terms, this is the shared mental matrix of the human race; in Indian terms, it is Godhead. But dreams of this sort are, to my knowledge, recorded only in myths. That is, we do not have proof that people have such shared dreams; all we have is proof that people like to think that such a thing is possible.[33] What is transmitted across the dream ether is therefore not dreams but myths. The dream ether is the warp that myths are woven on; the weft is individual human experience and art. Myths reflect our desire to believe that people really can dream the same dream, a desire that is a deep hope—a dream, if you will—that we all share. The myths that describe such experiences are shared dreams about shared dreams. The inner dream, told in the myth, is one in which love binds together inexplicably the hard and soft worlds of human perception. The outer dream *is* the myth, which nourishes our hope that it is possible to break out of the prison of our secret loneliness, to dream one another's dreams.

3 Myths about Illusion

Indian Texts

Nārada Transformed into a Woman

A well-known and well-loved example of the genre of myths about illusion is the cycle about the transformation of the sage Nārada into a woman. Heinrich Zimmer remarked of this tale, "The story is still told in India, as a kind of nursery tale, and is familiar to many from childhood."[1] Because the tale is part of the living oral tradition of India, there are many variants of it, each of which adds something to our understanding of the meaning the story has had for different Indian audiences. I will concentrate on one particular version, recorded in a medieval Sanskrit text, in which Nārada tells his own story:

> One day I went to play my lute for Viṣṇu and found the god joyously engaged in erotic play with his wife Lakṣmī. As soon as she saw me, Lakṣmī vanished from my presence. I wondered at this and remarked to Viṣṇu, "I am an ascetic, not a lecher; I have conquered illusion." Viṣṇu reminded me that a woman is never allowed to remain in the presence of any man but her husband; he also warned me never to say that I had conquered illusion, since no one, not even the gods, could conquer illusion. I then begged Viṣṇu to show me what illusion was, and he agreed to this. He took me to a beautiful pond and invited me to bathe in it. I entered the pool as Viṣṇu watched me, and in it I left my male form and became a woman. Viṣṇu picked up my lute and went away, and I forgot all about my former body.
>
> A king named Tāladhvaja ["Palm-Tree Banner"] came by; he married me, even though I confessed my total ignorance of my past, and he gave me the name of Saubhāgyasundarī ["She whose beauty is her good fortune" or, as we might say, "The woman whose face is her fortune"]. Then the king, who was a past master at the erotic skills, abandoned all his royal duties and made love to his queen night and day, losing all sense of time, drinking wine and immersing himself in pleasure. I, too, for twelve years that passed like a single moment, forgot my former body and former life as a sage.
>
> I became pregnant and had eight sons and then many grandsons. Sometimes I was happy, sometimes saddened by the quarrels

> of my sons and daughters-in-law; sometimes I was sick and in pain. One day an enemy attacked the kingdom, and all of my sons and grandsons were killed. As I lamented in an agony of grief, Viṣṇu took the form of a Brahmin and came to me and said, "Why are you so sad? This is just a mistake [*bhrama*] and a delusion [*moha*]. Who are you, and whose sons are these? Do not weep, but pull yourself together and perform the rituals for the dead, beginning with your own ritual bath." Then the king and I and the other relatives went with the Brahmin to the lake that was called "Male-ford" [Puṃtīrtha], and the Brahmin said, "You have had millions of sons who died in life after life, and millions of husbands and fathers, too. For whom will you grieve? It is all a mistake that arose in your own mind, like a dream." At these words, I entered the ford and instantly became a man, and Viṣṇu put my lute back in my hand.
>
> Then I remembered that I was Nārada, that I had been deluded by illusion and had become a woman, a terrible fate, and that at last I had become a man again.[2]

Nārada commits the intellectual transgression of insisting on learning about illusion despite Viṣṇu's warning that he should not look too deeply into the secret (because it is arrogant to expect to be able to conquer the magic that deludes even the gods). His experience of life as a woman ("a terrible fate," as the text tells us) is designed to cure him of this arrogance. (In other myths of illusion, which we will encounter in chapter four, the demeaning status is that of an Untouchable instead of a woman.)

Nārada's experience is said to be both happy and sad, and different variants of the story may emphasize either the happiness or the sorrow. One version remarks that, as a woman, Nārada "experienced the misery of worldly existence. Then she was separated from her husband and sons, and because of that sorrow she became Nārada again."[3] This text highlights the misery of worldly existence or married life, for the word *saṃsāra* can denote both of these conditions, a fact not without significance. The experience in the illusory world is a nightmare from which one wishes to escape; this is in keeping with the *mokṣa*-oriented argument that it is sorrow that enlightens and, finally, awakens one from the nightmare of existence. The story demonstrates the illusory nature of apparent happiness and the enlightening power of apparent sorrow.

Yet the version of the story with which we began seems at first to characterize Nārada's illusory world as sensuous and joyous, despite its sad ending, and this is in keeping with much of the folk and Purāṇic tradition, which is grounded in the *saṃsāra*-oriented point of view. Indeed, *mokṣa* is often depicted in life-affirming, even rapturous terms, but its basic view is that the world is a place one wants to depart from, not linger in. The text seems at first to depict a dream of the enjoyment of longed-for pleasures; Nārada remarks afterwards, somewhat wistfully, "As a woman, I drank wine and ate forbidden things."[4] The story is intended, however, not as a simple description of the delights of an erotic dream but, on the contrary, as a warning against sexual indulgence; the final weight comes down on the side of *mokṣa*, not of *saṃsāra*. The insidious dangers of sexual intoxication become evident after Nārada has been transformed; he forgets his true nature and loses all sense of time, because he is overpowered by sensuality. When Nārada loses his awareness of who he is, he loses his lute, which is the symbol of his "real" persona—of his art, his learning, and his religious work; for Nārada is always depicted as a homeless, wifeless sage, a wandering singer who carries a lute. In another version of the tale, when Nārada emerges from the water on the occasion of his retransformation, from a woman into a man, he still holds his hand above the water; it remains the hand of a woman, holding a mango. He then dives back into the water and immerses his hand, which turns into the hand of a man, holding not a mango but a lute.[5] In contrast with the lute, the mango symbolizes human cravings and sensual pleasures; when Nārada leaves the world of illusion, the soft, perishable mango must be transformed into a hard, enduring lute. The mango symbolizes nature; the lute symbolizes culture.

But there is a version of the story that is told from the mango's point of view, as it were. This text, which reflects the Vedic and Purāṇic values of *bhakti*—passionate devotion to the god—regards both sexuality and femininity as positive factors. The story, like our first version, is narrated by Nārada:

> Viṣṇu told Brahmā to bring me to him. As I went to bathe in a lake, I came out on the bank as a woman among other women. When they asked me who I was, I replied, "Who I am, and where I came from, and how I came to have the form of a woman—all of this seems like a dream, and I have no idea about it." One of the women said to me, "This is Vṛndā, the city of Kṛṣṇa." Then I went with the women to Kṛṣṇa, who could take the form of a woman. When he saw me, he said, "My darling! Come and embrace me!" I made love with him there for a year, and then Viṣṇu spoke of me to the goddess Rādhā: "This creature [*prakṛti*] used to have the form of Nārada, until he bathed in a lake of ambrosia. And I myself am Rādhā when I have the form of a woman, and I am Kṛṣṇa when I have the form of a man. There is, truly, no difference between the two of us, Nārada. This is the secret of Vṛndā." Then Rādhā took me back to the lake, and she went back to Kṛṣṇa, and by plunging into the lake I became Nārada again, with my lute in my hand.[6]

Here the image of bisexuality is adapted to play a part in a complex theology of sexual transformation.[7] Although the irrelevance of gender is here made explicit, Nārada's experience as a woman in the other world is far more "real" than his experience as a male Nārada in this world: it is an experience of the presence of God, not an illusion of yet another meaningless human birth. Significantly, Nārada remembers his previous existence as a kind of dream. The vision of sexual gratification that began the tale of Nārada as Tāladhvaja's wife but in that text quickly soured here encounters no obstacles at all. What sorrow there is in the story is simply the implicit sense of loss that Nārada feels when he leaves Kṛṣṇa and comes back down to earth—to an earth that he now realizes is not as real as he once thought it was. Significantly, Nārada has no children in the other world, to tie him to material life or to cause him sorrow; he has a purely erotic (spiritual) encounter, not an entanglement in fertility.

As a wandering musician and gossip, a confirmed bachelor and meddler in other peoples' love lives, Nārada himself often becomes at least temporarily embroiled in erotic escapades. Once, it is said, he saw a group of nymphs bathing in a river; he became excited and shed his seed.[8] Nārada's lust is cunningly satirized in the illustration of this episode (see plate 1): one hand is jammed into his crotch, while the other still desperately grips his lute; his thighs are tightly crossed, one ankle twisted behind the other, in a vain attempt to control himself. This image could stand as a visual embodiment of the unresolvable conflict between the claims of *mokṣa* and *saṃsāra*, the roles of ascetic and householder.

How do we know that Nārada experienced merely an illusion and not a real transformation into a woman and back again into a man? Such transformations often occur in Indian mythology and elsewhere as well, as in the Greek myth of Teiresias.[9] But there is a particular quality that distinguishes the Indian myths of transformation from other examples of this genre, such as the Greek, and that quality further blurs the already broken line between transformations and illusions. For Greek myths generally describe transformations that occurred once, long ago, *in illo tempore*; transformations of this kind serve to explain how things have been forever after: the human woman who spurned Apollo or provoked Hera's jealousy was changed into a tree or a flower, and ever since then we have the flower, not the woman. Indian myths, by contrast, describe transformations analogous to the change that turns a caterpillar into a butterfly: we keep having caterpillars, and they keep changing into butterflies. Indian transformations keep on happening.

In this context, we might well think that Nārada has in fact been transformed by his sea change, but gradually we recognize his experience as an illusion because of the conventions of the genre in which it is told: when Nārada returns to his state as a man, no time has elapsed for the people who knew him as a man. In one version, told by Sri Ramakrishna, Viṣṇu sends Nārada to fetch him some water; while going for the water, Nārada experiences not a transformation into a woman but a long life as a householder, whose wife and children are eventually destroyed by a flood. As Nārada struggles out of the flood and weeps, he hears Viṣṇu's voice saying, "Where is the water you went to fetch for me? I have been waiting more than half an hour."[10] This variant assimilates the tale of Nārada to the closely related story of the king who marries an Untouchable woman. In both of these tales, time stands still in the outer world while it moves swiftly in the world of the illusion. These texts lead us from our first guess, that a transformation has taken place, to the realization that experiences we often think are transformations might eventually be revealed to us as mere illusions if we knew the whole story.

However, in one sequel to the tale of Nārada, one of the criteria that in most versions identify his experience as illusory—the fact that all the people who participated in the illusory experience vanish when the dreamer awakens—is reversed; for now the people in the other world continue to exist when he leaves it, and there is, moreover, no disjunction between the rates at which time passes in the two worlds. This text also adds an important twist: it goes on to describe the quandary that the people in Nārada's illusory world experience when he leaves. This twist then prevents us from reclassifying the story as an instance of illusion after all; what is involved is, instead, a far more complex intermixture of reality and illusion.

In our first version of the tale, the story continues after the death of all of the sons and grandsons of Tāladhvaja's queen, Saubhāgyasundarī (the transformed Nārada). For in this story, it may be recalled, the king (Nārada's husband) does not die. The children die, and it is their death that triggers Nārada's retransformation; but the king survives. Nārada continues the narration:

> When I had entered the ford and become a man, King Tāladhvaja saw me and was amazed. He said, "Where has my wife gone? And how did this sage get here? My dear wife, did you drown, or were you eaten by fishes or turtles? And what will become of me now? Rāma found separation from his wife so unbearable that he left the earth. Women are fortunate, for the lawbooks allow them to burn themselves on their husbands' funeral pyres." As he lamented in this way, the Brahmin [Viṣṇu] said to him, "Why are you so sad? Have you never read any of the scriptures, and have you no wits? You won't bring her back by weeping over her; go and do your duties as you used to do. Use your mind to understand the nature of the soul. Animals have a weakness for the tongue and the penis, but only men have true knowledge." And so the king went home and attained knowledge of the true nature of things, and at last he retired to the forest.[11]

From Nārada's standpoint, the king and all the others in that world disappeared when Nārada became retransformed; this was the main factor that identified the experiences of Nārada-the-woman as an illusion or a dream rather than a transformation. We therefore assumed that the king ceased to exist when Nārada ceased to imagine him or to dream of him. From our original standpoint as we hear the story, Nārada is real—a part of the world in which the story is originally set—and Tāladhvaja is not—he is part of a world that is by definition and convention other. But the second half of the tale of Tāladhvaja forces us to turn the story inside out, to see Nārada appearing from another world into the life of Tāladhvaja. The simile used by the king is a significant one: he has lost his wife as Rāma lost Sītā. Like Tāladhvaja, Rāma married a woman who came to him from another world, the immortal woman who—like the Swan Maiden—stays long enough to bear a child and then vanishes forever.[12] (We will soon see texts that view the dream of Rāma from Sītā's point of view.)

But this is not all. If we do grant the king a degree of ontological status equivalent to Nārada's, we would assume that Queen Saubhāgyasundarī (née Nārada) vanished from the king's world when "she" became a man again. But now we learn that, from the king's standpoint, Nārada-Saubhāgyasundarī did *not* disappear—she became a man. Thus, from the king's point of view, Nārada experienced a transformation, not an illusion, and the king's own experience was entirely real. Though the text has not *argued* for the reality of the king's experience, it has tricked us into accepting it on an equal footing with the experience of Nārada, by treating it with the same narrative conventions.

Finally, in this one text Nārada's own experience takes on a further ambiguity, arising from the fact that the story is told by Nārada in the first person. This device is yet another factor in persuading us of the reality of Nārada's experience; he tells it to us himself, after all. But although Nārada never speaks to Tāladhvaja after he has become retransformed from Saubhāgyasundarī into Nārada again, we might assume that he did continue to see Tāladhvaja; for he tells us what Tāladhvaja said and did after that. Yet he may be speaking not as an eyewitness of the event but merely as the omniscient narrator Nārada, telling us things that, in retrospect, he realizes must have happened even though he himself (i.e., the Nārada in the story, rather than Nārada the narrator) did not see them happen.

These complexities of the tale of Nārada make us recognize the relativity of the standpoint of the observer, the relativity of illusion. The people among whom Nārada experiences his enlightening vision are *there*. When he wakes up from his dream, they miss him, and they try to construct a sensible way to explain what happened to him: he fell into the water and was eaten by turtles, and somehow a sage appeared on the spot at the same time. Viṣṇu explains Nārada's experience by quoting the standard Vedāntic dogma of the resemblance between dreams and illusion.[13] He does not, however, go on to explain in any detail why it was that the *king* experienced a relationship with Nārada, except, perhaps, by the unstated inference that the king was dreaming, too—that is, he was dreaming about Nārada's transformation into a woman. The real, transformative nature of the experience from the king's point of view contrasts vividly with Nārada's ambiguously illusory experience. Viṣṇu reminds Saubhāgyasundarī that "she" has had many lives, before and after, and many sons; he reminds the king, by contrast, of the hopelessness of bringing back his wife. Where Nārada forgets that he is really a man, King Tāladhvaja merely forgets that he is really a king, and he neglects his royal duties.

The problem of the reality of the experience of the other people in Nārada's dream world is ignored by most versions of the Nārada story. One text does, however, go on to explore a parallel problem in the very next tale it tells:

> A certain sage living on the banks of the Ganges was deluded by illusion and became an Untouchable girl [a Kirāṭa]. She married an Untouchable [Kirāṭa] man, had sons and grandsons, and lived for many years. One day she entered the Ganges and became a sage again. When her husband, sons, relatives, and friends noticed that she had been delayed, they deduced, from her pot and garment left beside the river, that she had been carried off by the current of the Ganges, and so they began to lament. The sage attempted to explain to them that he was the one whom they sought, but still they did not come to their senses. Finally he enlightened them, by means of many signs of recognition, so that they realized, "This is precisely the way it truly happened," and they overcame their sorrow and went away.[14]

Here the sage changes both sex (as in the Nārada story) and caste (as in many of the tales of the king and the Untouchables). When the people in his other world mourn for him, he is able to prove to them that his death has not in fact taken place. This proof is accomplished not through argument, which he tries in vain, but through signs of recognition (presumably by mentioning things that only the Kirāṭa woman would be expected to know). The townspeople, who are capable of deduction based on physical proof (for they infer, from the pot and garment on the bank, that the woman has been drowned), finally accept the sage's testimony on the basis of common sense: the signs of recognition.

The Hindi commentary on this story adds scriptural authority to common sense as a means of persuasion:

> Seeing them weeping and wailing, the sage went there and asked, "Why are you weeping? I was the Kirāṭa girl, and at the moment

> when I dipped into the Ganges my form changed into this form." The sage tried his best to make them understand, but their grief was too great. Then he cited traditional wisdom and tried to make them understand through illustration. After much effort, their grief was assuaged.[15]

In this text, sorrow does not bring enlightenment; on the contrary, enlightenment results in the removal of sorrow. This enlightenment, however, is not of a philosophical nature; it is merely the product of a clearer common-sense understanding of the hard facts of life and the acceptance of an apparently miraculous transformation as just such a fact. When mere argument fails, the sage tries scripture ("traditional wisdom") and then falls back on "illustration" (this may be another term for the signs of recognition, or it may refer to the more formal type of illustration represented by analogy, a classical Indian means of proof). Finally the family of the Kirāṭa girl understand the truth, and they are no longer full of sorrow.

These texts take into account the fate of the other participants in the illusory drama and regard them as physically real. No attempt is made to investigate or test the reality of the "other body" assumed by the primary figure—the reality of Saubhāgyasundarī or the Kirāṭa girl. Instead, these bodies—and their experiences—are simply assumed to be real, because we are imperceptibly led to accept the point of view of the other characters in the dream, who regard the "other body" of the dreamer as real. The reality of the dreamer's double is thus established by the other figures in his own dream; they haul him up by his own bootstraps, so to speak. These texts may thus be seen as mediating between the simple variants of the tale of Nārada, in which the dreamer awakens and assumes that his dream experiences were unreal, and the stories of the king and the Untouchable woman or the woman in the other world, in which the dreamer assumes that his experiences were real and proceeds to test their reality (as in the story of Vikramāditya in chapter two).

Nārada learns something of truth and value when he awakens from his own illusory experience, but he learns far more from his later awareness of the illusory experience of the people inside his other world. As he—knowing that he still exists—watches them mourn for him as if he were dead, he experiences both sides of the existential dilemma at once: he suddenly realizes that he simultaneously exists and does not exist. The image of the man helplessly watching those whom he loves mourning over his corpse, while he remains invisible and voiceless to them, is a poignant and recurring dream image.[16] It is also an image that was taken up by Indian sages of many sects to express the paradox of suffering and illusion. A powerful example of its use occurs in the Tibetan *Book of the*

Dead, which describes the experiences of a man from the moment of death until he is either enlightened or reborn. During this liminal period he watches as his relatives cry and weep, his share of food is divided up among others, his clothes are removed, his bed is taken to pieces, and his possessions are given away; "he can see them but they cannot see him, and he can hear them calling him but they cannot hear him call them, so he goes away in despair." He sees his family as though he were meeting them in a dream, and he tries to tell the mourners, "I am here; do not weep," but in vain. The intense pain of this experience, "like the pain of a fish rolling in hot sand," lasts up to forty-nine days. Finally he looks for a new body; for if he tries to reenter his old corpse, he finds that winter has frozen it, or that summer made it rot, or that it has been burnt or buried by relatives or given to birds and wild animals.[17] The final indignity comes when he observes the careless and unthinking way in which his funeral ceremonies are being conducted; his irritable criticism of this sloppiness is immediately compounded by his resentment of the people to whom his possessions are being given.[18] It is precisely to save the dead man from the experience of these emotions—grief, frustration, fear, pain, pettiness, jealousy—that the *Book of the Dead* keeps reminding him that everything he sees is merely a series of projections from his own mind and that even his mind does not truly exist.

Magic Doubles

One important cycle of stories about illusion revolves around the theme of the illusory double or shadow (*chāyā*), the look-alike created in order to delude someone into believing that someone who is actually absent is present. We have already encountered a kind of double in the tales of Nārada, together with the first stirrings of speculation as to the possible reality status of such a dream double as Saubhāgyasundarī, the wife of Tāladhvaja. The doubles in these myths serve several purposes. First of all, they shake the hero's confidence in the uniqueness and solidity of his waking persona. Second, they express the peculiar ambiguity of the experience of a dream, in which the dreamer sees himself simultaneously as subject (Nārada) and as object (Saubhāgyasundarī), the way the soul in limbo watches its own corpse in the Tibetan text. In more complex variants of this theme, which we will soon encounter, the double of the dreamer, who is both author and character, begins to press against the outer boundaries of the story, to melt away the line between the observer and the observed. The double in myths of dreams or illusion makes possible a witnessing of the dream, a process that *seems* to protect the dreamer from the dangers of complete solipsism, of enclosing himself in a world of which he is the only citizen. The dream double combats the *feeling* of solipsism by providing a second person to serve as a corroborating authority. Of course, since that person is merely another aspect of the dreamer, the double does not combat the *logic* of solipsism (which is, as we shall see, impossible to surmount). Bootstrap logic is not really logic at all, but it is dramatically effective.

Śuka and Śukra

In addition to dream doubles, magic doubles are created in various ways and for various purposes. The *Mahābhārata* tells of the sage Vyāsa, whose son, Śuka, was an ascetic of such unwavering chastity that he was able to use his yogic powers to transport himself to heaven, remaining indifferent to the charms of the nymphs he met on the way. Vyāsa, a less perfect sage, tried in vain to follow his son. Desolate on earth, he continued to grieve until the god Rudra came to him and created a shadow, just like Śuka, to follow Vyāsa everywhere in the world; and when Vyāsa saw the shadow, he rejoiced.[19] Rudra had at first tried to persuade Vyāsa not to grieve by citing the argument of *mokṣa*, that to be released from life is the source of the highest joy. But Vyāsa was too deeply tied to *saṃsāra*, to his love for his son, for this argument to reach him, and so Rudra switched to the opposite means of consolation: instead of weaning Vyāsa away from the illusion that consists of the emotional attachment to rebirth, Rudra *gave* Vyāsa an illusion: he created an imaginary son, a dream son, to keep Vyāsa happily deluded. The story ends abruptly at this point, and we hear nothing further of the fate of the shadow son. In this way, the experience that is normally used to trigger an awakening from a dream—the death of an *unreal* son—is transformed into an experience that triggers a reimmersion in the dream: the death of a real son proves so unbearable that it drives the father into a dream, the dream that his son is still alive. Despite the fact that the value of *mokṣa* is completely affirmed by Śuka's joyous entrance into heaven, the story of Vyāsa poignantly expresses the helpless attachment to *saṃsāric* values in face of the argument for *mokṣa*.

A similar ambivalence regarding the positive or negative value of human ties is found in another tale of a father and a son, one that takes some of the themes of the tale of Vyāsa and Śuka and develops them in a way that is metaphysically more complex.

> One day when the sage Bhṛgu and his son Śukra were performing asceticism in a deep trance together on a tableland of Mount Mandara, a beautiful nymph flew by them in the sky. Śukra fell in love with her, and she fell in love with him, as they looked at each other. Then Śukra closed his eyes and imagined that he had followed her

> to the palace of Indra in heaven. He reached the city of the gods, without dying, and forgot all about his former nature. He found the nymph, and they made love for a long time, living together for many eons. At last, when he had used up his merit, Śukra fell to earth and was reborn, first as a Brahmin, then as a king, and finally, after many rebirths, he became an ascetic boy on the bank of the Samanga River. Time passed as Śukra was engaged in this reverie.
>
> After a thousand years, Bhṛgu arose from his trance, but instead of finding his son beside him he saw a great skeleton, with worms crawling in the eye sockets. Bhṛgu became furious with Kāla, the god of time and death, and was about to curse him when Kāla appeared to him and explained that, during his trance, Śukra's mind had wandered along the road of his own desires and that he was now performing asceticism on the bank of the Samanga River.
>
> Then Kāla and Bhṛgu flew to the Samanga River, where they found the ascetic boy and awakened him from *his* trance. [See plate 2.] When Bhṛgu reminded the reborn Śukra of his former lives, the boy said, "Father, let us go and see the body on the tableland of Mount Mandara." When they returned to Mount Mandara, Śukra was sorry to see the body crawling with ants, for, though he had had many bodies, this was his first. Then, at Kāla's command, Śukra entered the withered corpse, the body of the boy fell to the ground, and Śukra rose up and embraced his father. They burnt the body of the boy who had been at the Samanga River, and father and son continued to live in that forest.[20]

The theme of the death of the son takes a different form here. To the father, the son seems to die, but he does not die; instead, he follows a nymph to heaven and lives in a dream world with a dream woman. While he is gone, his body seems to be a corpse; yet the body is not burnt, and the son eventually returns to it. It was a dream, not a death, that took the soul from the body; what seemed to be a transformation turned out to be an illusion. We thought that Śukra was just dreaming, but then we found that his corpse had decayed; we thought, then, that he had died, but then we saw his apparently intact body rise up again. Was he reborn, or was he dreaming that he was reborn? The text does not allow us to ask a question focused in that way.

Despite the fact that both father and son are eventually taught that the body is of no significance, the father becomes furious when he sees the rotting corpse, and the son, too, has a lingering sentimental fondness for it, since it was the first body he had inhabited. These emotions tie the two of them to the body in a *saṃsāra*-affirming way. Where Śuka had been impervious to the nymph, Śukra is entirely pervious. Śukra does not want to leave his nymph, but he falls to earth because of his emotional attachment to earthly pleasures (of which heavenly pleasures are simply a heightened instance). And so, instead of a double to replace the son by the father's side, this text creates a double (the ascetic boy) who has to be destroyed so that the real son can go on living with his father.

Shadows of the *Rāmāyaṇa*: Sītā and Rāvaṇa

A complex corpus of myths dealing with the theme of the shadow or double is associated with the *Rāmāyaṇa*, both in the original Sanskrit text attributed to the sage Vālmīki (c. 200 B.C.–200 A.D.) and in many of the folk versions in other Indian languages, as well as in the Sanskrit *Yogavāsiṣṭha*. The popularity of this theme demonstrates both that it is a basic Indian way of thinking about illusion and that Indian tradition regarded the *Rāmāyaṇa* as particularly fertile soil on which to raise new crops of stories about illusion. In Vālmīki's text, the demon king, Rāvaṇa, steals Sītā from her husband, Prince Rāma, and keeps her captive on the island of Lankā for many years. When Rāma finally kills Rāvaṇa and brings Sītā back home with him, both he and his people fear that her reputation, if not her chastity, has been sullied by her long sojourn in the house of another man. Rāma forces her to undergo an ordeal by fire, which vindicates her.[21] Already in the original Sanskrit text there are magic doubles of several of the main characters: Rāma and Rāvaṇa use magic weapons to produce images of themselves in battle, and Rāvaṇa's son creates an illusory Sītā that he kills in order to distract Rāma.

In several of the popular variants of the *Rāmāyaṇa*, however, Sītā has a false shadow or double that is designed to counteract the accusation that she failed to resist the virile and urbane Rāvaṇa or, indeed, that she lived in his home at all.[22] It is said that when Rāvaṇa attempted to carry off Sītā, she knew what he was about to do and she prayed to Agni, the god of fire, who took her away for safekeeping. Agni made a false (*māyā*) Sītā, whom Rāvaṇa abducted; after the war, the false Sītā, forced to undergo an ordeal by fire, was burnt to ashes, while the real Sītā came out of the fire (i.e., out of the protection of Agni) and was given back to Rāma. In these ways, attempts were made, even within the Sanskrit tradition, to deal with both levels of the problem: the hard level (that Sītā was actually seduced by Rāvaṇa) and the soft (that people thought she was seduced by Rāvaṇa). The tradition does not see any significant distinction between them.

A more striking, and at the same time more subtle, substitute for Sītā appears in Kampaṉ's Tamil version of the *Rāmāyaṇa*. The episode that is reworked is one that Vālmīki narrates briefly and brutally: The hideous ogress Śūrpanakhā fell in love with Rāma and propositioned him; he teased her by suggesting that only the presence of his wife, Sītā, prevented him from satisfying her desire. When Śūrpanakhā then attacked Sītā, Rāma commanded his brother, Lakṣmaṇa, to cut off the ogress's nose and ears, and Lakṣmaṇa did this.[23] In Kampaṉ's version of the incident, Śūrpanakhā, well aware of her ugliness, transforms herself into the image of Śrī, the divine form of Sītā. When the real Sītā appears, Śūrpanakhā tells Rāma that the other woman (the real Sītā) is a deceitful, meat-eating ogress who is skilled in the arts of illusion and has adopted a false form. But when Sītā, in fear and trembling, runs to Rāma and embraces him, Rāma rejects Śūrpanakhā. As David Shulman points out, both Sītā and Śūrpanakhā have a potential for violent, destructive action, and both are beautiful and seductive, but Śūrpanakhā cannot control her passion, while Sītā can.[24] In this sense, Śūrpanakhā represents the shadow side of Sītā's emotions (in the Tamil *Rāmāyaṇa,* Sītā is full of wild desire for Rāma when she first sees him), and so she becomes the shadow of Sītā's physical body.

Another Tamil *Rāmāyaṇa* presents a series of inversions of the relationships between the doubles: Rāvaṇa abducts Pārvatī (Śiva's wife) instead of Sītā, and he does not even manage to get the real Pārvatī:

> Rāvaṇa asked Śiva to give Pārvatī to him, and Śiva was forced to grant this wish to Rāvaṇa, who was a powerful devotee of his. But as Rāvaṇa was carrying Pārvatī south to Lankā, Viṣṇu took the form of a sage standing by a grove of upside-down trees, their roots in the air. When Rāvaṇa stopped to inquire about this strange sight, the sage asked him who he and the lady were. Upon hearing Rāvaṇa's answer, the sage said, "Śiva gave you Māyā [Illusion] and told you she was his wife." Rāvaṇa believed him and went off to a river to meditate in order to get the "real" Pārvatī, leaving the "false" one behind in the sage's care. As soon as Rāvaṇa was gone, Viṣṇu raced away with Pārvatī, bringing her to Śiva.
>
> When Rāvaṇa returned to the grove, to find the sage and the goddess missing, he followed the footprints but could not find Pārvatī, for she was with Śiva, who had rendered her invisible to Rāvaṇa by a wall of sacred ash. Śiva then appeared and gave Rāvaṇa a woman that he called the Māyāśakti [Illusion of Power, Śakti being a name of the wife of Śiva]. Rāvaṇa, believing that he now had the real Śakti, Śiva's wife, put Māyā in his chariot and went to Lankā. On the way, he saw the sage again, this time beside a grove of trees right side up. The sage said, "All this was *māyā.* Now you have received a real boon of a beautiful woman; there is no doubt of that." Rāvaṇa was content and went to Lankā with the Māyāśakti.[25]

Rāvaṇa, the master of illusion, is hoist by his own petard: he mistakes the reality for the illusion, and the reverse. As David Shulman remarks, "The nature of his delusion is clear from the moment he first catches sight of the upside-down tree—a classic Indian symbol for the reality that underlies and is hidden by life in the world, with its false goals and misleading perceptions."[26] The apparent inversions (the tree, and Śiva's true statement that the second woman is his delusionary Śakti) are in fact real; the apparent reality is what is a trick. Thus Viṣṇu, the greater master of illusion, tricks the tricky Rāvaṇa.

The ogress Śūrpanakhā is held responsible for the creation of another shadow image, this time not of Sītā but of Rāvaṇa:

> When Śūrpanakhā had been rejected and mutilated by Rāma, she resolved to get even with him. She took the form of a poor beggar woman and went to Sītā and asked her to draw a picture of Rāvaṇa. Sītā had seen only Rāvaṇa's feet [as a chaste woman, she would never raise her eyes to the face of a man other than her husband], so she drew only Rāvaṇa's big toe; but Śūrpanakhā completed the sketch and persuaded Brahmā to bring it to life. The shadow Rāvaṇa hid under Sītā's bed and emerged just as Rāma came into Sītā's bedroom. Rāma accused Sītā of having been unfaithful to him and threw her out.[27]

This tale, which is well known in Telugu folk variants of the *Rāmāyaṇa*, builds on several elements that we have seen in Vālmīki's text: Rāvaṇa's illusory form, which the naïve Sītā mistakes for a monk, and Hanuman's form, which the now cynical Sītā mistakenly thinks is *not* a monkey. Rāvaṇa's "big toe" (a euphemism?) may satirize other motifs from the Sanskrit epic: Sītā, as we have just seen, boasted that she would not touch Rāvaṇa even with *her* left foot, and Lakṣmaṇa could recognize only Sītā's anklets, not her earrings or bracelets, for he had seen only her feet.[28] Ultimately, the painted shadow Rāvaṇa, like the shadow Sītā, justifies Rāma's rejection of the real Sītā.

Another shadow of Rāvaṇa appears in a tale of intricate illusions that involves Hanuman as well. The *Śiva Purāṇa* refers briefly to a certain Rāvaṇa of the Earth (Mahī-Rāvaṇa), who was killed by Hanuman,[29] and the story is known throughout North India as well as South India.[30] But the most elaborate recorded version of it is in a Tamil text about Mayilirāvaṇaṉ (Peacock Rāvaṇa). This is the tale of a looking-glass world in which shadow figures and dangerous doubles pit their magic against one another:

> When Rāma had killed Rāvaṇa's sons and soldiers, Rāvaṇa was in despair until his minister reminded him of his brother Mayilirāvaṇaṉ [Peacock Rāvaṇa], who was skilled in deceit and illusion. Mayilirāvaṇaṉ came to Rāvaṇa and promised him that he would take Rāma and Lakṣmaṇa down to the Lankā of the underworld, where he reigned, and sacrifice them to Kālī.
>
> Rāvaṇa had another brother, the good demon Vibhīṣaṇa, who had defected to Rāma. Vibhīṣaṇa discovered that Mayilirāvaṇaṉ intended to take his [Vibhīṣaṇa's] form in order to deceive Rāma and Lakṣmaṇa. When Hanuman learned of this, he traced out the

walls of a fortress with his tail, surrounding the armies of Rāma. Mayilirāvaṇaṉ left the underworld Lankā through the stalk of a lotus. He took the form of Vibhīṣaṇa and waited until Hanuman opened his mouth; then he entered it and used his magic to put Rāma and Lakṣmaṇa into a box, which he locked tightly. Mayilirāvaṇaṉ [in the form of Vibhīṣaṇa] said to Hanuman, "Be on guard, Hanuman; Mayilirāvaṇaṉ will come here in a form like mine." Then he took the box with him to the underworld Lankā.

When Hanuman discovered the theft, he went down the lotus stalk and engaged in a battle with a demon named Matsyagarbha [Fish-Womb]. Hanuman lost the fight, surrendered, and asked Matsyagarbha who his parents were. Matsyagarbha replied, "I am the son of Hanuman, and my mother is a fish named Timiti." When Hanuman heard this, he was alarmed; he thought, "But *I* am Hanuman; there is no other Hanuman but me. This is very strange, for I have no wife; I have always been chaste. However, when I went to Lankā to look for Sītā, I did look at the wives of Rāvaṇa when they were lying about in a state of *déshabille*. Could this have resulted in the birth of my child without my knowledge?" Matsyagarbha then told Hanuman that when Hanuman was flying to Lankā over the ocean a demoness had swallowed his shadow; Hanuman had entered her belly and torn it apart, but a drop of his sweat had oozed out and had been swallowed by a fish, who had given birth to Matsyagarbha.

Hanuman revealed his true identity to his son Matsyagarbha and went on to find Rāma and Lakṣmaṇa. He woke them up and told them where they were and what had happened, whereupon they immediately fell asleep again. Hanuman then attacked Mayilirāvaṇaṉ, who called on Rāvaṇa to help him; but Rāvaṇa could not come, for the lotus stalk had been blocked. Hanuman killed Mayilirāvaṇaṉ and took the box back up through the stalk of the flower. At sunrise the box disappeared, and Rāma and Lakṣmaṇa awoke and stood up. That day, Rāma killed Rāvaṇa.[31]

This text plays a number of ingenious variations on themes in Vālmīki's *Rāmāyaṇa*. It expands on the episode in the Sanskrit text in which Hanuman leaps across the ocean to Lankā and is threatened, in mid-leap, by a goddess who attempts to swallow him; he enters her mouth and flies right out again.[32] In the Tamil text it is merely Hanuman's shadow that is swallowed (perhaps in response to the shadow Sītā, known from the popular variants), but this act of swallowing produces a child in the shadow world. Hanuman's insistence that he has no wife and, moreover, that he has no double leads him to construct a rational explanation for the apparently impossible son: it must have happened when (as Vālmīki has described in another famous scene) Hanuman spied on Rāvaṇa's harim.[33] This guilty memory satisfies Hanuman's need to dismiss the hypothesis of a double. (As we shall see in chapter four, the hero who dreams of another life often convinces himself of its unreality by insisting that, while the dream figure has a wife, he himself—the dreamer—is chaste.) Hanuman experiences the traditional dream adventure in the underworld, an adventure that involves him with a dangerous woman and a son whom he must abandon in the other world when the magic of that world fades at sunrise; the Tamil text says explicitly that Matsyagarbha wanted to come back up with Hanuman through the stalk, but Hanuman would not allow him to follow. If Hanuman experiences a dream, however, it is not his own dream; it is Rāma's dream. The fact that Rāma sleeps through the entire adventure in the underworld identifies that adventure as his dream; yet it is a true experience for Hanuman. When Rāma wakes up, his dream comes true: he kills the Rāvaṇa of the upper world even as Hanuman killed Rāvaṇa's dream double in the underworld.

A final Tamil text, closely related to the story of Mayilirāvaṇaṉ, depicts another shadow Rāvaṇa who is overcome by someone other than Rāma. This time it is Sītā herself, rather than Hanuman, who stands in for Rāma:

> The demon king Śatakaṇṭharāvaṇa [Rāvaṇa of the Hundred Necks] was sitting in his palace, watching the nymphs dance, when a messenger came and told the story of the *Rāmāyaṇa*, ending with the death of Rāvaṇa and the triumph of Rāma. Enraged, Śatakaṇṭharāvaṇa determined to attack Rāma. When Rāma learned of this, he was worried and expressed his fears to Sītā, who offered to destroy the demon for him. Rāma objected to this, arguing, "Listen, Lady Sītā. Because you are a woman, you do not know the tricks [lit., illusions, *māykai*] of the demons. Moreover, when Rāvaṇa kept you prisoner for ten months in Lankā, what did you do then? This is madness or stupidity; how could you kill that demon Śatakaṇṭha?" But Sītā persuaded him to let her take over, and with Hanuman's help she killed Śatakaṇṭharāvaṇa.[34]

Rāvaṇa appears here in an exaggerated form: he has a hundred heads, where Vālmīki's demon had only ten. Śatakaṇṭharāvaṇa is a double, or shadow, of the original Rāvaṇa in his actions—his attack on Rāma—and in his name; moreover, his story is an explicit double of Vālmīki's story: it is by hearing Vālmīki's story of Rāvaṇa that Śatakaṇṭharāvaṇa is drawn into the myth. There is another kind of double in this story, as well: Sītā's actions shadow the actions of Rāma in the Sanskrit epic. Shulman has pointed out the deep Tamil underpinnings of this implicit sex reversal, which actually becomes explicit at several points; for example, one of Śatakaṇṭharāvaṇa's sons, a great magician, remarks, "How masculine this woman is!" Thus Sītā becomes Rāma's double, as Saubhāgyasundarī is Nārada's double.

The story of the dream adventure is usually told from the standpoint of a man who becomes, or sometimes merely finds, a woman in the other world. The tales of Nārada are adventures of the first type (becoming a woman); tales of the second type (finding a woman) have been discussed in chapter two. In the first genre there are moments when the standpoint shifts to that of the male partner of the sex-changed hero; we see Nārada-as-woman from King Tāladhvaja's point of view. But in the second genre, in the tales of shadow women, such as the myths of the other Sītā, the standpoint of the woman comes into prominence and provides a kind of shadow to the theme of the male hero's dream adventure. For the hero in the dream adventure sees his tale as one in which he goes to the other world and makes love to his dream princess; but the shadow woman sees a demon come to her from another world and rape her. Once again we encounter the relativity of illusion, this time split into the contrasting viewpoints of the man and the woman.

Moreover, the myths of the shadow Rāvaṇa give us a third view of the dream adventure: the villain's view. If we put these various views together, we have a kind of Indian *Rashomon*, a multiple vision of the dream figure; since it gives us the impression that we are seeing the same figure from several angles, this multiple vision serves as a further apparent corroboration by group consensus. The dreamer from whose standpoint we view the myth at any moment is the one who has a double: when there are two women, it is her dream; when there are two heroes, it is his; and when there are two villains, it is the villain's. Each of these three figures has a kind of implicit double even in Vālmīki's *Rāmāyaṇa*. Rāma's brother Lakṣmaṇa does all the bad things that Rāma's paradigmatic character prevents him from doing,[35] while, conversely, Vibhīṣaṇa does all the good things that his brother Rāvaṇa will not do. Similarly, Śūrpanakhā may be seen as a kind of implicit double of Sītā, and the wicked hunchback Mantharā may be seen as a shadow of Queen Kaikeyī (who is herself a shadow of Queen Kausalyā). But the folktales bring these implicit shadows into the light, where they become strong and explicit: now Sītā has a literally identical double. And the Tamil tales show us two Rāvaṇas.

Sometimes the shadow is used against the demon rather than by him. In Tibetan Buddhism, the practitioner deals constantly with demons in the course of his mastery of illusion: "He may generate a person or a demon into an effigy and destroy it utterly . . . . A practitioner may exercise his reality-creating power, for example, to trick a demon into thinking that a 'substitute' or 'ransom' is—that is, 'appears as'—the real object of his malevolence."[36] That is, the yogin creates a double or shadow to absorb the demon—who is himself a kind of shadow. That double in this case is presumably the double of the yogin himself; in our stories, it is the double of the woman whom the demon covets.

If we compare the stories of Malayavatī and Uṣā, from chapter two, with the two types of stories about Sītā, we may see a kind of pattern of relativity. Malayavatī tries to kill the innocent hero, Vikramāditya; Aniruddha brutally rapes the innocent Uṣā. The argument as to whether Uṣā was mentally or physically raped applies equally well to Sītā: was her mind (and reputation) sullied by her mere presence in Rāvaṇa's house, or was her body sullied by an actual physical assault? The ordeal by fire, intended to resolve this quandary, cannot do so; the *Rāmāyaṇa* presents us with two very different outcomes of that ordeal. And where Uṣā argues that she merely *dreamt* that she was raped (despite the physical evidence of blood to be answered for), post-Vālmīki tradition suggests that Rāvaṇa merely "dreamt" that he raped Sītā or that Sītā merely dreamt that she was raped. The tales of Nārada go one step farther than this, however, for they combine *in a single story* the complementary points of view that appear elsewhere in Indian tradition only in one version or another. Where the folk tradition merely introduces a double into the basic story, the later variants on the Nārada story, and many of the tales in the *Yogavāsiṣṭha*, actually tell the story twice, from two points of view.

Double Women

Let us turn now to two more complex stories about double women. The first, the tale of Māyāvatī, is a continuation of the saga of Uṣā, for Māyāvatī's lover, Pradyumna, is the father of Uṣā's lover, Aniruddha, and Māyāvatī's tale, like Uṣā's, is told from the woman's point of view. The second story, the tale of the two Līlās, presents us simultaneously with the woman's view and with that of her double. In the first story, Māyāvatī has two husbands—a demonic husband, whom she despises, and an incestuous lover, whom she adores. In the second, the two women have a single husband—a good king—who is reborn instead of redreamt. The shadow women thus serve two very different functions in the two tales.

In most of the oldest variants of the tale of the shadow woman, the shadow serves to exonerate the woman herself from any possible defilement at the hands of a demonic husband. The shadow keeps the pure woman of the real world separate from the lustful, dangerous woman of the other world, the passionate woman in the dream.[37] These myths might be regarded as expressions of a kind of personality dissociation in reaction to a rape: "This happened to some other woman, not to me." This is one of the things that the tales of the shadow Sītā are saying. In these stories, the double implies that the "real self" did not experience the event. This emotional force field, placed between the self and the experience, frames and distances the pain. A similar protection is provided by the dreamer's statement, "This is all just a dream," when the nightmare becomes unbearable; the double is the narrative equivalent of the framing statement. The theory of illusion also performs this function. Viṣṇu, for example, tells Nārada, who is mourning for his dead dream family, "Why are you suffering? It is not *you* who have experienced this."[38]

In many Greek and Roman myths the sexually assaulted woman is permanently transformed into a plant or an animal; Ovid's *Metamorphoses* luxuriates in such stories. But even in Greek mythology these transformations are occasionally temporary rather than permanent; Helen of Troy, according to Euripides, was just such a shadow double.[39] Richard Strauss played new variations on the theme of the temporary transformation in his opera *The Woman without a Shadow*. In Indian myths about raped women the heroine is often permanently transformed into a goddess or into some supernatural creature who is literally a shadow of herself; significantly, this transformation usually takes place when a Brahmin woman is raped by an Untouchable man,[40] the inverse of the recurrent story (which we will see in chapter four) of the Brahmin man who is seduced by an Untouchable woman. But where the Brahmin man's transformation is almost always temporary, the woman's shadow may begin as an ephemeral creature but go on to endure alongside the original or even take over the central role.

Māyāvatī in the House of Śambara

Some of the sexual overtones of split personalities become more apparent in other variants of the myth of the shadow woman, of which a good and ancient example is provided by the cycle of myths about a woman who is actually named Māyāvatī ("Mistress of Illusion") and who is the wife of the greatest of all demonic magicians, Śambara. Māyāvatī's role varies in the different versions of the myth: sometimes she *is* the double, sometimes she *has* the double. Moreover, though her story is in many ways an explicit multiform of the story of Sītā, the chaste woman abducted by the lustful demon, Māyāvatī's shadow is Rati, the very incarnation of sexual passion.

> Pradyumna was the son of Kṛṣṇa and Rukminī. When he was six days old, Pradyumna was stolen by the demon Śambara, who threw him into the ocean. There he was swallowed by a large fish, which was caught and brought to Śambara's palace. Now Śambara's wife, Māyāvatī, supervised all the cooking, and when the fish's belly was cut open, she saw inside it a magnificent young boy. As she wondered who he was and how he had come to be inside the belly of a fish, Nārada said to her, "This is Kṛṣṇa's son, who was stolen by

Śambara. He was thrown into the ocean and swallowed by a fish. Take care of him; he is a jewel among men."

So Māyāvatī took care of the boy, and she was so deluded by his extraordinary beauty that she loved him passionately even when he was still a child. When he came to young manhood, she taught him all the magic that she had. But when the boy realized how ardently attached to him she was, he said, "Why are you acting like this, instead of acting like a mother?" Then she said to him, "You are not my son; that terrible Śambara stole you from your father, Kṛṣṇa, and threw you into the ocean, where a fish swallowed you. I took you out of the fish's belly, but your own mother is still weeping for you."

When Pradyumna heard this, he challenged Śambara to battle and killed him, using the magic that he had learned from Māyāvatī. Then he flew up into the air with her, using that same magic, and took her back with him to his father's palace. When they arrived, Nārada came there and said, "This woman, Māyāvatī, is the true wife of Pradyumna, and not the wife of Śambara. When Kāma, the god of erotic love, died, his wife Rati displayed her illusory form to Śambara and deluded him with lecherous acts and pleasures and lustful glances. Pradyumna is the incarnation of Kāma, and Māyāvatī is his wife, Rati." Then Kṛṣṇa and Rukminī rejoiced, for they had been reunited with a son who had been lost for so long.[41]

A number of stock folk motifs form the basis of this myth: the good wife of the wicked ogre helps the hero to kill the ogre; the infant hero is kidnapped and experiences an oedipal encounter with a woman he thinks is his mother; and a shadow woman substitutes for the heroine in order to preserve the latter's chastity. That the seductive shadow protects Māyāvatī's chastity is even more explicit in other variants of the myth: "Though Māyāvatī lived in Śambara's house, she was not truly his wife. For when Kāma was killed, and Kāma's wife, Rati, deluded the demon Śambara with an illusory form, Māyāvatī did not lose her virginity to him but made an illusory form in her own shape and sent that to him. Māyāvatī gave Śambara her shadow in bed."[42] Māyāvatī has two sorts of doubles. In one sense, Rati is her double, since Māyāvatī is Rati transformed. But Rati (who has now become Māyāvatī) creates yet another double, a seductive shadow who goes to Śambara when he thinks he is sleeping with the chaste Māyāvatī.

Pradyumna has only one persona, but he thinks that he has two. The one that he at first assumes to be real (that he is the son of Śambara and Māyāvatī) turns out to be an illusion, a dream from which he awakens to find out that his father is a god, not a demon, and that his "mother" is in fact his wife. This realization frees him from the torment he experienced when he thought that the woman so obviously in love with him was his mother. It protects him from experiencing an incestuous rape, just as Sītā's shadow protects her from the experience of being raped by Rāvaṇa. Several versions of the Māyāvatī myth express the mother's qualms as well; one creates yet another double, a wet nurse, to spare Māyāvatī the awkwardness of being both mistress and mother,[43] and in another the demon Śambara catches Māyāvatī and Pradyumna *flagrante delicto* and says to Māyāvatī, "You crazy whore, have you lost your mind, making love with your son?"[44]

A strange twist of the tale of Māyāvatī appears in two other texts, in which it is said that Rati herself was raped by Śambara. In the first of these two texts, Rati simply takes on the name of Māyāvatī when she lives with Śambara.[45] In the second text, however, Rati uses her powers of illusion to give Śambara a shadow for his bed, and this shadow is Māyāvatī.[46] In other words, Rati, who in the earlier texts had produced a double to protect Māyāvatī's honor, now uses Māyāvatī to protect her own honor. Since Rati is the incarnation of sexual pleasure, her original role in the Pradyumna myth is to provide the lustful counterpart to Māyāvatī's chastity; Rati is the seductive shadow of every virtuous wife. But now Rati herself is the chaste wife. And where Māyāvatī in the earlier texts was mistress of illusion (*māyā*), she now becomes merely the creature of illusion, herself an illusion. This inversion of the point of view may serve as a lesson for us, to make us realize that even the Indian authors sometimes found it hard to distinguish the original from the counterfeit.

The Two Līlās

The problem that the doubles themselves have in telling the original from the copy is vividly illustrated in the *Yogavāsiṣṭha* tale of Queen Līlā, in which the two aspects of the double woman confront each other face to face. Both of them are named Līlā, "Play" or "Art," a term used for the illusory sport of an artist, magician, or god.

> Queen Līlā was the wife of King Padma. When he died, Līlā prayed to the goddess Sarasvatī, who explained to her that in a former birth Padma and Līlā had been a sage named Vasiṣṭha and his wife Arundhatī; she also told Līlā that the king had now been reborn as King Vidūratha. Since Līlā had not been reborn, the king had taken a new wife, whose name just happened to be Līlā. Sarasvatī used her magic powers to transport herself and Queen Līlā through the air to the palace where King Vidūratha lived; invisible, they saw him in his court. When a great battle took place, they went to the battlefield; there Līlā caught sight of the second Līlā, who had the very

same form as hers, like a reflection in a mirror. Puzzled at this, the first Līlā asked Sarasvatī how there could be another woman just like her. The Goddess replied with a long lecture on the projection of mental images from inside to outside, as in dreams. These words were overheard by the second Līlā, who spoke to Sarasvatī and said, "In my dreams I have often spoken with a goddess of wisdom, and she looked exactly as you look to me right now." As they were speaking in this way, the battle commenced in earnest; and when Vidūratha seemed to be winning, the second Līlā said to the first Līlā, "See what a lion our husband is!" [See plate 3.]

But in the end, Vidūratha was killed by his enemy, King Sindhu; and, when he died, the second Līlā died, too, since, as Sarasvatī pointed out to the first Līlā, the second Līlā was merely a delusion, a dream of Vidūratha. This second Līlā was then transported back to the tomb of Padma, and Sarasvatī and Līlā also returned to Padma's tomb. Sarasvatī explained to the first Līlā that her own body, which had been lying beside the corpse of her husband for thirty days, had been taken to be a corpse and burnt by the royal ministers. Now, however, both the first Līlā and the second Līlā had spirit-bodies. Sarasvatī then revived Padma, who opened his eyes and saw two Līlās standing in front of him, alike in form and shape and manner and speech, and alike in their joy at seeing him alive. "Who are you? And who is this, and where did she come from?" he asked. The first Līlā said, "I am Līlā, your queen from a former life. This second Līlā is your queen by my art [*helayā mayā*], produced for you by me; she is just a reflection." Then Līlā embraced him, and he embraced her, and they rejoiced. And Līlā and Līlā and the king took as much pleasure in the stories of his former lives as in the pleasures of making love. Thus by the grace of Sarasvatī and by his own human efforts, King Padma won the happiness of the three worlds. Together with the two Līlās, the king ruled for eight thousand years.[47]

The text takes pains to distinguish the first Līlā from the second, calling them the "first" and "second" Līlā, or the "former" and the "latter" Līlā, or "Padma's Līlā" and "Vidūratha's Līlā," or, significantly, the "enlightened Līlā" (Prabuddhalīlā) and the "imaginary Līlā" (Saṃkalpalīlā). In contrast with the single king, who is reborn, the two Līlās exist simultaneously. Perhaps as a result of being thus anchored in both worlds at once, the two Līlās understand the vision, while the king is unaware of what is going on. The doctrines that Sarasvatī uses to explain these events are complex, and we will return to them in chapter four. Here, however, we may note that the Indian perception of these events is such that the king is able to experience a happy *ménage à trois* with his two wives, whom he receives not from two marriages (as in Noel Coward's *Blithe Spirit*) but from two incarnations. The second Līlā is a delusion of the second king, a dream that he dreams as a result of the magic of the first Līlā, who apparently projects an image of herself to function as the second wife of her erstwhile husband. The second Līlā is thus in a sense the product of the combined mental processes of Padma and his queen; she is a shared dream.

Double Universes

The two Līlās exist together at two different points of time in the same world. Though Līlā flies through the air to reach Padma's new court, she is flying through time, not through space. Yet, as we will see in chapter four, time, as well as space, is mapped in the Hindu cosmology; the two dimensions are parallel. It is therefore not surprising to find that Indian mythology tells not only of double people at two points on the spectrum of time but of double worlds that provide two layers of the spectrum of space.

Viśvāmitra's Upside-Down World

We have already encountered one variation of this theme in the tales of dream worlds, though these worlds might be said to mirror the waking world in time rather than space. There are, however, double worlds in Indian mythology that are clearly spatial. The most famous of these is the subject of a well-known myth that first occurs in the *Rāmāyaṇa*:

> King Triśanku undertook a sacrifice in order to go to heaven with his body. He asked the sage Vasiṣṭha to perform the sacrifice for him, but Vasiṣṭha protested, "It cannot be done." Triśanku then asked Vasiṣṭha's sons to perform the sacrifice for him, but they too refused; they also cursed him to become an Untouchable [Caṇḍāla]. And so during that very night the king was transformed into a Caṇḍāla, dark-skinned and bald, smeared with the ashes of corpses. When his ministers saw him thus, they ran away and abandoned him, and the citizens followed them.
>
> Then Triśanku sought the sage Viśvāmitra and begged him to help him. Viśvāmitra assured Triśanku that he would be able to enter heaven even with the body that he now had as the result of the curse. He summoned the other Brahmins to assist him; all of them agreed to come except the sons of Vasiṣṭha, who refused to touch an oblation offered by an Untouchable. Viśvāmitra then cursed the sons of Vasiṣṭha to die immediately and to be reborn as Untouchables, eaters of dog-flesh.
>
> At Viśvāmitra's command, all of the great sages began to per-

> form the sacrifice to bring Triśanku to heaven with his body. As Triśanku began to ascend to heaven, Indra came with the gods and said to him, "Triśanku, you fool, there is no place for you in heaven. Fall headlong down to earth, destroyed by the curse of your guru." Then Triśanku fell, crying out to Viśvāmitra, "Save me! Save me!" When Viśvāmitra heard him, he shouted to him furiously, "Stay there!" Then Viśvāmitra stood among the sages like a second Creator, and he created another Seven Sages [Ursa Major] in the southern sky. Crazed with anger, he created another garland of constellations, and then he said, "Now I will create another Indra, or else let the worlds be without Indra." And in his fury he began to create gods.
>
> The gods and sages were completely confused; they pleaded with Viśvāmitra and reminded him that Triśanku was unworthy of going to heaven with his body. Then Viśvāmitra said, "I promised Triśanku that he would get to heaven with his body, if you please, and I cannot go back on my word. Let Triśanku with his body have his heaven forever, and let all the constellations that I have made remain firm as long as the worlds endure." And the gods replied, "Your constellations will remain, and Triśanku will stay, head downwards, like an immortal," and Viśvāmitra agreed to this.[48]

The sage Viśvāmitra is driven by anger, as is King Triśanku, but the king is possessed by an unreasonable ambition, as well. The sage Vasiṣṭha, by contrast, is self-controlled; he remains calm, remarks, laconically, "Can't be done [*aśakyam*]," and walks away. The anger of Viśvāmitra is the stuff out of which he makes his alternative, illusory universe; the calm mind of Vasiṣṭha is what enables him to see through such illusions. The king's wish to enter heaven with his body arises from his illusions of grandeur. Although he is able to achieve his goal physically, he is stuck with his own literal-minded achievement, which is devoid of meaning or happiness. The ambiguity of his status as half king, half Untouchable is graphically expressed by his suspension midway between heaven and earth, upside down forever in the topsy-turvy world he has created by his own vain attempt to go against the natural order.

In a Purāṇic version of this story, Viśvāmitra explicitly refers to his secondary creation as "the world that I created when I was full of anger."[49] Not only is this world endowed with extra constellations (which can, after all, be fairly easily assimilated into the existing skies), but it is an exact replica of the world in which Triśanku was originally born: Viśvāmitra created, by his meditation, all the gods and men and serpents and demons and plants and trees; there were two suns at the same time in the sky, two moons that rose at night, a double set of planets, all crowding against one another, and a second set of all creatures. This caused a great confusion (*vibhrama*) among people, and it disturbed the gods. Brahmā persuaded Viśvāmitra to stop and to promise that no one else would ever again make such an alternative creation, though he granted Viśvāmitra's wish that the universe he had made would endure.[50] The confusion caused by this second world is described by the same word used in philosophical texts and poems to describe the error that one makes in mistaking something real for something else that is unreal: *vibhrama*. Seeing two moons is, like mistaking a rope for a snake, a metaphor for seeing a mirage.[51] In the case of Triśanku, however, the two moons seem to be not a mirage or a result of his faulty perception but rather a result of his faulty ambitions. The two moons are really there, but they should not be. Yet the fact that Viśvāmiṭra's world apparently still endures, though we no longer notice it, seems to imply that what he created was not real but merely seemed real at the time, by the power of his meditation. When Brahmā told him to stop, Viśvāmitra ceased to force his mental world upon everyone else; it continued to exist, but not within the scope of our mental perceptions. And this, in the context of Indian ideas about the mental grounding of all physical phenomena, is tantamount to saying that Viśvāmitra's world did not, in fact, exist. Moreover, no one else has ever been able to create such a world again, though (one assumes) other, lesser sages have succeeded in creating worlds less extensive, in time or space, than Viśvāmitra's. David Shulman has expressed the pathos of this episode; he speaks of "the king as Untouchable, trapped somewhere between heaven and earth, upside-down, a lonely, pathetic creature inhabiting his own uselessly self-contained world."[52] The solipsism of this universe is a quality that haunts the literature of dream worlds.

The *Devībhāgavata Purāṇa* tells a greatly expanded and complicated version of the Triśanku story but one that omits the actual creation of the duplicated universe:

> King Satyavrata was willful, lustful, slow-witted, greedy, and wicked. When he stole a Brahmin's wife, the king his father said to him, "Since you have acted like a dog-cooker in stealing a Brahmin's wife, go and live with the dog-cookers." And so Satyavrata lived with the dog-cookers, nursing a grudge against Vasiṣṭha for having urged his father to act as he did. Now, at this time Indra sent no rain for twelve years, and during the drought Viśvāmitra's wife and children were starving. Viśvāmitra's wife decided to sell one of their sons, named Gālava, but Satyavrata met her and dissuaded her, promising that he would bring her food. He killed animals and gave her their flesh; one day he killed Vasiṣṭha's wishing-cow, partly out of his anger against Vasiṣṭha and partly out of delusion. He gave some of the flesh to Viśvāmitra's wife and ate the rest himself, for he was hungry. When Vasiṣṭha found out about this, he said to

Satyavrata, "You have sinned greatly, acting like a ghoul [Piśāca, a flesh-eating demon]. Since you have committed three crimes—killing a cow, stealing a wife, and angering your father—you will be known as Triśanku ["Triple Sting"] and you will appear in the form of a ghoul to all embodied creatures."

As a result of that curse, Satyavrata became a ghoul, but he was devoted to the worship of the Goddess, who promised him that his father would make him king. Indeed, the king repented of having banished his son, summoned him back, installed him as king, and retired to the forest to meditate and die. He was able to do this even though Satyavrata had been transformed into a ghoul because, while Satyavrata had been in the forest, worshiping the Goddess, she had appeared to him and given him a celestial body, and he lost his evil along with his demonic form. Then even Vasiṣṭha became pleased with him.

Now, when Triśanku's son, Hariścandra, was born, Triśanku wanted to establish him as the crown prince and then to enter heaven himself, with his body, in order to make love with the celestial nymphs and to hear the sweet songs of the gods. Vasiṣṭha replied, "It is difficult for anyone to live in heaven with a human body, though heaven is a certainty for a dead man who has acquired merit. It is difficult for a living man to live with celestial nymphs, but perform sacrifices, and you will get to heaven when you're dead." When the king stupidly said, "If you won't do it for me, I'll get another priest who will," Vasiṣṭha lost his temper and cursed the king to become an Untouchable, a dog-cooker. And he added, "Since you have killed the wishing-cow and stolen a Brahmin's wife, you won't even get to heaven when you're dead!"

At the very moment when these words were spoken, Triśanku became an Untouchable; the sandalwood smell of his body turned to the smell of shit, and his golden body became black. He did not dare to go home, knowing that his wife and children would reject him, and so he remained on the banks of the Ganges. Meanwhile, Viśvāmitra returned home and told his wife what had happened to him while he was away: "Overcome with hunger, I had asked an Untouchable to feed me some dog's flesh, but the Untouchable reminded me of the *dharma* of a Brahmin [not to eat meat]. Just at that moment Indra sent rain, and I left the Untouchable's hut." Then Viśvāmitra's wife told him how Satyavrata had sustained them during the famine, and how he had killed Vasiṣṭha's cow and had been cursed to become an Untouchable.

On hearing this, Viśvāmitra resolved to free the king from that curse, and he found Triśanku living as an Untouchable in a village of Untouchables. When he heard that Vasiṣṭha had refused to send the king to heaven in his body, Viśvāmitra set out to do it himself. He transferred to the king all of his own accumulated good karma, and by that ascetic power the king flew up into the air like a swift bird, flying in the sky to the city of Indra. But when Indra saw that

> Triśanku had the form of an Untouchable, he said, "Filthy Untouchable, where do you think you're going in heaven?" Thus he reviled him even though he knew that it was Triśanku. At Indra's words, Triśanku fell straight down from heaven, and, as he fell, he called out to Viśvāmitra. Viśvāmitra heard him calling and saw him falling, and he shouted out, "Stay there!" By the power of the sage's asceticism, at these words the king stayed in the sky, even though he had fallen from the world of the gods. Then Viśvāmitra began to make a new creation, a second world of heaven. But as soon as Indra found out what Viśvāmitra was trying to do, he went to the sage and said, "What are you doing? We don't need this creation. Can't I do anything for you instead?" Then Viśvāmitra said, "Poor Triśanku is miserable now that he has fallen from your palace. Bring him there and be nice to him." Now, Indra was so terrified of the sage's powers that he said, "All right." He gave King Triśanku a divine body and took him to heaven.[53]

Triśanku is a three-time loser, hardly qualified for the extraordinary distinction of being translated to heaven with his body. He is cursed first to be a ghoul (Piśāca) and then to be an Untouchable (the equivalent of a ghoul in many myths of this type). Yet he has many virtues. Even as an Untouchable he is virtuous: not only is he explicitly said to have nourished Viśvāmitra's wife and children (as in other versions of this myth), but it is also implied that (perhaps in his second Untouchable incarnation) he saved Viśvāmitra himself from becoming a flesh-eater (i.e., an Untouchable or a ghoul), a fate which does actually befall Viśvāmitra in many other myths. In the present text, Viśvāmitra's wife is freed from the consequences of eating the cow because it is implied that she did not know what she was doing: "The sage's wife fed it to her sons. 'Surely this must be the flesh of a deer, not of a cow,' she said to herself to assuage her worry."[54]

Triśanku's flaws are offset by his virtues. Each time that he is cursed, he is restored: he is forgiven by his father and installed on the throne even after he has become a ghoul, because the Goddess retransforms him (through the power of devotion, *bhakti*); and he is forgiven by the divine father, Indra, and allowed into heaven, even after he has become an Untouchable, through the power of asceticism (*tapas*). It is, I think, significant that he is *not* retransformed out of his Untouchable form at the end, either because of the power of Viśvāmitra, a sage, cannot match that of the Goddess, or because the pollution of an Untouchable is somehow more enduring than that of a ghoul. Indeed, it is the fact that he is an Untouchable, not the fact that he is a human, that keeps him out of heaven at first; and, as Vasiṣṭha argues, what in the end will still keep him out of heaven—a place that good men *can* obtain—is the fact that he is a sinner (an adulterer and cow-killer).

This devotional text entirely unravels the point of the original story.

"Viśvāmitra's creation" (*Viśvāmitra-sṛṣṭi*) became a cliché for artificiality, in particular for various things said to have been created by Viśvāmitra in imitation of Brahmā's creation: the palm fruit for the human skull, the buffalo for the cow, the ass for the horse, and so forth.[55] This text ignores that entire development. All of these twists add up to a worldview in which extraordinary religious powers (asceticism and devotion) can work miracles, and Triśanku achieves his goal. Since this is so, it is not necessary for Viśvāmitra to create his alternative universe; he is able to manipulate the first one entirely to his satisfaction. But what is perhaps most striking about the ending of this variant is the implication that the gods fear the creation of a duplicate universe even more than they fear the consequences of allowing a cow-killing, adulterous, unfilial Untouchable and ghoul into heaven.

There is a Hindi folktale that satirizes the motif of the alternative universe by playing up the awkwardness of the presence of two identical wives, like the two Līlās:

> Kallū and his wife Raziyā were poor farmers. One day Kallū dug up a large pot, which he brought home to his wife. He dropped his tobacco pouch into it by mistake, and when his wife reached into the pot to take it out, she discovered not one but two pouches in it, each one filled with tobacco and the five rupees that Kallū had kept in the pouch. So into the pot they put their wool blanket (they had only one between them), and the single blanket became two. Then they put in an old coat, their tattered bedding, whatever they had, and the pot made everything double. They put the tobacco pouch in over and over again, until they were surrounded by a heap of pouches, each containing tobacco and five rupees. They spent much of the night counting their new wealth.
>
> On the next day, as Raziyā was cooking in the pot, she slipped on a pile of potatoes and fell into the pot. Kallū sprang forward and pulled her out, but then he saw a second Raziyā struggling to get her hands and feet out of the pot. He pulled her out, but Raziyā shrieked, "Where has this bitch come from? I'll never allow her to stay in my house. Why did you pull her out? Just stuff her right back in again." Abashed, Kallū said, "What have I done? One wife has always been plenty for me, but how could I leave her lying in the pot? And now if we stick her back, won't we just be making the same mistake again?" The new Raziyā sat frightened, head in hands, staring at the husband and wife; but when Kallū reached over to touch the original Raziyā, she pushed him away, and he lost his balance and landed in the pot. The two Raziyās jumped up and pulled him out; then they helped out the second Kallū, who was struggling to get out of the pot.
>
> Then Raziyā and Kallū used the pot to make a separate house for the new couple and to outfit it with all the necessary household

> goods. The neighbors were surprised to see how wealthy Kallū and his wife had become, and they were still more bewildered to discover that they had set up, next door to them, another couple, resembling themselves exactly. "It must be his brother," they concluded at last.[56]

This story is a comic variant of the widespread folktale of the magic horn of plenty. It is also a satire on the story of the creation of a second world, replete with all the details of the first world. More particularly, it satirizes the theme of the shadow bride by grafting it on to the Indian folk tradition of stories about jealous wives, co-wives, and wives and mistresses. For the world of Raziyā and Kallū, the folk world, is one of husbands and wives, kitchen utensils and nosy neighbors—the world of *saṃsāra*, which the folk tradition continues to celebrate. The events in the story challenge the assumptions of that tradition (the story is called "The Amazing Pot," and Raziyā and Kallū, as well as the neighbors, are amazed by it all), but in the end the miracles are taken in stride, and life goes on as usual.

Inside the Mouth of God: Yaśodā, Arjuna, and Mārkaṇḍeya

Another cycle of myths reveals a different sort of illusory universe or double world by laying bare the magical nerve in apparently everyday phenomena, peeling back the cover from ostensibly real experience in order to progress toward the reality of ostensibly mythic experience. Myths of this type often make use of the image of entering the mouth of God. Such a myth is the story of Kṛṣṇa (an incarnation of Viṣṇu) and Yaśodā (Kṛṣṇa's mortal mother):

> One day when the children were playing, they reported to Yaśodā, "Kṛṣṇa has eaten dirt." Yaśodā took Kṛṣṇa by the hand and scolded him and said, "You naughty boy, why have you eaten dirt?" "I haven't," said Kṛṣṇa. "All the boys are lying. If you believe them instead of me, look at my mouth yourself." "Then, open up," she said to the god, who had in sport taken the form of a human child; and he opened his mouth.
>
> Then she saw in his mouth the whole universe, with the far corners of the sky, and the wind, and lightning, and the orb of the earth with its mountains and oceans, and the moon and stars, and space itself; and she saw her own village and herself. She became frightened and confused, thinking, "Is this a dream or an illusion fabricated by God? Or is it a delusion in my own mind? For God's power of delusion inspires in me such false beliefs as, 'I exist,' 'This is my husband,' 'This is my son.'" When she had come to understand true reality in this way, God spread his magic illusion in the

> form of maternal love. Instantly Yaśodā lost her memory of what had occurred. She took her son on her lap and was as she had been before, but her heart was flooded with even greater love for God, whom she regarded as her son.[57]

The element in Yaśodā's vision that finally frightens and confuses her is the vision of herself in the second universe, for this calls into question her certainty that her original self (the one with the husband and the son) is the person she thought she was.

Hindu myths like the tale of Yaśodā and Kṛṣṇa open the barrier between myth and reality, a barrier expressed by the image of the mouth of God. On the narrative level of myth, in which gods participate as *dramatis personae*, the world of events that occur outside the mouth of God is regarded as real, a common-sense world with one moon and one sun in the sky. But we do not remain on this level for long. When the myth of Yaśodā opens, we think we know what reality is: it is the life of a harried mother with her mischievous child. Then, suddenly, when she glances into the mouth of the child, we learn that the child is God and that inside his mouth there is a world that appears to be mythical or at least unreal (since it replicates the world that we have assumed to be uniquely real). Yaśodā cannot sustain the vision of that world; she cannot bear the idea that *that* might be reality. She thinks it may be a dream or a hallucination of her own making or an illusion or portent sent by God. These are closely related phenomena, but the dream and the portent are regarded as partaking of a deeper kind of reality, while the hallucination and illusion are regarded as false in themselves, though they may be the signals of a truer reality. We who read the myth know that what Yaśodā has seen is a dream that is a portent sent by God. The rest of her life is an illusion, as she herself realizes while gazing into the mouth of God. This illusion is the divine magic that makes the phenomenal world seem real to us when it is not. Out of pity for her in her fear and confusion, Kṛṣṇa erases the vision of reality and substitutes for it the illusion that he is not God but merely her son. This illusion is made of maternal love.

A similar episode is described in the *Bhagavad Gītā*, where Arjuna asks Kṛṣṇa to reveal his true, eternal form. Arjuna's hair stands on end when he sees the transformation in Kṛṣṇa, and he says,

> In your body I see all the gods and all the crowds of every kind of being. As I look at you with your mouth wide open, I cannot bear it. All the heroes on this battlefield are rushing into your mouths that are terrifying with their enormous tusks. Some get caught between your teeth and their heads are crushed to powder. Like moths flying faster and faster into a blazing fire to be destroyed, all the worlds pour faster and faster into your mouths to be destroyed. I thought, "This is my friend," and so, rashly, I called to you, say-

> ing, "Hey, Kṛṣṇa! Hey, my friend!" for I did not know how great you are; it was because I was careless, or because I loved you. For the times when I teased you or joked with you when we played or rested together or sat or ate together—forgive me, O Lord. Bear with me, as a father with a son, or a friend with a friend, or a lover with his beloved.[58]

Here the mouth of God is seen as the mouth of devouring Time, and Arjuna cannot bear the vision. Kṛṣṇa takes pity on him and allows him to lapse back into the comfortable illusion that Kṛṣṇa is just his friend (or his father or lover), the way he allowed Yaśodā to relapse into the illusion that he was just her son. Arjuna thanks him for allowing him to return to his normal senses and his normal condition.[59] The vision of reality may be the only true sanity, but it *feels* like madess. Illusion is what feels normal.

The same misgivings that are voiced by Yaśodā and Arjuna are experienced by the sage Mārkaṇḍeya in another myth about the mouth of God:

> After Viṣṇu had burnt the universe to ashes at doomsday and then flooded it with water, he slept in the midst of the cosmic ocean. The sage Mārkaṇḍeya had been swallowed by the god, and he roamed inside his belly for many thousands of years, visiting the sacred places on earth. One day he slipped out of the god's mouth and saw the world and the ocean shrouded in darkness. He did not recognize himself there, because of God's illusion, and he became terrified. Then he saw the sleeping god, and he was amazed, wondering, "Am I crazy, or dreaming? I must be imagining that the world has disappeared, for such a calamity could never really happen." Then he was swallowed again, and, as soon as he was back in the belly of the god, he thought his vision had been a dream.
>
> So, as before, he roamed the earth for hundreds of years, and then again he slipped out of Viṣṇu's mouth. This time he saw, in the middle of the cosmic ocean, a little boy hidden in the branches of a banyan tree, a boy who blazed so like the sun that Mārkaṇḍeya could not bear to look at him. "I think I have seen this once before," mused the sage. "I think I'm being fooled by the illusion of God." In confusion and terror, Mārkaṇḍeya began to swim away, but Viṣṇu said, "Do not be afraid, my son. Come here. I am your father." Mārkaṇḍeya bowed to him with love, and Viṣṇu taught him His true nature and commanded him to return inside His belly. Then Viṣṇu swallowed Mārkaṇḍeya once more, and the sage lived there in peace.[60]

Like Yaśodā, Mārkaṇḍeya at first thinks that some sort of illusion is being foisted upon him, and, like her, he gets it backwards: when he falls out of the mouth, he feels that he has entered an illusion, not knowing that he has just escaped from the illusion. And when he has an intimation of *déjà vu*, which in his case is a true realization that he has in fact already experienced the vision once before, he is all the more convinced that he is at that moment experiencing an illusion. Both Mārkaṇḍeya and Yaśodā think that God is a child and that they themselves must be dreaming or crazy.

But the myth of Mārkaṇḍeya goes on to develop a different view. Gradually, Mārkaṇḍeya understands the truth of the vision and becomes identified with the enlightened narrator of the myth. As the myth progresses, the protagonist is gradually released from his delusions; he discovers that God is not (or not merely) a child, whereas the persistent belief that God is her child continues to ensnare Yaśodā. For her, the experience of the real hierophany takes place inside the mouth; for him, it takes place outside the mouth. The actual starting place is arbitrary, for the point of the myth is the transition, the motion across the threshold—in either direction. But Mārkaṇḍeya continues to vibrate back and forth between the two worlds until he ends up seeing the double image of both at once. The two images merge for him when he realizes that he and Viṣṇu are one and the same, the soul and God.

Géza Róheim has translated this story into psychoanalytic terms and classified it within the genre of dreams about doubles: "If we assume the identity of the ageless Markandeya and of Vishṅu, the first part of our myth is simple. The dreamer is withdrawn into himself, but out of his body he also forms a womb (ocean, lotus, etc.)."[61] Hindu mythology does assume the identity of the man and the Godhead, and it also describes an ocean that is both inside and outside Viṣṇu and a lotus that grows out of him and out of which he grows (see chapter five). Thus Viṣṇu is projected out of his own body when he spins the universe, and Mārkaṇḍeya, like all dreamers, is projected out of *his* own body when he imagines that he escapes from Viṣṇu's mouth. Each creates his external world and then inhabits it.

By contrast, Yaśodā's momentary experience of a new reality is never repeated, and she rejects it permanently. Since she is a woman and a mother, she cannot live for long on the plane of metaphysics; so she lapses back into emotional involvement. Since Mārkaṇḍeya is a man and a sage, he cannot live for long on any level other than the metaphysical. Yet the text is explicit on the following point: that Mārkaṇḍeya, like Arjuna, cannot bear the sight of God in his full powers, that he, too, has his moment of weakness. Moreover, later Indian traditions (particularly in Bengal) challenged Mārkaṇḍeya's position further by asserting that Yaśodā was the one who had reached the proper final resting point. It was right for her to return to the attitude of maternal love, still aware (even if not consciously aware) of both forms of God, the awesome (*aiśvarya*) and the intimate or sweet (*mādhurya*), the latter made all the more sweet and special because of the memory of awesomeness. The ascetic Mārkaṇḍeya, in this view, is aware of only the penultimate truth—the awesomeness; he has not yet returned to the relationship of attachment that is the ultimate—the only true—basis for the love of God. He does not yet know that the sweet form conceals the awesome form.[62] In this way, Indian tradition suggests a potentially infinite series of reversals and counterreversals; each branch of that tradition—Vedānta or *bhakti*, *mokṣa*-based or *saṃsāra*-based—finds its temporary resting place on some point of the spectrum. Though Arjuna is male, he ends up outside Kṛṣṇa and, like Yaśodā, he forgets the vision of being swallowed, for he must go on being involved in the world of action. Mārkaṇḍeya, by contrast, is free to wander, even free to wander out of the entire world. Where Arjuna's vision ends with the sight of doomsday, Mārkaṇḍeya's experience begins with doomsday and moves beyond it. Where Arjuna begs Kṛṣṇa to treat him as a father treats a son, Viṣṇu actually appears to Mārkaṇḍeya as a father and, in that form, goes on to teach him things that the warrior Arjuna cannot learn.

The myths of the mouth of God attempt to do within the frame of the story what the text does in the society: to teach the philosophical doctrine of illusion to nonphilosophical, worldly Hindus who dwell in the common-sense world of materialism, the world in which reality is defined by normal, social, conventional human existence ("This is my husband," "This is my son"). Within the myth of Yaśodā, this lesson is technically a failure; she does not change her view of what reality is, though her instinctive love of Kṛṣṇa is in fact the deepest expression of that reality. In that sense, she does not *need* to be enlightened; her emotional response is the correct devotional apprehension of God. Arjuna, too, learns to rely on his love rather than his intellectual apprehension of God. Even for the sage Mārkaṇḍeya, the love of God is a force that he cannot, and should not, relinquish, though it is not the way in which he comes to understand God; it is merely an instrument through which he finally achieves a full intellectual and metaphysical enlightenment.

Outside the myth, however, the situation is the reverse: the reader (or hearer) changes his view in the course of the myth of Yaśodā; he is moved to redefine his concept of reality. The persuasive power of the vision she sees is not logical but emotional; it dismantles our rational disbelief even though it fails to overcome her combination of rationality (she clings to the phenomenal world) and emotion (she backslides from her moment of pellucid enlightenment into the comfortable, familiar maternal love of the god). The myth of Mārkaṇḍeya, on the other hand, works in the opposite way: he does change his view of what reality is, and he does this by being shocked into a state of metaphysical rationality and a philosophically grounded love of the god. Many readers of the text would probably follow him on this path; others would not.

Both Yaśodā and Mārkaṇḍeya mediate between two points of view, that of the omniscient narrator or enlightened sage (who knows that reality is on the other side of the mouth of God) and that of the blinkered participant in the drama (the other villagers or inhabitants of Viṣṇu's stomach, who think that reality is on this side of the mouth of God). For us, as readers of the myth, several options are presented; we can play the role of Yaśodā or the role of Mārkaṇḍeya or still other roles from other myths, for each of us must find the level on which he prefers to live—or, rather, the level on which he is, unknowingly, living. In any case, the myth jars us out of simply accepting the level on which we happened to be before we encountered the myth.

Arguments

Indian: The Meaning of Illusion (*māyā*)

The two attitudes to reality and unreality that we have characterized as *saṃsāra*-oriented and *mokṣa*-oriented grow out of the rich ambivalence that is built into the doctrine of illusion as it has developed over the centuries in India. The more extreme form of the doctrine suggests that we all invent the same mental images (*māyā*) and project them on an empty reality—empty, that is, but for Godhead (according to the Hindus). The modified form of the doctrine would distinguish a particular mistake (*bhrama*, of which the classic example is mistaking a real rope for an unreal snake) from the more general illusion (*māyā*)—the illusion that there is anything there at all. According to this second form of the philosophy, God the magician makes the illusion; man the dupe makes the mistake. Implicit in the idea of the mistake is the belief that there is something there, for the term *bhrama* more precisely indicates mistaking one thing that is there for something else that isn't there. Within the entire illusion, there are many kinds of mistakes, but Indian philosophy always distinguishes between illusion or appearances within human experience—*bhrama*, which can always be corrected through further experience and hence might be called empirical illusion—and the transcendental illusion, or *māyā*, which is the gap between *all* experience and the transcendent reality of Godhead, *brahman*. Transcendent illusion can never be disproved or verified by any experience, for it is, by nature and definition, outside experience.

Both of the general forms of the doctrine of illusion, one extreme and one comparatively mild, are reflected in the myths of illusion and dreams, often within a single text. The extreme form of the doctrine places the burden of proof on the side of reality: one has to prove the reality of any phenomenon in time and space, for any phenomenon is presumed illusory until proven real. In this form, the doctrine maintains that the external world does not exist at all; this is the position, broadly speaking, of various Buddhist schools, such as the Yogācāras, Mādhyāmikas, and "No-Mind" movements. In denying the existence not only of gross material objects but even of God and the soul (the two things regarded as real by even the most extreme Hindu idealists), the Buddhists struck a truly radical position. It would take us too far afield to analyze these complex philosophies (which differ significantly from one another, as well as from various Hindu schools of idealism), but it may prove useful to summarize some of the basic forms of the Indian doctrine of illusion in order to provide a background for the spectrum of idealistic concepts that emerges from the myths.

A typical exponent of extreme idealism is the Mādhyāmika Buddhist philosopher Nāgārjuna, whose school thrived in Kashmir. This is his argument:

> Public reality—the arising, abiding, and perishing of events—neither exists nor nonexists: it is "like an illusion, a dream, a fairy city in the sky" . . . . Thus public reality and the divine image, a magical illusion and a dream, have no real existence, but they all occur and have real effects, and hence have no real nonexistence.[63]

Stephan Beyer describes the stance taken by Vasubandhu and other followers of Nāgārjuna:

> The Buddhist philosophers in India had long ago made an axiom of the "softness" of reality and given an ontological status to the omnipotence of the imagination: it devolved upon them to explain not why imagery is private but rather why reality is public. Much of Buddhist "ontological psychology" is an attempt to explain in historical terms why we make a systemic epistemological error in our apprehension of the world, why we attribute to it a solidity that in fact it does not possess.[64]

These Buddhist ideas entered the Hindu mainstream by influencing two great Hindu philosophers of the Advaita Vedānta school, Gauḍapāda and Śankara. Gauḍapāda maintained that the world is a dream and that all existence is unreal: "In dreams things are imagined internally, and in the experience that we have when we are awake things are imagined as if existing outside, but both of them are but illusory creations of the self."[65] Śankara later tried to explain away the more obvious debts to Buddhism in Gauḍapāda's work, but he himself was accused of being a "crypto-Buddhist."[66]

Absolute idealism is not, as it is often said to be, the typical Indian philosophical view, nor does it truly characterize even Śankara's thought

Hindu philosophers believed in the reality of the soul (*ātman*) and the Godhead (*brahman*)—as the Buddhists did not. (A possible exception to this generalization is furnished not by any idealists but by the school of materialists called the Cārvākas.) Hindus may have regarded the external universe as unreal either in comparison with these transcendent realities or because of its impermanence, but they did not regard it as unreal in the strict ontological sense. Indeed, even among the Buddhists the position of extreme idealism was felt by some to be logically absurd; a clown in a Tibetan text says to the monks, "All that you teach is untrue; what we perceive with the five senses is *not* an illusion."[67] In other forms of Buddhism, too, the worshipers experience a kind of reality backlash; in moments of crisis, they resort to various non-Buddhist forms of worship that fly in the face of their professed idealism and atheism.[68]

Even within classical, textual Buddhism, indeed, within the most extreme schools of Buddhist idealism, reality raises its head. Nāgārjuna himself, and others of his school, asserted that the distinction between *saṃsāra* and *mokṣa* (or *nirvāṇa*) is ultimately invalid; when you see the truth, you see that there is no distinction. This twist in the logic of idealism finds a parallel in another famous Buddhist paradox: it is necessary to give up desire, but then that means that you must also give up the desire to give up desire. In the end, we come up against a kind of relativity of illusion once more: if you perceive a barrier between *saṃsāra* and *mokṣa*, there is one, and it behooves you to struggle to stay on the right side of it (whatever you regard as the right side). If you perceive no barrier, there is none, and you are in *mokṣa* even while you are in *saṃsāra*.

There is, moreover, another way in which Indian idealism blurs the distinction between *bhrama* and *māyā*, between the assertions that there is or is not something there after all. If you think that the world is actually made out of mind, as many Indian philosophers do, then, when you mistake your own idea (of a snake) for a thing (a rope), you are experiencing not an illusion but a mistake; for although the snake for which you mistake the rope may not be real, and indeed (in the extreme doctrine) the rope itself may not be real, your mind, which makes you think you see a rope or a snake, is real. Therefore, the mistake (*bhrama*) consists in mistaking a real thing (mind) for an unreal thing (a rope or a snake). In this view, the reality status given to the mind first reverses the terms of the mistake and then erases the distinction between the mistake and the illusion. There is nothing but degrees of mistakes, and *everything* is real because everything is made of mind.

Most Indian philosophies, such as Mīmāṃsā, maintain that gross objects as a whole exist, because they are perceived.[69] In such views as these, the only thing that is absolutely unreal (*asat*) is a logical impossibility, expressed by such images as "the son of a barren woman" (see chapter six).

Only one Indian school of thought, the Advaita Vedāntins, regard the real (*sat*) and the unreal (*asat*) as equally impossible; they define the real as something that is never subject to change. The attitude of the rank-and-file Indian toward the extreme form of the doctrine of illusion may be gathered from the fact that, in Telugu, the term "Advaita" (i.e., the thought of philosophers from that school) comes to mean "illogical behavior, upside-down or contrary to normal thinking."[70] Thus most Indians consigned their philosophers to the topsy-turvy other world, the domain of illusion. Even mainstream Advaita Vedānta preferred a more moderate position, maintaining that our experiences are characterized neither by reality nor by unreality (*sat-asat-vilakṣaṇa*).

The average Hindu's attitude to soft-core idealism roughly approximates the average American's attitude to the theory of relativity; in both cases, most people would vaguely acknowledge the theory's "truth" as an abstract concept but would not use it as an operating principle. It has been suggested that the Indian man in the street (or, rather, man in the village) thinks that the universe is a real thing (*vastu*), that most philosophers think it is characterized neither by reality nor by unreality (*sat-asat-vilakṣaṇa*), and that only a few think it is totally empty (*śūnya*).[71] That is, while most people wrestle daily with the problem of particular errors of perception (*bhrama*), only a few of them are driven by this problem to consider the ambiguous nature of perception as a whole, and, of those few, even fewer come to the conclusion that what we perceive—and what we perceive it with—simply does not exist at all.

The attempt to mediate the ontological paradox is apparent from such expressions, so basic to the Indian philosophical enterprise, as *bhedābheda* (difference and nondifference), characterizing the relationship between spirit and matter or the soul and God (or the real and unreal aspects of the universe). This term is sometimes further qualified as *acintyabhedābheda*, "unthinkable difference and nondifference." This pattern of thought, which is a structural rather than a doctrinal parallel to the doctrine of the real-nonreal, is another expression of the mainstream Indian view that sees reality as both there and not there, a view that leaves the question somehow open in a way that Western materialist views do not accept.[72] This, rather than the pig-headed "Everything is illusion," is the basis of the ongoing idealistic argument in India.

Indeed, the word that (in keeping with general practice) I have translated as "illusion" (*māyā*) has many other meanings, and these lend it a power to denote much that is undeniably real. Originally it meant *only* what was real; through its basis in the verbal root *mā* ("to make"), it expressed "the sense of 'realizing in the phenomenal world'—and this implies: in three-dimensional space—by applying a special technique such as 'measuring' what was mentally conceived; converting an idea into dimensional reality."[73] Western scholars used to believe that *māyā* was related to another verbal root *mā* ("to measure"); this has recently been challenged.[74] But even if there is no etymological link, there is a conceptual link in ancient Indian thought between the ideas of making in the sense of creation *ex nihilo* and making (or finding) in the sense of redefining or measuring what is already there. In the *Ṛg Veda*, to "measure out" the universe was to create it, to divide it into its constituent parts, to *find* it by bringing it out of chaos. Viṣṇu "measures out" the three worlds by taking three strides.[75] Vedic myths in which the sun is "found" are myths about the original creation of the sun. In later myths, too, the theme of "finding the lost Vedas" or of finding the earth after it has been lost in the cosmic floods of doomsday is indistinguishable from the theme of myths in which the Vedas are first received by men or the earth is first created and set in the cosmic waters. Making is finding.

When *māyā* was gradually identified as the particular power of the gods to create, it came to express, as Jan Gonda has pointed out,

> a great variety of connotations which may, for want of something better, be expressed by such English terms as "power, wisdom, subtle device," and be defined as follows: "incomprehensible insight, wisdom, judgement and power enabling its possessor to create something or to do something, ascribed to mighty beings."[76]

Magicians do this; artists do it; gods do it. But according to certain Indian philosophies, every one of us does it every minute of our lives.

This concept of *māyā* as a kind of artistic power led gradually to its later connotation of magic, illusion, and deceit. Indeed, even in the *Ṛg Veda* there are passages where *māyā* indicates a trick, the making of something that is not really there.[77] It often means not merely bringing something into existence (as a mother would do: the Sanskrit word for mother, *mātṛ*, is derived from the same root) but manipulating the existent forces of nature or invoking the "power to create and achieve the marvelous."[78] Thus *māyā* first meant making something that was not there before; then it came to mean making something that was there into something that was not really there. The first describes the universe in the Vedic world-view; the second, the universe in the Vedāntic world-view. The first is *saṃsāric*; the second, *mokṣic*. In both cases, *māyā* can often best be translated as "transformation."

Arthur A. Macdonell's definition touches on the moral ambiguity in *māyā:*

> This term signifies occult power, applicable in a good sense to gods and in a bad sense to demons. It has an almost exact parallel in the English word "craft," which in its old signification meant "occult power, magic," and then "skilfulness, art" on the one hand and "deceitful skill, wile" on the other.[79]

To say that the universe is an illusion (*māyā*) is not to say that it is unreal; it is to say, instead, that it is not what it seems to be, that it is something constantly being *made*. *Māyā* not only deceives people about the things they think they know; more basically, it limits their knowledge to things that are epistemologically and ontologically second-rate.

But *māyā* has its positive as well as negative aspects. A similar cluster of meanings radiates from it as from the English derivatives of the Latin word for play (*ludo*)—de-lusion, il-lusion, e-lusive, and so forth—and from the word "play" itself—play as drama, as swordplay or loveplay, as the play of light that causes mirages, as the double image implicit in wordplay (as Johan Huizinga pointed out so brilliantly in *Homo Ludens*). These word clusters delineate a universe full of beauty and motion that enchants us all. All Indian philosophies acknowledge that *māyā* is a fact of life—*the* fact of life; but some (the *mokṣa*-oriented) regard it as a negative fact, to be combated, while others (the *saṃsāra*-oriented) regard it as a positive fact, to be embraced.

We will occasionally encounter, in texts such as the *Yogavāsiṣṭha* and the *Lankāvatārasūtra* (in chapters four and five, below), extreme forms of the doctrine of illusion, though such passages do not reflect the dominant viewpoint of those texts. Such extremes seem to invoke the problem of solipsism, "the view or theory that the self is the only object of real knowledge or the only thing really existent."[80] At first glance, *māyā* may perhaps be fairly accused of condemning us to solipsism. We in the West tend to reassure ourselves of the reality of the universe and of ourselves by taking refuge in the corroborating opinions of other people and by denying any status of reality to our private fantasies. Indians, by contrast, have often tended to reassure themselves of the reality of the universe by maintaining the reality of both private fantasies *and* public experience, and to do this they will sometimes dismiss the value of corroborating opinions as irrelevant to the reality status of both the external and the internal world. That is, they would not use corroboration to establish the reality of the external world, as we would do, and then be forced to let absence of corroboration demolish the reality of the internal world, as we would also do. They would ignore corroboration in both cases.

Indian myths present us with both the illusionist and the antiillusionist views of *māyā*, often in sequence. First there is a movement away from the objective view of reality; one learns that things are not as they seem, that the material world is more elusive than one had thought. This is what is achieved by the first episode in the myth of Nārada. But then one moves still further, toward the reality of the inner eye, as feeling, dream, and fantasy become ontologically legitimate.[81] This happens in the second episode of the Nārada story. In this way the inner world is brought forward to replace, in a sense, the outer world that has just been torn down. *Māyā* establishes the principle that reality is confusing, and less concrete than it looks; but while we are still recovering from the shock of this revelation, while we are flayed of our normal self-protective assumptions about the world and are newly sensitive to alternative views, *māyā* offers a balm for our ontological wounds; when it has emptied our material world, *māyā* rushes into our newly created metaphysical vacuum and assures us of the truth, and simultaneously the beauty, of our felt but unseen worlds.

David Shulman has captured an important aspect of the paradox of *māyā* in his study of the South Indian clown:

> The clown . . . argues for the reality of the inner worlds of vision, intuitive perception, hallucination, nightmare or dream. In a word, he exemplifies the world's status as *māyā*—at once tangible and real, and immaterial; entirely permeable by the imagination; always baffling, enticing, enslaving, and in the process of becoming something new and still more elusive. . . . The clown [has a] commonsensical and yet ridiculous acceptance of immediate, sensuous reality. The essence of *māyā* is contradiction—the incongruous wonder of the absolute transformed into sensible form; the innate, mysterious, dynamic contradiction of the clown. And this the clown shares with the Brahmin, with the latter's characteristic ambivalence toward a baffling and violent reality as well as his stance upon the border facing the ultimate on either side—transcendent wholeness through "outer" release, or the creative metonymy of *saṃsāric* form.[82]

The borderline between illusion and reality mirrors the borderline between *mokṣa* and *saṃsāra* (no matter whether you regard *mokṣa* or *saṃsāra* as the more real). It is also, therefore, the borderline between the "common-sensical and yet ridiculous acceptance of immediate, sensuous reality" and the philosophical sophistication that challenges that common sense. Indian culture at one level shares the Western common sense that regards material manifestations as the basis of reality, but at another level it moves beyond that common sense and, without entirely abandoning it, incorporates it into a broader view of the nature of illusion.

Yet the concept of "self," which lies at the heart of solipsism, is the joker in the deck when we attempt to construct an epistemological game that the two cultures can play together. The transhuman, theological implications of "self" in India do, I think, protect Indian philosophers from any true solipsism as it is found in the West. The assumed link between the mind of man and the mind of God (and, even more, between the body of man and the body of God) rescues the Indian idealist from the dangers of true solipsism: he, or his mind, cannot be the only thing in the world that exists. This link also rescues the believing dreamer from the dangers of madness, though not from the dangers of loneliness. Solipsism in its logical sense should not trouble the believing Hindu; but solipsism in its emotional sense—in the haunting fear that one might be physically alone and in the growing certainty that one is spiritually alone—can indeed trouble anyone, and this feeling can, as we saw in chapter two, be somewhat assuaged by the hope of a shared dream.

In the West, the loss of the sense of self (ego)—for which the Sanskrit *ahaṃkara* is a pejorative parallel—is often regarded as a sign of madness, but in India the loss of the sense of Self (*ātman*) as distinct from God (*brahman*) is the key to enlightenment. B. L. Atreya has argued this point in his defense of the philosophy of the *Yogavāsiṣṭha*:

> Solipsism seems to be the inevitable consequence of idealism. And there have been philosophers in India, the *driṣṭi-sriṣṭi-vādins* [those who argued that seeing precedes creating], who have held solipsism to be the most cogent doctrine. In fact, there cannot be any logical refutation of true solipsism. . . . The solipsist is refuted because he is not fully aware of the meaning and implication of the word "my" or "I" . . . . In discovering the real "I," he will find that the "I" is nothing less than the Absolute Whole looked at through the window of a particular and unique point of interest. The "I" is the Absolute Consciousness with the entire world present within it as an idea.[83]

Because they move as far away as possible from the terrifying brink of solipsism, Indians tend to rush to the other extreme of attributing an external reality to the internal mental constructions of other people. A delightful example of this appears in an argument in a Telugu devotional text:

> Vīraśaivism does not believe in *punarjanma* (rebirth) nor in *svarga* or *naraka* (heaven and hell). . . . Nevertheless, Vīraśaivism does apply the concept of *naraka* to those who deviate from the prescribed path. For example, the *Basava Purāṇa* states that a Śaivite enters twenty-eight-hundred-million *narakas* by uttering the names of deities from other religions. . . . The context of these statements suggests that anyone who deviates from the Vīraśaiva path falls into the hells which are provided by the other systems.[84]

In this way, it is possible to get gobbled up by dragons that *other* people believe in. This concept, when it appears in the West, appears only as a joke: A man complained to a psychiatrist that his brother thought himself to be a chicken; when asked why he did not seek a cure for his brother or have him put into an asylum, the man replied, "Well, we need the eggs." The Hindus get some very real eggs from their metaphysical illusions.

Western: The Hard and the Soft and Mr. Shlemiel

Myths about dream doubles and double universes, which dramatize the ambiguous nature of physical reality, have played a different role in the West. There are of course many European instances of such stories, but they are likely to be produced in the peculiar backwaters of our culture, whereas in India they are part of the mainstream. In the West, too, the tales of illusion are often satirical, poking fun sometimes at Western culture itself, sometimes at India. Even in India, as we have seen in the tale of the amazing pot, the theme of doubles provided material for satire, and the tales of illusion as a whole provide a more serious kind of satire on the complacency of the normal common-sense view of the world. But one example of a Western satire on this theme may prove useful as a reminder of at least one of the ways in which the West has resisted the implications of the theory of illusion.

A delightful spoof of the theme of the confusion between dream and reality and of the problem of multiple universes occurs in one of Isaac Bashevis Singer's tales of Chelm, the town of fools. In summary, the tale is this:

> Shlemiel, who lived in Chelm, set out for Warsaw. Along the way, he decided to take a nap, and he left his boots with the toes facing Warsaw, so as to be sure of taking the right direction when he awoke. While he slept, the blacksmith, a prankster, came along and turned the boots around. When Shlemiel awoke, he set off and soon came back to Chelm, where he recognized all the houses and the people and even found his own house and his wife and children, who greeted him. But he thought he had come to a second Chelm that was exactly like the first one. "Mrs. Shlemiel," he said, "I'm not your husband. Children, I'm not your father." "Have you lost your mind?" Mrs. Shlemiel screamed. But he continued to insist, "I am Shlemiel of Chelm One, and this is Chelm Two."
>
> Finally, one of the elders said, "Maybe there really are two Chelms." "If there are two, then why can't there be three, four, or even a hundred Chelms?" said another. And a third argued, "Even if there are a hundred Chelms, must there be a Shlemiel in each one of them?" When someone suggested that Shlemiel might have turned around and come back to Chelm, Shlemiel cried out, "Why should I turn around? I'm not a windmill." Finally they said, "Mrs. Shlemiel's husband, the real Shlemiel, must have left the day you came."

> They decided that Shlemiel should stay there until the real Shlemiel came back but that, of course, he must not live with Mrs. Shlemiel, though they hired him to take care of Shlemiel's children. Years passed, and everyone was convinced that Shlemiel had gone to the other Chelm, where he had had exactly the same experience as the Shlemiel in this Chelm: he had been hired by the local community and was taking care of the other Mrs. Shlemiel's children. Shlemiel wondered a lot about the other Shlemiel, and finally he realized, "All the world is one big Chelm."[85]

The situation that Shlemiel thinks he is confronted with is the situation that Nārada thought he was confronted with: two worlds claim that he lives in them, though there is only one of him. Shlemiel thinks that he has a wife and children in both worlds, unlike the Indian sages, who are chaste in one, married in another. As it turns out, Shlemiel does in fact remain chaste in what he thinks is his second world, his dream world: he is compelled to "renounce" his wife and children and is hired to take care of the latter. Indeed, in this story, as in the Hindu tradition, this renunciation is applauded: Shlemiel is much happier living apart from his shrewish wife, and she is relieved to be free of her foolish husband. The fools in the town are convinced that there are, in fact, two parallel worlds and perhaps even more than two, as in many Indian myths. But from the standpoint of the author and his readers, it is all mystical hogwash, metaphysical bullshit; there is only one Chelm, and only one Shlemiel—thank God. Jewish rationalism is impatient with this sort of metaphysical playfulness.

The doctrine of illusion in its crude form is not particularly well regarded in the West. Peter de Vries satirized an Indian holy man who went to midwestern cocktail parties and taught that "The world was not an illusion after all; it only seemed that way."[86] Western art historians and psychologists of illusion have trained heavier canons on *māyā*. Sir Roland Penrose remarks, "We have chosen . . . to probe into the nature of illusion and examine its effects to the best of our ability, rather than dismiss it in oriental fashion with the whole of existence as 'Maya,' the condition responsible for our presence in this disquieting yet intriguing vale of tears."[87]

Even the modified form of Indian idealism comes under attack in the West, for even the Indians who do not "dismiss . . . the whole of existence as 'Maya'" dismiss *some* aspects of it. We do this too, of course, but we do not label the *same* aspects unreal. Everyone feels that certain things are real and other things are not, but not everyone agrees on which is which—on where to draw the line along the spectrum of real and unreal. Even the stolidly realistic Sir Karl Popper is grudgingly flexible on this point:

> Realism is essential to common sense. Common sense, or enlightened common sense, distinguishes between appearance and reality. . . . But common sense also realizes that appearances (say, a reflection in a looking glass) have a sort of reality; in other words, that there can be a surface reality—that is, an appearance—and a depth reality. Moreover, there are many sorts of real things.[88]

Like equality in George Orwell's *Animal Farm*, reality is relative: some things are realer than others. In India, though people toyed with the idea of collapsing entirely the distinctions between inner and outer realities, some sort of opposition was always made at the beginning of the argument (if only to establish what it was that was going to be collapsed), and some sort of opposition was always made at the end of the argument, though this was often a very *different* opposition, one that divided up the territory in a totally new way.

If we look at Indian myths of creation, for example, we soon realize how misleading "hard" and "soft" are as keys to the ways in which Indians group their realities along the spectrum:

> When Brahmā made all this universe, he placed his seed in his wife, just as a man full of desire places his seed in a woman full of desire. She gave birth to the Vedas and the various branches of knowledge, such as logic and grammar; to the musical modes, the Four Ages, the year, the month, the season, the lunar day, the inch, the second, and other measurements. . . . She gave birth to the four kinds of doomsday, and time, and the maiden Death, and all the families of diseases, and she gave them all her breast to suck.
>
> Then Injustice [Adharma] was born from the Creator's back, and Misfortune from his left side. From his navel were born Viśvakarman, the guru of all artists, and the eight great gods of the sky; and from the mind of the Creator were born the four ancient sages. From Brahmā's mouth was born Manu, the ancestor of all mankind.[89]

At first, Brahmā uses physical parts of his body to create, and in this way he produces liminal creatures, abstractions (Injustice and Misfortune), which are visualized as personified figures, physical deities. But now he gives birth to material creatures, gods and men, and, to produce these physical objects, he creates miraculously and mentally, in contrast with the natural and physical techniques of creation that he and his wife had used to produce ideas. Thus physical creation gives rise to mental or ambiguous entities; mental creation gives rise to material entities. From the very start, therefore, dichotomies such as "hard" and "soft" fail to provide a useful conceptual framework for the Indian universe.

It might seem both more convenient and more honest to use Indian terms for such categories. The Tamil terms *akam* and *puram* refer, respectively, to the world of love, poetry, private emotion, and personal feeling and the world of war, inscriptions, public sentiments, and national issues. Though we might take "soft" as an approximation to *akam* and "hard" as an approximation to *puram*, to do so would reduce and distort the Indian terms, which provide for a subtle interaction between the two categories. Another Indian way of contrasting aspects of reality is one that we have already encountered: the reality of *saṃsāra* (the world of rebirth) and the reality of *mokṣa* (the nonworld of release from rebirth). And yet another taxonomy was suggested by the philosopher Śankara, who

> distinguished three levels of being—the highest level (*paramārthika*), which consists of exactly one entity, completely real, Brahman; the empirical level (*vyavahārika*), containing the objects we commonsensically call "real," like the shell [that we may mistake for a piece of silver]; and the illusory level (*prātibhāsika*), containing objects like the piece of silver [that we think we see in the shell]. . . . It would seem there ought to be a continuous scale of more or less, from Brahman, as the limit at the upper end, to negation (*asat*) as the limit at the lower end. . . . For example, . . . the objects confronted in dreams belong on the illusory level. But now suppose I have a dream in which I am walking along the beach and think I see a piece of silver, only to be disappointed in finding it only to be a (dream) shell. This dream piece of silver must surely be relegated to an even lower level than the *prātibhāsika*.[90]

We will encounter many Indian myths in which the levels of reality proliferate in the manner imagined here. Such compounding, or combination, is made possible by the fact that the *prātibhāsika* level (or the contradictory level, as it might be translated) contains, according to Śankara, three different sorts of unreal objects, which may be combined: objects of perceptual error (the snake for which the rope is mistaken), hallucinations or magical illusions, and the objects of dreams. A further multiplication of combinations is due to the fact that dreams are unreal in several different ways: dream experiences are canceled out by subsequent waking consciousness; they are mere memories that have no real object; they do not observe the rules of time, place, and causation; and they are self-contradictory.[91] Śankara here is arguing a very hard line indeed. This line continues in his discussion of the next level, the *vyavahārika*, or practical, businesslike, level—the level on which the rope is seen not to be a snake, the magical illusion is overcome, and one awakens from a dream. Yet, this too is part of the realm of *māyā*; it is canceled out and encompassed by the highest level, even as the dream is canceled out or sublated by waking consciousness. This highest level, *brahman*, is the reality that underlies the rope that is mistaken for a snake, even while it is the reality that demonstrates that neither the snake nor the rope exists. But then Śankara admits several respects in which dreams are, in fact, real. They do not satisfy either of the two criteria for unreality: dreams are not a logical impossibility (like the son of a barren woman), nor are they things that are never encountered in experience (like the horns of a hare). They are real because they are experienced, because they sometimes have real effects in waking life, and because they are said to be portents.[92]

Thus, like the grownups who moved beyond the realist views of the mature child, Śankara transcends his own arguments for the unreality of dreams, using them not to establish the sovereignty of waking life but to demolish that sovereignty. Moreover, the ways in which various levels of reality interact in arguments like those of Śankara caution us against accepting any rigid polar opposites (even subtle entities like *akam* and *puram*) as fixed stars by which to chart our course across reality. What we must settle for instead are tendencies, directions of movement, processes of reality and unreality.

In India, there are many different kinds of consciousness and many different kinds of reality: the realities of concrete experience, of inner vision, of dreams, memories, past lives, fantasies, and so forth.[93] These would have to be set out at various points on a spectrum that has no ends at all. A comparable, though different, range of perceived realities exists in the West, but the traditional Western way has been to assign each phenomenon to one or the other of the basic polar oppositions of hard and soft, real and unreal. This India refuses to do.

4 Epistemology in Narrative: Tales from the *Yogavāsiṣṭha*

In my approach to the Indian myths about illusion and dreams thus far, I have made a formal attempt to separate the texts from the arguments, the stories from the commentaries. This is in part a concession to a Western audience that is accustomed to viewing stories and arguments as two different genres; but it could also be argued, on one level at least, that in India, too, they are significantly different genres. Philosophy is not narrative; philosophy thinks out ideas in formal order, using arguments to indicate a proof. Narratives do not constitute proofs; they act out proofs. Narratives, such as myths, constitute a genre that views the same problems that are elsewhere treated philosophically, but views them through a story.

Myths do not prove anything; they merely tell you what is for them a truth, and you either accept it or you don't; it either matches an experience of your own, or it doesn't. The sequence of events is by its very nature compelling, and its philosophy is implicit. Narrative says: "This happened once." This is a basic form of human communication, because it makes an immediate contact, gathering the hearer into the speaker. The hearer then responds, either by saying, "Yes, it was like that with me, too, it happened to me, too," or, "It was different with me."[1] Narrative makes it possible for us to share our dreams by transforming them into stories and exchanging them for other peoples' stories. Narrative does not make it possible for us to prove that our dreams are real—it is, as we shall see in this chapter, impossible to prove the reality of a dream, philosophically or logically—but it makes it possible for us to imagine how we might try to prove that they are real.

Yet narrative does not function in dreams precisely as it functions in myth. The compelling causative sequence of events is absent from dreams; the thread of the plot is replaced by a pattern of images that suggest but never actually spell out the story. For this reason, too, proofs cannot be accomplished within dreams, for proofs depend upon the skeletal structure of cause and result that dreams lack. Myths add to dreams precisely the structure that makes such seeming proofs possible.

Narrative implicitly expresses a theory of causation through the sequence of its events. Nowadays, in the West, myth is boxed between history (which is regarded as true) and the novel (which is regarded as untrue), an ambiguous status. But *in illo tempore*, and in India, to say that something *happened* is to say that it is true, to force the hand of belief. The only place in which the power of narrative still functions in this way in Western culture is in psychoanalytic case histories—a sharing of dreams—where the truth of the past can often be expressed only when it is formulated as a story.[2]

Indian narratives have a peculiar penchant for incorporating into themselves elements that we would label philosophy: formal arguments and long discussions that interrupt the story. In our tradition, such matters would be relegated to textual commentaries. India has these, too; but much of what might be placed in a separate commentary is actually drawn into the narrative text, so that the text carries its own commentary around with it, the way a snail carries its house or a turtle its shell. To a Western reader, these passages often seem to spoil the story; such didactic ramblings in the great Sanskrit epics were invariably labeled "interpolations" by the Western scholars who stubbed their toes on them over and over again in the course of a good story. But to an Indian audience, there is no harsh break between the stories and the commentaries; indeed, the Indian audience tends to view the matter quite the other way around: it sees the philosophical argument as the basic genre and the stories as set into it like gems, as focal points, as moments when the philosophy gathers momentum and breaks out of a problem it cannot solve into a mode of thinking that at least allows it to state the problem and to share it in a parable. Ask a European scholar what the *Mahābhārata* is about and he will probably say, "The battle between the Kurus and the Pāṇḍavas." An Indian might give the same answer, but most Indians would say, "It is about *dharma*." What is foreground for one culture is background for another.

An example of the weight that Indians place on the philosophical content of their stories can be seen in the subject matter of the illustrations in the Chester Beatty manuscript of the *Yogavāsiṣṭha*. There are forty-one of these, and over a third of them (fifteen) depict not the events told in the stories but rather the people who are telling and explaining the stories. In other words, these illustrations depict what we would regard as the frame rather than the picture. Six illustrate the outer frame; of these, three involve Vasiṣṭha and Rāma. Sir Thomas Arnold, the editor of the catalogue, helpfully summarizes what it is that they are all talking about, but these summaries are entirely arbitrary; the pictures are just pictures of people engaged in conversation. These are the ideas that Arnold would print in invisible balloons above the heads of the figures in the drawings: Vasiṣṭha instructs Rāma "as to the means of attaining *moksha* (salvation)" or "how the Universe is nothing but a mode of the consciousness of Atma" or "how self-introspection may be attained." Other teachers are said to be telling other people about "the nature of true knowledge" or about "that bliss of perfect knowledge in which there is no pain" or "the true nature of Maya (illusion)." And the final illustration in the manuscript, a painting of two ascetics, apparently catches them at a moment when they are "discussing the origin of the Universe." To the Western eye, these are like frozen frames in a "talking" motion picture with the sound track turned off; but to the Indians, who already know the sound track by heart, they are highly evocative pictures, full of the motion, not of the body, but of the mind.

In the West, myth is usually the handmaiden of philosophy. Plato lapses into myth from time to time (as in the myth of the dream of Er in the *Republic*) to state things that, as he himself admits, can never be entirely spelled out in argument.[3] This is, I think, a valid parallel as far as it goes, but there are two important distinctions between the ways in which Plato and the Indian narrators fused philosophy and narrative. In the first place, Plato often invented his myths or called on myths that his audience was not familiar with, while the Indian narrator usually has only to remind his audience of a story that they already know well. Second, there was a complex system by which the Indian stories and commentaries were constantly interleaved, interpenetrating each other until we cannot really tell where the argument leaves off and the story begins. They have become each other, like salt placed in water (in the Upaniṣadic metaphor for the pervasion of the universe by the Godhead).[4]

In India, just as the commentaries are themselves regarded as a form of literature and are built right into the narratives, so, too, is the audience built into the story. Every Indian text is its own metatext, every Epic is its own epi-Epic, which tells you how to react to the text.[5] The story that we hear or read is told by a narrator to another person, who answers him and asks questions, speaking for the audience. Often this answerer is himself an actor within the story that is being told; sometimes the narrator tells his own story in the first person. We are familiar with this technique from the way in which Homer uses Odysseus as the singer of tales in his own story; in India, the process is elaborated and manipulated so that there are often several interlocutors on several levels, each raising different philosophical points that arise from the narrative. In keeping track of the story, one often has to supply a series of encapsulating quotation marks: "'"'"'". These tales are parables about parables, stories *about* storytelling as well as examples *of* storytelling. They build the philosophy into the story by placing a running commentary in the mouths of the characters on each of several different levels of narrative. In a similar way, the secondary elaboration is an explicit part of a dream.

In devotional literature, in particular, the speaker and the listener become collapsed into one as the narrative's functions of communication and communion merge together. People listen to stories not merely to learn something new (communication) but to relive, together, the stories they already know, stories about themselves (communion).[6] A. K. Ramanujan once remarked that no Indian ever hears the *Mahābhārata* for the first time;[7] here is a case of cultural *déjà vu*, a parallel to the *déjà vu* of lovers on the personal level. In the *Rāmāyaṇa*, Rāma listens to the two bards, who are his unrecognized sons, telling him his own story, and through the storytelling he eventually recognizes them.[8] And in the *Adhyātma-Rāmāyaṇa*, when Sītā is admonished by Rāma not to come with him to the forest, she replies in exasperation: "Many *Rāmāyaṇas* have been heard many times by many Brahmins. Tell me, does Rāma ever go to the forest without Sītā in any of them?"[9]

The fact that the audience can be expected to know the story has other uses, as well. The text can use the audience's assumptions and expectations to serve new purposes; it does not necessarily fulfill their expectations.[10] In this way, a philosophical text can manipulate stories to make a didactic point, using the stories against themselves, setting up traditional tales in order to undermine and change traditional ways of thinking about traditional philosophical problems. In India, philosophy is the context of narrative. We may, if we wish, seek other contexts as well—sociological, economic, psychological—but always the wave of the story casts us up on the sands of philosophy. As philosophy changes over the years, the same story may be asked to serve several different masters. Indians are not troubled by the simultaneous existence of several variants; they know that texts, too, have many doubles.

The *Yogavāsiṣṭha* is a text that makes use of traditional motifs in this creative way. The presence in it of numerous intricately intertwined scraps from the ancient Sanskrit and from contemporary folktales indicates that the author of the *Yogavāsiṣṭha* had a number of stories to call on to illustrate the points he wished to make. It is particularly striking that few of those earlier sources cared to make those points, to explain *how* it could be that dreams and waking life might interact as they seem to do. To some extent, it is a matter of priorities. The authors of the earlier texts doubtless knew about *māyā*; this knowledge adds the color and spice and profundity to the basic stories. They make their own points, both implicitly, in the narration of what happens to people, and occasionally explicitly, as when a character justifies his actions or the narrator comments on his actions. But the deeper philosophical points made in the *Yogavāsiṣṭha* are not drawn out in earlier Sanskrit texts and folktales.

This was because the philosophical arguments were either not yet fully enough developed or not widely enough diffused in the nonphilosophical segments of the culture to be slipped into a story. But, even more, it was because the story was always bigger, more profound, than any explicit argument that could be made to gloss it; the story always symbolized an insight that spilled over, beyond what the storyteller himself could say it meant. The story is a river whose fish keep jumping out. Paul Ricoeur has said that the symbol gives rise to thought; mythology precedes philosophy. More than that: philosophy is a vain attempt to catch up with mythology; philosophy races after mythology and gets closer and closer but never catches it, just as Achilles never quite reaches the tortoise in Zeno's paradox.

The story does not merely illustrate a theory, as, for instance, George Gamow wrote the tale of *Mr. Tomkins in Wonderland* to illustrate the theory of relativity. The story may give an example of the theory, but it also says things that the theory does not account for. There is a kind of mutual feedback between story and theory akin to the feedback that we have seen between myth and dream: each nourishes the other. The author of the *Yogavāsiṣṭha* hauls the tales in out of the Indian past and spruces them up to pass inspection by a very different judge. Their old meanings, always there if never fully understood, are dragged out to answer new questions, and they stand there squinting and awkwardly flinching in the unaccustomed light. In this new setting, the stories offer a poetic solution to certain metaphysical problems, creating a metaphysic out of imagery.[11]

The *Yogavāsiṣṭha* is a massive Sanskrit text, consisting of some 27,687 stanzas. It was probably composed in Kashmir, sometime between the sixth and twelfth centuries of our era (its date, like that of most Indian texts, is much disputed).[12] In the course of this long philosophical argument, the sage Vasiṣṭha tells about fifty-five stories; many of them are brief parables, but several are long, baroque, elaborately poetic renditions of complex adventures. These stories are both traditional and nontraditional; that is, they build on certain standard Indian narratives of illusion and dreams, but they build new stories out of the old themes, often with an entirely new philosophical point.

The stories in the *Yogavāsiṣṭha* are stories within another story. The full title of the *Yogavāsiṣṭha* is the *Yogavāsiṣṭha-Mahā-Rāmāyaṇa*, or "The great tale of Rāma as told by the sage Vasiṣṭha in order to expound his philosophy of yoga." This long poem is attributed to the poet Vālmīki (who is the author of the first Sanskrit *Rāmāyaṇa*) and is about an incident in the life of Rāma that was not dealt with in the earlier *Rāmāyaṇa*: a long conversation with the sage Vasiṣṭha. Thus, even the *Yogavāsiṣṭha* as a whole is a metatext, filling in the supposed gaps in the older text on which it purports to be based, just as many folk versions of the *Rāmāyaṇa* do. Similarly, Tom Stoppard's *Rosenkrantz and Guildenstern Are Dead* fills in certain gaps in Shakespeare's *Hamlet.*

The *Yogavāsiṣṭha* is well loved by Indians; it has been translated into many of the vernacular languages of India and has found its way into "anonymous" oral traditions.[13] In this way, although it is a highly sophisticated Sanskrit composition, it both grows out of folklore and grows back into folklore in yet another instance of mutual feedback. (A parallel might be seen in the way in which "Old Man River," composed by the sophisticated Jerome Kern and Oscar Hammerstein II, is based on folk themes and regarded by many Americans as a folk song.) The *Yogavāsiṣṭha* was (and may have been intended to be) a means by which sophisticated philosophical ideas were transmitted to an audience that was well educated (able to read Sanskrit) but probably not well trained in philosophy. The text is a curious blend of abstract, classical Indian philosophy and vivid, detailed Indian folklore, a kind of Classic Comics version of the doctrine of illusion.[14] In it, a philosophy that often seems hollow or arbitrary comes to life when the narrative spells out its widest implications. It is as if someone took the abstract concept "The universe is illusory" and made it somehow anthropomorphic, producing a kind of teaching device to make us understand what it *feels* like to realize that everything is an illusion. And it can't be done; in our hearts, we don't believe it. But the narrative does not merely discuss this problem; it enacts it. Like dreams, which are not so much thought (with logic and causation) as experienced (emotionally and in images), the *Yogavāsiṣṭha* presents us with experiences that make the thoughts real. The narrative allows us—nay, forces us—to imagine ourselves in a situation in which we *must* believe in the doctrine of illusion, in which we must act out the paradox.

Among the many tales in the *Yogavāsiṣṭha*, I have chosen a few that seem to me particularly powerful and beautiful examples of this genre.[15] Two of them are, I think, best read together, as expressions of the *Yogavāsiṣṭha*'s approach to the problem of psychology or epistemology; these are the tales of King Lavaṇa and the Brahmin Gādhi. Later we will look at other stories, such as the tale of the monk who met the people in his dreams, which reformulate these same problems and make a more direct approach to the problem of ontology.

Indian Texts

The King Who Dreamed He Was an Untouchable and Awoke to Find It Was True

Let us begin with the story of King Lavaṇa.

> In the lush country of the Northern Pāṇḍavas there once reigned a virtuous king named Lavaṇa, born in the family of Hariścandra. One day when Lavaṇa was seated on his throne in the assembly hall, a magician entered, bowed, and said to the king, "While you

sit on your throne, watch this marvelous trick." Then he waved his peacock-feather wand, and a man from Sindh entered, leading a horse; and as the king gazed at the horse, he remained motionless upon his throne, his eyes fixed and staring, as if in meditation. His courtiers were worried, but they remained still and silent, and after a few minutes the king awoke and began to fall from his throne. Servants caught him as he fell, and the king asked, in confusion, "What is this place? Whose is this hall?" When he finally regained his senses, he told this story:

"While I was sitting in front of the horse and looking at the waving wand of the magician, I had the delusion that I mounted the horse and went out hunting alone. Carried far away, I arrived at a great desert, which I crossed to reach a jungle, and under a tree a creeper caught me and suspended me by the shoulders. As I was hanging there, the horse went out from under me. [See plate 4.] I spent the night in that tree, sleepless and terrified. As I wandered about the next day, I saw a dark-skinned young girl carrying a pot of food, and, since I was starving, I asked her for some food. She told me that she was an Untouchable [a Caṇḍāla] and said that she would feed me only if I married her. I agreed to this, and, after she fed me, she took me back to her village, where I married her and became a foster Untouchable. [See plate 5.]

"She bore me two sons and two daughters, and I spent sixty years with her there, wearing a loincloth stinking and mildewed and full of lice, drinking the still-warm blood of wild animals I killed, eating carrion in the cremation grounds. Though I was the only son of a king, I grew old and gray and worn out, and I forgot that I had been a king; I became firmly established as an Untouchable. One day, when a terrible famine arose and an enormous drought and forest fire, I took my family and escaped into another forest. As my wife slept, I said to my younger son, 'Cook my flesh and eat it,' and he agreed to this, as it was his only hope of staying alive. I resolved to die and made a funeral pyre, and, just as I was about to throw myself on it, at that very moment, I, the king, fell from this throne. Then I was awakened by shouts of 'Hurrah!' and the sound of music. This is the illusion that the magician wrought upon me."

As King Lavaṇa finished this speech, the magician suddenly vanished. Then the courtiers, their eyes wide with amazement, said, "My lord, this was no magician; this was some divine illusion sent to give enlightenment about the material world that is a mere mental delusion." The king set out the very next day to go to the desert, having resolved to find once more the wasteland that had been reflected in the mirror of his mind. With his ministers, he wandered until he found an enormous desert just like the one he had known in his thoughts, and to his amazement he discovered all the exact details he had imagined: he recognized outcaste hunters who were his acquaintances, and he found the village where he had been a foster Untouchable, and he saw this and that man, and this and that woman, and all the various things that people use, and the trees that had been withered by the drought, and the orphaned hunter children. [See plate 6.] And he saw an old woman who was his mother-in-law. He asked her, "What happened here? Who are you?" She told him the story: a king had come there and married her daughter, and they had had children, and then the drought came and all the villagers died. The king became amazed and full of pity. He asked many more questions, and her answers convinced him that the woman was telling the story of his own experience of the Untouchables. Then he returned to the city and to his own palace, where the people welcomed him back.[16]

The Brahmin Who Dreamed He Was an Untouchable Who Dreamed He Was a King

The story of King Lavaṇa, though complete in itself, is further illuminated by comparison with the story of the Brahmin Gādhi.

There was once a wise and dispassionate Brahmin named Gādhi, who performed asceticism by submerging himself in a lake until the god Viṣṇu appeared to him and offered him a boon. [See plate 7.] Gādhi asked to see Viṣṇu's power of illusion, and Viṣṇu promised him that he would see illusion and then reject it. After Viṣṇu vanished, Gādhi came out of the lake and went about his business for several days. One day he went again to bathe in the lake, and as he went into the water he lost consciousness and saw his own body dead in his own house, being mourned by his wife and his mother and all his friends and relatives, and then he saw them carry his body to the burning grounds and burn his corpse to ashes.

Then, as he remained in the water, Gādhi saw himself reborn as an Untouchable [a Pulkasa] named Katañja: he saw himself squashed inside the disgusting womb of an Untouchable woman, then born, and then growing up as a child. He went hunting with his dogs, married a dark Untouchable woman, made love to her, had many children, and gradually became old. Then, since he outlived all his family, he wandered alone in the wilderness until, one day, he came to the capital city, where the king had just died. The royal elephant picked him up with its trunk, and he was anointed King Gavala in the city of the Kīras, since no one knew that he was an Untouchable. He reigned for eight years, until one day an old Untouchable saw him when he was alone and without his regalia; the old man addressed him as his friend Katañja, thereby identifying him as an Untouchable, and this encounter was witnessed by several people. Though the king repudiated what the Untouchable had said, all his servants refused to touch him, just as if he were a corpse; the people fled from him, his Brahmin ministers all committed suicide because they had been polluted, and the city was in chaos. Realizing that all this was his fault, Gavala decided to immolate himself along with his ministers. As the body named Gavala fell into the fire and became a tangle of limbs, the painful spasms of the burning of his own body in the fire awakened Gādhi in the water.

Gādhi came to his senses and got out of the lake, but he was puzzled when he recalled the wife and mother who had mourned for him, since his parents had died when he was an infant, and he had no wife, nor indeed had he ever seen the true form of a woman's body. He went home and lived as before, until, after a few days, a Brahmin guest came to his house and casually mentioned that in the Kīra country an Untouchable had been king for eight years until he was discovered and immolated himself, together with hundreds of Brahmin ministers. Gādhi asked him many questions and verified all the details, in amazement and dismay. Then he went to see for himself, and he found the country that he had thought of in his mind: the Untouchables' huts and all the rest. He asked about Katañja and was told that he had outlived all of his large family, left the village, and become king of the Kīras for eight years, until the citizens unmasked him and he entered the funeral pyre. The Brahmin Gādhi spent a month in the village and learned all the details from the villagers, just as he had experienced it. Then he journeyed to the city of the Kīras and saw all the places he had seen and experienced, and there too he asked and learned about the Untouchable king, who had, they said, died twelve years ago. Seeing the new king, as if he were seeing his own former life before his own eyes, Gādhi felt as if he were experiencing a waking dream, an illusion, a magic net of mistakes.

Then he remembered that Viṣṇu had promised to demonstrate the great power of illusion, and he realized that his enigmatic experience had been precisely that demonstration. He went out of the city and lived for a year and a half in mounting curiosity and puzzlement, until Viṣṇu came to him and explained the nature of his illusion. When Viṣṇu vanished, Gādhi went back to the Untouchables once more to test his delusion; more convinced than ever that he really had been there, and therefore more puzzled than ever, he propitiated Viṣṇu again, and again Viṣṇu explained how Gādhi had seen what he had seen. When Viṣṇu had vanished, Gādhi's mind was all the more full of agony; then Viṣṇu returned and explained it all to him a third time, and then, at last, Gādhi's mind found peace.[17]

Lavaṇa and Gādhi: Mutual Similes

These stories of Lavaṇa and Gādhi are long and complex; they occupy over sixty pages of Sanskrit text and are marbled with various metaphysical asides, to which we will turn our attention soon. It may seem perverse to combine two stories each of which is challenging enough on its own; in particular, it may appear to be asking for trouble to explain the story of Lavaṇa by having recourse to the story of Gādhi, which is so complex that the story of Lavaṇa seems a mere anecdote by comparison. Yet, when we set the stories side by side, they produce a double image of mutually illuminating similes, each standing for the other.

Comparison of the two stories is justifiable on the grounds that the Hindus themselves would have been likely to compare them. The *Yogavāsiṣṭha* tells over fifty stories, but these two are among the longest and the most important, and both of them are well known in India. Surely the Hindus would have noted, as did von Glasenapp, the striking similarities between the two tales.[18] Lavaṇa is a king who dreams that he is an Untouchable in a cremation ground and then goes back to being a king. Gādhi is a Brahmin who dreams first that he is in a cremation ground (his own death place) and then that he is an Untouchable in an Untouchable village, who pretends to be a king, goes back to being an Untouchable when he is unmasked, and ends up as a Brahmin once more. Lavaṇa's experience of the woman who appears to him in the desert and vanishes when he returns to court is structurally similar to that of King Tāladhvaja, the man to whom the female Nārada appears; Gādhi, on the other hand, is far closer to Nārada himself, undergoing his transformation under water and returning to his ascetic life at the end. When we set the Gādhi pattern against the Lavaṇa pattern, it might appear that Lavaṇa takes up the Gādhi story at midpoint: a king who remembers that he has been an Untouchable (see figure 2).

Certain things happen to both of them in the same way. From the standpoint of the onlookers in the outer scene, both are said to have spent only a few "moments" (*muhūrtas*) in the alternative reality, but, from the standpoint of the participants in the inner scene, they were said to have lived there for many years. Lavaṇa, when he is an Untouchable, forgets that he was a king, and Gādhi, when he is a king, forgets that he was an Untouchable. In addition to the fires in which both commit suicide, each experiences a major conflagration like doomsday: for Lavaṇa it is the forest fire that arises in the drought; for Gādhi it is the great communal immolation fire. And the verses describing the ghastliness of the Untouchables' villages are strikingly similar in the two stories.

Lavaṇa undergoes an initiation that is *like* a death and rebirth, but there is no clear break; he enters the Untouchable village in the persona of a king and only gradually sheds it (just as Gādhi enters the city as an Untouchable and changes into a king). This is the mild form of the transformation, brought about in a natural way by motion through space (by horse or on foot); it is the equivalent of the romantic adventure in which the hero simply rides his horse into the other world. Both Lav-

		Gādhi	Lavaṇa
Is born as a Brahmin		1, 8	
Enters water		2	
Enters cremation ground		3	3
Marries Untouchable woman		4	2
Sees Untouchable family	{ die / almost die	5	4
Becomes king		6	1,6
Enters fire		7	5
Tests dream		9	7
Is enlightened by	{ Viṣṇu / Vasiṣṭha	10	8

Figure 2. Lavaṇa and Gādhi: Mutual Similes

(Numbers indicate the sequence of events within each myth.)

aṇa and Gādhi experience mild transitions of this kind. Lavaṇa is recognized as a king in the Untouchable village; though he gradually forgets this identity, his mother-in-law remembers that a king had married her daughter. He can be recognized because the two adventures happen in a single time-span. Similarly, Gādhi (Gavala) is recognized as an Untouchable in the royal city, for the same reason, and he still remembers that he is an Untouchable; he lies, but he knows the truth.

But the mother-in-law does not recognize Lavaṇa when he returns to the village, nor do the townspeople recognize Gādhi when he returns to ask his questions. This is because each of them has experienced a return journey that is not a simple natural voyage but is, rather, a rude awakening, a violent transition by fire. On the way back, they have become reborn, losing in a single moment the many years they had amassed in the course of their gradual journey into the other world. To this extent, their experiences are roughly the same in their inner structure (a mild transition followed by a violent transition), though they are mirror opposites in the actual content of that structure: where Lavaṇa goes from king to Untouchable, Gādhi goes from Untouchable to king.

But the reversals are even more striking. What is real for Lavaṇa becomes a simile for Gādhi, and what is real for Gādhi is merely a simile for Lavaṇa. The stories are most vividly opposed in their outer structures. Before his mild transition, Gādhi actually dies; he is then reborn and experiences an entirely new life, beginning with his existence as an embryo. This transition (which takes place under water, like Nārada's transformation) never happens to Lavaṇa at all. Lavaṇa learns that his illusion is "like seeing one's own death in a dream,"[19] but Gādhi actually *does* watch his own death and rebirth. On the other hand, the death that Lavaṇa as Katañja really does experience (in the inner story), as a result of the drought and the forest fire, appears as a recurrent simile in the story of Gādhi as an Untouchable: Gādhi sees his corpse "like a leaf that has lost its sap, like a tree that has been brought down by a terrible storm, like a village in a drought, like an old tree covered with eagles"; when he grows old as an Untouchable, he is worn out like the ground in a drought, and his body dries up like a tree in a drought; his family is carried away by death, like forest leaves carried off by a torrent of rain, and he leaves the forest as a bird leaves a lake in a drought; death cuts away his whole family, as a forest fire cuts down a whole forest. The courtiers flee from Gādhi as Gavala, refusing to touch him, as if he were a corpse; yet when Gādhi as Brahmin sees the ruins of his old house, he is like the soul looking at its dried-up corpse.[20] One man's reality is another man's simile.

In this way, the Lavaṇa story, seen as framed by the Gādhi story, may imply another level, retroactively: A Brahmin may have dreamed that he was Lavaṇa, who dreamed that he was an Untouchable. On a simpler plane, the following questions might arise when we compare the two stories: Which is the object and which is the image of it? What is like what? What is a simile for what? The idea, on the philosophical level, that everything is merely a reflected image of something else (*pratibhāsa*) is supported on the rhetorical level by the compelling network of similes: everything is likened to something else.

The metaphysical stances of the two tales also differ greatly. Lavaṇa is *inside* his story and is entirely overwhelmed and mystified by it until the very end; to him, his persona as king certainly *seems* far more real than his persona as Untouchable, yet he forgets that he ever was a king. The creator of the mirage, the demon or god who is laughing at him, the puppeteer working the strings, remains offstage, invisible to Lavaṇa and to us. Gādhi, by contrast, is *outside* his story all the time, watching himself play out his scene like a television actor with one eye on the monitor. Sir Ernst Gombrich has suggested that, for visual phenomena, "Illusion, we will find, is hard to describe or analyze, for though we may be intellectually aware of the fact that any given experience *must* be an illusion, we cannot, strictly speaking, watch ourselves having an illusion."[21] Lavaṇa cannot watch himself having an illusion, though he later realizes that he has had one and comes to understand it and to extricate himself from it. But Gādhi quite literally watches himself watching. To Gādhi, his persona as an Untouchable is far more real than his persona as a king—which is merely a mask within a dream, twice removed from even apparent reality—but both are equally unreal in comparison with his true persona as a Brahmin.

For us, as Westerners, the finality of the Brahmin persona is challenged by the self-perpetuating layers of the story: Why could there not be a woman, say, dreaming that she was a king dreaming . . .? In fact, this cannot happen in our text. For the Hindu, the chain stops with the Brahmin, the linchpin of reality, the witness of the truth. To the extent that the Brahmin represents purity and renunciation, he is real, safely outside the maelstrom of *saṃsāra* and illusion. Our confusion about our own place in the frames of memory, one contained within another like nesting Chinese boxes, is shared by Lavaṇa until the very end of his tale. But to Gādhi, who is, after all, a Brahmin, the god who pulls the strings is directly manifest and takes pains to open up his bag of tricks right from the start; moreover, he returns three times at the end to make sure that Gādhi has understood his lesson properly.

One implication of this structure is that the entire series of frames is a model of society.[22] It is in the nature of social distinctions such as caste to allow each person to frame the whole set of the others. Caste is not a simple stratification but a set of interlocking hierarchies: each person's circle encompasses the circle of all others. If we turn for a moment from the *Yogavāsiṣṭha* stories to Hindu society in general, it is obvious that, from the standpoint of the Brahmin, the Untouchable is impure. It is less obvious, but equally true and equally important, that, from the standpoint of the Untouchable, the Brahmin is impure. Louis Dumont was the first to point out (in *Homo Hierarchicus*) some of the ramifications of this complex system, which is reflected in the metaphysics rather than in the muted social conscience of the *Yogavāsiṣṭha* (to which we will soon return). From the standpoint of caste and the criterion of purity, the Brahmin and the Untouchable live in a kind of symbiosis, a paradox of reciprocity. From the standpoint of power, which is so often the partner of purity in Indian conceptual schemes, the king and the Untouchable form such a reciprocal bond. And from the standpoint of society as a whole, the king and the Brahmin supply the double axis from which all other interrelationships are derived. Yet they alone cannot provide the entire grid on which the social cosmos can be mapped. Though the Brahmin provides the latitude and the king the longitude, the Untouchable provides a pole of pollution by which both of the others orient themselves. The Brahmin, the king, and the Untouchable are the players in the eternal triangle of purity, power, and pollution.

The dream of becoming either a Brahmin or a king is a very ancient theme in India. One of the earliest Upaniṣads, composed before 700 B.C., describes the paradigmatic dream in these terms:

> When he dreams, these worlds are his. Then he seems to become a great king. Then he seems to become a great Brahmin. He seems to enter into the high and low. As a great king takes his people and moves about in his own country just as he wishes, just so this one takes his own senses and moves about in his own body just as he wishes.[23]

Here the metaphor of the king preempts the metaphor of the Brahmin and becomes the basis of an extended somatic simile: the human body is indeed a model of society.

The experience of the king who becomes an Untouchable and the experience of the Brahmin who becomes an Untouchable share certain themes but diverge in several important ways. As we will see, either can be transformed into an Untouchable for any of a number of reasons: as punishment for a sin, or in order to learn something of value, or as part of an initiation. But just as the initiation of a king (royal consecration) is different in both form and purpose from the initiation of a Brahmin (preparation for sacred office), so, too, the kinds of transformations that Lavaṇa and Gādhi undergo are very different. The drama of Lavaṇa's transformation lies in the contrast between the splendor of his life at court and the squalor of his life in the village. The drama of Gādhi's transformation lies in the contrast between his purity as a Brahmin and his impurity as an Untouchable. In both cases, the fall in social status is extreme; but the king loses, in addition, what we might term economic or political status, while the Brahmin loses sacred or religious status. Let us deal separately with the different problems the king and the Brahmin face when each of them becomes an Untouchable.

The Suffering of the Hindu King

The problem encountered by the Untouchable king is reflected in the quandary described in the frame of the Lavaṇa story, the conversation between Rāma and Vasiṣṭha. The occasion for the discussion is this: Rāma has returned from a pilgrimage in a state of depression and madness (or so his father and the courtiers describe it). Rāma regards as a babbling madman anyone who says, "Act like a king," though he himself laughs like a holy man whose mind is possessed. He says that everything is unreal, that it is false to believe in the reality of the world, that everything is but the imagination of the mind. He is physically wasting away. The sage Viśvāmitra, who is called in by Rāma's father, the great emperor Daśaratha, says that Rāma is perfectly right in his understanding of the world, that he has been enlightened. Viśvāmitra then offers to cure him.[24]

We thus encounter, right at the start, several conflicting interpretations of human reality. Is Rāma crazy, or is he right? Is everyone else crazy? Why does Viśvāmitra offer to cure him if he is not mad? The *Yogavāsiṣṭha* suggests that enlightenment by a suitable spiritual authority will remove Rāma's depression while leaving his (correct) metaphysical apprehensions unimpaired. In Western terms, this is a kind of psychoanalysis that allows the fantasy to continue while making the patient socially functional; stated in *Yogavāsiṣṭha* terms, it allows the fantasy to be dispelled while making the patient socially functional. Thus Rāma's father calls in the sage Vasiṣṭha to assist Viśvāmitra, and Vasiṣṭha cures Rāma by assuring him that he is perfectly right. Viśvāmitra says, "What Rāma knows inside him, when he hears that from the mouth of a good man who says, 'That is true reality,' then he will have peace of mind."[25] In the tale of Lavaṇa, as in the framing story of Rāma, this corroborating function is performed by the sage Vasiṣṭha.

But the true nature of Rāma's madness is hinted at when people tell him to act like a king, and this madness can best be understood in the context of Indian mythology. Rāma's pilgrimage has been his first experience of suffering, and in reaction to this he has reevaluated his life as a king and found it to be unreal. The sage who persuades him to go on living his life despite this new insight is performing a role close to that of the incarnate god Kṛṣṇa in the *Mahābhārata*; for there, when Arjuna is depressed by the imminent death of his relatives (the situation that was used to extricate Lavaṇa and Nārada from their dream existences), Kṛṣṇa persuades him to go on anyway, to "act like a warrior." Several verses of this dialogue (the *Bhagavad Gītā*) are closely akin to some in the *Yogavāsiṣṭha* and may have been in the back of its author's mind.[26] To this extent, at least, the *Yogavāsiṣṭha* argues that the most important reality—that is, what is most valued, if not necessarily most solid physically—is social reality. This is, of course, a most orthodox Hindu point of view. In this logic, to know that a course of action is intrinsically unreal is an argument to *do* it, not an argument *not* to do it. When Arjuna realizes that he is not really killing his cousins, he can go on and kill them; when Rāma realizes that he is not really a king, he can go on and rule.

The Indian king found himself by definition in an ambivalent position. His basic *dharma,* or social duty, was to rule, to "act like a king," and this *dharma* is affirmed even in the myths of illusion. When Nārada returns to being Nārada after having been a queen, Viṣṇu advises his erstwhile dream-world husband, King Tāladhvaja, to stop neglecting his royal duties, and the king returns to his responsibilities. According to the Hindu textbooks on *dharma,* the king is not allowed to renounce his kingdom; in the *Mahābhārata,* King Yudhiṣṭhira agonizes over this problem for a long time and finally resigns himself to remaining king. In Buddhism, however, as we will see, kings do renounce their office. The Buddha himself set the example, and it is relevant to note that Yudhiṣṭhira, like the philosopher Śankara, was accused of being a closet Buddhist (*pracchannabauddha*). Moreover, the *Mahābhārata* heroes do spend twelve years in exile, and the Rāma of the Vālmīki *Rāmāyaṇa,* who has certain Buddhist leanings, is forced to renounce his throne for a while; he dwells among animals and demons in the forest and in Lankā (a kind of other world) before he returns to resume his duties as the true king. This theme of royal renunciation appears in the *Yogavāsiṣṭha* when Rāma returns from his pilgrimage and does not wish to be a king. Torn between the Hindu and Buddhist concepts of kingship and renunciation, what better compromise could an Indian king find than to *dream* of renouncing?

This compromise is also reflected in a subepisode of the tale of Lavaṇa in which the king creates a mental sacrifice. When Rāma expresses his puzzlement at the apparent contradictions in the story of Lavaṇa, Vasiṣṭha tells this story:

> Once, in the past, Lavaṇa recalled that his grandfather, Hariścandra, had performed the sacrifice of royal consecration, and he resolved to perform that sacrifice in his mind. He made all the preparations mentally: he summoned the priests and honored the sages, invited the gods and kindled the fires. A whole year passed as he sacrificed to the gods and sages in the forest, but then the king awoke at the end of a single day, right there in the palace grove. Thus by his mind alone King Lavaṇa achieved the fruits of the sacrifice of royal consecration. [See plate 8.] But those who perform the sacrifice experience twelve years of suffering through various tortures and hardships. Therefore Indra sent a messenger of the gods from heaven in order to make Lavaṇa suffer. This messenger was the magician, who created great misfortune for the king who had performed the sacrificial ritual of consecration, and then the messenger returned to heaven.[27]

Out of his compassion for King Lavaṇa, Indra substitutes for the real suffering he would normally have undergone an experience of suffering (a long period of existence as an Untouchable) that occupies just a moment in his life as a king. What is perhaps most striking in terms of the problem set forth by the text—the interaction between mental experience and physical evidence—is the fact that, in order to ground the king's mental experience in physical reality (so that he may have the fruits of the mental sacrifice in his real life), the gods send him *imaginary* sufferings that he may fulfill the (real) requirements of the traditional initiation. For his imaginary sufferings among the Untouchables are less real than an actual consecration, involving hardships, but more real than an imaginary consecration involving no hardships. Unhappiness is more real than happiness.

Lavaṇa's initiation bears a certain resemblance to shamanic initiations.[28] But there is a source for the theme of the imaginary consecration that is more specifically Indian than the Central Asian shamanistic corpus and is also more directly relevant to the tale of Lavaṇa. To this day, many Indian sects hold that anyone who dreams that he is initiated has in fact been initiated. This belief has an ancient precedent. In the Vedic sacrifice (the very one that Lavaṇa managed to perform mentally, though with the assistance of a number of mentally conjured priests, as the text and plate 8 demonstrate), one particular priest was employed as the witness. This priest, the Brāhman, did absolutely nothing; his job was to sit there and to *think* the sacrifice while the others *did* it. He was the silent witness, essential to the sacrifice, in particular because he was responsible for ensuring that no *mistakes* occurred. From this practice (three priests performing the sacrifice, while one—the "transcendent fourth" in Indian culture—performed it mentally) it was not a very large step to take to reach the practice in the Upaniṣads, where meditation on the sacrifice was far more important than its actual performance; and from there it was no great further distance to the purely imaginary sacrifice of the *Yogavāsiṣṭha*.

Hariścandra among the Untouchables

It is particularly ironic that Lavaṇa modeled his imaginary consecration on that of his grandfather, Hariścandra, since Hariścandra himself experienced a dreamlike initiation among Untouchables, like that of Lavaṇa himself, in addition to his conventional initiation. This story, which can be traced back to the eighth century B.C.,[29] is told more elaborately in the Purāṇas:

> One day when King Hariścandra was hunting in the forest, the King of Obstacles, who was jealous of Hariścandra's great achievements, entered him. As a result of this possession, Hariścandra in fury cursed Viśvāmitra to fall into a deep sleep. Viśvāmitra then became furious in turn, and Hariścandra became contrite and begged Viśvāmitra to forgive him. Viśvāmitra made Hariścandra promise to give him everything he had, and, in order to pay Viśvāmitra, Hariścandra sold his wife and son to an old Brahmin. Then Hariścandra said, "I am no human, but an ogre, or even more evil than that." Still Viśvāmitra demanded more payment, and then the god Dharma approached Hariścandra in the form of an Untouchable [a Caṇḍāla], foul-smelling and disfigured, and, in order to pay Viśvāmitra, Hariścandra sold himself in slavery to the Untouchable and went to work in the cremation ground, stripping the corpses of their clothing. With its jackals and vultures, heaps of bones and half-burnt bodies, the burning ground was like the world at doomsday. The singing of the throngs of vampires and ghouls sounded like the screams of doomsday, and the yells and moans of the mourners sounded like the cries of hell. Thus the king, while still alive, entered another birth, and thus he passed a year that seemed like a hundred years.
>
> One day Hariścandra fell into an exhausted sleep, motionlessly dreaming that he paid for his lapse by suffering for twelve years.

He saw a great wonder: He saw himself reborn as a Pulkasa [a different kind of Untouchable], out of the womb of a Pulkasa woman. He grew up, and when he was seven years old he went to work in the cremation ground. One day some Brahmins brought a dead Brahmin there, and when the boy asked them for the payment due him they refused, saying, "Go on and do your evil job. Once upon a time, Viśvāmitra cursed King Hariścandra to be a Pulkasa because he had lost his merit by injuring the Brahmin with sleep." They went on mocking him like this, and, when he could no longer bear it, they cursed him to go to hell. Immediately he was dragged off to hell, where he was horribly tortured, still in the form of a seven-year-old Pulkasa. He stayed there for one day, which was a hundred years, for that is what the denizens of hell call a hundred years.

Then he was reborn on earth as a dog, eating carrion and vomit. And he saw himself reborn as a donkey, an elephant, a monkey, an ox, a goat, a cat, a heron, a bull, a sheep, a bird, a worm, a fish, a tortoise, a wild boar, a porcupine, a cock, a parrot, a crane, a snake, and many other creatures; and a day was like a hundred years. Finally he saw himself reborn again as a king, who lost his kingdom playing dice; his wife and son were taken from him, and he wandered alone into the forest. At last he went up to heaven, but Yama's servants came to drag him away to hell with nooses made of serpents. At that moment, however, Viśvāmitra spoke to Yama about Hariścandra, and Yama told his servants what Viśvāmitra had done. Then the change in him that had come about from a violation of *dharma* ceased to grow. Yama said to him, "Viśvāmitra's anger is terrible; he is even going to kill your son. Go back to the world of men and experience the rest of your suffering, and then you will find happiness." These were all the conditions that Hariścandra saw in his dream and experienced for twelve years. And at the end of this period of twelve years of suffering, the king fell from the sky, hurled out by Yama's messengers.

As he fell, he woke up in confusion [*sambhramāt*], thinking, "In my dream I saw great suffering, with no end. But have twelve years passed, as I saw in my dream?" He asked the Pulkasas who were standing there, and when they said, "No," the miserable king sought refuge with the gods, praying, "Let all be well with me, and with my wife and son." Then he went back to work as a Pulkasa, selling corpses, and seemed to lose his memory; there was no wife or child within the range of his lost memory.

One day his wife came there, bringing the body of their son, who had died of snakebite. As she grieved over the little corpse, Hariścandra saw her and hastened toward her, thinking only to take the clothing from the corpse. She saw him, too, but they had been so changed by their sufferings in their long exile that they did not recognize each other; she was so transformed that she looked like a woman in another birth. But when the king saw the dead child, he remembered his own son, and when he heard the queen lamenting for her husband, Hariścandra, he recognized his wife and son. He spoke, and the queen recognized his voice; she also recognized the shape of his nose and the spacing of his teeth. But when she saw that he was an Untouchable, she clasped him around the neck and said, "O King, is this a dream, or is it real [*tathyam*]? Tell me what you think, for my mind is confused [*mohita*]." The king told her how he had come to be a dog-cooker, and she told him how their son had died. They resolved to immolate themselves together on the pyre of their dead son, but at that moment Indra and Dharma came there with all the gods and told them that they had won the right to eternal worlds, together with their son. Indra revived the boy and brought all three of them to heaven.[30]

In this story, metaphors and transformations replace one another, as do demons and Untouchables. Hariścandra says that he is *like* an ogre long before he becomes an Untouchable, and even that transition takes place not by magic (by a sudden transformation of his skin and body, as in the case of Triśanku) but simply by habit: he acts like an Untouchable, and so he is an Untouchable. Years of behaving like an Untouchable transform him until even his wife cannot recognize him at first. Her recognition involves physical evidence: she recognizes his voice and his physiognomy, hard material signs that shine through despite the dirt and disease and scars and wrinkles. But when she sees that he is an Untouchable, dark-skinned after years of working in the sun, and hideously clad, she rejects the reality of that vision, calling him "King" and hoping to dismiss the whole tragedy by saying, "It is all just a dream."

Many of the motifs in this myth appear in the tales of Lavaṇa and Gādhi. The death of a son and the decision to enter the fire lead to the sudden awakening, and the experience of life as an Untouchable purifies the king and gives him release. But in this text (which is set in the context of *saṃsāric* traditions and devotional values), that release is not *mokṣa* but physical transportation to heaven, and it is a worldly heaven, like Triśanku's, not an abstract merging with Godhead. In the end, Hariścandra and his wife do not go back to their original life, as Lavaṇa and Gādhi do; they leave both the earthly dream and the earthly reality, the royal pleasures and the Untouchable horrors. And Hariścandra's wife from the real world suffers with him inside the other world (though not inside the dream within the dream or even in the same part of the other world, the same Untouchable village). Hariścandra has no Untouchable wife, therefore, and no Untouchable child; his entire family moves into the nightmare with him, and at the end they move out of it with him to heaven. Even the child whose death precipitates the awakening is himself awakened from the dead in time to go to heaven, a *bhakti* twist that wipes out the final traces of any orientation toward *mokṣa*. The heaven to which they are all transported is probably not yet the eternal, infinite heaven of the full-fledged *bhakti* movement but simply the heaven of Indra, a place where earthly pleasures are greatly magnified and from which one must eventually return to earth.

The metaphor of transformation is acted out in several ways. Hariścandra is "like" an Untouchable and then becomes one; he is "as if" reborn and then dreams that he is actually reborn; the cremation ground is "like" hell, and then Hariścandra dreams that he is actually in hell. And the metaphor of the expansion and contraction of time is realized in several ways. Because of the ghastliness of the king's experience among the Untouchables, each year seems like a hundred years (a characteristic of dream adventures in general). But when the king dreams that he is in hell, he discovers that, in that world, there is another system of time reckoning: the people in hell call what we would call a hundred years "a day." And when the king dreams that he must suffer for twelve years to expiate his sin, he believes this; when he wakes up, he is deeply depressed to discover that twelve years have not, in fact, elapsed in the waking world; only one night has passed, the night in which he dreamed. He is convinced of this by some Pulkasas—the same Pulkasas who were there in his dream; now they are outside the dream, and they set the standard of reality. Unlike King Lavaṇa, Hariścandra must suffer in *reality*, in *real* time, the twelve years of suffering that are the traditional initiation of a king; the *dream* of twelve years does not count.

The Suffering of the Buddhist King
Vessantara's Gift

The tale of Hariścandra may well have been influenced by the *Vessantara Jātaka*, the famous Buddhist story of a king who was generous to a fault. As Richard Gombrich remarks, the tale of Vessantara is a thoroughly Buddhist story, but "it is interesting that another story of a man who gave away his family, Hariścandra, is extremely popular in Hindu Bengal. We posit that a story, like any other social phenomenon, is most likely to survive and flourish when it answers the most disparate purposes, in other words when its appeal is overdetermined."[31] In addition to the purposes that it served for the Buddhists, the tale of Vessantara clearly had meanings for the Hindus, meanings that we have encountered in other, related stories, and particularly in the tale of Hariścandra.

> King Vessantara gave away everything; one day he gave away the royal elephant, and for this excess he was banished. While he wandered in the forest with his wife, Maddī, and their two children, a wicked Brahmin named Jūjaka determined to ask Vessantara for

> the children. That night, Maddī dreamed that a black man wearing yellow robes, with red flowers in his ears, dragged her out of the hut by her hair, threw her down on her back, and, ignoring her screams, tore out her two eyes, cut off her two arms, cut open her breast, and tore out her heart and carried it away, dripping with blood. She awoke in terror and went to Vessantara's hut to ask him to interpret her dream. At first he asked her why she had violated her promise not to approach him at night except during her fertile season, but she said, "It is not improper desires which bring me here; I have had a nightmare." Then he asked her to tell him her dream, and when he heard it he realized that it meant that someone would ask him for his children, the final test and perfection of his generosity. But he said to Maddī, to calm her, "Don't worry; because you were lying in an awkward position, or perhaps because you ate something that disagreed with you, your mind was disturbed." She was deceived and consoled by this; she kissed the children and embraced them and left them in Vessantara's care.
>
> Then Jūjaka came and asked for the children, and Vessantara gave them to him. As Maddī returned to the hermitage, she thought about the nightmare she had had, and so she hurried home. Then her right eye began to throb, and trees with fruit seemed bare, and bare trees seemed to have fruit, and she completely lost her bearings. Eventually, Vessantara told her what had happened, and she praised his generosity. Indra then took the form of a Brahmin and asked Vessantara to give Maddī to him; he did so, but then Indra gave her back again. Finally, Vessantara was called back out of exile, and he and Maddī were reunited with their children. And the noble king Vessantara, full of wisdom after so much giving, at the dissolution of his body was reborn in heaven.[32]

Many of the elements in this story seem to be transformations of another famous Buddhist story that we have seen, the dream of Aśoka. Maddī's dream, like Aśoka's, is a textbook nightmare that foretells a tragedy that will befall a child, a nightmare that does come true. Vessantara lies to her about it, as Aśoka's wicked queen lies to him; the interpreter of the dream—Vessantara in the one tale, Aśoka's wife in the other—knows that the dream is truly prophetic but says that it is merely somatic. Maddī (like Aśoka's son, Kunāla) sees and rightly interprets a set of evil omens and the image of a topsy-turvy world. The roles are curiously mixed in their transformations: Maddī is like Aśoka in having the dream, but she is like Aśoka's wife in her sexual threat to the king, and it is Vessantara, not Maddī, who is the primary hero of the tale. In the end, all is restored; after his nightmare existence in the wilderness, Vessantara returns to the royal city. There he sets free all living creatures, even the cats, and gives everything away. This is what a king ideally, but never actually, does. The ambiguity of the king who gives everything away may be traced back to the Brāhmaṇas, where it is said that the ideal sacrificer (of whom the epitome is the king) should give everything away and go to heaven immediately; yet the sacrificer is warned *not* to do this, and he is explicitly told to make certain that he comes back from heaven when he goes there during the sacrifice.[33] The king's tension between renunciation and life in this world is already manifest in these early texts.

Vessantara returns to rule, but to rule as a renouncing king and perhaps not for very long. When he dies, he goes to a heaven like Hariścandra's, not a permanent release but a temporary way station full of superearthly pleasures. The ambiguity of this ending is retained in a Hindu retelling of the tale of Vessantara.[34] There the king is named Tārāvaloka, and he has twin sons named Rāma and Lakṣmaṇa, but he is still married to a woman named Maddī (Madrī, in the Sanskrit). When Tārāvaloka has been reunited with his children, he becomes king not of his own human kingdom but of the realm of the Vidyādharas, or celestial magicians, and he flies through the air to their land and learns all of their secret knowledge by the grace of the goddess Lakṣmī. This ending, with the hero flying away in the arms of a female magician, comes straight from the Hindu tales of dream adventures; it celebrates the worldly, *saṃsāra*-oriented values of that genre. But suddenly, at the end, the story is given a *mokṣa*-based (or Buddhist) twist: Tārāvaloka becomes disgusted with all worldly pleasures and retires to the forest as an ascetic.

Vessantara and Tārāvaloka do not live among Untouchables, as the kings in the Hindu paradigm do, because for the Buddhists, who are outside the caste system, the Untouchables cannot symbolize human reversals or royal sufferings. Yet suffering of one sort or another is still the key to the experience of the Buddhist as well as the Hindu kings. Suffering is what alerts us to the insubstantiality of *saṃsāra*, in part because it makes us want to believe that our pain is unreal, and in part because pain is a useful shock mechanism to awaken someone from a dream. A myth of cosmogony narrated in the *Yogavāsiṣṭha* expresses this power of suffering:

> When Brahmā made the universe, he created, in the land of India, all the people who are plagued by disease and pain. When Brahmā saw their misery [*duḥkha*], he felt pity, as a father feels pity for the unhappiness of his son. Realizing that there was no end to their misery except through *nirvāṇa* and release from rebirth, Brahmā created Vasiṣṭha and said to him, "Come, my son. For just a moment I will cause your mind, fickle as a monkey, to be engulfed in ignorance." As soon as he cursed Vasiṣṭha in this way, Vasiṣṭha forgot everything he knew; he was tortured by misery, sorrow, and confusion. Then he asked Brahmā, "My lord, how did such misery enter into worldly existence [*saṃsāra*], and how can a man get rid of

> it?" And in answer to Vasiṣṭha's question, Brahmā taught him the supreme knowledge. Then he restored Vasiṣṭha to his natural condition and said, "I used a curse to make you ignorant, and as a result of your ignorance you began to ask questions, my son. That was why you wanted to have this essential knowledge in order to help all people."[35]

Until Vasiṣṭha experiences suffering, he lacks the impetus to seek knowledge; the experience of the illusion of ignorance is necessary before one can understand the illusion of reality. The particular emphasis on ignorance (*avidyā*, or Pali *avijjā*) as the root of suffering, together with the exhortation to help all people, are clues to the Buddhist sympathies of this story.

The story of Lavaṇa involves just such an enlightening "curse," one that occurs in a brief moment (*muhūrtam*) but has effects that last for a lifetime. The key to Lavaṇa's enlightenment lies, moreover, not merely in his own suffering but in his exposure to other people who are by definition beyond the pale of comfortable Hindu society. These people are epitomized by the Untouchables, but other sorts of outcastes are assimilated to them, principally demons and women. Thus the king is enlightened in two related ways: by his own suffering and by being exposed to people outside his court; that is, he is forced to learn from people who are entirely different from him.

Ironically, this very theme—of learning from people who are "outside" (*bahiṣkṛta*)—comes to the author of the *Yogavāsiṣṭha* from people who are outside his tradition, the Buddhists. Another unmistakable hint of this heritage may be seen in the use of *nirvāṇa* ("extinction") as the term for release in the myth of Vasiṣṭha's suffering, for this is the Buddhist term for what a Hindu would normally refer to as *mokṣa*. So, too, *duḥkha* (suffering) is the key to Buddhist formulations of the nature and origins of the world. But a far more extensive Buddhist influence in narrative themes (as well as in the philosophical discussion of illusion) pervades the *Yogavāsiṣṭha* as a whole.

Gautama's Visions

For in early Buddhism as well as in Hinduism we find the paradigm of the king who is enlightened by suffering, and in light of the heavy Buddhist influence on the extreme form of the doctrine of illusion (and hence upon the philosophy of the *Yogavāsiṣṭha*), the borrowing of this Buddhist theme should not surprise us. Looming behind Rāma's experience of suffering—as behind that of Lavaṇa, whose debasement among the Untouchables is so graphically described—is the story of the Buddha, Gautama Śākyamuni, a king who never left his palace until he was a grown man and who did so then to discover the existence of suffering as the basis of enlightenment.

This episode is retold in Buddhist texts over many centuries, and the variations tell us much about the shifting spectrum of Buddhist concepts of reality and illusion. In one set of texts, within the Pali canon (and hence probably, but not certainly, the oldest version of the story), the future Buddha or Bodhisattva simply *thinks* about the three forms of suffering: old age, disease, and death. Indeed, he merely thinks about someone else thinking about these things. Gautama tells his own story in the first person:

> Monks, I was delicately nurtured. . . . I had three palaces. . . . In the four months of the rains . . . I came not down from my palace. To me . . . this thought occurred: surely one of the uneducated manyfolk, though himself subject to old age and decay, not having passed beyond old age and decay, when he sees another broken down with age, is troubled, ashamed, disgusted, forgetful that he himself is such a one. . . . When he sees another person diseased . . . [and] when he sees another person subject to death . . . .[36]

In another set of Pali texts, Gautama does not merely think about someone seeing an old man, a sick man, and a dead man; he himself actually sees such men:

> When the Bodhisattva was fourteen years old, he drove out of the eastern gate of the city and happened to see an old man with a white head. He asked his charioteer, "What is that man?" "It is an old man." . . . Some time later, he went out of the southern gate of the city and happened to see a sick man. . . . Some time later, he went out of the western gate of the city and happened to see a dead man. And as he returned home in his chariot, he happened to see a holy man, a renouncer.[37]

This text not only depicts the three men as physically real rather than imagined by Gautama; it also adds a fourth man, also physically real, who represents the answer to the question posed by the first three: the holy man, the transcendent fourth, who counterbalances the worldly triad.

A Tibetan text follows the pattern of this last version, with one significant variation: the Bodhisattva sees a (real) old man, sick man, and dead man, but the fourth is different:

> And yet on another occasion he met a deva [god] of the pure abode who had assumed the appearance of a shaved and shorn mendicant, bearing an alms-bowl and going from door to door. . . .[38]

Why did a god assume the form of a mendicant? One can imagine several good reasons: the transcendent fourth is of a nature different from the preceding three; the real mendicant—the Buddhist monk—does not yet exist, since the Buddha has yet to invent him. Yet our second text was not troubled by the first objection, and none of the other texts that we will encounter is troubled by the second; for if there were as yet no Buddhist monks in India, there were certainly other kinds of renouncers. A better answer to the question is, I think, supplied by the hypothesis that the Tibetan text has conflated the second version (in which Gautama actually sees the men) and the story as it is told in a number of other texts, beginning with the Pali introduction to the *Jātaka*, in which the gods take the form of *all four* of the men. The Bodhisattva goes in his chariot to a park, and at that moment the gods think, "The time for the enlightenment of Prince Siddhattha draws near; we must show him a sign." They change one of their number into a decrepit old man, visible to no one but Siddhattha. Subsequently the Bodhisattva encounters a diseased man whom the gods had fashioned, a dead man whom the gods had fashioned, and a monk whom the gods had fashioned.[39]

A Sanskrit version of this episode continues to regard the four men as products of the gods rather than as natural occurrences or thoughts, but the fourth man continues to be distinguished from the other three:

> When the gods saw the city as joyful as paradise itself, they made a man worn out by old age in order to incite the son of the king to go forth. . . . He asked the charioteer, "Is this some transformation in the man, or his natural state?" Then the gods deluded [*moha*] the charioteer's mind so that he spoke of what he should have kept secret, not seeing the fault [in speaking]. . . . The gods created a man diseased. . . . Then the Bodhisattva began to think about old age, and disease, and death. A man dressed as a monk [*bhikṣu*] came up to him, unseen by other men, and spoke to him. Then, as the king's son was watching, he flew up to the sky. For he was a god who had taken that form; he had seen other Buddhas and had come to him to make him remember.[40]

The charioteer, who answered freely in the first Pali text, now identifies the three men only because the gods have deluded him; yet it is because of this delusion that he speaks the truth instead of lying, as the Bodhisattva's father would have had him do. And where the gods *make* the first three men, one of them actually *becomes* the fourth and speaks to Gautama, which none of the others does. Moreover, though the first three men are visible to the charioteer as well as to the Buddha (and, presumably, to other men as well, as are the "real" men in the other versions), the fourth man is visible only to the future Buddha; he flies up right before the Buddha's eyes, just as Athena does in the *Odyssey* when no one but Odysseus knows that she is a god. Why must the gods make the first three men if they behave just like "natural" men (i.e., they are visible to others besides the Buddha, unlike dream images or thoughts)? Because, according to this text, the king had gone to great pains to remove from his son's path all of the real old, sick, and dead men that he might encounter. Thus the gods have to produce an illusion in order to replace the reality that has been unnaturally distorted, even as they have to delude the charioteer in order to make sure that he will speak the truth.

A final version of this episode further encases the four sights within the framework of other dreams; indeed, the chapter in which the prince encounters the four men is called "Dreams":

> King Śuddhodana, Gautama's father, had a dream in which he saw his son leaving the palace surrounded by gods, and he saw that he became a wandering religious mendicant, wearing an ochre robe. And so he had three palaces built and stationed five hundred men on the stairs so that the prince could not leave without being noticed. When the prince announced his intention to go out to the pleasure garden, the king stationed his men all along the prince's route; but at the very instant when the Bodhisattva [Gautama] came out of the eastern gate of the city, by the mental power of the Bodhisattva himself there appeared an old man. The Bodhisattva asked his charioteer who the man was, and the charioteer told him about old age. Another time, as the Bodhisattva went out of the southern gate, he saw a sick man, and another time, by the western gate, he saw a dead man. Finally, when he went out of the northern gate, the gods used Gautama's own mental powers to fashion on the road the image of a holy man. When the Bodhisattva saw him, he asked his charioteer about him, and the charioteer replied, "That is a man called a monk [*bhikṣu*]."[41]

Gautama's father, the king, has a predictive dream that he rightly interprets and tries to avert. Yet the Bodhisattva manages to escape all the same, and the dream comes true. By his own mental powers (*anubhāva*: authority, belief, intention) he produces the illusion of a man he has never seen and does not understand (for he asks the charioteer about him). Then he "sees" (a verb that can indicate the perception of a dream as well as a waking reality) a sick man and a dead man. The fourth man, the monk, is the ambiguous pivot: his ochre robe, always an evil omen in a Hindu dream, is a symbol of evil for King Śuddhodana; but for the Bodhisattva, and for the Buddhist reader, it takes on a new meaning as the emblem of the future order that Gautama is about to create. This fourth man appears first in the king's dream and then outside; he is visible to the charioteer, just as the other three men were. All four images are thus accessible to public corroboration, whether they are naturally there to be seen or are made by the gods or imagined by the Bodhisattva.

This last text goes on to describe other dreams that occur when the king continues to fight against the omens. This episode is also a part of our very first Pali text (in which the Buddha merely thinks of the three men), which tells it thus:

> When the Tathāgata [Gautama] was not yet wholly awakened but was awakening, he had five great dreams. He dreamt that the world was his bed of state, that the mountain Himālaya was his pillow; this meant that he was becoming fully awakened. Then he dreamt that grass came out of his navel and grew till it reached the clouds; this meant that he would proclaim the noble doctrine of the eightfold path as far as gods and men exist. He dreamt that white worms with black heads crept up over his feet to his knees; this meant that white-robed householders would find life-long refuge in him. He dreamt that four birds of various colors fell at his feet and became pure white; the four classes of society [*varṇas*] would take up renunciation and find release. And, finally, he dreamt that he walked on a great mountain of shit but wasn't dirtied by it; this meant that he would receive robes, alms, lodgings, and medicine but would not be attached to them.[42]

We have encountered several of these dreams in traditional Hindu dream books; indeed, the Buddhist commentator on this passage shows his awareness of this heritage when he rehearses the four causes of dreams: somatic disturbances due to bile, etc., will produce dreams such as falling from a precipice or flying or being chased by a beast or a robber; other dreams are caused by previous events, by possession by the gods (sometimes for one's good, sometimes otherwise), and as premonitions (the Buddha's dreams were of this fourth, premonitory, type). There are also a few personal or universal themes. But all of these motifs, personal or traditional, are given decidedly untraditional (i.e., non-Hindu) Buddhist glosses. The archaic image of the magic plant growing out of the navel (which appears in Hinduism as the lotus growing out of Viṣṇu's navel) becomes the doctrine of the eightfold path; the worms that surge over Gautama's feet are merely householders; the falling birds, so pregnant with meaning for ancient Indians as well as ancient Greeks, now become (by virtue of a pun on the word *varṇa*, "color" or "class") symbols of the classes of society; and the mountain of shit, which looms so ominously in Hindu dreams, is reduced to being a symbol of the material goods that Buddhist monks had perforce to receive from Buddhist lay people—a problem that is indeed highly charged for Buddhists, but culturally rather than personally charged.

In the Sanskrit text that tells of King Śuddhodana's dream, the dream that the Bodhisattva himself dreamed is also related, in terms somewhat different from those of the Pali canon:

> He saw enormous hands and feet waving about in the waters of the four oceans; the whole earth became a magnificent bed, and Mount Meru a crown. He saw the shadows of darkness clearing away, and a great umbrella, which came out of the earth to shed light on the triple world and dispel its suffering. Four black-and-white animals licked their feet; birds of four colors came and became one color. He climbed a great mountain of disgusting shit, but he wasn't soiled by it. He saw a river in spate, carrying along millions of creatures in its current, and he became a boat and carried them to the far bank. He saw many people suffering from diseases, and he became a doctor and gave them medicine and saved them all. Then he sat on Mount Meru, his throne, and he saw his disciples and the gods bowing low before him. He saw victory in battle, and a joyous cry from the gods in the sky.[43]

Some of the more dreamlike images from the Pali-canon version are omitted (the grass from the navel, the worms on the feet). The more conventional, culturally accessible images are retained and expanded. As a result of this editing, and perhaps also as a result of the assumption that the audience would be familiar with the Pali story, the explicit commentary is omitted; the secondary elaboration is subtly integrated into the dream itself.

This Sanskrit text had added, we saw, as a prelude to Gautama's own dream, a description of his father's dream, which consisted of a fairly simple, entirely realistic vision of the Bodhisattva's renunciation. It also added, as a kind of postlude to the half-illusory experience of the four men (and as a prelude to Gautama's own dream, which comes at the very end), the dream that Gautama's wife had on the eve of his awakening. This dream is more elaborate and surreal than Gautama's dream, but it, too, echoes many traditional Indian dream motifs:

> When King Śuddhodana learned that the Bodhisattva had seen these sights, he guarded him all the more carefully and ordered the women of the harim to double their efforts to seduce him. That night, as Gautama slept in the same bed with his wife, Gopā, she saw this dream: The earth shook, trees dried up and fell to earth, the sun and moon fell from the sky. She saw her own hair cut off, and her hands cut off, and her feet, and she was completely naked, stripped of her ornaments. . . . She awakened from this dream and asked Gautama what it meant, for, she said, "My own memory is full of error [*bhrānti*]; I can't see anything any more, and my mind is disturbed by sadness." He told her that the earthquake meant that she would be honored by all the gods, demons, and ghosts; the uprooted trees and torn-out hair meant that she would soon uproot from her mind the trap set by impure emotions. The fallen moon and sun meant that the enemies born of the emotions would

> soon be cast down. That she had seen her body naked meant that she would soon cease to be a woman and would become a man. . . . "Go to sleep, Gopā," he said; "these are good omens for you."[44]

Gopā's nightmare predicts her loss of her husband and hence her loss of status as a woman; the dream contains a number of images that traditional Indian dream books identify as bad omens—bad, that is, from the point of view of *saṃsāra*, which is the point of view of the dream books: loss of power, loss of beauty, loss of children, and so forth. Yet, from the Bodhisattva's point of view—the *mokṣa* standpoint—they are good omens. Once again we see that there is no such thing as a good dream from an absolute point of view; dreams, like everything else, are relative to the observer and to the interpreter. Gautama's interpretation of Gopā's dream is thus slanted (like Vessantara's interpretation of Maddī's dream), but the text accepts his view as the true one.

For our purposes, however, the importance of the dreams that Śuddhodana and Gopā and the Bodhisattva himself have is not so much their content as the implications of the context that they supply for the story. The fact that all three dream similar dreams (that is, dreams having the same latent content though somewhat different manifest content) establishes Gautama's experience as a kind of shared dream, shared by the two people closest to him, his father and his wife. That the dream is for them a nightmare and for him a happy dream demonstrates the way in which a single reality—the fact that Gautama is about to leave the palace—is differently reflected in different minds. But the fact that these three dreams appear in the chapter in which Gautama sees the four men has other implications as well. Does this mean that the four men, too, are his dreams? If so, these Sanskrit texts are direct expansions of those Pali versions in which the Buddha merely thinks about the four men (or three men). In any case, the Buddhist texts—of which the examples I have cited are just a few of many, though they cover the major patterns—do not seem to care whether the sights appear naturally or mentally or supernaturally. The Buddha's vision of reality is a vision of the suffering that the king has taken such great pains to conceal from his son, building ever higher dams to hold back the floods of human experience. The irony lies in the fact that this vision is sometimes real but sometimes just an illusion, created by the gods or by the Bodhisattva's own unconscious (the part of his mind that knows what he does not know that he knows) to replace the reality that he is unable to see. He sees only a shadow of the world in which men grow old and sick and then die, even though that world really does exist and is the world in which he is going to spend the rest of his life. It is illusion that shows him what is real.

Gautama rode out of his palace on his horse, Kaṇṭhaka, just as Lavaṇa rode out of his palace on the magic horse from Sindh, and the two figures have many other things in common as well. But there are great differences: the Buddha sought his enlightenment after the birth, not after the death, of his son; unlike Rāma and Arjuna, the Buddha did not go back to being a royal emperor but became instead a spiritual emperor; and the Buddha witnessed the sufferings of others, and pitied them, whereas Lavaṇa suffered primarily for his own sake, though he did witness the sufferings of the Untouchables. More important, where the Buddhist king may awaken *from* kingship, the Hindu king must, finally, awaken *to* kingship. David Shulman has shown why this is so:

> The king is linked with transcendence in more than one way. His "exile" opens up his world to the outside, i.e., to a deeper reality—one in which evil is tangibly revealed; in which truth is expressed bluntly; in which his normal social self is held up for scrutiny, and found wanting. This contact with a darker face of reality ultimately nourishes the king; his "descent" is painful, dangerous, unhappy, but clearly necessary. It leads directly to his rebirth: we have seen that there is a correspondence between the king's exile and his *dīkṣā* [initiation]. The ritual of kingship must include this stage; it is no less constituent of the king's role than his "white" periods.[45]

Once more we see the myths acting out a metaphor. Where the usual initiation is "like" a rebirth, the initiation of the king in the myth may involve actually becoming an embryo in a new womb. Midway between the two, between the *saṃsāra*-oriented consecration ritual and the *mokṣa*-oriented myths of complete rebirth, fall many of the stories in this corpus, in which the king keeps one foot in each world by dreaming of his rebirth.

Hariścandra and Tārāvaloka, like the Buddha, do not return to their kingdoms; Lavaṇa, Arjuna, and Rāma do. Triśanku and Vessantara are ambiguous cases. The myth of the king among the Untouchables thus remains open-ended, and this allows it to express both *saṃsāra*-oriented and *mokṣa*-oriented value systems. This same open-endedness is what enables the pattern to be applied not only to the king but also to the Brahmin who is transformed into an Untouchable—to Gādhi as well as to Lavaṇa. The Hindu king (like Lavaṇa) begins within *saṃsāra* and goes out of that world into Untouchability, which he experiences as a kind of renunciation; but he usually ends up back inside the material world. The Buddhist king—in the paradigm set by Gautama—begins inside the material world, too, but he ends up outside it, "released" either into renunciation on earth or into eternal bliss in heaven (or in *nirvāṇa*). Hariścandra, though a Hindu king, follows the Buddhist pattern or, rather, the early *bhakti* pattern, which owes much to Buddhism: though he ends up in a limited heaven, there is the possibility of a final release into a heaven that is infinite in time and space, a combination of *mokṣa* and the pleasures of *saṃsāra*.

A similar set of options is available to the Brahmin/Untouchable in these tales. The Brahmin householder (whom we will soon encounter in a folk variant of the tale of Gādhi) is like the Hindu king: he begins in the material world and then experiences Untouchability, but he returns to the world of the Brahmin householder. The Brahmin ascetic (like Nārada or Gādhi in the Sanskrit text) by contrast begins as a renouncer, outside the material and marital world, and experiences Untouchability as a kind of involvement in the world, complete with a wife and family that he does not have in his original life. In the end, he ends up outside the world again. Thus, of all four of the main protagonists—Hindu king, Buddhist king, Brahmin ascetic, and Brahmin householder—only one, the Buddhist king, undergoes, at the end of the myth, a final transformation, a complete change in his world. The other three undergo an experience that transforms their understanding of their lives, worldly or nonworldly, but does not lead them to abandon those lives. For them, the other world is a nice place to visit but not a place where they want to live forever. It is a place where they learn and from which they return.

But the world to which they return is not exactly the same as the world from which they began their journey; they have changed, and it has changed. We have seen that the child who believes that his dreams are real and the adult who believes that his dreams are real are only superficially alike; for the adult who returns to his belief does so only after he has passed through the stage of the grownup child who believes that his dreams are not real. So, too, the involvement in worldly life of the king who has passed through his stage of renunciation is quite different from the involvement of the king who has never known any other kind of life. After the journey, the king is in a sense released from involvement even while he is engaged in it. Kṛṣṇa in the *Gītā* taught Arjuna that, once he understood the truth, he would be free from the danger of amassing karma while performing his actions. He could, as it were, import a kind of *mokṣa* back into his life of apparent *saṃsāra*; he could have both at once. Similarly, Nāgārjuna taught that the truly realized person knows that *saṃsāra* and *nirvāṇa* are the same; he lives in *saṃsāra* but experiences *nirvāṇa*. And the Brahmin renouncer, Gādhi or Nārada, undergoes a similar transformation. His renunciation is flawed, at first, because he does not understand the nature of involvement; once he has experienced it and rejected it, he becomes truly free for the first time. The paradigm of Gautama, too, is more complex than it appears at first. Though Gautama goes from the world of involvement (as a king) into the world of renunciation (as a monk), he also can be said to go from an unreal world (the artificial ivory tower that his father constructs for him, the illusory palace in the sky) to a real world (the world of suffering). He goes *from* the other world into this world. We might chart these various paradigms as they appear in figure 3, where "O" stands for the other world, "S" for *saṃsāra*, and "M" for *mokṣa* (in the broad sense of freedom from the fruits of involvement rather than in the sense of final release and absorption into Godhead or *nirvāṇa*).[46]

Suffering among the Others

It is tempting for a Western reader to believe that the Hindu king's experience among the Untouchables was enlightening in a social sense—that he realized how the Untouchables suffered and resolved to use his kingship somehow to mitigate their sufferings. Such a resolution might well be supported, if not inspired, by the philosophical point of the story, that the caste distinctions between king and Untouchable are just as illusory as all the other mental structures that man imposes arbitrarily upon the universe. It must be stated, however, that this is *not* the point that the story is designed to convey; quite the contrary. Although caste has no ultimate reality, the text tells us, there are only two possible lines of action that one can take when one has come to this realization: either one withdraws from the social system entirely (this is the ascetic or *mokṣa* or Buddhist solution,[47] which Rāma is at first tempted to embrace) or one accepts it for what it is and does not worry about the enormous disparity between the king's riches and the Untouchable's poverty, since neither one is ultimately real (this is the *saṃsāra* solution). The doctrine of illusion could have been used to challenge the baseless strictures of the social system, but it was not; it was used, instead, to preserve the stability of the socioeconomic and political status quo, rechanneling whatever discontent there might be into abstract formulations.[48] Lavaṇa is said to experience pity when he returns to the Untouchable village, but he does not *do* anything about it (as a compassionate Buddhist king would do). Unlike King Lear, who experiences a less violent physical transformation but a more violent psychological transformation, Lavaṇa does not change his character or even his life. He does, however, become much more of what he was before—a wiser and more powerful king.

Mary Douglas has suggested that the Indian kings are an example of that group of people who want to grab and hold power, while the Brahmins represent that group who (like Isaiah Berlin's "intelligentsia") don't want power and try to keep their hands clean of it (also allowing themselves full license to criticize those who have it). Only the Brahmins could make the doctrine of illusion fundamental to their whole epis-

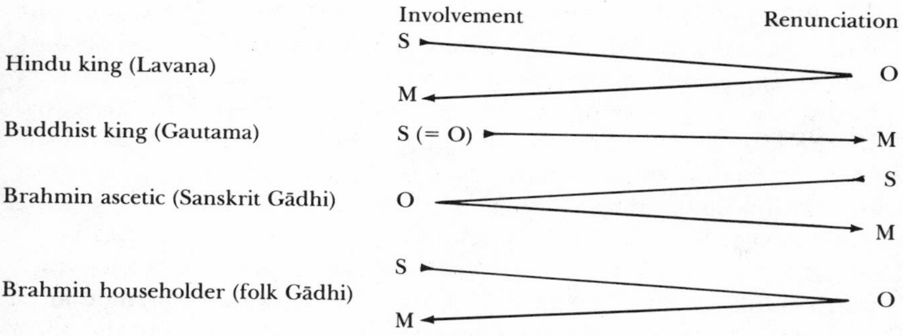

Figure 3. Hindu and Buddhist Kings and Ascetics

temology. Even so, the doctrine of illusion could provide a basis either for a hopeless revolt against tyranny or for an acquiescence in its inevitability.[49] India went the way of acquiescence, but not before managing to formulate a theory of ideal kingship in which kings were persuaded to take upon themselves the attitude more characteristic of Brahmins. Thus the kings were placed in a position where they had both to exercise power and to shun it.

For a Hindu who reads the *Yogavāsiṣṭha*, the gruesome description of the life lived by the Untouchables shows not how unhappy they are but how horrid they are. The *king* is the one whose sufferings, caused by the Untouchables, matter. He is the one whose suffering is therefore real; theirs may be, or may not be. The myths of illusion reveal the vanity of society and the hollowness of proof by consensus, but they do not challenge the cruelties brought about by society.

The bias of the myths of the Untouchable kings is also demonstrated by the fact that the transformation works in only one direction: the hero, whether king or Brahmin, can fall into Untouchability, but we have no tales of Untouchables who succeed in "dreaming" themselves into being kings or Brahmins (though in some South Indian village myths Untouchables masquerade as Brahmins). In the inner frame of the Gādhi story, where an apparent Untouchable rises to kingship (not by dreaming or dying but simply by masquerading), he is unmasked and destroyed, like Triśanku in the *Rāmāyaṇa*. That the *Yogavāsiṣṭha* is not primarily concerned with the problem of caste as a social problem is, I think, indicated by the casualness with which the question of pollution is treated. Why do the courtiers not reject King Lavaṇa when they learn that he has lived so many years as an Untouchable? This could be because they do not treat his miraculous experiences as *really* real; for, in contrast, when it was revealed that King Gavala had been *born* as an Untouchable and had merely walked from his Untouchable village to the royal city, without crossing any ontological barrier, he was indeed treated as a polluted man. Similarly, in the *Devībhāgavata Purāṇa* version of the tale of Triśanku, the Goddess purifies Satyavrata (after he has become a flesh-eating ghoul) so that he may ascend the throne. These instances demonstrate that the Hindus were aware of the pollution that resulted from the king's sojourn among the Untouchables or nonvegetarian demons. Yet, against these examples, we have, in addition to the story of King Lavaṇa, many tales of kings who became kings again after being Untouchables and even—like Hariścandra—went to heaven after being Untouchables. Either the dream experience is treated as unreal—which is not, I think, the case in the *Yogavāsiṣṭha*—or the king is purified after his sojourn (by asceticism, or by devotion, or by coming to understand the basic unreality of *all* experience, not the dream experience in particular). In any case, it is the mental, not the social, transformation of the king that is stressed in all of the myths of illusion.

A key to this distinction lies in the fact that, though the king may be an Untouchable, his wife may not. Hariścandra and his wife do not return to the palace after their sojourn among the Untouchables, nor can Lavaṇa bring his Untouchable wife back to court. Conveniently, as well as traditionally (in dream tales the world over), the polluting wife dies in her own world. For the hard, social reality that would be implied if the king were to bring the wife back into the waking world goes against the grain of everything the text is trying to demonstrate. Only the far softer, more elusive reality of enlightenment clings to the king as he crosses the barrier back into his court. The context of the myth is philosophy, not sociology.

The people with whom the king undergoes his sufferings represent the experience of the extremity of misery; they also represent the reversal of normal social values, reversals that take place in time of crisis and may provide the stimulus for religious conversion. But these people are also a source of unorthodox knowledge. The Untouchables are closely associated with women and demons, both of whom are purveyors of valuable, if dangerous, antinomian doctrines. In the *Yogavāsiṣṭha*, Queen Cūḍālā is the heroine of a long story in which she manipulates a series of complex illusions in order to enlighten her husband (see plate 9).[50] Several other women also appear as interlocutors: besides Līlā, whom we have already encountered, there are Surucī, Viśucī, and Sarasvatī, to name a few. The translator, Mitra, regards this as "curious" in view of the fact that, after the time of the Upaniṣads, "female education was subsequently abrogated by law."[51] Women do, indeed, appear as teachers in the Upaniṣads, the fountainhead of Hindu misogyny, so the paradox is an ancient one.

Moreover, in the *Yogavāsiṣṭha*, two of the key figures in the tales of Lavaṇa and Gādhi are simultaneously women and Untouchables (the women whom Lavaṇa and Gādhi marry). Another character is at once a woman and a demon: the ogress Karkaṭī, who narrates many of the tales in the *Yogavāsiṣṭha*. Many texts, Buddhist as well as Hindu, describe female spirits (Yakṣinīs) who come to men in the night and give them magic powers in return for the sexual gratification that these succubi so ravenously crave.[52] In one text it is said: "He who desires to have intercourse with supernatural women can evoke with his mantras all kinds of female demons and live with them in the nether world [*pātāla*] for a complete world period [*kalpa*]."[53] Teun Goudriaan comments on the composite image of demon and damsel:

> It is perhaps striking that experiences similar to those just described, viz. the appearance at first of demons evoking fear and afterwards of beautiful damsels offering their love, were part of the Buddha's "temptation by Mara"; and siddhis like these also occur to the yogins or Buddhist monks who strive after release by way of a course of introspective psychical exertion. A yogin might be able to make use of these siddhis if he chooses to do so; but he should abstain from them if he really clings to liberation from existence as his direct goal.[54]

There are two ways of viewing this ambiguity. The phrase "offering their love" may be regarded as a threat (to Hindu or Buddhist yogins headed for *mokṣa*) or as a reward (to folk heroes committed to *saṃsāra*). The dream may therefore represent an initiatory test, conveying (to the ascetic) powers that should be rejected or (to the prince) magic powers that are highly prized. Conventional, *saṃsāra*-oriented Hinduism viewed women in general (and demons in general) as bad, while antinomian, *mokṣa*-oriented Hinduism generally viewed both women and demons as good (or at least as potentially good).

Yet *mokṣa*-oriented Hinduism also regarded women, particularly demonic women, as the root of all evil. Women were considered illusion incarnate, the sexual power that deludes and maddens otherwise sane and rational men. The saint and poet Kabīr called Māyā a demonic woman, an ogress (*ḍākiṇī* or "hell-cat, hungry for flesh"): "Māyā is an Ogress, / she eats up everything: / You whore, I'll knock out all your teeth, / if you dare come near the Saints!"[55] Thus, depending on one's point of view, women are the perpetrators of illusion or the people who teach one to become free from illusion. Apparently it takes one to know one.

Demonic women are of course particularly ambiguous in this regard. The ogress Karkaṭī met a king in the Himālayas and was about to devour him when she discovered that he had supernatural knowledge; the king invited her to his palace and provided her with the bodies of murderers and other criminals so that she could continue to indulge her carnivorous tastes while devoting herself constantly to her meditations (see plate 10).[56] In this tale there is a direct correspondence between the antisocial sin of eating human flesh and the (also antisocial) seeking of superhuman knowledge. Uneasy about this connection, the text attempts to rationalize it by providing Karkaṭī with the bodies only of evildoers, a familiar maneuver in Indian theodicies.[57] Another attempt to deal with the combination of cannibalism and special demonic knowledge appears elsewhere in the *Yogavāsiṣṭha*: a male vampire addicted to human flesh but nevertheless deeply ethical would not eat anyone who could answer certain questions (of which one is, "Countless lives are generated like dreams within dreams; whose dreams are they?"). He met a king who answered his questions brilliantly, and so the vampire did not eat him (see plate 11).[58] (The story of the king and the vampire is a well-known Indian tale; in one famous variant, the king is Vikramāditya.)[59]

A special kind of magic power is somehow held by these creatures who live beyond the human pale and beyond human laws. As the traditional masters of *māyā*, demons know better than anyone else how treacherous and how convincing it can be. Since they use it themselves, they are less likely than anyone else to be taken in by it; they alone can see through it (though they are sometimes outillusioned by the gods, hoist by their own petard).[60] Moreover, as outsiders, as antinomian figures, challengers of the householder establishment, demons are in many ways analogues of the ascetic sages—people like Nārada and the Buddha—who wandered about ancient India, teaching doctrines of *mokṣa* that challenged the values of the world of *saṃsāra*.[61] And the experience of life among the demons, or of life as a woman or as an Untouchable, is the experience of the shadow side of humanity and of happiness, an experience that breaks through the deluding surface of seductive pleasures to expose an underworld that expresses the treacherous flimsiness of life.

Finally, there is a power that inheres in the demons' addiction to human flesh and in their position outside the Hindu pale, and that is a power they share with Untouchables. Throughout the *Yogavāsiṣṭha*, the equation between Untouchables and demons is explicit. Lavaṇa's Untouchable wife tells him, "I am like a female ghoul, an eater of men, horses, and elephants; . . . my father is like a vampire."[62] Lavaṇa says, "I acted like a vampire, prowling about for fish on the banks of the river, . . . and I was so horrible that even the vampires ran from me in terror."[63] So, too, in the tale of Gādhi, the Untouchable who becomes a king is said to be like a flesh-eating ogre from whom all the people flee, and the people among whom the Untouchable lives are called Bhūtas ("ghosts" or "has-beens").[64] The demonic illusory power is deeply ingrained in the world: the universe is said to be like a ghoul made to frighten children.[65]

As the Untouchables are demons, so their village is the home of demons: it is hell. The king says: "The girl brought me to her father, as if the Fury of Torture (Yatanā) were leading me to hell. I was like a man who had fallen into hell, and after escaping from those foul hell-grounds, I lay exhausted, as if I had escaped from hell."[66] The descent into hell appears throughout Indian mythology (and beyond) as a metaphor for the spiritual journey of initiation; elements of that pattern are clearly relevant here. In the tale of Gādhi, when the Brahmin returns to the village where he lived as an Untouchable, he regards it as hell.[67]

The experience of suffering takes place among liminal people in a liminal time and place. Geographically, the king crosses the threshold into his other life in the Vindhyas, the mountain range that forms the southernmost border of the "Aryan land" of the north and hence the boundary of classical Hindu civilization. Temporally, the time is doomsday, the moment of the death and rebirth of the universe or, more precisely, the moment when all the things that seemed to be real are reduced to the nothingness that was always their true nature, the moment when the magic picture-show machine is turned off at last. The recurrent image of doomsday in these myths serves to emphasize the insubstantiality of the world; the things we think of as hard and permanent are constantly destroyed and recreated.

Doomsday images bombard us: the magician's wand whirls like a cloud of fire at doomsday; the king rides the horse like a doomsday cloud on a mountain shaken by earthquakes; the king is carried along as swiftly as the floods of doomsday; the desert is burnt out like the universe at doomsday; the king wanders in the jungle as Doom wanders over the empty universe at doomsday; the huts of the Untouchables are like the clusters of ghosts at doomsday; famine comes to the village as doomsday comes to the material world; an untimely doomsday leaves the place a burnt-out shell, like the universe burnt by the fire of the twelve doomsday suns.[68] And in the tale of Gādhi, the cremation fire burns Gādhi's corpse as the submarine doomsday fire burns the ocean waters; when his city is filled with fires in which people commit suicide, it is like the doomsday blaze; when he returns to the Untouchable village, it is broken down and ruined like the universe at doomsday.[69]

One particular doomsday image recurs throughout the story of Lavaṇa: the image of Mārkaṇḍeya slipping out of the mouth of the sleeping Viṣṇu. King Lavaṇa's attendants and ministers question him as he awakens from his trance, just as the gods questioned Mārkaṇḍeya when he was terrified by the doomsday flood; Lavaṇa reaches the tree from which he is about to be suspended, just as Mārkaṇḍeya reached the great banyan tree after wandering about in the universal ocean, and Lavaṇa spends the night—which seems an eternity—by that tree; he is also plunged into delusion, just as Mārkaṇḍeya plunged into the universal ocean.[70] Like Mārkaṇḍeya, too, he loses touch with what he initially thinks of as reality; he experiences a new vision of reality but loses it again when he returns to his first world. For both of them, the transition represents not merely the death of the individual, the dreamer, but the death of the entire world of the dreamer: doomsday.

The world of the Untouchables is, therefore, not merely the place where people at the bottom of the Indian social scale dwell; it is symbolic of the shadow side of the entire universe. The symbolism of the king's adventure among the Untouchables is all the more compelling because the story is an ancient one in India, so widespread as to be almost a set-piece. We have already encountered important variants of it in the tales of Triśanku and Hariścandra, but there are other texts that link the theme even more closely to the *Yogavāsiṣṭha*, both through the names of the protagonists and through the motifs that recur throughout the corpus. The *Rāmāyaṇa*, in particular, narrates several cycles of stories of this type, all of which revolve around the two sages, Viśvāmitra and Vasiṣṭha, who are the doctrinal anchor pins of the *Yogavāsiṣṭha*.

Vasiṣṭha is a Brahmin, like Gādhi. Viśvāmitra is a king, like Lavaṇa, but he is a king who becomes a priest and who competes with Vasiṣṭha as royal sage versus Brahmin sage. In the Epics, Viśvāmitra is connected by birth with a king named Gādhi ("Singer") and another named Gālava.[71] Viśvāmitra thus provides in his person a link between the split personalities of Gādhi and Gavala, the Brahmin and the king. Viśvāmitra and Vasiṣṭha are also closely involved in the saga of Lavaṇa's grandfather, Hariścandra, and Viśvāmitra himself is implicated in several myths in which he moves among Untouchables who eat not only dogs and cows but people.[72] In all of these tales, Viśvāmitra and Vasiṣṭha interact with kings who are cursed to sojourn among Untouchables in another world that is an inversion of our waking world.

This other world is an upside-down world in which people eat people. This practice is, more than anything else, the mark of the world of the Untouchables, but it is also the mark of *all* human society under extraordinary circumstances. For many Indian texts relate that in time of drought—and particularly during droughts that last for twelve years, the period of the king's sufferings or initiation—people eat one another; parents even eat their children, and children their parents.[73] For children to eat their parents is the milder form of the violation of normal codes of behavior, because Indians believe that the child in the womb eats the body of the mother and, of course, once born drinks her milk (which is made of her blood).[74] But for parents to eat their children is a particularly extreme reversal of normal behavior; this is the sin that plagued the ancient Greeks (as in the theme of Thyestes' feast in the *Oresteia*). It appears in India as a metaphor for the upside-down world of the saints: "the cow is sucking at the calf's teat."[75]

The other world is equated with the part of this world that is beyond the pale, the village of the Untouchables; it is also equated with the part of all of us that is normally held in bounds by society but that bursts out in times of emergency. The other world is a place where those whom we eat in this world eat *us*.[76] The nightmares that haunt the unconscious mind—the mind that dreams—appear in the writings of Plato and Freud as their version of the other world, the shadow of rational human experience. In the poetry of the Indian saints, the normal, illusory universe is itself characterized by such inversions of normal action, in verses designed to shock us out of our faith in the world that has such social forms; thus Kabīr speaks of a "jolly woman eating her neighbors for breakfast" along with a buffalo smoking a pipe and leeches who cough.[77]

Folk Variants on the Tales of Lavaṇa and Gādhi

The relationship between this world and the other world and the relationship between the world of social reality and the world of dreams are differently conceived in some of the folk variants of the stories of Gādhi and Lavaṇa. Gādhi appears as a Brahmin householder rather than a Brahmin ascetic in a story recorded by John Hinton Knowles in Srinagar, Kashmir, in 1893. Knowles calls this tale "Metempsychosis," and he reports that he heard it from Narayan Kol of Fateh Kadel (who did not associate it with the *Yogavāsiṣṭha*):

> A young man who had fasted for twelve years and thought that he had "perfected himself in religious matters" rested under a tree. A crow perched above him and shat on his head. He was very much annoyed at this and turned toward the bird; and the bird died. The young man continued his journey and reached a house, where he begged for food. The woman of the house asked him to wait until her husband arrived; the holy man was angry at this reply and was about to curse her when she interrupted him by saying, "I am not a crow, that you can burn me with your angry looks." The young man fell silent, wondering how she had come to know of the incident of the crow. Her husband returned, they all had dinner, and afterwards the man of the house told this tale:
>
> "A Brahmin prayed for years to know something of the state of the departed. At last the gods complied with his request. Early one morning, while he was bathing according to custom, his spirit left

> him and went into the body of an infant, the child of a cobbler. He grew up, married, and had many children. One day, he was made aware of his [former] high caste; he went away and became king when he was chosen by the royal elephant and hawk.
>
> "But the wife he had had as a cobbler got to know of his whereabouts and went to join him. When it became known that he and his wife were cobblers, people fled or burnt themselves to death, and the king immolated himself, too. His spirit went and reoccupied the corpse of the Brahmin, which remained by the riverside, and the Brahmin went home. 'How quickly you have performed your ablutions this morning!' said his wife. The Brahmin wondered if he had seen the future state or merely experienced a dream. A few days later, a beggar came with the tale of the king who was a cobbler. The Brahmin mused, 'How can these things be? I have been a cobbler for several years. I have reigned as a king for several years—and this man confirms the truth of my thoughts. Yet my wife declares that I have not been absent from this house more than the usual time; and I believe her, for she does not look any older, nor is the place changed in any way.'
>
> "Thus ends my story, whereof the explanation is this: The soul passes through various stages of existence according to a man's thoughts, words, and acts, and in the great Hereafter a day is equal to a *yug* [Sanskrit *yuga*, aeon], and a *yug* is equal to a day."
>
> At the end of the story, the woman asked the stranger if he wanted anything more. He replied, "Only happiness." She advised him to go home to his parents, "who," she said, "have wept themselves blind because of you."[78]

This folk variant transforms several elements of the Sanskrit text. The frame story acts out a simile that plays an important part in the explanatory portion of the Gādhi story, the maxim of the crow and the fruit in the tree, a symbol of inexplicable coincidence that we will meet in chapter six. Women are more important in this text than in the Sanskrit version. The frame story contains a good wife, the purveyor of special wisdom, like the female interlocutors in the *Yogavāsiṣṭha*, but also of worldly wisdom: it is this woman who points the final moral and sends the boy back to his worldly life with his parents, even as Vasiṣṭha sends Rāma back to his duties as a young king. In doing so she invokes yet another frame for the story: from the standpoint of the parents, who are "weeping themselves blind," the young man is the lost son in yet another story, one that we are never told. In the innermost story, a woman is also important. The cobbler—Untouchable because he handles leather, the skin of the cow—has a wife who does not die, as Gādhi's dream wife does; she is the instrument of his unmasking as a king. But the most striking departure from the Sanskrit text lies in the fact that the Brahmin in the intermediate layer—the Brahmin who is imagined by the householder and who imagines the cobbler—has a wife. Gādhi does not; indeed, it is this fact that Gādhi uses as the basis of his argument when he first dismisses his dream life: it does not correspond with the chaste circumstances of his waking life. Nārada, too, has no wife in his waking life, but in his dream life as a woman he has a husband who, like the cobbler's wife, survives. Finally, Hanuman vehemently denies that he can be the same as the "shadow" Hanuman who has a wife. The wife of the Brahmin in the Kashmiri text is, moreover, the pivot of his argument. It is because of her that he does *not* trust or attempt to prove (as Gādhi eventually does) his vision as a cobbler/king, for she has persuaded him to reject and therefore not to attempt to validate this vision. The Brahmin here dismisses the report of the man who "confirms his vision," a man who is, significantly, merely "a beggar" in this text and not, as in the Sanskrit, "a Brahmin guest"—the ultimate authority for verification. Instead, he is completely won over by the common-sense, banal details of his wife's arguments and by the unchanging quality of his bourgeois life, even though the storyteller does offer a perfectly good explanation for the validity of the cobbler/king episode: the soul moves very fast, and therefore many things can actually happen to the soul when it is out of the Brahmin's body, while just a moment passes for the body in its slower time frame. The qualities of the transmigrating soul are more explicitly relevant here than in the Sanskrit tale of Gādhi; here the cobbler goes to the city as a result of his recollecting his previous high caste (the high caste of the Brahmin who is dreaming that he is a cobbler) and not as the result of the death of his family (one of whom, the wife, remains alive to expose him). The text does not tell us how it is that the cobbler realized he was part of a Brahmin's dream or why he tried to regain his waking status inside his dream life instead of waking up. Nor are the text's explanations ever actually narrated to the Brahmin, the way Gādhi's experiences are explained by Viṣṇu. The worldly values of the Kashmiri folk tradition have twisted the point of the story and given the Brahmin both a wife and the down-to-earth skepticism appropriate to a married man.

In this Kashmiri folk version, the validity of the dream episode is never tested and, therefore, never proven. It is most likely that the folk variant represents the original version, on which the *Yogavāsiṣṭha* has rung an important change, for the tale lacking the test at the end is found elsewhere in India as well. R. K. Narayan tells the story of Lavaṇa, "From the Yogavasistha," but it ends at the moment when the king, waking up and crying, "Where is that magician?", finds that the magician has vanished.[79] The point of the story in these simpler variants is that the whole thing *was* just an illusion, and so it never occurs to anyone to test it.

A similar transformation takes place in the tales of Nārada; the earlier ones merely describe the illusion, while only one later version begins to investigate the reality status of the people in the illusion. So, too, in a late Sanskrit retelling of the tale of Lavaṇa, the point is simply that some people can enter into other peoples' bodies.[80] Appropriately, the king is here called not Lavaṇa ("Salt") but Sravaṇa (a "renouncer," particularly a Buddhist monk):

> There was a king named Sravaṇa, who sat in his assembly hall surrounded by his ministers and attendants. He was deluded by a magician: he mounted a splendid horse and wandered over the whole earth until the horse threw him in a deserted place. Overcome by hunger and thirst, he met an Untouchable [a Cāṇḍāla] girl and promised to marry her if she would give him food and water, which she did then and there. He had many children with her, but after some time they all began to starve. Thinking, "Let them eat my cooked body," he entered the blazing fire. Then in a moment, as he opened his eyes, he was filled with amazement, and to the assembled ministers and servants and kings he narrated that whole adventure in a single moment. This is the story in the *Vāsiṣṭharāmāyaṇa*, and there are many other stories of this type, which tell about people who enter another body.[81]

This text is doubly attributed, rightly to the *Yogavāsiṣṭha* and wrongly (I think) to the *Varāha Purāṇa*. This vague pedigree is encouraged by the text's assurance that "there are many other stories of this type." The Hindi commentary makes explicit the point about the finality of the illusion: "It was *māyā* after all. The moment he opened his eyes, the king became what he was: the same gathering, the same ministers. The king narrated the happenings to the courtiers from the beginning to the end. Everyone was astonished at the magician's feat and made lavish promises to him."

These folk variants clearly present the first half of the *Yogavāsiṣṭha*'s implicit argument, that certain illusions and dreams seem quite real until we wake up; but they ignore the second half of the argument, that even when we are awake we can sometimes establish the reality of the dream/illusion.[82] The *Yogavāsiṣṭha* goes into this proof, this vindication of the shared dream, through complex arguments, to which we will turn our attention below.

In contrast with the simplifying tendencies of the folk variants, there is a rather recent and more sophisticated rendition of the story of Lavaṇa that goes even farther than the *Yogavāsiṣṭha* in developing the second half of the story. This variant was composed at the end of the nineteenth century by the Telugu poet Guru Jada Appa Rao; it is called "The Dream of King Lavaṇa," and is one of a group of poems called *Strings of Pearls* (*Mutyala Saralu*).

> King Lavaṇa was in his court when a magician approached him and said, "Great king, I will show you a magic feat. Watch!" He waved

his peacock-feather brush and there appeared a white horse that stole the king's heart. While the amazed king looked at the horse, which stood before him, he sat as still as if there were no sign of life in him. His courtiers were upset, but he came back to life in a short while. As he looked around and saw his court, his disturbed mind gradually pieced together the past events, one by one. The king said, "Where is the magician, and where is the horse? Years have gone by." But his courtiers said, "Lord, it was only seven minutes." Then the king matched in his mind the illusions of being and non-being, and in wonder he realized the power of time. He said,

"Have seven minutes lasted seven years? Or have seven years been captured in seven minutes? Does the mind cause all of this, the little things and the big? A king mounted a magic horse and was swept away by his mind, speeding to unknown lands. At dawn, he grabbed a vine that hung from a tree, and the horse sped away. The exhausted king fell asleep, and when he awoke, as if reborn into another life, he saw before him a new world full of beauty. He heard a voice singing a song and felt as if his past memories were calling him. He forgot his hunger—which burned in him like the underwater doomsday mare—as he listened in bliss and saw the beautiful dark young girl who was singing. Who was the lucky person she was singing for? I thought I heard her sing his name—Lavaṇa. Boldly I said to her, 'I am starving for food, but a different, more powerful hunger burns me and makes me follow you.' The girl said, 'You want me, but you do not know who I am. I am an Untouchable girl. My heart breaks when I see that I cannot feed you. And I could give this food to a man only if I were married to him.' I grabbed her hand and took her in my arms and kissed her, stroking her braided hair. 'I will marry you,' I said. 'Give me food.'

"She gave me food more delicious than the nectar that Viṣṇu gave the gods. Her father said to me, 'Son, I have been looking for you all this time. Take my daughter, who is dearer than my life. We came from that world, and we want to go back there; but this daughter has kept me here, chaining me to her golden love.' Through many harvests I lived in heavenly pleasure with that girl, and we had sons fit to be emperors. Knowing that the love of grandchildren would be a new bondage to life, her father left this world, taking the path of renunciation. Then there was a famine, and our children were starving. My wife came to me and said, 'Do not grieve, for we will die by fire, and there is no better fortune than death. We will have in the future what we think of when we die. I will live in your company all my future lives until the day of final release.' And so we thrust aside our grief and entered the fire, hand in hand."

This is the story that Lavaṇa told with deep sorrow in his eyes. Then the pandits in his court said, "Do not grieve. This is illusion." The king frowned in anger and replied, "What do you mean, 'Do not grieve. This is illusion'? Does grief disappear if you just say, 'It

> is illusion'? You pandits speak like parrots, repeating words you learned in books. You do not have experience; you do not know what it is like. Whatever is experienced is *real* for that time. In the future, everything will be unreal, but what about now? The mind is rooted in thoughts that shake you in constant grief and hit you on the head. But no one can explain how this happens. Where is that mysterious land? Where are my dear children? Can anyone show me my wife, who is dearer to me than life?"
>
> Overcome with sorrow, the king covered his eyes with his hands and sat there, lost in grief. Then, suddenly, there was a flourish at the door of the court, and the guard came to announce, "A sage and a lady on a horse have come to see you, O king." "Show them in right away," said the king. And no sooner had he spoken than a woman as beautiful as a celestial nymph [*apsaras*] entered the court hall, mounted on a pure white horse and accompanied by a sage. The sage blessed the king and said, "May you have great happiness. The Yavana king of Sindh, who was a friend of your father, has sent you a gift: this girl, his beloved daughter. He also sends you this horse—there is nothing like it in the world." The king did not even hear these words. He looked at the girl in amazement and walked to her, saying, "My dear, have you come?"[83]

The theme of death and rebirth, which is woven in and out of the background of the Sanskrit version of the story of Lavaṇa, is brought into sharper focus in this Telugu version. The king seems to be dead while he is in his trance and then to come back to life; between this death and rebirth he falls asleep (under the tree) and awakens. A corollary of the rebirth motif, the theme of the memory of past lives, appears in the king's statement that the girl's song seemed to awaken such memories in him and that she seemed to remember him (or at least his name) from her own previous lives. And when the girl's father speaks of "that world" to which he wishes to return (and, apparently, does return, when he renounces life), he may be referring to his own memories of a former life or of another world.

The king angrily rejects the simplistic statement of the doctrine of illusion and refuses to apply it as a balm to his grief: he will not say "It was just a dream" to erase the pain of losing his happy dream, the way one would say "It is just a dream" to escape from a nightmare. Yet he does not deny the illusory nature of his experience or, like the Sanskrit Lavaṇa, try to prove its reality; nor does this text state or even imply that the girl and the Untouchable village were really there, as they are in the Sanskrit text. Instead, this Telugu Lavaṇa argues that even an unprovable illusion that is valued is emotionally real; everything that is experienced is real, he says, and it has a power and meaning that the pandits, who know only books, not life, can never comprehend. The Telugu king takes no active part in holding on to his illusory happiness; he experiences it passively and helplessly. Nor does the girl who comes to him at the end prove to the courtiers the reality of his dream experience. From their standpoint, she is a different girl, the daughter of a king of Sindh, not the daughter of an Untouchable villager. But the king knows, privately, that she is the same girl, keeping her promise to live with him in all his future lives. Though the text merely invokes a tired cliché when it says that she was as beautiful as an *apsaras*, a woman from heaven, the king knows that she really does come from the other world. Similarly, when the horse reaches the court, he is reduced to being a merely metaphorically otherworldly horse, not a truly magic horse, like the horse in the dream. The horse and the girl share the same ambiguous earthly ties, and both of them come from Sindh, like the horse in the Sanskrit tale of Lavaṇa. The fact that the girl has the horse with her when she comes to court might be evidence that she is the girl in the dream—if we were sure that the horse in court was the horse in the dream. In the end, the king simply recognizes the girl—or, rather, he thinks he does. The story ends on a question. Nothing has been proved, but everything has been felt.

This Telugu text apparently combines the theme of the king who dreams of his princess and finds her and the theme of the king who has a dream adventure with an Untouchable woman. Such a combination, resulting in the final reunion of the king and the woman, would have been unthinkable during the classical period in which the Sanskrit texts were composed, and it was not even possible in the nineteenth-century Kashmiri text; for there, when the Untouchable woman (the cobbler's wife) comes to court, the king is ruined. Indeed, the king does not really have an Untouchable wife even in our Telugu text, for the girl who comes to him in his court is not, literally, an Untouchable girl. She is a rather clever compromise, by which the modern Telugu poet takes advantage of the social reforms of his time without actually trampling on Brahmin sensibilities. The girl is said to be the daughter of a Yavana, a Greek (or other foreigner),[84] and thus is technically a non-Hindu and hence an Untouchable in the broadest sense. In fact (or, rather, in history), many Indian kings did marry Greek princesses, from the time of Alexander the Great's entrance into India in 321 B.C., and they did so without any loss of caste.

Despite this manipulation of the caste of the girl whom the king marries at the end, the Telugu poet works a major transformation on the Sanskrit text's attitude toward the Untouchables. The world of the Untouchables in this Telugu text is a world of beauty, not a world of horror, and a world of goodness, not a world of evil. This is spelled out in two long speeches, as well as in the general description of Lavaṇa's dream.

When the girl first protests to the king that she is an Untouchable, he mentally runs through all the Hindu law books (*śāstras*) to find some justification for marrying the girl, and this is what he comes up with:

> "Are the Untouchables really impure? If people who kill animals are low in caste, how can those who persecute human beings be high? If a system gives low status to people whose bodies are unclean but high status to people whose minds are unclean, that system is surely unfair. There are only two castes among human beings, the good and the bad. If good people are Untouchables, then I would rather be one of them."

Then, when he meets the girl's father, the father immediately speaks these reassuring words:

> "I am a low-born Untouchable, yet by the grace of my guru I rejected the unclean profession of Untouchables. I live by feeding cows. I taught my kinsmen to reject all their unclean acts. We do not kill cows. Our religion is peace."

The father even speaks words from the Vedas to join the king and the girl in holy matrimony. This part of the text goes directly against the grain of the Sanskrit story, giving it a social message that is not only irrelevant but antithetical to the point of the *Yogavāsiṣtha*. The Telugu poem at last provides a sociological context for the tale of Lavaṇa, but it is not the context of the original story. Moreover, it still constitutes only a distant background; the philosophical and poetical contexts are the foreground.

Indian Arguments

Ways of Knowing for Sure: Authorities

In all of the versions of the stories of Lavaṇa and Gādhi, different and often directly contradictory points of view are presented. Sometimes one will be chosen over another, and the grounds for such a choice are the degree to which each argument rests on one or more of the traditional Indian authorities—not authorities in the sense of persons but in the sense of types of evidence. (Authoritative persons are merely one of the several types of evidence.) The choice between several points of view, bolstered in this way by traditionally accepted ways of knowing, is further complicated by the fact that these ways of knowing are themselves hierarchically ranked, and ranked differently by different schools of epistemology.

The tension between *saṃsāra*-oriented and *mokṣa*-oriented value systems gives rise to a conflict between the social validation of experience ("Be a king") and the private validation of experience ("Believe in your unshared dream"). Throughout Indian mythology we find both a willingness to tolerate the inner tension of a personal reality shared by no one else and a desire to "validate" that reality by public corroboration. Thus, as we have seen, when Rāma's father, King Daśaratha, wants to persuade Rāma to take up his royal duties once again, despite Rāma's (true) perception of the unreality of those duties, Daśaratha calls in Viśvāmitra, who says, "What Rāma knows inside him, when he hears that from the mouth of a good man who says, 'That is true reality,' then he will have peace of mind."[85] The "good man" is one of the classical Indian sources of validation, on the social rather than the private side of the spectrum. The text deals at length with this and other forms of validation.

When Vasiṣṭha tells Rāma that Lavaṇa was able to establish his kingship through an imaginary consecration, Rāma is puzzled by the implicit paradox. He asks Vasiṣṭha, "What authoritative way of knowing for sure [*pramāṇa*] could there be for this consecration, since it was achieved through a magic web of imagination?" Vasiṣṭha said, "At the time when the magician arrived at the palace hall of Lavaṇa, right then I myself was living there and saw it with my own eyes. And when the magician had gone, I myself, in the presence of the assembled people, asked the king what had happened. As a witness I saw all of this with my own eyes. I did not hear it from someone else."[86] Vasiṣṭha here simultaneously invokes three forms of evidence: the evidence of "another" corroborating witness (Vasiṣṭha, to corroborate Lavaṇa); the evidence of his own eyewitness participation in the event; and, by implication, the evidence of his spiritual superiority. (The fact that Vasiṣṭha was present only at the *telling* of the adventure, not at the adventure itself, is a point to which we will return.)

The question of reliable authorities or "good reasons" (*pramāṇas*, ways of knowing and proving) is one that is central to all Indian philosophical enterprises. Different philosophers have held distinct views about the number and nature of the various *pramāṇas*, and a good analysis of them is given by Karl Potter.[87] The most important ones are inference (*anumāṇa*), argument (*tarka*, or, as Potter defines it, "the use of various and assorted forms of reasons to indicate absurdity in the opponent's thesis"), perception (*pratyakṣa*, direct witnessing with one's own eyes), and verbal authority or *śabda*, "which consists in knowledge gained from hearing authoritative words, which usually means the *śruti* or sacred scriptures, such as the Vedas and Upanishads."[88] Of these various forms, argument (*tarka*) is usually ranked below inference (*anumāṇa*); both are less reliable than direct perception and verbal authority, and verbal authority generally outranks perception. Potter points out why perception is not ranked at the top:

> All sources of immediate experience, and not only the awareness born of the functioning of the sense-organs, are included [in perception, *pratyakṣa*] (although there are those who would limit perception to knowledge born of sensation). . . . Memory is a kind of perception, although of a second order. . . . But there is disagreement among the schools of Indian philosophy as to whether each or any of these nonsensory forms of experience is trustworthy, and indeed as to whether it is proper to class them as *pratyakṣa*.[89]

Among these "nonsensory" perceptions, Potter inclues the yogin's special awareness (*alaukika*, "uncommon, not of this world, or not within the scope of normal people") and the "mental perception" (*mānasapratyakṣa*) of the Buddhists. These are generally, though by no means always, accepted as authoritative, but both they and the more conventional forms of perception may be erroneous.[90]

Of the many possible ways of knowing (*pramāṇas*), the *Yogavāsiṣṭha* recognizes three of the classical four: direct perception, inference, and verbal authority. It ignores the fourth, disputation (*tarka*). There is no structure in the *Yogavāsiṣṭha* in which true dialogue could take place; the people whom Vasiṣṭha and the other sages address do not fight back or keep interjecting puzzled pleas for clarification or even mutter, "Yes, of course you are right, Socrates," though they do ask the questions that trigger the long explanations. In place of disputation, the *Yogavāsiṣṭha* makes frequent use of another classical way of knowing: analogy (*upamāna*). The particular form that analogy takes in the *Yogavāsiṣṭha*—which is, after all, a poem—is simile or example (*dṛṣṭānta*).[91] The work is a tissue of similes; some, which we will examine in chapter six—the rope and the snake, the magic city in the sky, the child of a barren woman, and the crow and the palm tree—occur so often that one begins to accept them as proven facts rather than mere poetic suggestions.

Though the *Yogavāsiṣṭha* accepts the authoritative word (*śabda*) as a means of knowledge and mentions various canonical works and traditionally revered types of wise men as bearers of this kind of authority, the proof that is regarded as by far the best is that of direct experience (*pratyakṣa*): "Of all proofs, eyewitness evidence is the one basic proof, as the ocean is basic to all rivers; analogy and the others are just aspects of direct perception."[92] This would seem to challenge the traditional hierarchy, in which verbal authority is higher than perception. But perception is dependent on what we would call authority, for the reliable eyewitness proof "is not the direct perception of an ordinary individual but that of a Yogi,"[93] i.e., it is the perception of someone who can be relied on to know the difference between reality and illusion. Moreover, according to the *Yogavāsiṣṭha*, the other means of knowledge are only auxiliaries of the one reliable form of direct perception, which is "the result of a sustained personal effort of a qualified aspirant."[94] Finally, the authority of *pratyakṣa* is undermined on the most basic level by the implicit contrast between *pratyakṣa* and *parokṣa*, between what is visible and what is invisible. For *parokṣa* means not only what is invisible but what is mysterious and secret, and the gods love what is *parokṣa*. *Pratyakṣa* is therefore what is most profane and most material and hence, in Indian terms, least real. *Pratyakṣa* lacks divine support.

The concept of authority may seem an inappropriately culture-bound criterion to interject into a scientific argument. But Peter Berger and Thomas Luckmann have shown how deeply social influences predetermine our construction of reality, and Thomas Kuhn has demonstrated the social nature of much of the inspiration (and proof) of scientific theory. And it could be argued that in the West our scientists are our Brahmins; they are the authority figures whom we believe even when they tell us such unlikely things as that space is curved and full of black holes.[95] Thus, though some texts seem to regard direct perception (*pratyakṣa*) as the best authority, while others regard scripture (*śabda*) as the best authority, there is no real contradiction between them. For, as we will see, perception is best for lower-level problems, while scripture is best for high problems. Finally, since scripture is regarded as embodied in persons of known wisdom—Brahmins or yogins—the ultimate authority is a combination of perception and scripture: it is the direct perception of a man deeply versed in scripture.

Unreality-Testing

But this proof—the authoritative person's eye-witness account (*pratyakṣa*)—is, after all, a subjective one: "I saw it with *my* eyes," says Vasiṣṭha. And it will be the ultimate work of the *Yogavāsiṣṭha* to undermine the value of both personal perception and corroborating witnesses as proof. An apparent reality may in fact be an illusion even if you see it with your own eyes, or even if other people agree with you that they saw it with *their* eyes, too. In arguing that the universe is illusory, the *Yogavāsiṣṭha* says that the world is like an experience that has no witness (*adraṣṭakam*).[96] The *Yogavāsiṣṭha* teaches us that we need other people to assure us that what we think we see is *not* there; we need assistance in our public unreality-testing. And the key to this quandary is *whose* eyes have witnessed the events; what matters, in the end, is the spiritual authority of the corroborator.

Karl Potter has discussed the ways in which Advaita philosophers like Śankara approached the problem of testing reality. In discussing this same topic, I have often used the instance of the snake and the rope, but Potter uses the classic example favored by Advaita, where someone sees a piece of shell and mistakes it for a piece of silver.

> For the Advaitin, gaining knowledge is like finding that silver is really shell, or like waking up from a dream. It is important to ask how we know we have discovered an object to be more adequate than another. What is the *test* of the relatively more true (real, adequate) according to Advaita? It is not at all obvious that the correction of common illusions like the shell-silver case is the same process as correcting dream-illusions. To test the former error, we bend down and reach for the object; if we are still deluded, we carry it to the market and try to get a metallurgist to assay its worth. When do we perceive our error? We may perceive it when our senses show us that its qualities are different on closer examination than we had thought previously, but we may not—sometimes it will take the force of public or trained opinion, e.g., the metallurgist's, to convince us that we are the victim of an illusion. (This analogy may help to explain the importance of the *ṛṣis* or wise men who wrote the Vedas and Upanishads: they are to Truth what the metallurgist is to truth in our stock example.) Discovering an illusion, then, is a more drawn-out process, frequently, than waking up from a dream.[97]

Testing a mistake (a temporary illusion) is a more complex process than testing a dream, because there are a series of steps that one is instructed to take, steps that involve a series of corroborators and authorities. Testing a dream or the all-encompassing Illusion is quicker, but it is also harder; there are no other people to whom one can appeal.

Is there, nevertheless, a relationship between the process of correcting a mistake and the process of emerging from an illusion? Indian tradition suggests that a person who becomes aware of a minor distortion, such as an optical illusion, may be unwittingly taking the first step on the path toward becoming aware of a more general kind of distortion that is built into all experience. Unexpected results in the trivial sphere may occasionally inspire a reformulation of the values implicit in one's definition of reality; a mote that troubles the mind's eye may eventually shake the entire edifice of perception. Within the entire illusion that the *Yogavāsiṣṭha* depicts there are numerous mistakes. The characters in the drama are at first aware of neither the mistakes nor the illusions; they come to recognize that there must have been some mistakes; finally, they recognize the entire illusion.

Rāmānuja discussed the relevance of various forms of authority for overcoming both minor and major distortions. He argued that if one sees two moons or mistakes a rope for a snake, no amount of testimony or any quantity of "reliable bystanders" saying, "That is not a snake, but a rope," would be of any use to the deluded person. Only proper experiential knowledge would convince him that there is only one moon or a rope. But when one attempts to dispel illusion itself, neither bystanders nor experience is of any use; here, only scripture can help; only scripture can lead us, after death, to *brahman*.[98] Thus, though it is impossible to test Illusion through experience, it is not impossible to test illusions—to test mistakes and mirages. Or, more precisely, as we saw in chapter one, it is possible to falsify a dream—that is, to verify the fact that it is "merely" a dream and not a reality—by waking up. But it is not possible to verify a dream—to prove that it is a reality and not a dream—by never waking up. All that we can do is to prove that the data provided by several different dreams form a coherent whole, and this is a very limited sort of test. To verify the dream as a dream would be to verify the entire illusion—which is, as we have seen, impossible. No amount of testing or arguing can accomplish such a proof.

We have seen a possible link between the two levels of disconfirmation in Indian epistemological theory in the suggestion that small bits of disconfirming data, facts that do not fit the existing paradigm, build up until the entire paradigm is thrown into question. Yet it is argued by other philosophers that such minor incidents alone, no matter how often they occur and how much pressure they may build up, do not overthrow paradigms; only a change in world-view, a leap of imagination, can do this. The question of steps versus leaps is much debated in Indian philosophy: How many rope/snakes does it take to make us realize that even the rope does not exist? Karl Potter has used this as the criterion by which to distinguish certain Indian doctrines of enlightenment as "leap philosophies" (*ajātivāda*), in which faith can be gained only by a sudden leap of insight, in contrast with "progress philosophies," in which such conviction or faith can be gained progressively by action, devotion, or understanding.[99]

Advaita Vedānta is a leap philosophy. By assimilating illusion to dreams, it invokes an analogy: the final awakening from a dream or an illusion is both faster, once it happens, and slower, in beginning to happen, than the partial awakening from minor perceptual errors:

> It is not as a result of any conscious decision on the part of either the dream-self or the waking self that we wake up from dreams—this just seems to happen. The analogy with respect to gaining release ought to be that it just happens, and this leads fairly directly to leap philosophy, perhaps of that type which makes release dependent upon the grace of God.[100]

Yet the progress schools imply, by their very existence, that *bhrama*-awareness leads to *māyā*-awareness. This is the point of the discipline of yoga and the teaching of Indian metaphysics, of the devotion to the guru and the painstaking memorizing of sacred texts: effort counts. These efforts generally take place within the realm of *saṃsāra*: one works gradually toward *mokṣa* within the realm of material commitment; it is not necessary to leave one's wife and children in order to find God. Yet other Indians regard enlightenment as an all-or-nothing affair: they leave their families and wander about naked, defying all human conventions. Such violent divorces from conventional life may be reflected in the violent transitions from caste Hinduism to Untouchability in our myths. Thus the Indian evidence suggests that the cumulative awareness of *bhrama* sometimes does, and sometimes does not, lead to an awareness of *māyā*. Even if, logically, *bhrama* cannot force the hand of *māyā*, being of an entirely different order of argument, *bhrama* may be capable, illogically, of triggering the response to *māyā*, of short-circuiting the wires that normally protect us from seeing *māyā* for what it is.

Is man helpless in the face of this dilemma? Is the process by which one is or is not drawn through the awareness of *bhrama* to the awareness of *māyā* accidental or not? This argument was taken up in South India in the form of a debate about the nature of divine grace. The Cat School argued that one need not work at salvation, for God picks up the sinner as a mother cat picks up a kitten; all the kitten has to do is to go limp. (Indeed, according to certain extreme branches of this school, one *interferes* with the process of grace if one makes any effort at all to bring it about.) But the Monkey School argued that one did have to work at it, for God picks up the sinner as a mother monkey picks up a baby monkey: the baby monkey has to hang on for dear life. The problem of *bhrama* is a monkey problem: we can work hard, with good results, at ironing out our mistakes, at falsifying our theories, at testing our dreams. But the problem of *māyā* is a cat problem; either we wake up from the dream—and there is no effort that we can make to do so—or we go on dreaming forever.

Lavaṇa and Gādhi do attempt to test their dreams. Moreover, their reactions to their illusory experiences and their use of public and authoritative corroboration are significantly different. As soon as Lavaṇa has his vision, he is persuaded by the emotional impact of his experience as an Untouchable, and therefore he is immediately troubled by what he perceives as a contradiction: the courtiers thought he was on his throne, while he thought he was living in an Untouchable village. He sets out the very next morning to "find the wasteland that had been reflected in the mirror of his mind," yet he was at that time the only one who regarded his vision as real, and he had not a shred of evidence with which to defend his faith in it. Gādhi, on the other hand, is not surprised at his vision inside the water, but he assumes that it is nothing but a vision. Gādhi does nothing at first to test his vision, nor does he tell anyone about it.

Only when someone else offers him evidence of the reality of his dream does he decide to test it. Even then he is puzzled, not by the massive paradox of his simultaneous experience of two lives, but by the nagging detail of the inconsistency of one particular aspect of his "second" life: he is puzzled by the fact that his visionary self has a wife and a mother, while he himself has none. He decides to set his mind at rest by going to look into the matter of his own existence as an Untouchable.[101] Because he is a wise man, free of passion, Gādhi is all the more able to recover physically the land of his imagination. As Vasiṣṭha remarks of him, "Wise men who exert themselves win even the kingdom of the mind; Gādhi went to find what he had seen in a dream, and he found it all. Seeing the illusion of the universe, Gādhi made an effort to make it an object of authoritative knowledge [*pramāṇa*]."[102] In this, Gādhi is acting not like the Hindu yogin who dispels illusion but like the Tibetan Buddhist yogin who creates reality.

When statements are made in India about a person's being in two places at once or a person's remembering his past lives, usually no one bothers to prove or disprove the statement. This may be because such statements are not taken as cognitive propositions or theorems in need of proof; they present no challenge to cognitive consistency or scientific rigor because they are not even apprehended in those terms. They are apprehended, rather, in terms of the value that such beliefs have for the people to whom they are told. Even if one assumed that it was possible to prove that a person really was in two places at once and that material evidence of this could be presented, there still might be no attempt actually to carry out a proof, any more than there would be, on the part of the realists, an attempt to prove that such a thing is *not* possible. For most people simply do not bother to test their basic cosmological assumptions; when the presupposition is so deeply ingrained, proof seems superfluous.

But the possibility that one might believe that it could be true that someone could be in two places at one time and might go ahead and attempt a proof of this is what is imagined in the *Yogavāsiṣṭha*. India offers various philosophical explanations for the paradoxical experiences of Lavaṇa and Gādhi. We will discuss in chapter five the question of ontology—what reality *is*; here it is useful to pursue the question of epistemology—how reality is *perceived*. When faced with experiences that cannot, apparently, be real, why is it that some people ignore them, others accept them on faith, and still others—like Lavaṇa and Gādhi—set out to prove them?

Before beginning to answer this question, we must recall that the myths of Lavaṇa and Gādhi do not demonstrate that ancient Indians performed experiments to prove that their dreams were real. These myths, like the myths about shared dreams, demonstrate only that the ancient Indians *imagined* episodes in which people set out to prove that their dreams were real. Moreover, even within the stories, the actors do not set up experiments; they merely follow up a chain of events that is set in motion by a chance circumstance that might never recur. If anyone ever did actually try to validate a dream in ancient India, we have no records of it. What we have are records of predictive dreams that came true, and this is evidence of a quite different order. At best it is evidence for the validity of the theory; it is not evidence that anyone ever set out to prove the theory. The Hindus knew an unfalsifiable hypothesis when they saw one quite as well as Sir Karl Popper; unlike him, they did not let that knowledge stop them from believing in it.

Lavaṇa and Gādhi, like many scientists, are driven to carry out their investigations by their refusal to tolerate what Leon Festinger has called "cognitive dissonance": a discord that results when religious faith maintains a valued belief in the teeth of overwhelming factual data that contradicts it.[103] Lavaṇa and Gādhi want their religious and their practical views, their sacred and their profane experiences, to be brought somehow into harmony. Their refusal to tolerate cognitive dissonance is, in one sense, a refusal to accept a contradiction: *either* Lavaṇa was in court *or* he was in the Untouchable village. Yet, as we have seen, Indians often seem able to live comfortably with such contradictions without attempting to resolve them. (This might be yet another reason why one would not think of proving one's assumptions about such a contradictory experience.) It would seem, therefore, that we have stumbled on yet another cultural spectrum of ideas about a basic epistemological assumption. Let us look at this spectrum more closely.

Common Sense and Contradiction

What are the assumptions with which the hero of the story begins? What are the assumptions of the author, and what assumptions does he expect his audience to have? To answer these questions, we must return to the problem of common sense that we touched on in the Introduction. Indians did not regard common sense as an element that ought to be taken into account in constructing a proof. Common sense is not one of the classical authorities (*pramāṇas*) or ways of knowing; direct perception (*pratyakṣa*) may include common sense by implication, but technically it is an entirely separate way of knowing. There are exceptions to this general rule; some people did regard common sense as formally significant. Jayaśrī, for example, who was a skeptic rather than a mystic, demolished all philosophical arguments and finally maintained that we must rely on normal common sense, the consensus of the people (*laukika mārga*).[104] So, too, many mystics argued that truth (*brahman*) is self-evident (*sapra-*

kāśa) and need not be philosophized about. Such thinkers were very much in the minority among philosophers, but they may have represented a general, popular level of feeling; people do, after all, tend to take common sense seriously, even if philosophers do not. Indeed, our stories begin precisely at the moment when direct perception comes into violent conflict with common sense—*Indian* common sense.

Since peoples' responses to experiences such as Lavaṇa's and Gādhi's are, at least to some extent, socially conditioned, it is necessary to try to take into account, in attempting to understand their attitudes, what most people in that society at that time would have expected. Only when we have some idea of what would have been surprising to most people can we begin to wonder why some people were more surprised than others (about such experiences) or why some people did something about their surprise and others did not.

There are two clusters of evidence in the data we have already encountered that indicate that the Indian man in the street at the time of the composition of the *Yogavāsiṣṭha* had two kinds of cultural common sense available to him; evidence of this is provided by the general literature of ancient and medieval India and by the *Yogavāsiṣṭha* itself. We know that the philosophy of illusion in its basic form (as in our myths of illusion) was well known in India from the time of the Upaniṣads, a millennium and a half before the *Yogavāsiṣṭha* was composed. We know, therefore, that most Hindus would not find the tales of Lavaṇa and Gādhi as surprising as we do; they have heard that sort of story before, though probably not in so striking a form. It is also evident that the author of the *Yogavāsiṣṭha* has great sympathy for the doctrine that reality is illusory, illusion real; this appears not only from his explicit philosophical arguments but from the power with which he depicts the vivid dream experiences.

Yet this doctrine of illusion may not have been the predominant cultural assumption, the shared common sense, in India at the time the *Yogavāsiṣṭha* was composed. We know that there were many skeptics in India who took reality to be as solid as any Victorian empiricist would have taken it to be. Once again we encounter evidence for these ideas: that no one can believe that he does not exist or that the universe does not exist; that illusion must always be defined by contrast with what is real; and that *something* must be real.

Throughout the Sanskrit texts, people express amazement at the miracles that are performed by various gods and yogins. A typical incident occurs in the *Bhāgavata Purāṇa*:

> Akrūra seated Kṛṣṇa and Balarāma in his chariot and took his leave of them. But when he went to bathe in the river, he saw the two of them, Balarāma and Kṛṣṇa, together there, and he thought,

> "How can the two of them be in the chariot and also be right here? If they are here, they cannot be in the chariot." And with this in mind, he got out of the water and looked for them. But he saw them there in the chariot, just as before, sitting there. He plunged back into the water, thinking, "Was my vision of them in the water, then, false?" . . . He praised Kṛṣṇa, who withdrew his form from the water, like an actor playing a part. And when Akrūra saw that Kṛṣṇa had vanished from the water, he came out and returned to the chariot in amazement. Then Kṛṣṇa, who was in the chariot, asked him, "Have you seen some miracle on the land or in the sky or in the water? You look as if you had."[105]

Like Gādhi, Akrūra has a vision when he is in the water, and the vision is sent by Viṣṇu (Kṛṣṇa). This vision, however, is in direct conflict with his common sense, which tells him that one person cannot be in two places at the same time. He tests his hypothesis twice: he looks for Kṛṣṇa and Balarāma on the land and then, finding them there, returns to see if they are also still in the water. When he *still* finds them in both places, he becomes amazed (at first, apparently, he was just puzzled). The fact that such things *happen* in India does not mean that everyone *believes* in them. (The opposite situation, where people *do* believe in things that *don't* happen, arises in many Buddhist texts that explicitly forbid the aspiring Bodhisattva to perform miracles of levitation, clairvoyance, etc. They assume—through common sense—that people are perfectly capable of levitation, etc., but they regard such showing-off as neither tactful nor safe.[106] These considerations led the Buddha to ground his monks.)

A second body of evidence also indicates that common sense in ancient India did not normally stretch to accommodate the possibility that a person could be in two places at one time. This evidence comes from the *Yogavāsiṣṭha*, from the words spoken by the unenlightened witnesses of the various metaphysical paradoxes. When Līlā returns to her palace after traveling with the goddess Sarasvatī to the scenes of her dead husband's future lives, she wonders which of the worlds she has seen is an erroneous perception (*bhrāntimaya*) and which partakes of the true essence of things (*pāramārthika*); she cannot tell the artificial from the nonartificial. When Sarasvatī asks her to explain what she means by these terms, Līlā replies, "That I am standing here, and you are near me—this is the unartificial world; this is what I know. And when my husband now stands by me, that is the artificial world, I think, since what is empty cannot be filled with time and place and so on." And even when Sarasvatī explains it all to her, Līlā accuses her of lying, since it cannot be that all the things she saw could somehow fit into the small room she was in when she saw them.[107]

When, much later, Līlā has overcome her common-sense objections and has projected her astral body into the palace where her husband has been reborn in another body, the miracle is ignored by everyone there, whose common sense blinds them to the truth of what they are seeing. Rāma wonders about these people and asks Vasiṣṭha, "When the people who lived in the palace saw Līlā, did they think her to be real or imaginary?" And Vasiṣṭha replies, "They would have thought, 'This sad queen standing here must be some friend or other of our queen; she must have come here from somewhere.' What doubt would they have? For cattle are without discernment; they think things are as they appear. Why would they puzzle about it?"[108] Similarly, in the Hindi folktale about the magic pot, those who see the doubles of the peasant and his wife simply assume that they are the peasant's brother and sister-in-law.

The amazement that is constantly expressed by the characters within the *Yogavāsiṣṭha*—including the amazement of Lavaṇa and Gādhi, who are greatly reluctant to accept the extreme idealistic explanations offered to them—surely indicates that the Indians' cultural consensus about common sense at that time included a stubborn disinclination to believe that the visions of Lavaṇa and Gādhi were materially real. And in the tale of the monk's dream, which I will discuss in chapter five, the text repeatedly insists that the characters in the story were amazed to find that the lives they had taken for real were merely parts of someone else's dreams or, contrariwise, that people they had just dreamed about turned out to be real people they could talk to. They are amazed at both implications: the implication that their real lives are dreams and the implication that their dreams are real—or, rather, as real as their waking lives. They had assumed, as we usually assume, that dreams are unreal and that lives are real. Even at the very end of the story of the monk's dream, Rāma cannot understand how the dream figures could become real, and the commentator explains his quandary: "Rāma asked his question because he did not think it was possible that the matter could be as it seemed and as it had just been said to be, or that in that way Rudra could make a hundred people by making the monk have a hundred dreams."[109] Even Rudra himself is said to have been amazed by his realization that the people in his hundred dreams had thought themselves to be real, though he then conquers his amazement and carefully figures it all out.[110]

It must be granted that the narrator's insistence on the amazement of the characters in the story is, in part, simply a literary device, employed also in Christian miracle tales, to emphasize the importance of the extraordinary event and to provide us with doubting fools, fall guys, or "stupid disciples," set up either to be converted or to serve as a foil for those who are converted. Nevertheless, these amazed participants and bystanders must also represent the point of view that the narrator expected to find in at least some of his audience. One might argue that the experience of surprise at reality-switching is more common—and hence less surprising—in India than in the West, since Hindus' basic epistemological assumptions make it possible to cross these borders more easily and more often.[111] Yet the boundary itself is taken for granted, even in India.

The fact that we Westerners also experience amazement or even disbelief when we first hear this story is not, I think, irrelevant. In any case, we will read ourselves into any text that we read. Not only *may* we ask our own questions of the text; we cannot *help* asking our own questions. But the common sense of the text itself is indicated not by the questions that it inspires in us but by the questions that it inspired in the interlocutors who are part of the text. It is gratifying to note that many of the questions asked by the characters in the story are the very questions that would occur to an American first encountering the story—literal-minded, earthbound, flat-footed questions. But we also ask questions that they do not ask, and they ask questions that would not occur to us. Moreover, we ask them at different points; they bother us before, or after, they drive the Indian audience to interrupt the narrative. This is because, in addition to the common sense that the two cultures share, each has its own peculiar kind of common sense as well. And their common sense leads Indian thinkers to deal with contradiction in ways different from ours.

In order to explain how, and why, Lavaṇa's illusion was produced, Vasiṣṭha offers Rāma various explanations, various relevant bits of the doctrine of illusion that the story is meant to illustrate. How did Lavaṇa's dream come to be witnessed by others? Vasiṣṭha, who was present in Lavaṇa's court when the king had his vision, tells Rāma what he had told Lavaṇa himself:

> Vasiṣṭha said to Rāma, "In the morning, the king asked me, 'How can a dream become something right in front of one's eyes? I was amazed when everything was told [by the Untouchables] just the way it had been [in my dream], with all the precise details of reality.'" And, hearing, the story, Rāma asked Vasiṣṭha, "How *did* the dream become real? Tell me, good Brahmin." Vasiṣṭha said, "Ignorance gives rise to all of this, so that what has not happened happens, as when one dreams of one's own death. The mind experiences precisely the things that it itself has caused to arise, though such things do not truly exist, nor, on the other hand, are they unreal. What happened in the Untouchable village to King Lavaṇa appeared as an image in his mind and was either real or unreal, or else the delusion that Lavaṇa saw immediately became a conscious perception in the mind of the Untouchables. The image of Lavaṇa climbed into the mind of the Untouchables, and the conscious perception of the Untouchables climbed into the mind of the king. For just as quite similar sayings appear in the minds of many people, even so, similar time, place, and even action may appear in many

> peoples' minds, as in a dream. And, just as the mind can forget things that have been done, no matter how important they may be, so, too, one can certainly remember something as having been done even though it has not been done."[112]

This is not an explanation; it is a cornucopia of explanations, containing all the possibilities on the spectrum of *māyā*: mass hallucination or, more precisely, dual hallucination, the *rêve à deux*; the projection of an image from one mind to another; archetypal images, universally shared; the simple tricks of memory; and the sense of *déjà vu*.

These various explanations account in part for various different sorts of mistakes that are made by different characters within our story, and the way that these different explanations pull against one another produces a tension in the plot. When Lavaṇa has awakened on his throne, after his supposed adventures among the Untouchables, and the magician has vanished (and the courtiers have suggested that the magician was an instrument sent by the gods to teach the king about illusion), we might expect the story to end, as many of the simpler tales of Nārada and as many of the folk variants of the tales of Lavaṇa and Gādhi do end. But our text goes on to make an extraordinary statement: "King Lavaṇa, realizing the mistake [*bhrama*], set out on the very next day to go to the great desert. For, he reasoned, 'I remember that wasteland as it was reflected in the mirror of my mind, and so it can be found again somehow.'"[113]

What does the text mean when it says that the king has realized his "mistake"? On the first, superficial, level, it would mean that he has been mistaken in thinking that he had really lived among the Untouchables, since all his courtiers assure him that he had never budged from his throne. But if this were the case, the king would *not* go to find the wasteland; he would regard it as a mere fantasy and dismiss it as a mental aberration without a physical basis. Instead, he regards it as a reflected image (*pratibhāsa*), which here implies that it was reflected (imaginarily) from a place where it was *real*, and this is what the king sets out to prove. This is the second level of mistake, and in some parts of the multifaceted explanation it is the accepted level: there was a real Untouchable village, and the king felt its reflection in his mind; this is the village that he seeks and finds. On a third level, however, both the king's court and the Untouchable village are imaginary reflections of something else—or of nothing; Lavaṇa never comes to see this, but, outside the frame, Rāma (and, through him, the wider audience of the *Yogavāsiṣṭha*) transcends this final mistake as well as the more obvious first-level mistake.

The ambiguities in the text mount up and cluster into opposed groups until they constitute a contradiction, a paradox, an incongruity, or simply a situation that thumbs its nose at common sense. Either Lavaṇa was sitting on his throne at court or he was living in the Untouchable village:

how can both things be true at once? The contradictions in the text are met with contradictory explanations, as we have seen: either Lavaṇa and the Untouchables projected and received images of real people or they imagined unreal ones.

The tale of Gādhi is similarly glossed by several overlapping theories of illusion:

> Viṣṇu said, "Gādhi, not a single thing is external, not the sky, mountains, water, earth, or anything else; everything is in one's own mind. Since the glory of the mind can establish the infinite universe, why does it amaze you that its magic should reveal Untouchableness? The quality of being an Untouchable was fastened on to you by the power of the image. And the Brahmin guest who came to you and ate and slept and told a tale—all this that you saw was a mistake [*sambhrama*]; and when you went back to the village of the Untouchables and saw the ruined house of Kaṭañja, and when you went to the Kīra city and heard the story of the Untouchable who became king—all of those things were merely a mistake that you thought you saw. There was no guest; there were no Untouchables, no Kīras, and no city; it was all a delusion." When Gādhi thought about this for six months but was still quite confused, Viṣṇu returned and offered him the explanation of the phenomenon of mass hallucination and archetypal images. Again he vanished, leaving Gādhi more confused than ever, and finally he returned and said, "Now listen, and I will tell you how it really was, with no mistakes. A certain Untouchable named Kaṭañja built a house at the edge of that village once in the past. He lost his family in the very way [that you imagined] and went to another country and became king of the Kīras and entered the fire. When you were in the water, the image of that very form of Kaṭañja entered your mind, and the things that happened to Kaṭañja became an image." Then Viṣṇu disappeared, and Gādhi became serene.[114]

Viṣṇu begins by giving Gādhi the soft-line Vedāntic view: nothing at all is real, and one might therefore just as well substitute one illusion for another, since they are all equivalent. This serves primarily to confuse Gādhi, however, and so Viṣṇu returns to flesh out his first gloss with the compatible theory of the archetypes. But when Gādhi finds this still too difficult to take (as the rank-and-file Hindu must have done), Viṣṇu gives him a much harder version of the doctrine: There *was* a real Untouchable, but it was not Gādhi; and Gādhi (also real) somehow tuned into the experiences of the other man, as one might tune into another telephone conversation on a party line. In the first version, the experience of the life of the Untouchable (and the life of the king) was all *māyā*; in the third version, the Untouchable episode was merely *bhrama*, a mistake interjected into what was otherwise, for all intents and purposes, a real life.

We have seen that Indians are not, in general, troubled by contradiction. The various contradictory explanations offered by the *Yogavāsiṣṭha* derive in part from the Indian theory that there are many different true ways of understanding any single phenomenon, each suitable for one sort of person at one level of metaphysical acuity. This doctrine, which appears in Buddhism as the concept of "skill in means" (*upāya*), assumes that anyone can be taught anything if you go about it correctly; it corresponds roughly (quite roughly) to our belief in "different strokes for different folks." But when the explanations pile up too frenetically, they serve in part to make us permanently distrustful of *any* explanation. Freud taught us to be suspicious of too many excuses for a single fault (like the man who borrowed a horse, brought it back lame, and argued that the horse was sound now, that the horse had been lame when he borrowed it, and that he had never borrowed it).[115] Yet the *Yogavāsiṣṭha* does not leave us with a hermeneutics of suspicion; for between the soft line (that everything is unreal) and the hard line (that everything is real, but we mistake it for what is unreal), there is also a middle path. This middle line represents the common-sense view of the *Yogavāsiṣṭha* in general.

The text presents us with an extreme form of the philosophical doctrine of illusion, and it states that "truly enlightened people" will *not* be amazed by such phenomena. But then it presents us with a number of people who *are* astonished when presented with evidence that the doctrine of illusion might be literally true. In order to suggest the possibility that experiences like Lavaṇa's and Gādhi's might in fact be real, the author imagines that someone has actually tested this possibility, and he imagines what would happen if the test proved positive. He draws on the "toolbox" of beliefs—the full range of possible explanations available to Hindus. He sets up a conflict and picks a fight in an area where most people had long ago made a tacit peace with ontology. The people in Lavaṇa's court were skeptics; it was for their sake, as much as for his own, that Lavaṇa had to prove the reality of his vision. The author of the *Yogavāsiṣṭha* projects the presumed skepticism of a large part of his audience onto the characters in the court, including the central figures. But the author himself is maintaining (in his heart, or for the sake of a pretty story—who can tell?) the stance of idealism, both absolute and modified. The decision to apply criteria of skepticism to this idealism is brought about by his knowledge of the cultural common sense of his audience.

In the light of this cultural cognitive dissonance, built in even before the adventure begins, we might view the adventures of Lavaṇa and Gādhi as designed not merely to test the particular dreams but to introduce more clarity and self-awareness into the internally inconsistent model as a whole. The contradiction is not eliminated, for the final result is even more ambiguous than the starting point—but it is explicitly so; and it is precisely this explicitness that is its achievement. It forces into the open the conflicting assumptions that its society usually keeps hidden. The net effect, therefore, is to validate and support the original value system, despite its internal contradictions.

Was Lavaṇa sitting on his throne at court, or was he living in the Untouchable village? How can they both be true at once? This contradiction is the key to the process of enlightenment. The word that I have translated as "reflected image" (*prātibhāsika*), as when the image of Lavaṇa was projected into the minds of the Untouchables, might also be called a "contradictory image." The word refers to light rays that are bounced "back" or "against" other images. Dasgupta discusses the term as it relates to the nature of the world-appearance according to Śankara:

> The world-appearance is not, however, so illusory as the perception of silver in the conch shell, for the latter type of worldly illusions is called *prātibhāsika*, as they are contradicted by other, later, experiences, whereas the illusion of world-appearances is never contradicted in this worldly stage and is thus called *vyavahārika* [from *vyavahāra*, practice, i.e., that on which all our practical movements are based]. So long as the right knowledge of the Brahman as the only reality does not dawn, the world-appearance runs on in an orderly manner, uncontradicted by the accumulated experience of all men, and as such it must be held to be true. It is only because there comes a stage in which the world-appearance ceases to manifest itself that we have to say that, from the ultimate and absolute point of view, the world-appearance is false and unreal. . . . Thus the *prātibhāsika* experience lasts for a much shorter period of time than the *vyavahārika*.[116]

In other words, it is easier to correct mistakes than to correct illusions; or, as Karl Potter has pointed out, we will be moved more quickly to test a temporary contradictory illusion (the *prātibhāsika* experience) than to awaken from a dream or from a larger uncontradicted illusion (the *vyavahārika* experience), though the process of extricating ourselves from the contradiction takes longer than extricating ourselves from the uncontradicted illusion, once we begin. The obvious contradiction, which sooner or later exposes the distorted image for what it is, is the clue to a hidden contradiction that we may never step back far enough to see. Gādhi's contradictory experience lasts far longer than Lavaṇa's, though Gādhi is, from the start, far more sophisticated metaphysically than Lavaṇa. We see the mistake right away, for it is contradicted by common sense; but the illusion, which is supported by our common sense (*vyavahāra*), may never be dispelled.

In the stories of Lavaṇa and Gādhi, the author of the text, unable to sustain the position of pure idealism, lapses into a modified materialism; this materialism, the need to say that *something* is real, may take different forms, sometimes in favor of the subjective, sometimes denying the subjective. In the end, however, the position of absolute idealism simply becomes top-heavy and falls by its own weight. In the old animated Tom and Jerry cartoons, the cat, fleeing madly from some terror devised by the mouse, runs off the edge of a cliff and continues to run in the air, in a line parallel to the earth, until he happens to look down and discovers that he is standing on the air, in defiance of all the laws of gravity and of his own common sense; he then plummets to earth. The idealism of the *Yogavāsiṣṭha* runs on, carried forward by the impetus of its own complex narratives and elaborate metaphors, until, every once in a while, the author looks down and sees that he is walking on idealistic air—flying, in other words, as he did not believe it possible to fly but as one so often does in a dream. Sometimes he then falls bathetically into skepticism, but sometimes he does not; sometimes he keeps on flying.

Western Arguments

Reality-Testing

When we turn back to examine our Western common sense regarding dreams and proofs, we might look first at our attitude to our own stories about these matters. Stories demonstrating the reality of dreams dart in and out of the history of Western literature, though often at an oblique angle; they have been taken seriously enough to be suppressed.[117] One has only to glance at Gnosticism, Chrétien de Troyes, and E. T. A. Hoffmann, to say nothing of our surrealists (whom I will discuss in chapters five and six), to realize that any superficial contrast between India and the West on the issue of the reality of dreams is, more precisely, a contrast with only one of the positions taken in Western discourse and philosophy. Arabic sources tell many tales in which a sleeping man awakes to find himself in a situation designed to prove to him that he is dreaming while he is, in fact, awake. Stories of this type were also known in Spain and in China and Japan. But there is, I think, a significant difference of tone between the Indian and Western examples of this genre.[118]

In the first place, when we look at the distribution of the specific theme of the dreamer who takes his dream for real until he awakes or who finds that it *was* real even after he awakes, we begin to see a pattern, a complex *maṇḍala* that has India as its center. The Chinese and Japanese stories were based on tales carried to the East by Indian Buddhists, and the Spanish stories were retellings of tales brought by Islamic traders from India. This is, at heart, an Indian theme. However, it is a theme that serves a different purpose in India and the West. The story of the dream adventure was regarded in the West primarily as an exotic and rather off-beat delicacy, an appetizer to titillate the mind for a while before getting down to serious philosophizing. In India, however, it was the main course, philosophically speaking; it was taken very seriously indeed, as an elusive clue to a real truth. Moreover, this truth was stated far more positively in India than it was in the West. As Roger Caillois remarks of the dream adventure in European romantic literature,

> Very frequently the dream remains a fairy tale that is dispelled by the awakening and to which at times a cumbersome allegorical value is attributed; it has nothing in common with the intellectual complications of the Oriental dream. "It was only a dream," the sleeper cries out upon awakening, occasionally disappointed, occasionally relieved, all according to whether the dream gratified or oppressed him. It is never more than an illusion, which may have been pleasing or distressing, but which the opening of the eyelids suffices to send back into nothingness.[119]

In India, by contrast, the dream adventure often proves the very opposite point; it proves the "nothingness" of the world that we see when we open our eyes, or it proves the substantial reality of the dream itself.

One good reason why such stories about the reality of dreams occupy a less respectable place in Western culture than they do in India can be surmised when we look at the common-sense view that dominates (though it never entirely permeates) Western thought. The empiricists and realists have been quick to label nonempiricists and nonrealists as lunatic dreamers. The leader of this group is Sir Karl Popper, whose reaction to idealism was the typical Western abhorrence of solipsism: "To me, idealism appears absurd, for it also implies something like this: that it is my mind which creates this beautiful world. But I know I am not its Creator. . . . Denying realism amounts to megalomania."[120] Here Popper fails to take into account the possibility (basic to all Indian thinking) that "my mind" and the mind of the "Creator" are one, a basic Indian assumption that we first encountered in chapter three and will meet again in chapter five. A very similar assumption underlies Michael Polanyi's answer (both to solipsism and to Popper):

> Any presumed contact with reality inevitably claims universality. If I, left alone in the world, and knowing myself to be alone, should believe in a fact, I would still claim universal acceptance for it. . . . I may rely on an existing consensus, as a clue to the truth, or else may dissent from it, for my own reasons. In either case my answer will be made with universal intent, saying what I believe to be the truth, and what the consensus ought therefore to be. . . . This position is not solipsistic, since it is based on a belief in an external reality and implies the existence of other persons who can likewise approach the same reality.[121]

As we will see, Polanyi's confidence in the universality of his private truth rests on his faith in the existence of a Power who is part of our minds.

Thus Polanyi argues that even when one is alone one may be confident of an uncorroborated belief. But what of the opposite situation? What happens if a whole group corroborates a delusion? This is the apparent situation in the story of Lavaṇa. It is also, as we shall see, the situation of those scientists who are locked into a Kuhnian paradigm and of the people in Festinger's study of cognitive dissonance who prophesied a doomsday that did not take place:

> The individual believer must have social support. It is unlikely that one isolated believer could withstand the kind of disconfirming evidence we have specified. If, however, the believer is a member of a group of convinced persons who can support one another, we would expect the belief to be maintained and the believers to attempt to proselyte or to persuade nonmembers that the belief is correct.[122]

This was in fact the case with the group that Festinger studied: when their doomsday predictions failed to come true, they did not relinquish their beliefs, nor did they try to hide from public ridicule; instead, they rededicated themselves to proselyting. Festinger remarks upon this syndrome: "Consider the extreme case: if everyone in the whole world believed something, there would be no question at all as to the validity of this belief."[123] It is interesting to compare Festinger's "extreme case" with Polanyi's statement about faith: "If I, left alone in the world, and knowing myself to be alone, should believe in a fact, I would still claim universal acceptance for it."[124] Where Polanyi would maintain his belief despite the group, Festinger would argue that a delusion looks like a truth if enough people believe in it.

But the existence of a group that corroborates an opinion is not, in itself, regarded as sufficient evidence in Western science, though it weighs heavily. Testing is what distinguishes the madman from the mad scientist. Bertrand Russell argued that the inductive method, rather than the weight of group opinion, was the essential element in determining truth: "If not, there is no intellectual difference between sanity and insanity. The lunatic who believes that he is a poached egg is to be condemned solely on the ground that he is in a minority."[125]

In the West we fall back ultimately on the consensus of the group for the verification of phenomena that cannot be tested. Such phenomena include, according to Thomas Kuhn, scientific theories. It was once generally held that scientists were led to change their paradigms when they were faced with disconfirming data; Kuhn has argued, with a qualified success, that scientists hold on to their paradigms despite almost any amount of disconfirming data. The first view involves *bhrama*: sooner or later, the evidence convinces us that the snake is in fact a rope. In Kuhn's view, what is involved is *māyā*: no amount of evidence can convince us that the rope exists. The first view is generally held (especially by scientists) to be scientific; the second is religious. The *Yogavāsiṣṭha* demonstrates that science is useless in addressing the problem of reality.

Yet, when we look more closely at science and religion, we find that their difference is generally a matter of degree: at *some* point, *some* weight of data becomes decisive for most people. At least for some, long practice at eliminating errors eventually leads to an understanding of the truth. Scientists like to think that they have a lower "disconfirmation" threshold than religious believers have, and indeed this may be the case. It may be that scientists are monkeys while theologians are cats; or it may be that scientists address monkey problems while theologians address cat problems.[126]

Kuhn suggests that it is peculiar that so many scientists agree about their findings:

> No wonder, then, that in the early stages of the development of any science different men confronting the same range of phenomena, but not usually all the same particular phenomena, describe and interpret them in different ways. What is surprising, and perhaps also unique in its degree to the field we call science, is that such initial divergences should ever largely disappear.[127]

These differences of opinion are gradually eroded by the pressure of the group—and not just any group:

> The solutions that satisfy [the scientist] may not be merely personal but must instead be accepted as solutions by many. The group that shares them may not, however, be drawn at random from society as a whole, but is rather the well-defined community of the scientist's professional compeers. One of the strongest, if still unwritten, rules of scientific life is the prohibition of appeals to the populace at large in matters scientific.[128]

In other words, it is the Brahmins who supply the authority. The circularity of the scientific authority structure, like all authority structures, is evident when we realize that the authority who validates the solution is a man whose authority is validated by the fact that he has produced solutions the validity of which has been established by authorities who . . . . Once again we enter the phenomenon of mutual feedback; the scientist is the chicken and the test is his egg. Paul Feyerabend has pointed out that the "auxiliary hypothesis of intersubjectivity"—the belief that several scientists see the same thing and therefore establish its validity—underlies scientific authority:

> But this hypothesis is *false*, as is shown by the moon illusion, the phenomenon of fata morgana, the rainbow, haloes, by the many

> microscopic illusions which are so vividly described by Tolansky, by the phenomena of witchcraft (*every* woman reported an incubus to have an ice-cold member), and by numerous other phenomena.[129]

In other words, the whole group may be wrong. Even when they share dreams—or scientific hypotheses—they may all be sharing a false dream.

From the materialist point of view—what the Indians call the *vyavahārika* or practical level—our definitions of reality are functional; they help us to avoid bumping into things. Sir Karl Popper defends his faith in the validity of testing thus:

> The disappointment of some of the expectations with which we once eagerly approached reality plays a most significant part in this procedure. It may be compared with the experience of a blind man who touches, or runs into, an obstacle, and so becomes aware of its existence. *It is through the falsification of our suppositions that we actually get in touch with "reality."* It is the discovery and elimination of our errors which alone constitute that "positive" experience which we gain from reality.[130]

Halfway through the paragraph, reality takes on quotation marks; this is apparently what makes Popper nonnaïve. But these quotations marks do not remain in place for long; nor do they succeed in generating an illusory force field around material objects. The objects are there, and we know it because we bump into them. Science in this sense is very practical.

Everyone knows how to avoid bumping into chairs. But even within the realms of science, the plot begins to thicken when we engage in enterprises more complicated than navigating in drawing rooms, when we begin to hypothesize scientific forces and processes that cannot be measured by radar and sonar. And though there is no scientific problem about validation when people have a negative attitude to material reality (we can tell when people bump into chairs they think are not there), there is a validation problem when people have a positive attitude to ideal reality (when they think they bump into chairs we think are not there). The latter is the situation of Lavaṇa and Gādhi, and it is a situation to which not only Western idealists but Western historians of science, and philosophers, have devoted much attention. The problem arises because, though there may perhaps be a way of testing a real discovery, there is—according to materialist theory—apparently no way of testing an unreal discovery; there is no way of testing a dream. And we would do well to recall that all of our visual perceptions are based on guesses, most of which are seldom if ever tested and some of which cannot be tested. Yet the tale of Lavaṇa demonstrates how one might test—and prove—the validity of an illusion. It may be madness to go on dreaming and never want to wake up, to hang on to a belief and never want to test it; but Lavaṇa does wake up, and he does test his dream.

The use of straightforward tests is sufficient, in R. L. Gregory's opinion, to demonstrate to any sane man the difference between illusion and reality:

> It is sometimes said that "all is illusion." But perception allows us to avoid bumping into things; perceptions are predictive, and check with the behavior or testimony of other people, and with instrumental data. If we call perception illusion, the word "illusion" ceases to have significance. So this is not a profitable gambit.[131]

Yet, as we have seen, when the precise factors that concern Professor Gregory—prediction and the testimony of others—are taken up by more sophisticated exponents of the Indian theory of illusion, such as the *Yogavāsiṣṭha*, that theory does indeed become a "profitable gambit."

The literature of dreams, in Western as well as Eastern traditions, attempts to come to terms with the demands of scientific verification. As Roger Caillois writes, one approach to the problem of the relationship between the dream and the waking world "involves the possibility of bringing back from the world of dreams some object—a scar, a mark, a token—which will be proof of the dream's reality, something solid and tangible which will survive after the illusions of the dream have faded away, to attest to the unimpeachable existence of the world from which it had been brought."[132] The bridle that Bellerophon found after his dream of Pegasus is an example of this "solid and tangible proof"; the huts in Lavaṇa's Untouchable village are another.

Western science would accept the evidence of Bellerophon's bridle but not the evidence of Pindar's description of a bridle as "proof" of a dream. The implication is that the dreamer can project his mental images (his desires, his memories) into his dream but cannot project a physical object (a material bridle) out of his dream. As we have seen, Indians do not share this assumption. But even in the West we have become increasingly aware of the ways in which mental projections influence our perceptions of physical objects. J. S. Bruner and Leo Postman constructed an experiment that demonstrated the power of such a projection. They showed people a series of cards, among which was a red six of spades. Most people simply projected onto the incongruent card their own image of either a black six or a red heart, but under repeated exposure they began to waver, and some of them became quite upset. One subject finally blurted out, "I'm not even sure now what a spade looks like. My God!"[133] So strong is the power of mental projection that it will often completely neutralize the data that we receive from the external world; this is *bhrama*. But when we come to perceive the projection, we may come to question the nature of the actual data—to wonder if we have ever, in fact, seen a spade. This is *māyā*.

Sir Ernst Gombrich has taught us much about the way in which the process of projection applies not only to our manipulation of sense data (as in the case of the red six of spades) but to our experience of art, where "we tend to project life and expression onto the arrested image and supplement from our experience what is not actually present."[134] Projections of this sort appear in India as the reflected or contradictory images (*pratibhāsa*) that cause landscapes that exist in a distant place or in someone's mind to be perceived as if they had come to life before our eyes. Indian and Western theories of projection seem to suggest that we perceive illusion and reality in the same way, a way characterized by memory, hypothesis, and emotion. This view is at variance with that of classical nineteenth-century empiricism; it is a metaphysical rather than a physical approach to reality.

As Thomas Kuhn has demonstrated, for scientists to break out of one paradigm and into another requires the same kind of self-awareness and bootstraps shift of perspective that is required for the dreamer to realize that he is dreaming in order to wake up. It requires a leap. As we saw at the close of chapter one, adults can retain the child's ability to make such a paradigm shift in redefining the reality status of dreams. The process of shifting paradigms is closely akin to the process of religious conversion:

> These facts . . . have most often been taken to indicate that scientists, being only human, cannot always admit their errors, even when confronted with strict proof. I would argue, rather, that in these matters neither proof nor error is at issue. The transfer of allegiance from paradigm to paradigm is a conversion experience that cannot be forced.[135]

This conversion experience often takes place in the middle of the night or even during sleep.[136]

Once the scientist has dreamed his new dream, he is faced with the problem of converting everyone else, just like the people in Festinger's doomsday group. We may find other parallels in the structures of some of the myths of illusion. Many of the myths of the mouth of God, such as the tale of Mārkaṇḍeya falling out of Viṣṇu's mouth or the story of Nārada's transformation, depict highly individual or even alienating or antisocial experiences; so do the initial episodes of the myths of the shared dream, when the hero is still the only one who believes that his dream is real. In these tales the individual must defend his own private vision against society as a whole forever, or at least until he finds proof, either in the actual existence of his dream companion or in some other kind of physical evidence. These myths may be contrasted with the better-known genre of the myths of social charter, the myths of shared experience; in these tales the group reminds itself of events that happened to it as a whole and became the basis for its existence as a group.[137]

The transition from what Kuhn calls extraordinary science (the discovery of a new paradigm) to normal science (the period in which all scientists in a given field are working within that once-new paradigm) is the transition from the solitary dreamer (the man who has fallen, alone, out of the mouth of God) to the group that shares the dream (the myth of social charter).

Arthur Koestler likened scientists to sleepwalkers acting out their dreams. In the Egyptian universe, eclipses were regarded as the enactment of cosmic, mythic tragedies, "But these tragedies were, like those in a dream, both real and not; inside his box or womb, the dreamer felt fairly safe."[138] That is, if challenged, the scientist could always draw back and say, "It's only a dream." Since Galileo, however, scientists have come out of their boxes and insisted that their dreams are real, not merely abstract speculations on what might be real. The shift from one paradigm to another is then not just the shift from one dream to another dream but the shift from dreaming to waking up. Yet we have seen the problem involved in any attempt to prove that one is finally awake.

Scientists since Galileo have claimed to be constantly awakening from a series of dreams; this process is called progress. In this view we do not merely swap one dream for another but continue to wake up from each dream; we do not feel that each subsequent dream is simply a linear variation on its predecessors but that each new dream encompasses all the others. In all the centuries since Galileo until our own, each new scientific paradigm has been presented as a full and final awakening: now at last we were no longer dreaming. But the twist has come with the more recent paradigms, those of Einstein and Heisenberg and Gödel, who have argued that we are, in fact, dreaming after all and that the very nature of the process of scientific observation makes it impossible for us ever to wake up. At last we are in the position that Plato and the Indian sages argued for: we are dreaming still, but now we *know* that we are dreaming. The transition from pre-Galilean to Galilean to post-Einsteinian science is not, therefore, a transition from science as dream to science as waking and then back to science as dream. Just as adults who believe their dreams are real are not the same as young children who believe their dreams are real, so, too, the scientists who are now aware that they are dreaming know that they are still capable of getting closer and closer to the state of awakening, though they can never reach it. They can approach, but not reach, the point where the subtle awareness of mistakes (*bhrama*) leads to the awareness of illusion (*māyā*).

Michael Polanyi's thought represents a kind of synthesis of the views of Popper and Kuhn. Though Polanyi holds, like Kuhn, that the scientist in some sense dreams the world, he also holds, like Popper, that the world is out there and that the scientist then goes out and finds it—and finds that it is, in fact, as he had dreamed it. This extraordinary coincidence is made possible by the fact, always implied by Polanyi, that the mind of the scientist and the form of the universe are made in the same way—indeed, probably by the same Power. The dream and the physical reality correspond, not only in general structure but even in minute detail, because both the structure and the detail are made by that same overarching Power. If the universe is, in a sense, made of mind, then, even if science remains within the realm of mind, it is in direct contact with the world. The universe is a dream that we share with God.

We must beware, therefore, of placing too much faith in the tests that scientists carry out after formulating their hypotheses; for we learn, both from Indian texts like the *Yogavāsiṣṭha* and from historians of science like Thomas Kuhn and Paul Feyerabend, that these tests are ultimately beset by the same uncertainties that devastate all mental perceptions of the world. Tests, too, fall within the range not only of *bhrama* (which many scientists admit) but even of *māyā* (which most scientists do not admit). The characters in the *Yogavāsiṣṭha* go about systematically proving their unrealities, and they succeed, just as scientists succeed: they make predictions that contradict their own common sense, and they test them and find them valid. But the lesson that the *Yogavāsiṣṭha* teaches us is that these tests do not prove anything at all, because common sense, the arena in which the game is played, constantly recedes.

The Receding Frame

The technique of the tale within a tale, like nested Chinese boxes or Russian dolls, allows the storyteller to dramatize the closely related theme of the dream within the dream:

> Someone, in a dream, wakes up—or rather believes that he has awakened, although he continues to dream—and now lies expecting another awakening, which this time may be real but may also be as illusionary as the first. In this way he will be transported from one dream to another, from one awakening to another, without ever being absolutely certain whether he has finally arrived at the true awakening, the one that will restore him to the world of reality. . . . Since, at every moment of the dream, the sleeper is unaware of the fact that he is dreaming, and is even convinced that he is awake, it is clear that there can never be a moment in which a person who believes himself to be awake does not have to entertain the suspicion of a doubt that he might perhaps at that time actually be dreaming. This problem has benefitted from a long and complex philosophical history.[139]

Stories about dreams, like scientific proofs, often deliberately obfuscate the understructure of common sense in such a way as to leave the reader uncertain which is the real level. The joker in the deck of unreality-testing is the level of the frames: *within* the dream or vision it is always possible to prove that something is real, but all the author need do is to point out that the *whole* dream is an unreal part of something else, and all subproofs are then rendered irrelevant. One cannot win the game of unreality-testing, for it is always possible that someone will come along and change all the rules. The reality of the world is not a falsifiable hypothesis. Even when scientific principles are applied inside a paradigm, faith encompasses the paradigm on the outermost layer—or, rather, on what appears, at any given moment, to be the outermost layer. Faith can never be grounded. Not only can we never know when we have awakened from the last frame; we can never know how we might go about trying to awaken from it even if we did know that we were in it.

As we have seen, the hypothesis "This is real" can be falsified (when we wake up) but not verified, while the hypothesis "This is a dream" can be verified (again, when we awaken) but not falsified. To this extent, if we accept falsification as the only reasonable criterion (as Popper would have us do), we are doomed to realism, to the only falsifiable hypothesis. Although one's mistakes may be subjected—successfully—to scientific falsification, this test does not verify or falsify the reality of the life of the scientist (the Brahmin or king) who is inspired to seek that proof. The extreme form of Indian idealism regards tests such as Lavaṇa and Gādhi carried out as a mere arbitrary construction of reality, the conjuring-up of just one more set of mental images to set against the given set of mental images. When Gādhi was finally convinced by the report of his Brahmin guest and the testimony of the Untouchables and the words of the people in the city of the Kīras, he thought his dream was real. But then Viṣṇu came and told him not only that his dream was *not* real but, indeed, that the people who had corroborated his dream, who had witnessed his test—the Brahmin guest, the Untouchables, and the Kīras—were all equally unreal. By implication, Lavaṇa's second trip to the Untouchable village did not really prove that he had been there before, since that trip, too, might have been a dream—this time a dream that his courtiers happened to share. (This is a view of scientific method that might be regarded as an extreme reduction of the attitude of Thomas Kuhn.) The more moderate and realistic form of Indian philosophy, on the other hand, regards the testing as an actual attempt to seek data whose existence is predicted by the hypothesis, data that either do or do not exist; and whether they do or do not exist is a question that will be decided one way or another by the experiment. (This is a view of scientific method that bears the same general relationship to the theories of Sir Karl Popper that the first view bears to those of Kuhn.) In the case of Lavaṇa and Gādhi, the hypothesis is that the visionary experiences actually did take place.

It is impossible to verify the reality of the scientist verifying the test; it is also impossible to verify the reality of the lives of us who listen to his story. This must be taken on faith, and the *Yogavāsiṣṭha* argues for such faith, though it also argues against it and implies that there is no reason to believe that our lives are real. It presents both the argument for the destruction of faith and the argument for the creation of faith. The original complacency of Lavaṇa and Gādhi is undermined; they are taught that reality is not as real as they thought it was. This was the message of the myths of the mouth of God, too. But in the outer frame, Rāma is taught that reality is realer than he thought it was, or at least that it can survive in a contingent fashion; he is convinced of the necessity of carrying on with a life whose intrinsic vanity he has, correctly, perceived. This was the message of some of the myths of the king and the Untouchables. The first argument, undermining the reality of waking life, is *mokṣa*-oriented; the second, affirming the reality of dreams, is *saṃsāra*-oriented.

The shock of enlightenment comes when the text suddenly changes the lens on the telescope through which the story is being viewed, drawing back and bracketing (as the phenomenologists say) the entire action that has led us to suspend our disbelief. A striking example of the way in which the frame can be removed from a test of reality in order to negate everything that has preceded it is provided (unconsciously) by Sigmund Freud. Having stated his hypothesis that all dreams are wish-fulfillments, he begins to defend himself against his critics, among whom are several of his patients:

> A contradiction to my theory of dreams produced by another of my woman patients (the cleverest of all my dreamers) was resolved more simply, but upon the same pattern: namely that the non-fulfilment of one wish meant the fulfilment of another. One day I had been explaining to her that dreams are fulfilments of wishes. Next day she brought me a dream in which she was travelling down with her mother-in-law to the place in the country where they were to spend their holidays together. Now I knew that she had violently rebelled against the idea of spending the summer near her mother-in-law and that a few days earlier she had successfully avoided the propinquity she dreaded by engaging rooms in a far distant resort. And now her dream had undone the solution she had wished for; was this not the sharpest possible contradiction of my theory that in dreams wishes are fulfilled? No doubt; and it was only necessary to follow the dream's logical consequence in order to arrive at its interpretation. The dream showed that I was wrong. *Thus it was her wish that I might be wrong, and her dream showed that wish fulfilled.*[140]

Within the myth or dream, reality is defined by a consistent set of rules, in which one may build up increasing confidence. But when the author interjects himself into the scene, applying the same rules but on another level of reality, one that encompasses and supersedes the previous one ("It was only a dream" or "It was her wish that I might be wrong"), the inner scene is exposed in all of its softness. The memory of a non-wish-fulfilling dream dreamt *before* we encountered Freud might be taken as counterevidence; but this *Freud* cannot provide, because anyone who tells him a dream is telling it to *him*. We might do it, of course; but now we have read Freud . . . .

In fact, the Freudian frames recede still farther. After remarking on the relentlessness with which his patients continue to produce "counter-wish dreams" precisely in order to stymie him, Freud comments:

> During the last few years similar "counter-wish dreams" have repeatedly been reported to me by people who have heard me lecturing, as a reaction to first making the acquaintance of my "wishful" theory of dreams. . . . Indeed, it is to be expected that the same thing will happen to some of the readers of the present book: they will be quite ready to have one of their wishes frustrated in a dream if only their wish that I may be wrong can be fulfilled.[141]

Here Freud leaps right off the page, out of the frame of the story that he is telling, into the life of the reader. There is no frame that Freud cannot ultimately pull back far enough to produce a focus that will validate his hypothesis. This is science at its very softest.[142]

Sir Karl Popper has nothing but scorn for the problem of the receding dream frame:

> Common sense is unquestionably on the side of realism; there are, of course, even before Descartes—in fact ever since Heraclitus—a few hints of doubt whether or not our ordinary world is perhaps just our dream. But even Descartes and Locke were realists. . . . In its simplest form, idealism says: the world (which includes my present audience) is just my dream. Now it is clear that this theory (though you will know it is false) is not refutable: whatever you, my audience, may do to convince me of your reality—talking to me, or writing a letter, or perhaps kicking me—it cannot possibly assume the force of a refutation; for I would continue to say that I am dreaming that you are talking to me, or that I received a letter, or felt a kick. . . . Of course, this argument for realism is logically no more conclusive than any other, because I may merely dream that I am using descriptive language and arguments; but this argument for realism is nevertheless strong and *rational*. . . . This, of course, does not refute an idealist, who would reply that we are only dreaming that we have refuted idealism. . . . I do not think it worth pursuing these exercises in cleverness; and I repeat that, until some new arguments are offered, I shall naïvely accept realism.[143]

Naïve or nonnaïve, Popper is not naïve enough to fall into the trap that Freud set for himself; Popper *knows* when he is pulling back from the receding frame and knows also when an idealistic opponent can pull the frame out from under him. Yet, like the Bellman in *The Hunting of the Snark* ("What I tell you three times is true"), Popper hopes that, by affirming again and again that he does not *care* if the frame recedes from him, he will convince us that it has not, in fact, receded. By defining reality *only* in terms of value, he sidesteps the ontological issue; he shuts his eyes and hopes that the problem of the receding frame will recede.

Yet Popper does trip himself up in the inward-spiraling loops of his own ropes when he tries to tie down his idealistic opponents. Though he admits that "Common sense typically breaks down when applied to itself" and that "The attempt to establish (rather than reduce) by these means the meaning (or truth) [of certain theories] leads to an infinite regress," [144] he insists on making that attempt himself:

> The relativistic thesis that the framework *cannot* be criticially discussed is a thesis which *can* be critically discussed and which does not stand up to criticism. I have dubbed this thesis The Myth of the Framework, and I have discussed it on various occasions. I regard it as a logical and philosophical mistake. (I remember that Kuhn does not like my usage of the word 'mistake'; but this dislike is merely part of his relativism.) [145]

Popper's maneuver in the final sentence of this statement—itself a fine example of frame reasoning—is strongly reminiscent of Freud's attempt to extricate himself from his "clever" patient. Popper goes on to argue that, although we are indeed prisoners of our theoretical frameworks, "if we try, we can break out of our framework at any time. Admittedly, we shall find ourselves again in a framework, but it will be a better and roomier one; and we can at any moment break out of it again." [146] How are we to break out? Popper's suggestion takes the form of a mixed metaphor: "This is how we lift ourselves by our bootstraps out of the morass of our ignorance; how we throw a rope into the air and then swarm up it—if it gets any purchase, however precarious, on any little twig." [147] Bootstrap-lifting is precisely what the Indian mystics are trying to do with their paradoxical stories; and who but the Indians would throw a rope (or a snake?) into the air and try to climb up it? It is typical of Popper to suggest that this might be accomplished only if the rope caught on a twig; the whole point of the Indian metaphor is that one must climb up on thin air—on faith.

Kuhn recognized the inevitable circularity that tends to trap us within a paradigm, even as he recognized the fact that we do, in fact, break out; but, unlike Popper, he argued that it was persuasion of an emotional rather than a rational nature that catapulted one out of the frame.[148] As usual, Paul Feyerabend takes the Kuhnian stance to a mischievous extreme:

> How can we discover the kind of world we presuppose when proceeding as we do? The answer is clear: we cannot discover it from the *inside*. We need an *external* standard of criticism, we need a set of alternative assumptions or, as these assumptions will be quite general, constituting, as it were, an entire alternative world, we need a dream-world in order to discover the features of the real world we think we inhabit (and which may actually be just another dream-world).[149]

The dream is what helps us to crash through the frame of apparent reality—the last visible frame—even though the dream, too, is a frame, and not the last frame, either. This is Feyerabend's hotheaded counterattack against Popper's cool assumption that he can simply reason himself out of the final frame.

The problem of breaking out of the paradigm is the problem of watching yourself having an illusion; as Gombrich puts it, "I cannot make use of an illusion and watch it."[150] Douglas Hofstadter explains why this is so:

> It is important to see the distinction between perceiving oneself and transcending oneself. You can gain visions of yourself in all sorts of ways—in a mirror, in photos or movies, on tape, through the descriptions of others, by getting psychoanalyzed, and so on. But you cannot break out of your own skin and be on the outside of yourself. . . . This is reminiscent of the humorous paradoxical question, "Can God make a stone so heavy that he can't lift it?"[151]

In India, as we will see in chapter five, God *can* make a stone that he cannot lift, and He can dream a dream from which He cannot awaken. Moreover, in India, as we learned from the tale of Gādhi, it is possible to watch onself having an illusion.

The problem arises when one tries to watch not the dreamer but the *dream*, not as Rāma watched Gādhi, but as Rāma watched Katañja (the Untouchable as whom Gādhi was reborn in his dream). Dement was aware of the pitfalls in his attempts to obtain "direct verbal descriptions of ongoing REM periods":

> Would the dreamer narrate the activity? Or would he speak only as one of the characters in the dream fantasy? Is the whole idea as absurd as asking an actor to describe a scene while he is in the middle of acting it out?[152]

It is impossible to be inside the dream and outside the dream at the same time; yet we *are* inside and outside, in another sense, every time we dream. The best way to express this paradox, perhaps, is to imagine what it might be like to live the dream and to tell it at the same time, and this is what the Indian myths attempt to do.

The ever-widening circles of the receding frames never seem to end; they indicate, though of course they do not reach, infinity. Zeno's paradox is the paradox of the receding frame: one can jump half way to the shore, then half of the remaining distance, and then half of that . . . , but one never reaches the shore. You can, however, get *closer and closer*, and this is what the scientist with his ever-more-refined guesses, and the theologian with his ever-more-subtle metaphors, hopes to do. In the myths, the adding-on of circle after circle produces a kind of obfuscation effect: you wear out your listener until he thinks that you have come to a conclusion, though in fact the problem remains unsolved forever. In the Upaniṣads, this technique is both used and mocked. When the sage Yājñavalkya is asked, "How many gods are there?", he answers, at first, "Three thousand three hundred and six"; then, pressed further, he reduces the number to thirty-three, six, three, two, one and a half (!), and one.[153] But when Gargī asks him what water is woven on (wind), and what wind is woven on (the atmosphere), and so on, through the sun, moon, stars, gods, and, finally, *brahman*, and when she asks him what the worlds of *brahman* are woven on, he replies, "Gargī, do not question too much, or your head will fall off."[154] There is a pedagogic point in pressing on toward the infinite; the Zen Buddhists perfected this technique of setting the mind in motion toward something that it could not, by definition, ever reach. But if one actually tries to reach it, one's head falls off.[155]

The attempt to approach infinity, to produce the illusion that one has described infinity, drives us inevitably into narrative, into parable and metaphor. James Joyce's famous description of hell suggests infinity in this way: There is a mountain of sand a million miles high and a million miles broad and a million miles thick; and at the end of every million years a little bird carries away in its beak a tiny grain of that sand; and when the bird has carried it all away, not even one instant of eternity could be said to have ended.[156]

The infinity of space may be approached in a similar manner, through a visual metaphor that suggests what it cannot possibly represent. The Hindu cosmos is a series of receding frames (see figure 4), circles within circles, expressed as a series of concentric oceans of various fluids (salt water, milk, honey, and so forth). This arrangement apparently exasperated Thomas Macaulay, who felt that his government should not "countenance, at public expense, . . . geography made up of seas of treacle and seas of butter."[157] But, as Diana Eck has pointed out, India has a kind of "systematic geography" in place of our systematic theology. It is not surprising that there should be an analogy between cosmology and the concentric loops of narrative structure, since both geography and mythology map the world and thus, either implicitly or explicitly, order it.[158]

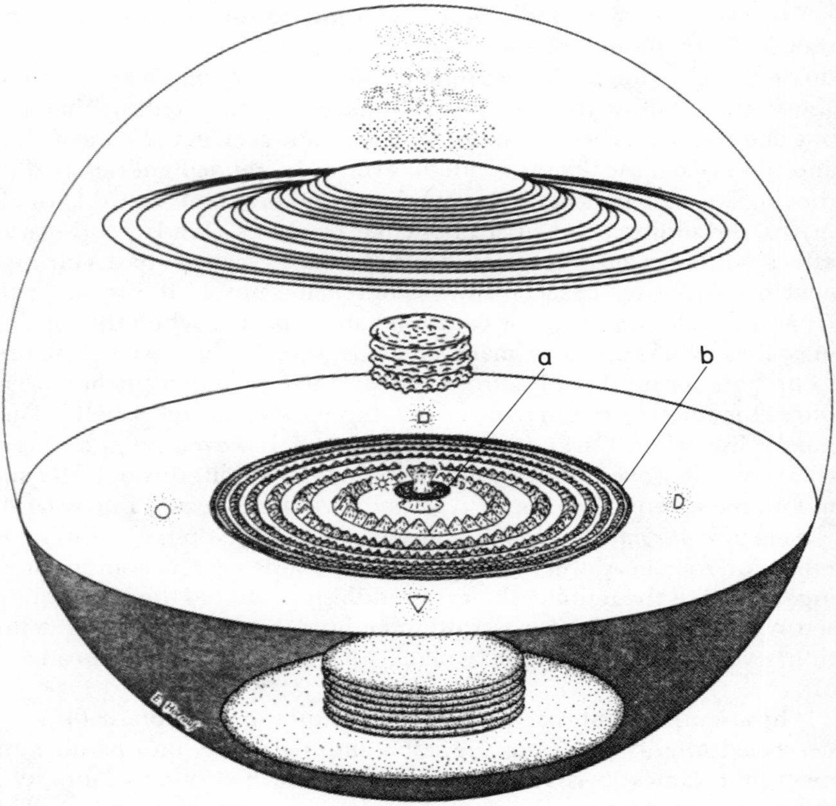

Figure 4. One Kind of Indian Universe
a = Mount Meru, the *axis mundi*
b = Lokāloka, "World-non-World," the encircling mountain

This chart includes many other features, such as something that resembles a stack of flapjacks on the bottom, a cupcake suspended in midair above the world beneath a flying saucer, a swarm of mosquitoes above the flying saucer, and various triangles, squares, crescent moons, and suns scattered here and there. These all represent physical and spiritual dimensions of the Buddhist cosmos that are not relevant to my present argument. The points I wish to make are limited to the general complexity of the scheme and the relationship between Mount Meru and the World-non-World range. This chart, which is part of Paula Richman's Ph.D. dissertation, "Religious Rhetoric in *Maṇimekalai*" (University of Chicago, 1982), is the result of Ms. Richman's collaboration with Eugene Hoerauf, cartographer, Department of Geography, Western Washington University. I am grateful to Ms. Richman, who holds the copyright on this chart, for permission to reproduce it here.

Moreover, the charts of cosmology (like the implicit charts of the narrative) offer a spatial representation of time as well as space.[159] It is our notions of time that are most violently assaulted in the tales of illusion, perhaps because we tend to think that time is irreversible, while space is not. Long before Einstein suggested that we think of time as a fourth dimension, Indians mapped time onto their mythological globe and then flattened it out, with the inevitable distortions, in a story.

The outermost circle of the Indian cosmology is a ring of mountains called World-non-World (Lokāloka), the point where the world and whatever is not the world meet. This is a boundary that is not a boundary; it is a spot where the map lapses into what in our code would be a series of elipsis dots. This is the moment when centrifugal force takes over, when the drone of the great numbers begins to make reason doze, and we *feel* the stirrings of infinity.

The ring of mountains named World-non-World is a paradox that allows us to stop drawing circles. It is a statement that spits in the face of anyone trying to get to the end of the system, the equivalent of the threat that your head will fall off. Such paradoxes always proliferate on the boundaries of cultural systems, as Don Handelman has pointed out:

> As the limits of such systems are approached, there is a radical increase in paradoxes of cognition and perception—mechanisms which permit the system to be self-limiting, and so systemic, while hiding this knowledge from itself. The boundaries of such cultural systems are composed of such paradoxes, which cannot be resolved in accordance with the underlying logic of the taken-for-granted features of everyday life.[160]

The paradoxes that bound such systems may be visual or verbal. Sometimes they involve a peculiar twist or strange loop, an inversion, as we will see in chapter five. Sometimes, however, they involve nothing more than a statement of simple faith: "God exists" or "I think, therefore I am." If we try too hard to puzzle it all out, we trip over our own feet, as Gargī did. It either happens to you or it doesn't. And to reach the spot from which it can happen to you, you must pass through common sense and go beyond it, just as one must pass through a concept of *māyā* as the force that empties the material world to the concept of *māyā* that fills the mental world (chapter three) and as one must also pass through the ten-year-old's concept of the dream as unreal to the adult's concept of the dream as real (chapter one). Common sense is the star by which we navigate the shoals of *bhrama*; faith is what steers us across the ocean of *māyā*.

5 Ontology in Narrative: More Tales from the *Yogavāsiṣṭha*

When we ask our own questions of Indian tales of dreams, we may try to concentrate on the epistemology of the problem—the question of how people think about the world—only to find ourselves drawn back over and over again to the ontology of the problem—the question of what the world really is. That is because the two problems are in fact a single problem; epistemology is the shadow double of ontology. The Indian texts treat it as a single problem from the very start; they ask how our minds affect the world and how the world exists in our minds. They take the quandary of nested dreams (the question of whether we have awakened from the last of a series of dreams) and twist it in upon itself to present a more baffling problem, the enigma of the dreamer dreamt: If we cannot determine whether we are the final dreamer, in the outermost frame, can we determine whether or not we are part of someone else's dream, part of the dream of the dreamer in the next frame outside ours? Although this question is not directly posed by the myths of Lavaṇa and Gādhi, it is in a sense implicit in them. For if we look at the story from the viewpoint of Lavaṇa, for instance, it is apparent that he might well wonder not only whether he has finished waking up from a series of dreams (first that he is an Untouchable and now that he is a king), but whether he is not the king in the dream of a Brahmin who dreamt he was a king. If we are not sure that we are in the outermost frame of a nested dream, we cannot be sure that we are the final dreamer.

Indian Texts and Arguments

One myth in the *Yogavāsiṣṭha* tackles this dilemma more directly and powerfully than any text I know. This myth builds our minds—the minds of us, the audience, as we listen—into the story, and it does so by drawing us deeper and deeper into the tale within the tale. In this way it embodies, as well as talks about, the paradox of the author who is a character in someone else's story, the dreamer who is a figure in someone else's dream.

The Monk Who Met the People in His Dream

Once upon a time there was a monk who was inclined to imagine things rather a lot. He would meditate and study all the time, and fast for days on end. One day, this fancy came to him: "Just for fun, I will experience what happens to ordinary people." As soon as he had this idea, his thought somehow took the form of another man, and that man wished for an identity and a name, even though he was just made of thought. And by pure accident, as when a crow happens to be under a tree when a palm fruit falls from it and hits him, he thought, "I am Jīvaṭa." This dream man, Jīvaṭa, enjoyed himself for a long time in a town made in a dream. There he drank too much and fell into a heavy sleep, and in his dream he saw a Brahmin who read all day long. One day, that Brahmin fell asleep, worn out from the day's work, but those daily activities were still alive within him, like a tree inside a seed, and so he saw himself, in a dream, as a prince. One day that prince fell asleep after a heavy meal, and in his dream he saw himself as a king who ruled many lands and indulged in every sort of luxury. One day that king fell asleep, having gorged himself on his every desire, and in his dream he saw himself as a celestial woman. That woman fell into a deep sleep in the languor that followed making love, and she saw herself as a doe with darting eyes. That doe one day fell asleep and dreamed that she was a clinging vine, because she had been accustomed to eating vines; for animals dream, too, and they always remember what they have seen and heard.

The vine saw herself as a bee that used to buzz among the vines; the bee fell in love with a lotus in a lotus pond and one day became so intoxicated by the lotus sap he drank that his wits became numb; and just then an elephant came to that pond and trampled the lotus, and the bee, still attached to the lotus, was crushed with it on the elephant's tusk. As the bee looked at the elephant, he saw himself as an elephant in rut. That elephant in rut fell into a deep pit and became the favorite elephant of a king. One day the elephant was cut to pieces by a sword in battle, and as he went to his final resting place he saw a swarm of bees hovering over the sweet ichor that oozed from his temples, and so the elephant became a bee again. The bee returned to the lotus pond and was trampled under the foot of an elephant, and just then he noticed a goose beside him in the pond, and so he became a goose. That goose moved through other births, other wombs, for a long time, until one day, when he was a goose in a flock of other geese, he realized that, being a goose, he was the same as the swan of Brahmā, the Creator. Just as he had this thought, he was shot by a hunter and he died, and then he was born as the swan of Brahmā.

One day the swan saw the god Rudra, and he thought, with sudden certainty, "I am Rudra." Immediately that idea was reflected like an image in a mirror, and he took on the form of Rudra. This Rudra indulged in every pleasure that entered his mind, living in the palace of Rudra and attended by Rudra's servants. But the Rudra that he had become had a special power of knowledge, and in his mind he could see every single one of his former experiences. He was amazed by the hundred dreams he had had, and he said to himself, "How wonderful! This complicated illusion fools everyone; what is unreal seems to be real, like water in a desert that turns out to be a mirage. I am something that can be thought, and I have been thought. There happened to be a soul that, by chance, became a monk in some universe, and he experienced what he had been thinking about: he became Jīvaṭa. But because Jīvaṭa admired Brahmins, he saw himself as a Brahmin; and since the Brahmin had thought about princes all the time, he became a prince. And since that prince was inclined to do things in order to run a kingdom, he became a king; and because the king was full of lust, he became a celestial woman. And that fickle woman was so jealous of the beautiful eyes of a doe that she became a doe; and the doe became a vine that she had noticed, and the vine saw herself as a bee that she had observed for a long time, and the bee was trampled under the feet of an elephant that he had seen, and he wandered in and out of a series of rebirths. At the end of the round of a hundred rebirths is Rudra, and I am Rudra, I am he, the one who stands in the flux of rebirths where everyone is fooled by his own mind. For my amusement, I will raise up all those creatures who are my own rebirths, and I will look at them, and by giving them the ability to look at the matter as it really is, I will make them unite into one."

When Rudra had decided on this, he went to that universe where the monk was sleeping in his monastery, like a corpse. Joining his mind to the monk's mind, Rudra woke him up; and then the monk realized the error he had made (in believing his life as Jīvaṭa to be real). And when the monk looked at Rudra, who was the monk himself and was also made of Jīvaṭa and the others, he was amazed, though one who was truly enlightened would not have found cause for amazement. Then Rudra and the monk went, the two of them together, to a certain place in a corner of the space of the mind where Jīvaṭa had been reborn, and then they saw him asleep, unconscious, still holding a sword in his hand: the corpse of Jīvaṭa. Joining their minds to his mind, they woke him up, and then, though they were one, they had three forms: Rudra and Jīvaṭa and the monk. Though they were awake, they did not seem to be awake; they were amazed, and yet not amazed, and they stood there in silence for a moment, like images painted in a picture.

Then all three of them went through the sky to the place, echoing in the empty air, where the Brahmin had been reborn, and there they saw the Brahmin in his house, asleep with his wife, the Brahmin lady, clasping him around his neck. They joined their minds to his mind and woke him up, and they all stood there, overcome with amazement. Then they went to the place where the king had been reborn, and they awakened him with their mind, and then they wandered through the other rebirths until they reached the swan of Brahmā. And at that moment they all united together and became Rudra, a hundred Rudras in one.

Then they were all awakened by Rudra, and they all rejoiced and looked upon one another's rebirths, seeing illusion for what it was. Then Rudra said, "Now go back to your own places and enjoy yourselves there with your families for a while, and then come back to me. And at doomsday, all of us, the bands of creatures who are part of me, will go to the final resting place." And Rudra vanished, and Jīvaṭa and the Brahmin and the others all went back to their own places with their own families; but after a while they will wear out their bodies and will unite again back in the world of Rudra.[1]

This story is a highly sophisticated variant of a much-loved Indo-European folk motif, which includes the story of Chicken-Licken (who told Henny-Penny who told Foxy-Loxy . . . that the sky was falling) and The House That Jack Built. The theme also appears in European literature as the motif of "Magic: Man Magically Made to Believe Himself Bishop, Archbishop, and Pope," otherwise known as Stith Thompson's Motif D 2041.5.[2]

We have already encountered a more specifically Indian reflection of this theme in the variant of the Hariścandra story, in which the king dreamed that he was reborn many times as many things. Indeed, like the theme of which the Hariścandra story is an example (the king among the Untouchables), the tale of the chain of rebirths is a kind of set piece in India. A shorter myth, though with a longer chain of rebirths, appears elsewhere in the *Yogavāsiṣṭha*:

An ascetic named Long Asceticism [Dīrghatapas] died, and his wife committed suicide. One of their two sons, named Puṇya [Merit], was immune to grief, but the other son, named Pāvana [Purifying], was not. To assuage Pāvana's grief, Puṇya pointed out that, if Pāvana wished to be consistent in his mourning, he must mourn not only for his recently deceased father and mother but for all the parents he had had in his other lives, and Puṇya reeled off the list: Pāvana had been a deer, a goose, a tree, a lion, a fish, a monkey, a prince, a crow, an elephant, a donkey, a dog, a bird, a fig tree, a termite, a rooster, a Brahmin, a partridge, a horse, a Brahmin again, a worm, a fly, a crane, a birch tree, an ant, a scorpion, a tribal hunter [Pulinda], and a bee. Puṇya added that he himself could

> clearly recall his own births as a parrot, a frog, a sparrow, a Pulinda, a tree, a camel, a lovebird, a king, a tiger, a vulture, a crocodile, a lion, a quail, a king, and the son of a teacher named Śaila. [See plate 12.][3]

Difficult as it is to tell when people of another culture are joking or serious, it does seem that there is at least an element of humor in Pāvana's list. For Hindus were so familiar with the motif of the chain of rebirths that they could poke fun at it, just as they could satirize the theme of the double universe in the Hindi tale of the pot, recounted in chapter three. Whether or not they believe in it, Indians have a joking relationship with illusion. The theme of the dream of the chain of rebirth was mocked by the poet Rājaśekhara in his play *Karpūramañjarī*. A conversation takes place, at the start of act three, between a love-sick king and his jester.

> KING: I am thinking about a vision I saw in my sleep.
> JESTER: Tell me about it.
> KING: I thought a beautiful girl stood within my field of vision, even within the range of my hand, as I lay on my bed. I grabbed for the end of her sari, but she went away leaving the sari in my hand, and then my sleep vanished too.
> JESTER: [*Aside*] I should think it would! [*Aloud*] You know, I had a vision last night, too.
> KING: What was your vision?
> JESTER: I dreamt last night that I fell asleep by the Ganges and was washed away by her waters and absorbed by a cloud.
> KING: How amazing!
> JESTER: The cloud rained me into the ocean, and the oysters absorbed me and I became an enormous pearl. I was a drop of cloud-water in sixty-four oysters in succession, and finally I became a perfect pearl. All of the oysters were fished out of the water, and a merchant bought me for a hundred thousand pieces of gold.
> KING: What a wonderful vision!
> JESTER: The merchant had the jeweler drill a hole through me—that hurt a bit—and then I was strung with the other sixty-three pearls to make a necklace priced at a million pieces of gold. The merchant—who was named Sāgaradatta [Gift from the Sea]—went to King Vajrāyudha, in Kanauj, and sold the necklace to him for ten million pieces of gold. The king put the necklace on the neck of his favorite wife, and at midnight he began to make love to her. But her breasts were so big and hard that I was hurt [by the pressure of the king against her body], and so I awoke.
> KING: You knew that my vision, in which I met the woman who is as dear to me as my very breath of life, was not real

> [*na satyam*], and so you tried to drive it away with your countervision.[4]

The king dreams a classic erotic dream and wakes up just as he strips the woman, holding her dress in her hand—but the dress is not there when he wakes up. His dream is *not* real; the king acknowledges this. The jester then interprets the king's dream as a monk would do, and he brings the king down to earth by presenting him with a fun-house-mirror distortion of a dream of rebirth. He tells first of a dream within a dream (for he dreams that he falls asleep) and then of a dream of transmigration. The king keeps expressing amazement, as people do when they are told of dreams that come true; but apparently he is just as amazed at the high price brought by the pearl as at the fact that the jester became a pearl at all. (The term for pearl, *muktā*, may also be a pun on *mukta*, the released soul or soul that has reached *mokṣa*.) The theme of the pain or suffering that causes awakening or enlightenment appears here as a satire on the moment of awakening from the orgasmic dream: the sexual climax (not of the jester/pearl, but of the king of Kanauj) causes pain, not pleasure; the pearl is squashed between the woman's breasts. Thus the jester mocks both the theme of suffering (for it also hurts him when a hole is drilled in the pearl) and the theme of the chain of rebirths, in order to show the king how ridiculous it is to pay any attention to your dreams.

But the story of the monk who dreamed of the hundred Rudras differs from the usual varieties of this theme in at least two important ways: instead of piling up barnyard animals or clergymen, it piles up nested figments of the imagination. And instead of piling them up in a line, it piles them up in a rope that snakes back in upon itself.

The story of the monk's dream, like all of the stories in the *Yogavāsiṣṭha*, is told by Vasiṣṭha to Rāma, and Rāma asks Vasiṣṭha a number of questions. These questions elicit both explicit discussions of the metaphysical implications of the text and supplementary episodes that explain some of the events in the basic story (just as the tale of Lavaṇa's imaginary consecration helped to explain his experience among the Untouchables). For example:

> Rāma said, "How did Jīvaṭa and the Brahmin and the other forms that the monk imagined become real? How can an object of the imagination be real?" Vasiṣṭha said, "The reality of the imagination is only partial; do not take it for something entirely real. What isn't there, isn't there. Yet the true nature of what is seen in a dream or visualized by the imagination exists at all times. Everything exists in a corner of the mind. . . . A person sees a dream as if it were a solid, hard thing, and then from that dream he falls back into another

> dream, and from that into yet another dream, and each time it appears hard and solid."[5]

Elsewhere Vasiṣṭha gives a different explanation of the monk's dream:

> Then Rāma asked, "What became of the hundred Rudras? *Were* they all Rudras, or weren't they? And how could a hundred minds be made from a single mind? How could they be made by that Rudra who was himself made in someone's dream?" Vasiṣṭha replied, "The monk visualized a hundred bodies in a hundred dreams. But all those forms in the dream *were*, in fact, Rudra, a hundredfold Rudra. For those who have removed the veil from reality can imagine things so precisely that those mental perceptions are actually experienced. And because of the omnipresence of the universal soul, something that is experienced in a particular way and in a particular place by a mind with true understanding will actually come into existence in that way at that very place."[6]

On the one hand, the text seems to say, all the things that we think are real are only parts of a dream—our dream, or someone else's dream. On the other hand, there *is* a reality in dreams, for the things that we imagine or dream are reflections of some reality, which does exist at all times and in all places and happens to get into *our* minds "by accident," like the accident that makes the monk think that he is Jīvaṭa. In this view, mental images are reflections of an underlying reality; there *was* a Jīvaṭa, and the monk dreamt of him; it remained then only for Rudra to find the Jīvaṭa that the monk had dreamt of and to introduce them to each other. Though the monk dreamt of a hundred people, those people did exist as a part of the god Rudra. Yet the text also implies that the monk had the power to dream them into existence from his mind upward, all the way up the line from the monk to the swan to Rudra; and Rudra had the power to think them all into existence as part of himself, from his mind downward, all the way from the swan to the monk. The text tells us that all the people in the dream are part of Rudra, physically; and it also says that they are part of his mind, his dream. These are not contradictions. For Rudra to think of something is for him both to make it exist and to find that it has always existed as part of him. These two kinds of creation—making and finding—are the same, for in both cases the mind—or the Godhead—imposes its idea on the spirit/matter dough of reality, cutting it up as with a cookie-cutter, now into stars, now into hearts, now into elephants, now into swans. It makes them, and it finds them already there, like a *bricoleur*, who makes new forms out of *objets trouvés*.

Rudra's mind is the mold that stamps out the images, all of which derive from him. He stamps this mold on the spirit/matter continuum of the universe in such a way that it breaks up into the separate (or, rather, apparently separate) consciousnesses of all of us. The images that he sketches in our minds were already there—in the continuum, and in our minds; but we cannot know them until his mind touches ours, until he "joins his mind to [our] mind." Finally, when we *really* know Rudra, the images vanish, and the continuum is seen as it really is, devoid of the fragments of individual figures in the landscape. Then the background becomes the foreground.

Despite Rudra's extraordinary ontological status, his actual mental processes are flawed like those of even the best of his dream creatures, the monk. The monk, who unknowingly imitates Rudra's "play" (*līlā*), begins dispassionately enough; but as soon as he imagines a person with passions (the earthy Jīvaṭa), he is caught up in those passions himself and forced to follow the game into realms he had not intended to explore. So, too, Rudra is caught up in his own sport; he is "amazed" to see what creatures people the brave new world of his imagination. Though he is the mold that cuts the forms, those forms also create themselves, beyond his control, once the process is set in motion. Like the monk, Rudra discovers that creation inevitably leads to imperfection, to the self-perpetuating desire to go on creating. Like the monk, Rudra indulges his frivolity, his creative urge. Not even Rudra can remain deaf to the songs of the sirens he imagines. Someone else is pulling *his* strings.

For pure play does not remain pure for long. Rudra begins to act "for the sake of play/sport/amusement/fun," or "for the sheer hell of it" (*līlārtham*)—a term we might also translate as "art for art's sake." This same art is implicit in the term *māyā*, derived from the Sanskrit verb "to make." *Māyā* is what Rudra makes (or finds) when he imagines the universe; *māyā* is his art. Yet *māyā* is often associated with evil in Indian texts, for it is the trick of the mind that causes us to become, literally, deadly serious about what begins in a spirit of play. *Māyā* is what makes it possible for Rudra to use his art, but it is also what blinds us to that art. *Māyā* is what makes us dream, and die.

The *Yogavāsiṣṭha* tells us of other Hindu gods who have had powers like Rudra's:

> While Viṣṇu remained asleep in the ocean of milk, he was born as a man on earth; while Indra remains on his throne in heaven, he goes down to earth to receive the sacrifice; though Kṛṣṇa was only one person, he became a thousand for the many kings who are his devotees, and for the thousands of women who were his mistresses, by indulging in the game [*līlā*] of partial incarnation. In this same way, through the power of the understanding of Rudra, Jīvaṭa and the Brahmin and all the others who had been imagined by the monk went to whatever city they had imagined.[7]

The imaginings of gods are a thousandfold more powerful even than the imaginings of monks. And Rudra in this text is the supreme god.

Rudra is the warp upon which we all weave our dreams; he is the fluid in which we all flow together like the particles in a suspension. He is the place where we all meet in our dreams, the infinity where our parallel lives converge. Rudra is the dream ether that we saw in chapter two, the medium for the *rêve à deux* in psychoanalysis. The text tells us that the lives that the monk imagined could not see one another, living as they did in separate universes, except through the knowledge of Rudra.[8] This last phrase is, I think, purposely ambiguous. It means that only people who know Rudra—in particular, who know that they are Rudra—can meet the people in their dreams or meet the people that they were in their former lives and will be in their future lives. But it also means that only through the fact that Rudra knows them can they hope to bridge the gap between the apparently separate souls; Rudra will show them that they are one another because they are he. For though, as Rāma points out, Rudra is merely a character in someone's dream—the monk's dream at first, the swan's dream at last[9]—he is also the dreamer of all dreams, including the dream of the one who dreams him, the dream of the monk. Thus, when the text says that Jīvaṭa lives in a universe in a corner of the mind,[10] the immediate meaning is that it is a corner of the monk's mind. But as the tale unfolds, we come to understand that the monk himself exists only in the corner of another mind: Rudra's mind. Moreover, where the monk merely dreams of Rudra, Rudra produces the monk in a more direct fashion: the monk is a partial incarnation of Rudra, an atom flowing in the veins of Rudra. Rudra is "made of" Jīvaṭa and the others, we are told.

Karma and Rebirth

Do the people in the monk's dream exist for just the one episode that Vasiṣṭha tells us about, which occupies perhaps a few months of an adult life, and do they then suddenly vanish when the monk wakes up or dies? Or do they live entire lives, from birth to death, of which the monk witnesses only a brief fragment? Both situations are possible at once, according to this text, for we can find outside ourselves the things that we imagine inside our heads; they exist before we think of them, but we bring them into existence by thinking of them. This is a story simultaneously about dreams that tune into an already existing reality and about rebirths that create a new reality.

When we reach the point where Rudra begins to retrace his footsteps, he refers to the "flux of rebirth [*saṃsāra*] in which one is deluded by one's own mind" and "the various wildernesses of rebirth" through which one has wandered.[11] Rudra then goes from one universe to another to find the place where the *re*birth of Jīvaṭa, the Brahmin, and so forth had taken place or, even more significantly, had begun; and, at the end, they all wander together in the grounds of the other rebirths. For *saṃsāra* primarily denotes the physical world in which creatures circulate through their repeated births and deaths.

The figures at the very beginning and the very end of the chain of the monk's dream—that is, the figures who are directly inside the outer frame formed by the monk and Rudra—are a man named Jīvaṭa and a swan. Jīvaṭa (the only character in the dream who is given a proper name) is a derivative of *jīva*, the ordinary Sanskrit word for the individual life or the transmigrating soul. The swan[12] is an ancient Indian symbol for the soul, and particularly for the returning soul, the transmigrating soul, perhaps because of the natural symbolism of the swan's seasonal migration. The swan is also a liminal bird, able to live in two worlds, land and water, or matter and spirit. The swan comes to symbolize the memory of past lives, as in a verse from a Sanskrit poem describing the moment when a princess came of age: "When the time came for her to learn, all that she had learned in her former life came back to her, as the rows of swans come back to the Ganges in the autumn."[13] In another myth of the dream of rebirth, King Purañjana is, like Nārada, reborn as a woman. One day he meets a friend from his previous life as a king, who tells him, "Don't you remember your old friend? You and I, my dear, were two swans who lived together in the lake of the mind until you left me to wander on earth. I created the illusion that made you think you were a man or a woman; our true nature is as two swans." And when the swan of the mind is awakened by the other swan, he wins back the memory that he had lost.[14] Here the swans are explicitly identified with the individual soul and the universal soul and are explicitly said to be one and the same.

In this sense, each of the levels within the monk's dream is a complete rebirth of a single soul, which goes from Rudra to the monk to Jīvaṭa to the Brahmin, and so on, until it subsides back into Rudra again. This mechanism is clearly at work in the second half of the cycle, when the animals die and are reborn, presumably as young animals that grow up. On the other hand, it appears that the monk transfers his consciousness into an already existing Jīvaṭa, taking up Jīvaṭa's life *in medias res*, as it were, and Jīvaṭa joins consciousness with an already existing middle-aged Brahmin, and so forth. This mechanism would explain how all of them continued to exist when the monk awoke and how they were able to meet and talk together when Rudra found them all. Once again, the text says both that the soul makes each new life (from birth to death) and that it finds its new lives (in midstream). There is one single soul, and there are a hundred different souls, and yet they are the same.

We do not see the entire rebirth of each of the characters; none of them is born, and most of them do not die within the story. The monk falls into a deep trance; Jīvaṭa passes out in a drunken stupor; the Brahmin falls asleep after a hard day's reading; the king and the celestial harlot are exhausted by pleasure; and so forth. These people dream and become what they have habitually dreamt about and are thinking of as they die. The belief that you become what you are thinking of at the moment of death is one that we have encountered in the Telugu story of King Lavaṇa and in the Tibetan *Book of the Dead*, the express purpose of which is to make the dying man dream the right dream so that he will be reborn in the right way—released, if he is heading for *mokṣa*, or at least born well, if he is to remain enmeshed in *saṃsāra*.

Yet, near the end of the chain, some of the animals do seem to die and become what they happen to see at the moment of death: the bee is pulverized on the tusk of an elephant, the elephant is cut to pieces by a sword, the next bee is trampled by another elephant. This elephant's fate is ambiguous, almost certainly designedly so: he falls into a pit and becomes the favorite elephant of a king. Did he die in the pit and become reborn to an elephant cow in the king's elephant stables, or did he fall into a trap set by a king to catch a wild elephant, who was then tamed and made into the king's favorite elephant? We do not know. In any case, these animals experience violent accidents of various sorts. The penultimate transition is explicitly said to be a death: the goose dies, shot by a hunter, and becomes the swan of Brahmā. The swan then experiences the final, and most subtle, transition: as soon as he realizes that he is Rudra, his idea is instantly reflected like an image in a mirror; that is, it is projected from him and becomes a solid figure, or, if you prefer, it becomes reflected in the already existing figure of Rudra himself.[15]

It would appear that the figures are arranged in a kind of hierarchy and that the higher consciousnesses merely dream of a partial rebirth, while the lower ones must actually die—must endure, physically, what the others have experienced only mentally. Setting aside for the moment the monk, as a special case to which we will return, we can see that the characters form three groups, which exhibit decreasing degrees of metaphysical acuity (see figure 5). Jīvaṭa is defined as an ordinary sort of man who loves life; hence he is the logical starting point for an odyssey that is designed to dramatize for ordinary people (the ones who are amazed when the dividing line between dream and reality melts away) the doctrines of illusion and rebirth. He is, moreover, the random sample, the man in the street; the monk thinks of him "by pure chance."[16] Jīvaṭa is the literal embodiment of the transmigrating soul—of Everyman. Paired with Jīvaṭa is the highest human type: the learned Brahmin. In the tale of Gādhi, it is the Brahmin who is the pivotal figure, the dreamer of the outermost dream, but Gādhi experiences the dream helplessly, albeit with understanding. In the tale of the monk's dream, by contrast, the dreamer (the monk) actively sets out to produce the dream experience and to materialize it; this activity is proper only to perfected monks, not to ordinary Brahmins. Thus the Brahmin and Jīvaṭa are rightly paired as puppets, rather than puppeteers, in this particular episode. (There is, of course, one other Brahmin in the story—Vasiṣṭha; but his role is even more peculiar than that of the monk, and we must postpone for the moment an analysis of his status in the hierarchy.) After the Brahmin come the prince and the king. The royal image is divided into two, of which the first is lower than the second, as was the case with our first pair. These four men roughly (quite roughly) symbolize the four classes (*varṇas*) of ancient Indian society: the Brahmin, the king, the ordinary citizen

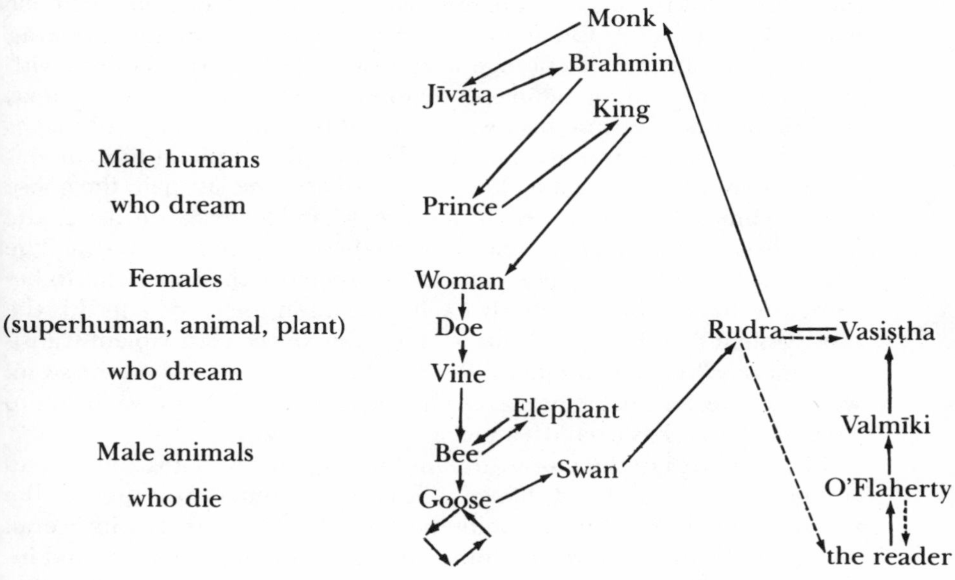

"x→y" signifies "x thinks about y"

Figure 5. The Dreamer Dreamt

Reproduced by permission of the journal *Daedalus* from Wendy O'Flaherty, "The Dream Narrative and the Indian Doctrine of Illusion," *Daedalus* 111:3 (Summer, 1982): 104.

(Jīvaṭa), and the servant (the subsidiary feudal lord). It is, I think, significant that there are no Untouchables in this group, for the group represents the system, and Untouchables are out of the system entirely—in another world.

Below the king is a triad of females, who form the transition from higher to lower consciousness, one semidivine (the celestial woman), one animal (the doe), and one vegetable (the vine). These three figures are still part of the higher echelon who dream rather than die and who become what they have always known, not what they see as they die. The text tells us that animals do dream; so, too, the vine is conscious; she is said to see in herself the embodiment of the loveliness that had been asleep and numb inside the doe for a long time.[17] The vine is the incarnation of the metaphor of female beauty (graceful women are always like clinging vines in Sanskrit poetry), even as Jīvaṭa is the embodiment of the soul.

The next quartet, like the first, is divided into two pairs. The elephant and the bee are animals closely associated with violence and eroticism; the wildness of the male elephant in rut carries fairly obvious symbolic meaning, and bees in Indian love poetry are said to form the bowstring of the god of lust and to plunge deep inside the flowers that ooze with sap even as the rutting elephant's temples ooze with musk. In our text, the bee perishes because his lust for the lotus stupefies him and makes him stick to her even in death.[18] The bee and the elephant find violent deaths, over and over again. Then we encounter the last pair, the goose who becomes a swan. Here the hierarchy doubles back on itself; the lowest becomes the highest, and the swan becomes the god, Rudra. The true break comes within this pair: the goose has to be shot dead to become the swan. This is the only explicit death in the story, and it is the most violent transition; by contrast, the swan, in the least violent transition, merely "reflects" itself into Rudra. Once we have reached the swan, we are home. At this point there is no more dreaming; now we begin to unravel all that has been dreamt.

The creatures in the monk's dream form a pattern that is a masterful combination of order and chance. They are distributed so as to cover the full spectrum of creatures, a point that the text emphasizes by its overall groupings: human males, nonhuman females, and male animals and insects. These groups are, I think, meant to depict a steady general decline in status. Yet within each group are upswings: Jīvaṭa moves up when he becomes a Brahmin or a prince; the bee improves his lot when he becomes an elephant; and the goose becomes a very special swan. Moreover, there are switchbacks (the elephant who relapses into beehood), redundancies (several bees), and, finally, a catchall group of "etceteras" at the end. These irregularities convey the richness and randomness of the process of reincarnation.

This random variation also characterizes the pattern through which all of us will, at some time before the end of infinity, become incarnate as that same monk. Yet, although anything *can* happen, certain things are more *likely* to happen; this is how karma skews and orders the chaos of the universe. When the same dream gets into different people's heads—in this case, the dream of the monk who meets the people in his dreams—there may be minor variations on the theme, minor changes in the manifestations of the archetype: "Again and again these lives revolve in creation like the waves in water, and some [rebirths] are strikingly similar [to what they were before], and others are about half the same; some are a little bit the same, some are not very much alike at all, and sometimes they are once again just the same."[19] This flexibility, together with the elements of pure chance and the gravity of karmic tendencies, makes certain coincidences not only possible but probable.

Midway through the round of rebirths, the text moves from dreams to deaths and then begins to talk about them simultaneously, using the image of one to illustrate the other: death is like a dream (or, rather, like an awakening), and a dream or an illusion is experienced as a kind of death. We awaken from ignorance, or from sleep, or from life; the same verb covers all three. In the end, the contrast between creatures who dream and creatures who die is exposed as being as meaningless as the contrast between one transmigrating soul or a hundred dreamt souls.

Our story takes place on three levels of thought that are also three levels of existence. We begin on the most obvious level, with our assumption that dreams are basically different from reality; on this level animals actually change from one form to another form when they die. Mind and matter are distinct; though they may interact and influence each other, they are made of different stuff. On the middle level we encounter the possibility of transforming mind into matter and matter into mind; this is the level where people dream, or think, about assuming another form and so assume it. This middle level has two subdivisions. Truly enlightened people, who understand that mind and matter are not essentially different things, may intentionally use their minds to bring about a change in the forms of matter (or, rather, an apparent change): the monk changes his dreams into living people. But those who are not truly enlightened are forced to undergo what they think are real changes of form, though these changes, too, are merely apparent: the woman is changed into a doe. Finally, on the highest level, we find the undifferentiated substance that is always both mind and matter, the substance that underlies both the apparent changes of material form and the less obvious transmutations that mental forces exert on apparent matter. On this level we realize that nothing ever changes into anything else, that everything was always there all along, and that everything was, for want of a better word, God.

Illusion and rebirth melt together from the very start, in the short poem with which the commentary introduces the whole story: "The story of Jīvaṭa is about the way in which people wrongly believe that they have obtained various bodies; such a wrong perception operated in the mind of the monk as a result of his various karmic memory traces [*vāsanās*]."[20]

What are the karmic memory traces? They are the "unconscious memory of past lives."[21] In classical Indian philosophy, they are the bits of experience that adhere to the transmigrating soul and that predispose it to act in one way or another in its new life; they may also be experienced as inexplicable, tantalizing memories, the uneasy aftermath of a dream that has been forgotten by the conscious mind but that continues to haunt the deeper mind—the unconscious mind. The karmic memory traces are "the impressions of anything remaining unconsciously in the mind, the present consciousness of past perceptions; fancy, imagination, idea, notion, false notion, mistake."[22] The second half of this definition indicates how closely karma is associated with illusion: karma is what makes us make mistakes.

It was the karmic memory traces that kept alive the knowledge that returned to the princess when she came of age, like swans returning to the Ganges in autumn; she did not recall her past life, but she recalled what she had known in that life. Our text tells us that after the bee had become an elephant and was then reborn again as a bee, he went back to the same lotus pond where he had previously met with his unfortunate accident, "because people who are not aware of their karmic traces find it hard to give up their bad habits."[23] So, too, when the beautiful woman becomes a doe because she envies the beauty of the doe's eyes, Rudra remarks, "Alas, the delusion that results from the karmic traces causes such misery among creatures."[24] All of the people in the dream chain are reborn in a particular form *because they want something*. There is a hunger, unsated in their present lives, that propels them across the barrier of death into a new birth, where this still unfulfilled longing leads them to do what they do.

The cause of rebirth—excessive attachment to the ways of the world—is also the cause of the failure to see through the deception and illusion of the world. The qualities that make the soul cling to rebirth or to illusion are vividly encompassed by a Korean word, *won*, which has a cluster of meanings, including resentment, ingratitude, regret for lost opportunities, and a knot in the stomach; this state of the soul results from being poorly treated or unappreciated while living or from any of the many situations covered by the rubric "to die screaming."[25] The unwillingness to let go, the inability to leave things unavenged and unfinished, is the drive to rebirth. Though monks and great sages and poets and gods can project themselves into physical bodies whenever they want to, all of us—princes and harlots and bees and professors—helplessly spin, out of our desires, the lives that we have inherited from our former selves. Sooner or later our dreams do become real, whether we want them to or not, whether they are nightmares or wishes that we long to have fulfilled.

Déjà vu: Memory and Emotion

Karma is a ready-made classical Hindu explanation for the phenomenon of *déjà vu*. The karmic traces produce a kind of half-recalled memory from past lives: if you think you have been somewhere before and know that it was not in this life, it was in a preceding life. Each birth makes the others seem unreal, dreamlike, until one gains the knowledge (particularly the knowledge of past, present, and future, which the Hindus call *trikālajñāna*) to see their reality. The fragmented, imperfect, tantalizing sense of memory, the complete knowledge that hovers just out of reach of the mind's eye, is interpreted, in India, as the incomplete memory of former lives. These lives are unreal, illusory, not because they are false (in the sense that they never happened at all) but merely because life, like illusion, is by its very nature impermanent.

The sense of *déjà vu* is surely one of the inspirations of many myths of the dream adventure. A "shock of recognition" appears in the form of *déjà vu*: we are shocked to recognize, intuitively, something that we feel that we remember—like the dream lover, in chapter two—though we cannot be remembering it, since it has just happened for the first time.[26] One is suddenly caught up in a moment so intense that it triggers a sense of memory as well as a sense of experiencing something for the first time. There are many ways to explain this feeling. On the psychological level, it can be seen as an example of retroactive feedback: we dream of something archetypal; then it happens to us in a particular way; then we remember the dream, but now the dream is filled with the details of the actual event, details that now seem to have been in the dream from the very start. We also remember the incident itself differently, investing it with the pattern that we had brought with us from that first dream. On the physiological level, it has been suggested (by Freud, and others) that in a split second we construct a long dream to account for a physical sensation that has just occurred (such as a dream of drowning to accommodate the sensation of wet feet in bed, or a dream of being guillotined in the French Revolution to accommodate a blow on the neck from a collapsing headboard). This overlap between physical and psychical phenomena (or mistaking wet feet for drowning, as one might mistake a rope for a snake) is similar to the overlap explained by the sleep-laboratory analysis that we saw in chapter one: we process physical and mental data in the same way; we process new experiences and memories in the same way. Such double exposures might be triggered by random brain impulses or selected by certain intense emotional events.

And there is a third level on which *déjà vu* can be explained, after the psychological and the physiological: the theological. Myths like the tale of the monk's dream affirm that there is some sort of memory that links the past to the present, even over the chasm of death. This force is more basic even than the karmic memory traces themselves: it is the memory built into the divine nature of our mental substance, our mythical DNA. The dream ether holds forever the echoes of all the voices and images that have been transmitted over it. Though we can seldom reach down to touch it, it is always there for us to touch.

A well-known Indian (and Greek) motif associated with this theme is the fish that swallows a ring. We have seen variants of this motif: Hanuman's shadow was swallowed by a fish, and Pradyumna was brought to Māyāvatī inside a fish (chapter three); the reborn jester became an oyster and was fished out of the sea (chapter five). Usually the fish swallows not the reborn person himself but his symbol, the ring. In tales of this type, the loss of memory may take place not as a result of death and rebirth but merely as the result of a curse within a single life. In "The Recognition of Śakuntalā," the king seduces a girl in the forest, has a son by her, returns to his palace, and forgets all about her (as the result of a magic curse) until his memory is reawakened: a fish that swallowed the magic ring *he* had given *her* to remember *him* by is caught and served up at the royal table; when the king sees the ring, he remembers the girl in the forest. He realizes then that it has been delusion that made him reject her, or madness, or a dream, or a demon, or fate; and he regards his amnesia as a dream from which he has now awakened, though now he meets her only in his dreams.[27] Elements of this story are milder versions of elements in the tale of Lavaṇa: the king's sojourn in the forest, which is brief in the story of Śakuntalā, is the equivalent of Lavaṇa's full life in the desert, and Śakuntalā's rusticity corresponds with the full-fledged Untouchability of Lavaṇa's consort. But what is particularly relevant here is the implication that each of us, in our present lives, may at any moment be awakened to the memory of another, lost life. The fish symbolizes the persistence of memory, perhaps because the fish's unblinking, staring eyes suggest a consciousness that never falters for a moment, as ours does when we alternately sleep and wake. Indo-Europeans measure time by the blink of an eye (cf. the German *Augenblick*, Sanskrit *nimeṣa*); but for fish, who do not blink, time does not erode memory. The fish is an ancient symbol of liminal consciousness in India: "As a great fish goes along both banks of a river, both the near side and the far side, just so this person [the dreamer] goes along both of these conditions, the condition of sleeping and the condition of waking."[28] And as the fish swims deep in the ocean, it symbolizes deeply submerged memories.

A. K. Ramanujan's poem "No Amnesiac King" grows out of these themes. The central stanzas are these:

> One cannot wait anymore in the back
> of one's mind for that conspiracy
>
> of three fishermen and a palace cook
> to bring, dressed in cardamom and clove,
>
> the one well-timed memorable fish,
> so one can cut straight with the royal knife
>
> to the ring waiting untarnished in the belly,
> and recover at one stroke all lost memory.[29]

The story of the fish with the ring in his belly is a widely distributed Indo-European motif; Stith Thompson lists it by reference to the Greek tale of the ring of Polycrates.[30]

In India, the theme of the fish that restores lost memory is enhanced by the theological echoes of Viṣṇu's avatars: Viṣṇu appears both as a fish who grows from a minnow to a whale and saves Man from the flood, and as a fish or horse-headed aquatic figure who dives down into the depths of the cosmic ocean to bring back the lost Vedas when they have been carried off by a demon.[31] The myth of Viṣṇu as the fish is closely tied to the tale of the fish with a ring:

> The magic fish [is] the unlikely harbinger of potential good fortune, the symbol of the remote possibility, the unlikely occurrence, the finding of something which had been irretrievably lost, the silvery receptacle of the lost ring, and the reminder to humans that nothing can ever be permanently forgotten, ignored, or submerged in ignorance or non-being.[32]

Of all the things that we lose, memory is the most precious; it is also the most recoverable, if one knows how to go about it. The myth of the fish and the flood thus extends the motif of the fish with the ring to include not merely the temporary flood, which washes away one individual memory within a lifetime or at death, but the universal flood, which washes everyone away at doomsday. Even then, the myth assures us, Man survives; memory survives.

The problem of memory, linked to the problem of personal identity, is one that has plagued the karma theory from its inception and is particularly a thorn in the side of the Buddhists. Even for the Hindus, there always remains a certain amount of psychological uncertainty[33] and cognitive uncertainty[34] about one's previous karma. One cannot know why one has the karmic destiny that one has; moreover, if one cannot feel responsibility for what one has done in a previous life because one cannot remember that life (and therefore, it could be argued, one is not the same person), one cannot feel the justice in being punished for a crime that someone else did (the other, previous self, lost to one's present memory). One can be *told* about it and believe it, but that is something else; that is sharing the dream only on the weakest level. But this is not, I think, an insurmountable problem for South Asians. For one thing, the concept of personal identity is in India so fluid that one could very well *feel* a part of someone else—one's own ancestor or child or even someone with whom one has had intimate exchanges of food or sex and therefore of "coded substance."[35] If people become a part of strangers in daily intercourse and give parts of themselves in return, the emotional reality of the karmic transfer across the barrier of death and rebirth could be very vivid indeed. The bonds with members of one's family, one's own "flesh and blood," in the past and the future, are even stronger; one's family, and one's caste, *are* one's self in India. And through the unifying substance of the Godhead, one is linked with the consciousness of all embodied creatures.[36]

This dissolving of the individual boundaries of the self is what makes it possible for one person to dream for another person, as we saw in chapter one. It also supplies the rebuttal to the challenge of solipsism, as we saw in chapter three: that even if the self *is* all that exists, the self is not merely one person. Salman Rushdie expresses this concept in his own way:

> I am the sum total of everything that went before me, of all I have been seen done, of everything done-to-me. I am everyone everything whose being-in-the-world affected was affected by mine. I am anything that happens after I've gone which would not have happened if I had not come. Nor am I particularly exceptional in this matter; each "I," every one of the now-six-hundred-million-plus of us, contains a similar multitude.[37]

The Western rebuttal of solipsism consists in distinguishing the self (the ego) from the external world, as Freud and Piaget have taught us to do. But Freud's ego functions in ways very different from the Hindu self (*ātman*) or ego (*ahaṃkara*). *Ahaṃkara*, literally "The making of an 'I,'" is best translated as egoism; it is a mistaken perception, the source of the whole series of errors that cause us to become embroiled in *saṃsāra*. Once we realize that "I" does not exist, we are free from the most basic of all illusions. It is the Western assurance that the ego is real that drives us to assume that this is the point from which all other frames radiate outward, like the "ego" that anthropologists use to designate the point on their charts from which kinship terms are calculated (ego's parents, affines, children, etc.). In India as in the West, the ego (*ahaṃkara*) is the center of the family (or of *saṃsāra* as epitomized in the family). But the family is the basis of reality in Western psychology and the basis of the illusory material world (*saṃsāra*) in India. The self (*ātman*), by contrast, links one not merely to a certain group of other people but to everyone and, further, to the real world (*brahman*), which transcends everyone.

For the Buddhists, however, rebirth poses an even more baffling problem, since Buddhists do not believe in the existence of the self (or the Godhead) at all. How can you experience rebirth if there is no self to transmigrate? In addition to the many philosophical gymnastics that Buddhist philosophers have performed, over the ages, to circumvent this problem,[38] stories like the myth of the monk's dream suggest a compromise that might be palatable to some Buddhists: there is no material self, but there is a mental substance that maintains a continuous illusion of self in a kind of cluster of emotional mist that wanders from life to life.

The key to the persistence of memory, and hence the persistence of rebirth, lies in the persistence of emotion. Here, as so often, the *Yogavāsiṣṭha* tries to do two different things at once, to move in two different directions at the same time. Though it tells us to cut off certain kinds of emotion—lust, in particular—it plays on other emotions throughout, especially amazement, and it exhorts the reader to strive toward a state of enlightenment that is described in many texts as the highest bliss (*ānanda*), often expressed in sexual terms. As we saw in the mythology of Kṛṣṇa in chapter three, emotion is the key to salvation in *bhakti* mythology, which does not accept *mokṣa* as a final goal. But the *Yogavāsiṣṭha* is not a *bhakti* text; it is a Vedāntic, *mokṣa*-oriented text. It asks us to replace the wrong emotions with the right emotions, the wrong sort of lust with the right sort of ecstasy. It simultaneously delights and chastises us; it moves us and stirs us up with its stories, but its goal is to still us and quiet us with the peace (*śānti*) that comes at the end of a great religious text. The emotion is in the story; the peace is in the commentary.[39]

Gādhi's detachment, colored though it is by amazement, pulls him out of the story and makes him an observer, alongside Rāma and Vasiṣṭha and ourselves. Lavaṇa's helpless involvement is more like our own involvement in the dramas of our own lives. The monk begins the story detached from emotion and firmly (as he thinks) perched on the frame of the story; he is drawn into the vortex and made to experience, rather than merely to think about, his ontological quandary.

The *Yogavāsiṣṭha* exhorts us to cut off emotion so that we can cut off delusion. Here (as in classical Buddhism and Vedānta) the focal point is hatred of women. Rāma regards women as destruction and cannot be tempted by lovely women; old age is like a worn-out old harlot; longing is a crazy mare that wanders about out of control, like a lecherous old woman who runs in vain after one man and then another and another.[40] Both Gādhi and Lavaṇa must abandon the women with whom they have contact in the pivotal episodes of both myths, for they must break the spell of the illusion, a spell made of emotional attachment. Gādhi in his original, waking life does not even know what a woman looks like. The descriptions of his marriage to the Untouchable woman are sensuous: she has breasts like clusters of blossoms, limbs as graceful as young sprouts; he awakens her desire for the first time and lies with her on beds of flowers. But later, when he returns to the Untouchable village, he is full of shame and disgust when he remembers how he embraced her on a bloody lion skin when he was drunk on wine spiked with the aphrodisiac made from the musk of elephants in rut.[41] The dream values *saṃsāra*, but Gādhi's waking life is devoted to *mokṣa*.

A man in the grip of illusion and emotion will be the victim of other people's *māyā* (as Lavaṇa was overwhelmed by the image projected by the Untouchable Katañja), and, insofar as everyone projects the images of his own emotions, he will project dangerous realities on others (as Lavaṇa projects his own image on the Untouchables). The *Yogavāsiṣṭha* tells a vivid tale about the power of lust to project material images:

> Once upon a time there was a king named Indradyumna, whose wife, named Ahalyā, had heard the story of the seduction of Ahalyā, wife of the sage Gautama, by Indra, king of the gods. Now, in that city there lived a pimp named Indra, and because of all the stories of Indra and Ahalyā, the queen Ahalyā fell passionately in love with the pimp Indra, sent for him, and made love with him night after night. The king found out about the affair and had the couple tortured: they were thrown into cold water in winter, placed on a heated iron pan, tied to the feet of elephants, whipped, and tortured over and over with everything the king could devise, but they merely laughed, delighting in each other. Indra said to the king, "Your punishments do not bother us, for the universe is made of my beloved, and she thinks the universe is made of me." Infuriated, the king commanded a sage to curse them, but the lovers merely said, "You are foolish to waste your powers by cursing us, for though our bodies may be destroyed, our inner forms will be unhurt." As they fell to the ground because of the curse, they were reborn as deer, still firmly attached to their illicit passion, and then as birds, and then as a Brahmin married couple. And because of their karmic impressions and memories and their delusion, they were always reborn as a married couple, for their love was real [*akṛtrima*]."[42]

The love of Ahalyā the queen and Indra the pimp is, at the start, an imitation of another, more classical, story: the archetypal adultery of Indra, the king of the gods, and Ahalyā, the wife of Gautama.[43] The text does not, however, romanticize the queen and the pimp; it merely demonstrates how their passions kept them together despite all opposition. It may or may not be a good thing to be reborn over and over again, helplessly in love; but clearly the lovers think it is a very good thing indeed (as did King Lavaṇa and his Untouchable wife in the Telugu variant of the tale). People do get what they want; that is what karma is all about. The force of Yaśodā's maternal love gives her a god who is her child, while Mārkaṇḍeya gets a god who is a father. Sages, too, get what they want; the lustful Nārada is vividly contrasted with the detached Vasiṣṭha, while Viśvāmitra hovers liminally between them.

Lust and suffering represent the two ends of the emotional spectrum in India, a spectrum that is then itself set in opposition to the pole of detachment. Just as lust may draw the unwary man into an illusion, so suffering may draw the receptive man out of one. The unpleasantness of life among the Untouchables is the turning point for both Lavaṇa the king and the Brahmin Gādhi. At first this suffering is what makes their lives seem so very real to them; but when the suffering becomes intolerable, with the experience of the death of a son or the disgrace of dethronement, the recording needle leaps right off the paper; then Lavaṇa and Gādhi wake up and say, "It was only a dream." So, too, it is suffering that first draws us into the story, makes us read on, and makes the story real to us; but it is also suffering that makes us finally look up from the page: "Only when we want to resist the pull of the illusion, when what we read becomes too unpleasant, we . . . tell ourselves that after all we need not submit to words on paper."[44] Only when we fear that the hero will not survive do we say to ourselves, "It's only a story, after all." The reader's conscious suspension of disbelief is quite different from Lavaṇa's unwitting immersion in a dream. Yet the two awakenings are similar enough to explain each other in ways that we will explore in chapter six and the Conclusion.

Emotion is what drives karma forward; it is what causes us to be reborn. We have seen the close connection between dreams and rebirth; it is therefore not surprising to learn that, according to the Upaniṣads, emotion is also what causes us to dream: dreamless sleep occurs when someone has no desires whatsoever and therefore sees no dream whatsoever.[45] It is emotion that makes us *want* to see things when they are not there, emotion that makes us project our wishes onto material reality. A vivid instance of the emotional power of illusion—or, more precisely, of mistakes—occurs in the *Yogavāsiṣṭha* during a famine, when people and animals driven to the extremities of hunger, thirst, and fear fall prey to ludicrous misperceptions: "Buffaloes plunged into the 'water' that was a mere shining mirage of specks of light; people devoured scraps of hardwood trees in the mistaken apprehension that they were flesh, and fragments of forest stones that they thought were cakes; people ate their own blood-smeared fingers in their frenzy at the smell of flesh."[46]

The *Yogavāsiṣṭha* also uses emotion to explain the distortions of time that take place in dreams and trances. Playing on the well-known phenomenon of the expansion and contraction of waking time—time drags when we are unhappy and flies when we are happy—the *Yogavāsiṣṭha* demonstrates how mental time drags while physical time flies. That is, dream time is long compared with waking time (a long dream adventure takes place while less than a single night elapses), and yogic time is even longer than dream time (many centuries pass for the yogin's mind, while only a few days pass for his body; hundreds of years pass during the monk's twenty-one-day meditation). Both dream time and yogic time are contrasted with physical, emotional, passionate time, in which, as the text insists over and over again, the whole night passes in what seems like just a minute, and many years pass like a single day. Sensuality shrinks time and erodes life; we awaken from the dream of lust to find that we have become old. But we awaken from the dream of enlightenment to find that we never aged at all.

The contraction and expansion of time under the influence of emotion is manifest in other ways that are relevant to the problem of dreams and narratives. It is often said, in the Epics and Purāṇas, that listening to a good story well told makes the whole night pass as if it were a single moment.[47] The passion involved in hearing a good story makes time pass quickly, like the passion involved in making love all night, rather than making it pass slowly, as it would in a night spent dreaming. One might have thought that the link between stories and dreams would be closer than the link between stories and love-making—that stories would expand time rather than contract it. But stories and love-making are often connected. In the story of the two Līlās, in chapter three, the king and his queens find equal pleasure in making love and in telling stories of their former lives, and traditions such as the one surrounding Scheherezade and her thousand and one stories demonstrate that women (as well as men) may use stories as a substitute for sex. This ambiguous quality of stories, linked to dreams on the one hand and sex on the other, may also be seen in the ambiguity of the orgasmic dream: to the extent that it is a sexual experience, it shrinks time, but to the extent that it is a dream, it expands time. Indeed, according to Śankara, all dreams are ambiguous in this respect: some make time pass faster, and some make time pass slower.[48] Perhaps yogic dreams make time pass slower, while orgasmic dreams make time pass faster. Perhaps, too, philosophical stories (like the *Yogavāsiṣṭha*) make time pass slower, while adventure stories (like the *Rāmāyaṇa*) make time pass faster. Perhaps good stories shrink time, while bad stories stretch time. Happiness is quick; sadness, slow. It is emotion and content, rather than form or genre, that primarily determine the direction in which time will be distorted.

A vivid example of the manner in which lust shrinks time may be seen in the tale of King Yayāti. Yayāti succeeded in obtaining youth after he had become old, in order to satisfy his lust for his young wife; when he fell from heaven, he was suspended for a while between heaven and earth, like Triśanku.[49] He then resolved not to strive for heaven but to make heaven on earth, and he managed to remain physically young despite his years, like Dorian Grey, until one day Kāma himself and the Gandharvas and celestial nymphs and Old Age incarnate appeared to Yayāti as dancers and singers. They deluded him, and, when the dance was over and the dancers had gone away, the king had become an old man.[50] It was Yayāti's religious virtue that kept him young, against the grain of normal time; and it was his lust that snapped the thread and brought him back into the sway of time once more.

We have seen that the Indian map of the cosmos is as much a diagram of time as it is of space, that the infinity that it attempts to describe extends in the fourth dimension as much as in the first three. If everything changes constantly (as the Buddhists teach us), then change is the only thing that never changes; time is all that is real. The regressive twist that we will soon see in the universe is also a flashback in time. *Déjà vu* tells us that memory can work into the future as well as into the past; the Indian sage, like Lewis Carroll's White Queen, has a memory that "works both ways": "It's a poor sort of memory that only works backwards," the Queen remarks.[51] Contrariwise, as Salman Rushdie points out, "No people whose word for 'yesterday' is the same as their word for 'tomorrow' can be said to have a firm grip on time."[52] (The Hindi word *kal*, literally "time," designates either yesterday or tomorrow, depending on context.) It all depends on what sort of time one wishes to grip.

The Indian *rāga*, a traditional musical theme with infinite possibilities of individual variation, is another example of a self-referential cultural form. A *rāga* does not usually end at all; people wander in and out of it and fade away on the periphery, like the World-non-World mountain that flickers in and out of the material world. The *rāga* never ends; but the musicians, sooner or later, stop playing it; the audience dozes off or goes home. Since the end of each variation is the beginning of the next, it does not really matter where you leave off or where you begin again. The *rāga* as it exists in sound—when it is played—expresses the paradox of time that circles back on itself.[53]

Karma is a memory that works both ways: emotions in the present carry us back into the past and project us into the future. The sage who is free of emotion is free of time; this is the express goal of yoga. The mind can also project us sideways through time in the present; this is what allows Lavaṇa to be in two places at the same time. Time is the key to what appear to be spatial paradoxes in the *Yogavāsiṣṭha*.

The relevance of the doctrine of karma to the study of the mythology of dreams needs no further belaboring. The central metaphor of the dream adventure, the flight to another world, is commonly used to describe the movement of the soul from one body to another. In the Upaniṣads, the soul is depicted as a bird returning to its nest, and the *Yogavāsiṣṭha* says, "Flying up and flying up, enjoying one body after another, the particles of life finally go back to the place that is their own nest."[54] Yet the popularity of the story of the dream adventure in cultures where reincarnation is *not* generally accepted must make us pause before placing too much emphasis on karma as a generating, rather than simply a reinforcing, element of the story in India. For the paradox of the dreamer dreamt poses a challenge that is not entirely met by the theory of karma.

The Monk and the Narrator

The monk is said to be free from the emotions, the unfulfilled longings, that animate and reanimate the creatures in his dream. His involvement in rebirth seems at first to be different from that of all the other characters in Vasiṣṭha's story (or within the monk's dream). The text insists that the monk himself was born purely by chance and that, again by chance, he became Jīvaṭa.[55] That is, the monk did not become reborn to quench a thirst; he dreamed of another life out of pure intellectual curiosity. In other words, he became Jīvaṭa merely in play or for amusement (*līlārtham*), the word for purposeless sport being the same as the one used to describe why it is that God, who has no desires, bothers to make the universe at all. Rudra insists that the monk indulged in pure play when he imagined Jīvaṭa, and it is this same spirit of pure play that leads Rudra himself to decide to travel through the universes to wake up all the figures in the monk's dream.[56] The purity of the monk's mind gave him the ability to become whatever he thought of; that is, he emptied his mind of everything but the one thing he wanted to become, with the result that he became that thought. The commentator adds that the monk assumed the form of another man in the manner of ascetics (*yatis*),[57] for yogins can enter other peoples' real, existing bodies.

Yet the monk *is* caught up, like the others, in his own imaginings; like them, he is astonished when brought face to face with the people in his dream, and Rudra says that the monk became Jīvaṭa because of his still-decaying karmic memory traces. The monk experiences precisely what they all experience, even though, unlike them, he sets out to do it on purpose. He was the victim of a mistaken perception (*vibhrama*); as soon as he wanted to become someone else, his mind lost its calm, like an ocean stirred by a whirlpool; his form changed because of the emotion that moved him at that time.[58] Rāma is puzzled by this problem and asks Vasiṣṭha how a monk of such spiritual distinction could be caught up in the web of delusion.[59] Vasiṣṭha does not answer this question specifically, but the subsequent analysis makes it clear that the monk's great degree of mental control, though temporarily swept aside by the intensity of the dream, reasserted itself so that the monk could realize the dream of Rudra, could become awakened. The commentator introduces the last chapter with this verse: "In this chapter, the body of the monk is destroyed when he has been released through his meditation; just as the monk was first bound by and then released from his false perception, so, too, other people become bound and are released at their own awakenings."[60] The monk is part of the chain gang of rebirth, like all the rest of us, but he is first in line; and the story in the *Yogavāsiṣṭha* describes the moment when he breaks out, to set an example for all of us. At the end of the story, the monk is described as one who has become released from the wheel of rebirth during his lifetime.[61]

The monk is a Buddhist monk; he lives in a Buddhist monastery in a northern country called Jina, perhaps China. He is thus probably a Tibetan or Mahāyāna monk and, moreover, a shaman and a magician. But the power that he has is one that is possessed by Hindu yogins as well: "By their own powers over time and space, yogins and female yoginīs here can stand somewhere else, wherever they wish."[62] Vasiṣṭha is a Hindu Brahmin and a yogin; but he is also a storyteller. Like the monk and Rudra, Vasiṣṭha is able to make his dreams come true—and not merely his dreams but even his conscious, didactic examples. Moreover, Vasiṣṭha is not amazed at the things that happen in his story—not even at the fact that his story turns out to be true. He creates not out of idle curiosity or even in a spirit of playfulness but to teach Rāma a lesson. Unlike the Brahmin in the monk's dream, who, albeit a Brahmin, was not a particularly subtle theologian or accomplished sage, Vasiṣṭha knows all the answers; he alone never seems to be fooled.

Or so it seems. But when Vasiṣṭha replies to another of Rāma's questions, the dilemma moves onto another plane altogether:

> When Vasiṣṭha had finished speaking, Rāma asked, "*Is* there such a monk? Search within yourself and tell me right away." Vasiṣṭha said, "Tonight I will go into a deep trance and search the universe to find out if there is such a monk or not, and tomorrow morning I will tell you." When they met again on the next morning, Vasiṣṭha

said, "Rāma, I searched for that monk for a long time yesterday, with the eye of knowledge, the eye of meditation. Hoping to see such a monk, I wandered through the seven continents, and over the mountains of the earth, but no matter how far I went, I could not find him. For how could something from the realm of the mind be found outside it?

"But then, near dawn, once more I went north in my mind, to a glorious country named Jina, where there is a famous monastery built over an anthill. And in that monastery, in the corner of a hut, there was a monk named Far Sight [Dīrghadṛśa], who had been meditating for twenty-one nights. His own servants did not enter his firmly bolted house, for they feared that they might disturb his meditation. In his own mind he was there for a thousand years. (In a former eon there was once another monk of this very sort, just as I described him, and this one today is a second.) And when, just in play, I searched through other universes, I found, in a universe in the corner of space in the future, another monk just like that, with the same powers. And even in this very assembly there are people who will someday have the very same experiences and take on such a form and do such things, when this illusion will cast its spell over them."

Then Rāma's father, Daśaratha, said to Vasiṣṭha, "Greatest of sages, let me send my men to the hut of that monk to awaken him and bring him right back here." Vasiṣṭha said, "Greatest of kings, the body of that monk no longer has the breath of life in it; it is dissolved with rot; it is no longer the vessel of a living creature. The soul of that monk has become the swan of Brahmā; during his own lifetime he has been released and is no longer subject to rebirth. At the end of a month, the monk's servants, longing to see him, will force open the bolts, and they will wash his body and throw it away. Since the monk himself has left that body and has gone somewhere else, how could anyone wake up that ruined corpse in the monastery?"[63]

What are we to make of this epilogue? Rāma's questions begin to consider the possible reality not of the characters in the monk's dream but of the monk himself, that is, the reality of a character in a story told by Vasiṣṭha. And in his response to Rāma, Vasiṣṭha jumps out of the frame of narration and into his own story, just as the monk jumps out of the frame of his dream to meet the people he dreams of—or, perhaps, as Rudra jumps out of the frame of his divine mind to meet the thoughts in it. This adds a new dimension to the nested levels of the dream, for now we have Vasiṣṭha thinking of Rudra, who is realizing the monk, who is dreaming of Jīvaṭa and the others. It also adds another figure, Vasiṣṭha, to the list of those who are privileged to manipulate the strings of the puppets within the cosmic drama by giving physical form to their mental images.

Vasiṣṭha is at first skeptical of any possibility that his own mental constructs could be real; as he says to Rāma, "No matter how far I went, I could not find such a monk; for how could something from the realm of the mind be found outside it?"[64] It would appear that, at this point at least, Vasiṣṭha aligns himself with those who are amazed to find their mental creations coming to life. Yet he *does* go to look for the monk, nevertheless. By seeking the monk, Vasiṣṭha acts out the idealistic assumptions of the text, assumptions that have already been challenged by the skepticism of Rāma and by Vasiṣṭha's own initial doubts. But Vasiṣṭha finds the monk, and, by finding him, he not only discredits that skepticism but greatly strengthens and enhances the idealistic argument; for he demonstrates that works of artistic creation—the stories that we make up to prove a point—reflect some aspect of reality, one that most of us do not have the powers to prove, as Vasiṣṭha did. This is an important extension, for it implies that this reality is reflected not only in dreams—which we take to be real while dreaming but retroactively define as unreal when we awake—but even in stories which we take to be unreal from the start—artistic creations, which we think we control. The artist, like the god, catches the wave of *māyā*; the things that he imagines are real.

Why did Vasiṣṭha think that he could find the monk, since the monk was merely a creature in a story he had told and, presumably, made up himself? The commentary suggests that Rāma might have wrestled with this problem before framing his question to Vasiṣṭha:

> Rāma was full of doubt and curiosity. He praised his guru and recognized the purpose of his instruction, but he said, "Search within yourself and ask yourself this question: 'Even though I imagined this monk and spoke about him in order to enlighten you, Rāma, nevertheless did he actually come into existence somewhere?' For it is simply not possible that a person that you would talk about would not have some sort of true essence."[65]

Rāma was amazed by the tale of the monk's dream; that is, he shared to some extent our common-sense intuition that dreams are not real. Yet Rāma's question and Vasiṣṭha's implicit affirmative answer—for he does go to look for the monk—suggest that both of them were at least half convinced of the real existence of the monk; that is, they shared to some extent the philosophy set forth in the text, in flagrant violation of their common sense. Their ambivalence is explicitly stated: they were amazed and not amazed. They wanted to find out for sure, and so Vasiṣṭha set out to test his hypothesis. Both Rāma and Vasiṣṭha felt that there was, in fact, a possibility that Vasiṣṭha's mental creations *might* have a physical reality. The fact that it never occurred to Vasiṣṭha to go and look for the monk until Rāma asked him to do so, and the brusqueness of his initial reply to Rāma—"How could you expect to find . . ."—probably indicate Vasiṣṭha's belief that it does not really matter at all if one finds the specific real monk of the dream; Vasiṣṭha's didactic point lies elsewhere. People do not usually test such basic assumptions, as we saw in the context of unreality testing in chapter four. Nevertheless, to please Rāma, he does go and look, and he is not at all amazed in the end to find that the monk does exist. This is the psychology of the text, and it is similar to the psychology of the stories of Lavaṇa and Gādhi.

The monk's existence might be explained in two ways, one corresponding to Rudra's finding the figures in his dream, the other to his making them. The two explanations imply different things about the nature of reality; together they provide an expression of the ontology of the text. The first is the possibility that certain people might have the power instinctively to "tune in" on some real, already existing physical phenomenon while apparently just imagining such a phenomenon in a spirit of pure play or by pure chance. This is what Rāma means when he says, "Whatever a person like *you* [i.e., the great sage Vasiṣṭha] would talk about," must have some sort of true essence; such a sage would instinctively make up something *real*, even when constructing a hypothetical case. The second explanation is one that the text has already dwelt on at some length: certain people, of whom Vasiṣṭha is apparently one, have the power of making their mental projections, their dreams, become real physical objects—objects that had not existed until the powerful dreamer dreamed them into reality. In the context of our story, these two explanations are mutually supportive, not contradictory.

For either or both of these reasons, the monk is real. When Daśaratha, the king, asks Vasiṣṭha to bring the monk to court, Vasiṣṭha gently points out the stupidity of the question, not on the basis of the argument that one could hardly expect to find the monk at all (the tentative, and quickly disproved, hypothesis with which Vasiṣṭha had at first ridiculed Rāma's question about the reality of the monk), but rather because the monk's body was so *very* real that it had, like all real bodies, eventually ceased to exist; it had rotted away.

The Girl inside the Stone

Vasiṣṭha is unable to stop imagining things. In classical Hindu mythology, he is the archenemy of Viśvāmitra. Where Viśvāmitra creates illusory double worlds and supports King Triśanku's deluded ambition to go to heaven with his body, Vasiṣṭha sees through all illusions. But in the *Yogavāsiṣṭha*, Vasiṣṭha and Viśvāmitra have joined forces in order to enlighten Rāma, and Vasiṣṭha creates a double world far more subtle and complex than the one that Viśvāmitra created in the earlier texts. Vasiṣṭha tells Rāma about this world:

> One day, long ago, I decided to leave this busy world and go to a quiet, out-of-the-way place where I could enter into a deep trance, free from all imaginings, where I would be invisible to everyone. I went off into a far-distant corner of the space of emptiness, and there, through my yoga and my imagination, I created a little hut, where I lived, sitting in the lotus posture, as if I had entered a deep sleep. A hundred years passed like that as if it had been a moment, and yet even then I was not free from the ghoul of egoism [*ahaṃkārapiśāca*]. In my meditation I saw the thousands of universes that are nested one within the other, even inside the smallest atom of a stone.
>
> Then I awoke from my meditation and I heard the sweet voice of a woman. I wondered how anyone could be singing there in the midst of pure emptiness, and I was amazed. I went into the space of my mind and saw countless worlds, all unable to see one another. After many years of wandering I heard the sound of a lute, and I followed it until I saw a beautiful young woman singing sweetly. The woman, who was a magician [*vidyādharī*], approached me, and I asked her who she was and why she had come to me. She said:
>
> "At the outer rim of the universe there is a mountain called World-non-World [Lokāloka], which encircles the disks of the worlds. On the peaks of that mountain there are many stones, and in a tiny atom in one of those stones is my home, where I live with my husband. He has spent his life studying the Vedas, and he knows nothing of worldly life; but since the textbooks said that he must marry, he created a wife for himself in his imagination, and that is who I am. But still he does nothing but study the Vedas. He cares nothing for the needs of a woman; he is a chaste old Brahmin, all his passion burnt out. Our lives are therefore entirely pointless. For I am the most beautiful woman in the universe, and I never grow old, though I have lived a long time, yet I have never tasted the pleasures or comforts of life, and my youth is wasted. So I have given up all desires, and I seek only release. To do this, I practiced yoga and learned to fly, in order to visit great sages, and this is how I found you. Teach me and my husband how to find release, for our lives have no purpose, and it is better not to exist than to lead such a life. Have pity on us."
>
> When this girl, whom I had created in my imagination, said this to me, I replied, "How could a girl like you live inside a stone? How can you move around? How can you occupy space?" But she described to me in great detail the whole universe that was in that rock, and all the people there with her, and then she asked me to do her the favor of going with her to that universe. One has great

curiosity about such marvels, and so I consented and went with her through the sky, flying through vast emptiness. We reached the mountain of World-non-World, and she brought me to her stone, but I didn't see any universe. I said to her, "A universe has to have an earth and sky and hell, and a sun and moon and stars, and human beings and animals and plants, and gods and demons. But all I can see is a big rock. Where is your universe? Has it disappeared?" She replied, "How strange it is that you cannot see the world of my experience, which I see even now reflected inside me like an image in a mirror. Even though you are omniscient, you cannot see the stone-universe, though I, a mere stone-girl, can see it. For I have been experiencing it all my life; but since your experiences have been different, you do not perceive it as I do. In my youth and my inexperience I perceived this illusory world; but you are so wise that you cannot see the world that is illusory. Yet if you recall your own experiences, you will also see the world that I see in this stone. You must concentrate." Then I went into a trance, and I saw, as in a dream, a great stone and a whole universe inside it.

She entered that universe, and I entered it with her, and she said to me, "This is my husband. He created me mentally in order to marry me, but now we are both free from passion and want to go to the final place. Doomsday for this universe is coming soon. Enlighten him and me and set us on the right path." As she spoke, her husband came out of his trance and opened his eyes. He said to me, "I am the Creator of this universe. As you are to me, so I am to you; this is a mutual story. For a man who is dreaming becomes a man in another man's dream. This woman got caught in the whirlpool of worldly life [*saṃsāra*]. Through her own karmic memory traces and deep desires, she constructed a world of her own in her universe of stone and desired me for her husband. But in fact I am not her husband, nor is she my wife. Today is the day set for the doomsday of this universe and the end of my own karmic memory traces. Vasiṣṭha, go back to your own universe." As he spoke, he withdrew his mind from all ideas of the external world, and as soon as the ideas of hardness and fluidity and motion and so forth were withdrawn, the external world, with all its contents, disappeared. Doomsday engulfed it; I watched until the fires and floods subsided and there was nothing but a great stillness.

Then I remembered the stone and the girl and the confusion between the two, and I was amazed, like a country boy standing at the door of a palace. I looked at the stone again, and everywhere I looked, in every single atom of it, I saw a whole universe. Each of these worlds was different from the others; some had a few resemblances, some more, some no resemblance at all. Some were made entirely of rock, some of water, some of air. In one of them I saw Rāma killing Rāvaṇa, and in another I saw Rāma being defeated by Rāvaṇa. Then I understood that all of these worlds were the ideas of various people. Each person imagines his own world, and that becomes his world.

Then I turned away, with great effort, and went back to the hut in the corner of emptiness. I didn't see my own body anywhere, but I saw the body of a magician [*siddha*] sitting there in meditation. I began to wonder about it all, thinking, "This is a great magician who has come to this part of the sky, wandering around, just as I did, to find a lonely spot where there was some peace and quiet. Because he had the power of imagining what was real, he saw this hut, and, since he didn't think I would come back for a long time, he threw out my body (which had become a corpse) and took its place here. Now, if I go back to my own world and stop imagining this place, the hut will disappear; there will be nothing but space, and this magician will have no ground to stand on. Then he will fall down—still in meditation, falling like a stone." Then I went, in my mind, from the sky to earth, and he did fall from the sky, still sitting in the lotus posture. I had to work hard to wake him up, using rain and thunder and hail, but finally he woke up. When I asked him who he was and what he was doing, he looked around him for a moment, trying to recall his previous state. Then he said, "Wait for a moment while I remember my own adventures, and then I will tell you." After a moment he remembered everything, and he told me the long story of his life, ending, "And after all that I was worn out, and longing for solitude, just as you were. And I came here and saw your hut. I never thought you would come back, for I thought, 'Some magician has abandoned his body and gone to *nirvāṇa*.'"

Then, out of friendship for that magician, I said, "You are not the only one who didn't think it through; I, too, failed to consider the matter fully. For if I had thought about you, I would have made that hut firm in the sky; I knew that as long as I imagined, 'Let there be a hut,' there would be one. Then you would have had a firm place to stay. Get up, and let us two live together in the world of the magicians." We both agreed to this and went through the sky, and after a while we bowed and parted. He went to his favorite spot, and I went to mine. And that is the end of that story.[66]

Vasiṣṭha's initial purpose is to find a place so empty that his mind will be empty, both of external annoyances and of internal strivings; he wants to go into a trance where he will be free from imagination (*nirvikalpa*).[67] Yet he is seized by a ghoul—not a material ghoul, such as seized Triśanku or Hariścandra, but a metaphysical ghoul, the ghoul of egoism. Possessed by himself, literally, he imagines everything. He had intended to enter the deep, dreamless sleep that is the stage closest to *brahman*; instead, he entered the stage before that, the dreaming sleep in which we create, as the gods create, by emitting images.

At the start, therefore, we have Vasiṣṭha imagining that he is sitting in a hut imagining the universe. He wakes up from the second trance, but he is still in his hut, inside the first trance, and in this trance he meets a woman whom he had imagined in his second trance, as she explicitly points out. She lives on the border between the world and whatever is outside the world, just as a dream takes place on the borders between consciousness and unconsciousness. Apparently the world continues to exist even when Vasiṣṭha has awakened from the trance in which he created it, just as the monk continues to exist in Vasiṣṭha's story after he has told it. One reason why the world continues to exist, however, is that Vasiṣṭha is not the only one who created it; its own creator, the husband of Vasiṣṭha's dream girl, also created it, just as that creator created, mentally, the girl that Vasiṣṭha had created mentally.

In fact, once we get inside the stone-world, we find two contradictory stories about who created whom. The girl insists that her husband created her mentally in order to marry her; he maintains, however, that she created *him* mentally in order to marry him, and he therefore denies the validity of their relationship; he is *not* her husband, he maintains (even as Gādhi insisted that he was not the husband of the woman inside his own dream). The two worlds inside the stone are the *saṃsāra*-oriented world of the woman (who is dying for lack of physical pleasures) and the *mokṣa*-oriented world of the man (who wishes to die in order to be free of everything physical). That each of the two creates a different world, even though they live in the stone-world together, could be taken as a rather mild statement of the power of emotional projection—a statement of the sort often encountered in the West—and Vasiṣṭha's statement that "each person imagines his own world" could also be interpreted in this vague way. But the myth also makes a sharper statement about the physical existence of these mental worlds; it describes them as things that other people can see and live in, and it speaks of them in terms that remind us of the various monks seen by Vasiṣṭha: some look very much alike, some not so much alike, and some have *us* inside them. Two of the stone-universes had Rāma fighting against Rāvaṇa (winning in one, losing in the other), as Vasiṣṭha tells Rāma himself.[68] Yet, on the other hand, we cannot live in someone else's world unless we can enter into someone else's experiences. This, too, can be taken in a more literal or a less literal sense; the text takes it in both senses: in the general archetypal sense (all of us share the same sort of human consciousness) and in the specific manifestational sense (some people can actually live, in detail, all the events of other people's lives).

The text also presents us with these alternative, if not necessarily contradictory, ontologies: some mental worlds cease to exist when we stop imagining them; others continue to exist even when we stop imagining them. Vasiṣṭha's dream girl continued to exist when he ceased to imagine her world. His hut, on the other hand, did not stay up in the sky when he stopped imagining it; it fell from the sky when he stopped believing that it was in the sky, just as the cat fleeing the mouse fell from the air when he ceased to believe that he was walking on firm ground. The stone-world, by contrast, exists even when Vasiṣṭha stops thinking of it, but when *its* creator ends *his* trance, it disappears, devoid of the mental energy that has maintained it; its creator turns it off as one would turn off a movie projector. This disappearance takes the form of an elaborately described doomsday, the same image that pervades so many other stories in the *Yogavāsiṣṭha*, either as a metaphor or as an actual enlightening event. Thus the creator of the stone-world universe achieves his release not by having Vasiṣṭha stop imagining him (an event that has already taken place, with no effect on the stone-universe), nor by having Vasiṣṭha enlighten him (as the girl had suggested, but as the creator himself apparently had no need or desire for), but simply by using up his own karma. His independence of Vasiṣṭha is expressed when he remarks, cryptically but clearly, that both he and Vasiṣṭha are creators, and both are dreamers, mutually creating and dreaming each other and telling each other's stories.

Vasiṣṭha then produces a slapstick doomsday within his own little world. He does this not to demonstrate his metaphysical prowess but simply to evict a magician who has been camping in his hut in his absence. Coming as it does after the majestic description of the doomsday within the rock, Vasiṣṭha's petty action is rather bathetic, and he himself comes to realize how thoughtless and small-minded he has been.

This story, which Vasiṣṭha tells about himself, reveals the sage's feet of clay, both epistemologically and ontologically. Though Vasiṣṭha does not marry the woman in the other world, her siren song lures him from his trance (as the song of the girl lured Lavaṇa in the Telugu version), and he flies through the air with her by means of her magic powers, as Pradyumna flies with Māyāvatī and Aniruddha flies with Citralekhā. It is fair, if perhaps misleading, to say that Vasiṣṭha follows home a woman who has just told him that she is the most beautiful woman in the world and that her husband refuses to sleep with her. (Her predicament, the young girl rejected by her ascetic husband, is a common one in ancient Indian mythology.)[69]

Vasiṣṭha is susceptible. His attempt to maintain a trance free of mental images fails spectacularly. On the other hand, he is unable to enter the girl's world at first because, as she argues (to flatter him?), he is *too* pure; he sees so clearly that he sees right *through* her illusory world. He must recall his own impure karmic traces in order to materialize her imaginary world, to stain, as it were, her own transparent universe with the dye of his own experiences in order to see it. Vasiṣṭha does have such karma; elsewhere in the *Yogavāsiṣṭha* it is said that Queen Līlā's husband, King Padma, had in a previous incarnation been a Brahmin named Vasiṣṭha—perhaps our own Vasiṣṭha—and this Brahmin was so tied to his mental world that when he died his unsated desires became incarnate as demons and hovered above his own house.[70] (See plate 13.) And we have seen how Brahmā clouded Vasiṣṭha's mind with ignorance in order to teach him the meaning of suffering. In light of these weaknesses in his character, it is not surprising that Vasiṣṭha cannot resist leaping into the story of the hundred Rudras to find the monk (who, like Vasiṣṭha himself in the story of the stone-universe, is attempting to hide out in a hut). The stone-universe teaches Vasiṣṭha that the people he is dreaming about are also dreaming about him. He meets his double when he encounters the Brahmin in the stone, and he meets yet another double when he encounters the magician camping out in his own imaginary hut.

The Möbius Universe

Vasiṣṭha is the key to the paradox of the dreamer dreamt. Vasiṣṭha tells the tale of Rudra to Rāma in order to enlighten him, but, later in the *Yogavāsiṣṭha*, Rudra appears to Vasiṣṭha in order to enlighten *him* (see plate 14). The process of awakening from the dream is expressed, in narrative terms, as the movement from one frame of discourse to another frame, which envelops the first. The *Yogavāsiṣṭha* is a story within a story within a story. We have seen the complex set of nested frames in the tale of the monk's dream, but that story is itself nested in ways we have not yet considered. The very first verses of the *Yogavāsiṣṭha* tell us that the sage Agastya told Sutīkṣna about a Brahmin named Kāruṇya, the son of Agniveśya, to whom Agniveśya told the story of a nymph named Suruci, who learned from a messenger of Indra that the sage Vālmīki had told Bharadvāja the story of how Rāma had heard from the sage Vasiṣṭha a lot of stories . . . the stories of this text. Vasiṣṭha is thus the pivotal point. He is inside several of the stories; he is also the narrator to whose level of narration the text most often refers. Vasiṣṭha's ambivalent status as author and character thus raises the question of our own status: are we the dreamers, or are we part of someone else's dream?

The tale of the monk is one in which each dream seems to be nested inside another until we encounter the final, innermost dream and find that it is identified with the outermost dream: Rudra is the monk who is dreaming about Rudra. What we thought was a spiral turns out to be a kind of Möbius strip. A Möbius strip is a one-sided surface formed by holding one end of a rectangle fixed, rotating the opposite end through

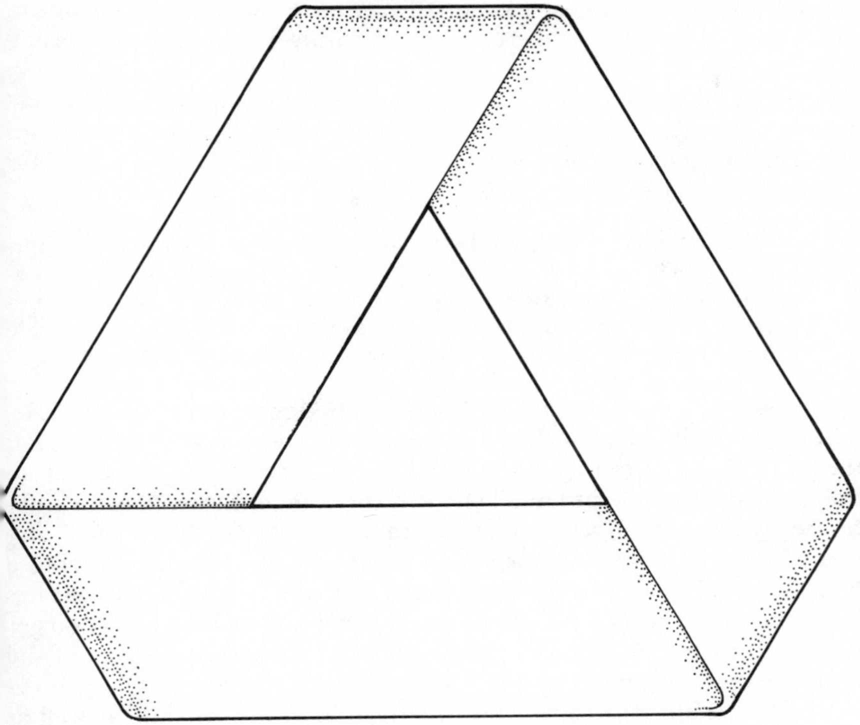

Figure 6. A Möbius Strip

180 degrees, and then attaching it to the first end (see figure 6).[71] This form has two sides but only one surface: it bends in on itself forever.

The Hindu universe is a kind of four-dimensional Möbius strip, finite but unbounded, negatively curved (as our own universe is now said to be, according to some scientists).[72] The Lokāloka, or World-non-World Mountain, where the stone-girl lives, is the nonboundary, a place where you can wander around forever and never get out. The World-non-World Mountain becomes identified, through the implications of the story, with the World Mountain, Mount Meru, which is the center of the familiar universe. The outside is thus the same as the inside. Indeed, Mount Meru is said to be twice as wide on top as it is at its base (32,000 and 16,000 leagues, respectively).[73] Thus it is shaped like an inverted cone, widest at the top, where most mountains are narrowest. This calls to mind the inverted world-tree at the center of many Indo-European cosmologies, but it also suggests the Möbius universe, in which the inside is the outside.

Such a universe is described by C. S. Lewis at doomsday for Narnia, his imaginary Christian and Platonic kingdom. The children go through the door of a small stable ("It is more like a mouth," says one), and find the inside bigger than the outside. In it is a garden:

> This garden is like the stable. It is far bigger inside than it was outside. . . . The farther up and the farther in you go, the bigger everything gets. The inside is larger than the outside . . . world within world . . . like an onion: except that as you go in and in, each circle is larger than the last. . . . The dream is ended: this is the morning.[74]

This inside-out onion is also implicit in the design of the Hindu temple. The outer periphery, which represents *saṃsāra*, is rich in detail; from it the worshiper passes through a series of courtyards, which diminish in both size and detail, until finally he enters the inner sanctum or "womb-house" (*garbha-gṛha*), which may be empty or may contain a small aniconic image, symbolic of *mokṣa*. And although one has moved from a large physical space to a small physical space, the feeling is that one has been moving outward all the time, spiritually, into larger and larger spaces, until one encounters, in the still center, the stark symbol of the totality of the universe.[75]

In all of these images we encounter the inversion of time as well as space. The ouroboros, the snake biting his tail, is a symbol of both spatial and temporal infinity. When Kekulé, the organic chemist, was wrestling with the problem of the structure of the benzene molecule, he dreamt of a snake biting its tail and awoke with the discovery of the benzene ring. His dream turned out to correspond to something real; the archetypal image supplied one of the very few possible basic answers to a problem in which he had immersed himself for a very long time. The Hindu god Śiva wears as bracelets and anklets snakes biting their tails, particularly when he dances his dance of doomsday—the moment when the end becomes the beginning again and a new Golden Age follows the holocaust. The ouroboros is also the symbol of logical paradox, as Patrick Hughes has pointed out:

> The ouroboros, the snake with his tail in his mouth, is the prototype of the vicious circle. What could be more vicious than to bite yourself, with a view, presumably, to eating yourself. Furthermore, this is impossible. Jaws can't devour jaws, the stomach can't digest itself. . . . This task . . . is a good definition of paradox. . . . The

> "Endless Snake" depicts an ouroboros who has become one with himself. It has fallen into the mathematical sign for infinity.[76]

This sign, a figure eight on its side, needs but a flick of the wrist to turn it into a Möbius strip, another example of a vicious circle. The snake that we mistake for a rope is not just any old serpent; it is the symbol of the riddle that we can never solve. The final twist comes when the snake, which symbolizes infinity, the Möbius universe, the ouroboros, and logical paradox, is also revealed, on closer inspection, to be, perhaps, a rope. The frontispiece to this book depicts such a snake, who even goes so far as to cast a rope-shadow with his snake half and a snake-shadow with his rope half.

The Möbius strip, then, is the shape of time and space in India. As Vasiṣṭha plunges farther and farther into that boundary that is the center, he pulls away the layers one by one, in a kind of Möbius striptease, until he finds himself back again in his own hut—the center of his own universe. Like the monk and like Rudra himself, Vasiṣṭha finds himself caught on the treadmill of the center and the periphery. He realizes that you never know which is which—that in fact there is no difference between the center and the periphery.

The implications of this twist bother Rāma, who asks, "How could a hundred Rudras be made by a Rudra who was himself made in someone's dream?" We are tempted to step back in rhythm with all the other characters who leap from frame to frame: we move from Rudra, who is dreamt by the swan (who is dreamt by the goose, . . . who is dreamt by Jīvaṭa), to the monk, who is imagined by Vasiṣṭha, who is a character in a book (the *Yogavāsiṣṭha*) that is said to be a lost part of another book (the *Rāmāyaṇa*) that is attributed to the poet Vālmīki, whose work has been translated into English by me and is now being read by you. (Take another look at figure 5.) When we reach Vasiṣṭha, we think we have reached the outermost level, but this turns out not only to be the first of several apparently "outermost" levels but also to be inside several inner levels.

Up to the point where we end, with all the characters crowded together around Rudra, the story of the monk's dream seems to be a cumulative tale; but as we look deeper, we see that the structure is not linear but concentric, that the story is not a cumulative tale but a nested tale, with a meshwork of interwoven threads that must be unraveled, not merely unknotted.[77] And, when we look closer still, we see the switchback loop. In a similar sequence, we can at first depict the line of transmission beyond Vasiṣṭha as a straight line: Vasiṣṭha to Vālmīki to O'Flaherty to you, the reader. But one of the things that the story teaches us is that the frame can always pull back from what seems its natural resting place to reveal yet another level within which it is nested; this was the moral of the tales of Lavaṇa and Gādhi, and it is even more vividly illustrated by the monk's dream. When we finally realize that there is no way of knowing whether we are in the final frame, the final awakening, we realize that the nested frames are infinite. One way of depicting this endlessness, as we saw in chapter four, is to imagine ever widening circles that never end; there is always another circle encircling the last visible circle. But another way to depict such an infinity would be to bend the outer limit in upon itself, to close up the spiral of dreams. This is what happens in the monk's dream.

This story forces us to consider the possibility that the outer level is identical with one of the levels that we had considered to be inside the outer level, or farther down the linear sequence; the dreamer, Rudra or the monk, is identical with the dreamt, Rudra or the monk. If we apply this twist to the line of transmission in the outward-bound direction, we must draw at least a dotted line from our putative ultimate point (ourselves) back to Rudra. This implies that Rudra is imagining the person who is reading this story about Rudra. It also implies that Vālmīki, the author of the *Yogavāsiṣṭha*, is imagining not only Vasiṣṭha but the readers of the *Yogavāsiṣṭha* and, moreover, that Vasiṣṭha is imagining Vālmīki. And if we apply the twist to the narrator of the book that you are at this moment reading, we might draw a dotted line back from O'Flaherty to the reader,[78] a step that the reader may not wish to take. The story of the monk's dream is not only circular (like the shared dream of Vikramāditya and Malayavatī in chapter two) and nested (like the dreams of Lavaṇa and Gādhi in chapter four), it is also looped. The two dreamers are giving each other mutual feedback.

We may avoid being tricked into accepting the involuted twist in Vasiṣṭha's story, which occurs at the moment when the monk leads us back to Rudra, back once more into the secret heart of the labyrinth, from which the characters in the story can never escape. But do we escape, after all? I think not. Vasiṣṭha experiences doubts about the monk's nonexistence, and so he cannot resist acting in his own play, just like the monk and Rudra. Authors are caught up in their stories, and so are readers. If Vasiṣṭha can plunge into the page and come face to face with the monk in his own story, as Rudra can go into his dream and wake up the people who are dreaming him, we cannot rest confident in our assumption that our level of the story is the final level.

If there *is* a final level, it is the level of the Godhead, *brahman*, the impersonal, transcendent continuum beyond even Rudra. This is the level of the universal soul, the source of all mental images that assume material form. Indeed, the hypothesis that there is a dreamer dreaming of us, or an author writing us, is a deciding factor in establishing these stories as Hindu rather than Buddhist, despite the fact that a (Buddhist) monk is the hero and despite the clearly discernible Buddhist influence on the

Hindu philosophy of idealism. For the Buddhists do not have the theological hypothesis to fall back upon. The Buddha refused to discuss precisely what it was that one found when one entered *nirvāṇa*; this refusal left a metaphysical void (*śūnyatā*) into which all later Buddhist philosophers eventually rushed. What would the story of the monk's dream be like if it were told by a Buddhist and therefore lacked the substructure of Godhead? The closest the Buddhists could come was the *Lankāvatāra-sūtra* and certain Zen *koans*, but these are not *narratives* on the grand scale of the *Yogavāsiṣṭha*. Without God (or, at least, gods) there can be no story, no myth.

Western Texts and Arguments: The Furies and the Red King

What would the story of the monk's dream be like if it were told in the West? Like the doctrine of illusion and the theme of the dream adventure, the paradox of the dreamer dreamt is known in the West. Recently the theme of the dreamer dreamt has been taken up by surrealist artists like René Magritte, surrealist playwrights like Pirandello (with his characters in search of an author), and writers like Jorge Luis Borges,[79] as well as by popular authors like Ursula LeGuin, Tom Stoppard, and John Barth and even by the creators of science fiction and comic books. Jung claimed to have dreamt of a yogin whose dream Jung was. Yet when we weigh the attention paid to this theme in Western literature, it appears to have been tackled only intermittently and rather nervously. Aeschylus provides a very early example both of the treatment of this theme by a major writer and of the problems that it has raised for subsequent Western readers.

A complex circle of shared dreams occurs in the second and third plays of Aeschylus's *Oresteia* trilogy, which retells the myth of the betrayal of Agamemnon by Clytemnestra. Aeschylus makes use of two closely related dreams, one explicit and the other, I think, partly explicit and partly implicit. In the first, Clytemnestra dreams that she has given birth to a serpent; when she offers it her breast to suck, it draws forth clotted blood with the milk. Orestes, her son, interprets the dream: "Since she has nursed this horrible portent, she must die violently. For I have become a serpent, and I will slay her, as this dream says." Orestes knows that he is the serpent, and Clytemnestra concurs in his interpretation. When Orestes says that he is going to kill her, she cries out, "Oh no! This is the serpent I gave birth to and suckled!"[80] This is not a shared dream; it is, however, a dream in which the dreamer and the person dreamed of agree on the interpretation, and it is a dream that comes true.

Soon, however, a more mysterious dream occurs. Aeschylus merely sketches this, but the Indian parallel fleshes it out. In the concluding episode of the second play, Orestes, who has just killed Clytemnestra, cries out, "Look! There they are, covered with serpents!" When the chorus insists that what he sees are just his fancies (*doxai*), that he is out of his mind because there is blood on his hands, Orestes answers, "You don't see them, but I see them. They aren't just fancies to *me*. They are clearly angry dogs from my mother."[81] The serpents from Clytemnestra's dream have now become part of Orestes' dream; now it *is* a shared dream. And that it is "just" a dream is clear from the fact that the members of the chorus think he has gone mad; they cannot see his dream, because it is only inside him.

This situation is dramatically altered as the final play of the trilogy opens. The chorus, which at the end of the last play consisted of old men, unable to see the avenging females covered with serpents, now consists of that very group of females: the chorus that we, the audience, now see is the group of Furies that was invisible to everyone but Orestes at the end of the second play. Everyone can see them now. Moreover, everyone agrees that *they are asleep*[82] and that they are dreaming of Orestes. This is evident from the passage in which the Furies cry out in their sleep, "Grab him! Grab him!" and Clytemnestra's ghost says to them, "You are just hunting your prey in a dream; what have you actually *done*?"[83] Thus we have a circle: Orestes dreams of the Furies, and they dream of him.

But this is not the only circle. The ghost of Clytemnestra appears, sees the Furies, and sees that they are asleep. Indeed, she begins her speech to them by saying, "You are sleeping, but what do I need sleepers for?"[84] She then tries to wake them up. These first words of her speech are the formula used throughout the Homeric epics and later Greek literature to introduce the statement the dream figure makes to the sleeper who is dreaming of that figure. In the Homeric formula the ghosts of the dead appear to people as dreams; and just as the ghost of Patroclus appears to Achilles, standing by his head (as a ghost or a dream would do),[85] so the ghost of the dead Clytemnestra appears in a dream to the Furies. Her introductory phrase thus indicates that the Furies are dreaming of her and that she is trying to wake them out of their dream of her. The formula becomes explicit a few lines later, when she says, "I, Clytemnestra, am calling to you in a dream right now."[86]

But Clytemnestra is also dreaming of the Furies. This is implied by the close association of ghosts and dreams in ancient Greece. Just as Clytemnestra dreamed of her murderer (Orestes), who would avenge the man she had murdered (Agamemnon), so she dreams of the Furies who are to avenge *her* death (at the hands of Orestes). George Devereux argues this point:

> The Erinyes [Furies] are, in a sense, Klytaimnestra's ghost and, in another sense, a product of her shed blood. This leads to the *seemingly* perplexing insight that the *dreamed* Klytaimnestra is *a product of* her own products: of the Erinyes. Her vengeful "ghost(s)" dream(s) of her vengeful double.[87]

Thus we have still another shared dream. People here are dreaming of one another as Vikramāditya and Malayavatī dreamed of each other. Nor is this merely a shared dream; it is also a circular dream, in which people conjure up people who conjure up the first dreamers. The Furies arise both out of Clytemnestra's mind (her dream) and out of her body (her blood).

It is not, perhaps, so surprising that the Furies all dream the same dream; they are, in a sense, a single person.[88] (We have encountered the Indian argument that *all* of us have the same basic consciousness, which enables us all to dream the same dream of the universe.) But in Greek terms it *is* strange that the Furies are dreaming of Clytemnestra, who is dreaming of them, and that Orestes is dreaming of the Furies, who are dreaming of him. Moreover, there is a third circular dream in the *Oresteia*, and this forms a circle when joined with the other two: Clytemnestra and Orestes are dreaming of each other. Clytemnestra dreams first of Orestes (the serpent who will kill her), but then, I think, one could argue that Orestes dreams of the ghost of Clytemnestra. Devereux suggests that Clytemnestra's double (*eidōlon*), the image of her that is enacted in the third play, is "both a dream and a haunting."[89] Here, again, the ghost is a dream. The ghost of the murdered woman haunts the son who murdered her; Clytemnestra is Orestes' nightmare.

The human Clytemnestra and Orestes share the dream of the nonhuman Furies even as they shared the dream of the suckling serpent. The Furies are thus mediators between the mother and the son; they are the supernatural place where the two dreams meet, and they, in turn, dream explicitly of both the mother and the son. The metaphysical element that supplements the psychological web emerges only when Aeschylus decides to depict on stage all three of the participants in the oneiric triangle (see figure 7).

This may indicate that Aeschylus is granting a kind of concrete physical status to all of the dreams, comparable to that which Indian dream theory postulates. But it may be only a dramatic convention, used to make the dreams more vivid than they would have been if the dreamers had merely narrated them. For the circularity of the dreams is deeply submerged in the *Oresteia*; it is certainly not central to the drama. Aeschylus may have realized that he was depicting a circular dream, but he did not stress it. He had other points to make that were more important to him.

Devereux does not think much of this metaphysical tangle:

> This is clearly a "boxes within boxes" situation: the image in one mirror replicates the image in another mirror and vice versa. Each turns the "potential" energy of the other into "kinetic" energy. . . . This "boxes within boxes" statement is therefore one which passes for "wisdom" in theology and in metaphysics. It is a kind of idle "wisdom," that fascinates the child quite as much as the adult, because it produces a mental vertigo.[90]

In earlier Western literature these boxes within boxes were not always dismissed quite so scornfully as they are by Devereux, but they were treated in a desultory way. Saint Augustine tells the story of a man who saw, in his own house before he went to bed, a philosopher who came to him and explained certain points in Plato that he had formerly refused to explain. When the man later met the philosopher and told him what had happened, the philosopher argued, "I did not do it; I merely dreamed that I did." This, says Saint Augustine, shows that what one man saw in his sleep was displayed to the other while awake, by means of a phantom appearance.[91] It is, I think, most fitting that this mutual dream should have been about Plato, whose complex idealism fueled one side of the schizophrenic Western approach to the problem, the idealist approach, in contrast to the empiricist approach, represented by Devereux.

Bishop Berkeley, whose philosophy owed much to Plato, is perhaps the most notorious Western theologian to have taken up the problem of idealism. Berkeley had no problem with his own reality; he could rest on Descartes's assertion of the existence of the self: Cogito ergo sum. (Of course, this is, as we saw in chapter four, not an argument but rather a statement of faith that cuts off argument.) But Berkeley was concerned with the continuing existence of things besides himself when he stopped thinking of them, and to this solipsism the bishop found the mind of God to be a satisfactory solution (another statement of faith). If Berkeley did not see a tree hidden in a deep forest, and if no one else saw it, did the tree still exist? Only if God saw it.[92]

Berkeley was immortalized and satirized in Lewis Carroll's *Through the Looking Glass*, which mythologizes several themes from Plato. The central skirmish takes place when Alice comes on the Red King asleep, and Tweedledee tells her that the king is dreaming about her and that, if he left off dreaming, she would go out like a candle. When Alice protests that she is real, begins to cry, and then argues that she wouldn't be able to cry if she weren't real, Tweedledum retorts, "I hope you don't suppose those are real tears?"[93] As Martin Gardner glosses this passage,

> Alice takes the common-sense position of Samuel Johnson, who supposed that he refuted Berkeley by kicking a large stone. "A very

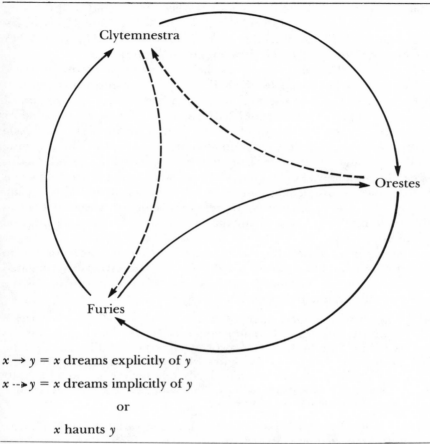

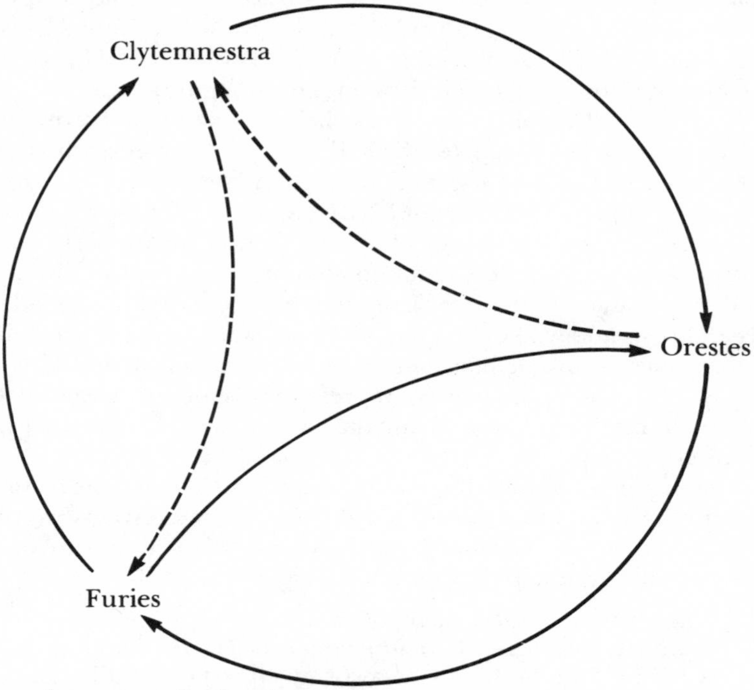

$x \rightarrow y$ = x dreams explicitly of y

$x \dashrightarrow y$ = x dreams implicitly of y

or

x haunts y

Figure 7. The Circular Dream in Aeschylus's *Oresteia*

> instructive discussion from a philosophical point of view," Bertrand Russell remarked, commenting on the Red King's dream in a radio panel discussion of *Alice*. "But if it were not put humorously, we should find it too painful." The Berkeleyan theme troubled Carroll as it troubles all Platonists.[94]

Alice does not kick a large stone; she cries. In this she may be invoking (consciously or unconsciously) the classical Indian touchstone of reality: suffering. If nothing else is real, tears are real. Indeed, the idea that we are all figments of the imagination of God (alias the Red King) does not trouble Indian idealists, though they do laugh at some aspects of the doctrine of illusion (as we have seen in the story of the magic pot and the dream of the court jester who became a pearl). And the particular image that Tweedledum uses to describe what Alice's fate would be if the king were to awaken—"You'd go out—bang!—just like a candle!"—is an Indian one. (Carroll uses the same image in "Down the Rabbit Hole.") For the blowing-out of a flame is the literal meaning of *nirvāṇa*.

At the end, Carroll takes the Berkeleyan theme and twists it: Alice wakes up from her dream (of the Red King) and wonders who it was that dreamed it all, she or the Red King: "He was part of my dream, of course—but then I was part of his dream, too!"[95] The question is never answered, for there is no way of telling whether we are part of someone else's dream. Miguel de Unamuno attempted to envelop the dreaming God in yet another dream: "I say that we are a dream of God. God is dreaming us and woe to that day when he awakes! God is dreaming. It is better not to think of that, but continue to dream that God is dreaming."[96] Thus Unamuno places a regressive twist on the dreaming God, as Carroll himself does, by implying that, as long as *we* do not wake up, God will not wake up.

The theme of mutual dreaming has continued to appear from time to time in the West, but it has usually done so only in response to repeated infusions from the Orient. A good example of such an infusion is the story of the Chinese philosopher Chuang Tsu:

> Once upon a time Chuang Tsu dreamed that he was a butterfly, a butterfly fluttering about enjoying itself. It did not know that it was Chuang Tsu. Suddenly he awoke with a start, and he was Chuang Tsu again. But he did not know whether he was Chuang Tsu who had dreamed that he was a butterfly, or whether he was a butterfly dreaming he was Chuang Tsu. This is an example of what is called the Transformation of Things.[97]

Woody Allen has created a delightful modern variant of this Chinese myth of the nested and circular dream:

> The Emperor Ho Sin had a dream in which he beheld a palace greater than his for half the rent. Stepping through the portals of the edifice, Ho Sin suddenly found that his body became young again, although his head remained somewhere between sixty-five and seventy. Opening a door, he found another door, which led to another; soon he realized he had entered a hundred doors and was now out in the backyard.
>
> Just when Ho Sin was on the verge of despair, a nightingale perched on his shoulder and sang the most beautiful song he'd ever heard and then bit him on the nose.
>
> Chastened, Ho Sin looked into a mirror and instead of seeing his own reflection, he saw a man named Mendel Goldblatt, who worked for the Wasserman Plumbing Company and who accused him of taking his overcoat. From this Ho Sin learned the secret of life, and

> it was "Never to yodel." When the emperor awoke, he was in a cold sweat and couldn't recall if he dreamed the dream or was now in a dream being dreamt by his bail bondsman.[98]

Despite the characteristically Allenesque zaniness, the story emerges as a myth through its use of the themes of the confusion of dreams and reality, the seductive song of the swan maiden, the man who sees his own double, the ambivalent experience of youth and old age, and the doors beyond doors.

In addition to the lighthearted satires of Woody Allen and Lewis Carroll, there is the grumpier tirade of George Devereux, in his comment on the circular nested dream in the *Oresteia*:

> As a child, I was entranced by the picture of a girl holding a picture, etc. In the lycée I became fascinated with the notion that our heavenly bodies may only be the atoms of larger bodies, etc., and our atoms the heavenly bodies of a smaller universe, etc. . . . I do not propose to waste time on refuting *Scheinprobleme*. I hold that any endless vista of "wisdom" of the "boxes within boxes" type, which cannot be adequately solved by an application of Russell's theory, is *a priori* nonsensical.[99]

The picture Devereux saw "as a child" may have been Velasquez's painting that shows a man holding a mirror in which he sees himself holding a mirror. The painting is ingeniously hung in the Prado on a wall facing a mirror, so that the observer can trace the images inside the painting and then outside it again, with himself as the ambiguous pivotal level of reality—the only level that seems to interest Devereux. The metaphysical implications of this *mise en abîme* make use of that peculiar juxtaposition of the banal and the sublime that serves not only the humor of Lewis Carroll and Woody Allen (and eludes Devereux's humorlessness) but a far more serious purpose. Indeed, Devereux has missed the point of the *Oresteia* paradox: what is troubling is not that the dreams expand in ever widening circles but that they twist in upon themselves: the outside joins the inside.

This paradox is largely relegated by our culture to the fantasies of children, who still believe that their dreams are real. The mental vertigo that fascinates children, in Devereux's indictment, continues to produce some of the most imaginative literature in our day, in books written not by children but for children. Writers like Lewis Carroll, C. S. Lewis, and Russell Hoban (whose "Last Visible Dog" presents the image of infinite regress on a Bonzo dogfood can)[100] continue to preserve the insights that we have traditionally set apart in the sacred space of the nursery, in fairytales and children's myths. These stories are ostensibly intended for people who have not yet learned that their dreams are not real, but they may also be read by people who (as we saw in chapter one) have grown old enough to understand how real their dreams are.[101]

The Dreamer Dreamt

The dreamer dreamt is an instance of the theme of recursion or self-reference, which is itself one variant of the paradox of infinite regress.[102] The existence of several levels of reality allows us to pop out of a play within a play or a fantasy within a fantasy into a "realer" world—though one that is still, perhaps, one level away from the most real world.[103] But then these levels twist back in what Douglas Hofstadter has characterized as a Strange Loop or a Tangled Hierarchy, a transformation of the paradox of the receding frame. Tangled Hierarchies abound in logic as a special kind of self-referential paradox, of which perhaps the most famous is the Paradox of Epimenides, the Cretan who said, "All Cretans are liars." (One might also note the unconsciously self-referential paradox of Plato, the poet who said that all poets are liars.) A sharper form of the paradox is the simple assertion "This statement is false." Hofstadter finds examples of Strange Loops in the fugues of Bach, the staircases of M. C. Escher, and Gödel's mathematical theorem, all of which "appeal to very simple and ancient intuitions"[104]—intuitions that, as we have seen, are preserved in the Hindu texts.

M. C. Escher depicts simultaneous worlds, impossible worlds, and infinity; he was once even accused of having illustrated reincarnation.[105] One of his most famous paradoxical drawings, *Drawing Hands*, is a hand drawing a picture of a hand that draws the first hand (plate 15), a concept that also appears in the drawings of Saul Steinberg. And Escher's *Picture Gallery* depicts a man looking at a painting of a town that contains a gallery in which *he* is looking at a painting.[106] Once the loop doubles back on itself, we have a dreamer dreaming of a dreamer who is dreaming of *him*, which is the paradox of Alice and the Red King or of the monk and Rudra. We have a picture of a man watching himself have an illusion.

The paradox of mutual hierarchy—the relationship between two things, each higher than the other—is an old one in India, and we have already seen several different instances of it, on several different levels. In chapter two we saw lovers dream of each other; each regarded the other as part of his or her mind, and each was right. On the formal level, too, myths and dreams gave rise to each other. In chapter three we saw stories in which each of two people regarded the other as an illusory figure who had entered the real world and then vanished. In chapter four we saw how Untouchables and Brahmins mutually polluted each other; here, too, we saw folktales and court literature giving each other mutual feedback. And now in chapter five we have encountered people and worlds who not only dream of each other but create each other. Again and again we have been thrown back into the paradox of the chicken and the egg; but we have seen how some people are able to get real eggs from their illusory chickens.

It should be noted that mutual influence of this kind produces a true paradox only on the level of creation. There is nothing peculiar about chickens being born out of eggs (an egg, it has been said, is just a chicken's way of making another chicken), but the riddle goes, "Which came *first* . . . ?" Similarly, to have two people dream of each other is not *logically* troubling, though it challenges our concepts of the possibilities of certain types of mental communication. It is when two dreamers *create* each other in their dreams that the problem becomes a logical paradox: which of the two dreamers is the first dreamer? This is the paradox posed by the monk's dream. The Indian version of the chicken and the egg, the seed and the tree, is negated and used as an instance of "Upside-Down Language," language that laughs at itself, together with other metaphors of illusion: "Sprout without seed, branch without trunk, fruit without flower, son born of a sterile womb, climbing a tree without legs . . . ."[107] That sprouts and seeds should give rise to each other is a natural paradox; that they should not is an unnatural paradox. It is also a violation of the normal function of time, a switchback in the loop of time, for the sprout to grow before the seed or without the seed.

Hofstadter suggests that we can untangle the Strange Loop in a narrative or a picture if we step far enough back.[108] He speaks of a "protected" or "inviolate" level: if there are three authors, each of whom exists only in a novel by one of the other two, the three of them are caught in a Strange Loop or Tangled Hierarchy; but if they are all characters in yet another novel, by a fourth author, that author is "outside of the space in which that tangle takes place—author H is in an inviolate space," unassailable by the rules that apply on the other levels. The three authors have access to one another but not to the fourth author:

> They can't even imagine him—any more than you can imagine the author of the book *you're* a character in. If I were to draw [the fourth author], I would represent him somewhere off the page. Of course that would present a problem, since drawing a thing necessarily puts it *onto* the page.[109]

According to this, the answer to Lewis Carroll's question, "Which dreamed the dream?" (the Red King or Alice), is: "Lewis Carroll." Hofstadter would encompass the Strange Loop within a receding frame. A similar solution is offered for Escher's *Drawing Hands*: M. C. Escher is the hand drawing both hands. As Hofstadter remarks, "One could further Escherize the Escher picture by taking a photograph of a hand drawing it, and so on."[110] The theological implications of this solution are clear from what Hofstadter says next:

> The illusion is created, because of the Tangled Hierarchy of symbols, that there is no inviolate level. One thinks there is no such level because that level is shielded from our view . . . ; [it is] analogous to the invisible "prime mover" Escher.[111]

We go along assuming that we are in a simple hierarchy until the levels "take [us] by surprise and fold back in a hierarchy-violating way." At this point, the only thing that can extricate us from the tangle is the hypothesis of a prime mover behind the scenes. What the prime mover moves is the infinitely receding frame. In a way, these paradoxes constitute an attempt to force the reader or watcher to construct a proof of the existence of God. Similarly, the tales of illusion force the reader or listener to imagine that he is part of someone else's dream. The apparently self-created object must be created by someone else; someone outside the frame *and inside it* must be drawing the picture or dreaming the dream. Other minds—or Another Mind—may be dreaming us.

Hofstadter's solution to the puzzle fails because it can still be outflanked by another move: the receding frame (which now encases the Strange Loop) can be turned into yet another Strange Loop by twisting the new outer frame back in upon itself. Though Hofstadter rightly senses that the Buddhists have thought long and hard about the same paradoxes that he has chosen to tackle (he cites several Zen *koans*), he does not really understand how much farther they have gone than he has gone. He states one of the rules of his game:

> Inside a fantasy, any theorem from the "reality" one level higher can be brought in and used. It is as if a "No Smoking" sign in a theater applied not only to all the moviegoers, but also to all the actors in the movie, and, by repetition of the same idea, to anyone inside multiply nested movies! (Warning: There is no carry-over in the reverse direction: theorems inside fantasies cannot be exported to the exterior! If it weren't for this fact, you could write anything as the first line of a fantasy, and then lift it out into the real world as a theorem.)[112]

But this final twist is precisely what is achieved by the *Yogavāsiṣṭha*: the fantasies do move in both directions. The rules created inside the "movie" are taken out and applied to the people in the theater: the people that exist inside Vasiṣṭha's story (the monk, for instance, or the husband of the girl in the stone) come out and interact with people on the "reality" level (the level of Vasiṣṭha), and the actors inside the monk's movie (the people in his dream) are also "exported to the exterior." Moreover, the "fourth author" is *inside* the story of one of the other authors. God is in our mind while we are in His.

The final twist that closes the paradox up again is implicit in the myths of the mouth of God (chapter three): Yaśodā is inside Kṛṣṇa, and Kṛṣṇa is inside her; Mārkaṇḍeya is inside Viṣṇu, and Viṣṇu is inside him. The relationships between these two pairs do not seem to be precisely the same: Yaśodā and Kṛṣṇa create each other, while Viṣṇu and Mārkaṇḍeya are dreaming of each other. But in terms of the Indian equation between mental creation and physical creation, between dreaming and being reborn, finding and making, we can see that they are, after all, the same.

Mārkaṇḍeya and Yaśodā at first think that God is their son and that he is inside them, just as the world-soul (*brahman*) is identified with the individual soul (*ātman*) and, more particularly, as a child is contained inside the seed or womb of the parent. Both of them come to learn that God is their parent and that they are inside him. Yet this second vision does not replace the first view; it supplements it. God is both inside and outside them, is both their child and their parent. This image of mutual parenthood, each one creating the other, is basic to Indian thinking. It appears first in the *Ṛg Veda*, in a series of riddles about people who are the parents of their parents. Thus it is said, "From Puruṣa, Virāj was born, and from Virāj came Puruṣa,"[113] and, again, "From Aditi, Dakṣa was born, and from Dakṣa, Aditi."[114] Sāyaṇa, in commenting on the second of these verses, cites Yāska's assertion[115] that, by the *dharma* of the gods, two births can be mutually productive of each other.

The term by which a child addressed his father, "Tāta," also came to be used as the term by which a father addressed his son, though the first usage remained as well. "Tāta" first means "my son" and then comes to mean "my father" *or* "my son." This etymological confusion appears also in the (false) gloss for the word for wife (*jayā*) as the woman in whom the husband is once again born (*jāyate*) as his own son.[116] In Hindu mythology the argument as to who is the father and who the son—an argument that is only implicit in the episode of Mārkaṇḍeya in the belly of Viṣṇu—becomes explicit in a subsequent episode in the same story. On one occasion, after Viṣṇu had reabsorbed Mārkaṇḍeya and continued to sleep in the ocean of chaos, Viṣṇu and Brahmā became embroiled in an argument. Brahmā maintained that, as the primeval Grandfather (Pitāmaha), he was the father of us all; yet, as Viṣṇu pointed out, Brahmā was born from a lotus that grew out of Viṣṇu's navel (as Mārkaṇḍeya "grew" out of Viṣṇu's mouth). As they continued to argue, Viṣṇu went in and out of Brahmā's mouth, but Brahmā then went in and out of Viṣṇu's belly (exiting through the navel).[117]

This argument takes on interesting iconic aspects because of the ambiguity of the image of the lotus growing from Viṣṇu's navel. Since in Indian mythology the lotus is a symbol of the womb, Viṣṇu acts as the mother of Brahmā, which is what Viṣṇu insists is the case; but if one interprets the image anthropomorphically, it is apparent that the lotus stalk is a cord that connects the navel of Viṣṇu to a womb-lotus that is part of the body of Brahmā, and this, in human terms, would make Viṣṇu the child of Brahmā, which Brahmā insists is the case. This simple physiological metaphor is then further complicated by the fact that, in India (and elsewhere, as Eliade has shown), the navel is often a symbol of the center or womb of the world, the place of origin. If Viṣṇu's navel is a womb-symbol and Brahmā's lotus is a womb-symbol, the two gods are at a standoff. At this moment in the argument, Śiva appears in the form of a cosmic phallus, proving once and for all that *he* is the father of *both* Viṣṇu and Brahmā; he is the One who draws the hand drawing the hand drawing the hand.

But this solution is only temporary. For in one version of the story of the cosmic phallus, when Śiva appears, Brahmā calls him, "My son," whereupon Śiva immediately beheads Brahmā.[118] In another story, Brahmā merely asks Śiva to become his (adopted) son, and still Śiva beheads him.[119] Yet in many myths Śiva is quite content to be, and to be known as, Brahmā's son.[120] The fact of mutual paternity is basically accepted as an underlying assumption of all these myths; from time to time, certain gods choose to make an issue of it, but for the most part it causes no trouble.[121] When, in the *Bhagavad Gītā*, Arjuna asks Kṛṣṇa how he can have existed both before and after Vivasvan, Kṛṣṇa simply replies, "I have passed through many births, and so have you; but I know them all, and you do not. I become born by my own creative power [*māyā*]."[122]

The mutual creative dream in the tale of the monk and the tale of the girl in the stone differs in this respect from the shared dreams in chapter two: in the shared dream, one person dreams of another who already exists, while the dreamers of the mutual creative dreams dream each other into existence. The element of mutual creation is also present in the myths of the mouth of God, but these myths involve physical projection of one person out of another rather than mental projection of one dream into another. Since, as we have seen, the processes of physical and mental projection are not basically different at all, the myth of the shared dream and the myth of the mouth of God can be superimposed on each other. And when we then add the theme of the receding frame, we have the mutual creative dream, or the myth of the dreamer dreamt (figure 8).

In graphing the myth of the mouth of God, I have used a broken line for mankind and a solid line for God. This was intended to reflect the Indian emphasis on what is relatively more real. In the West, one would

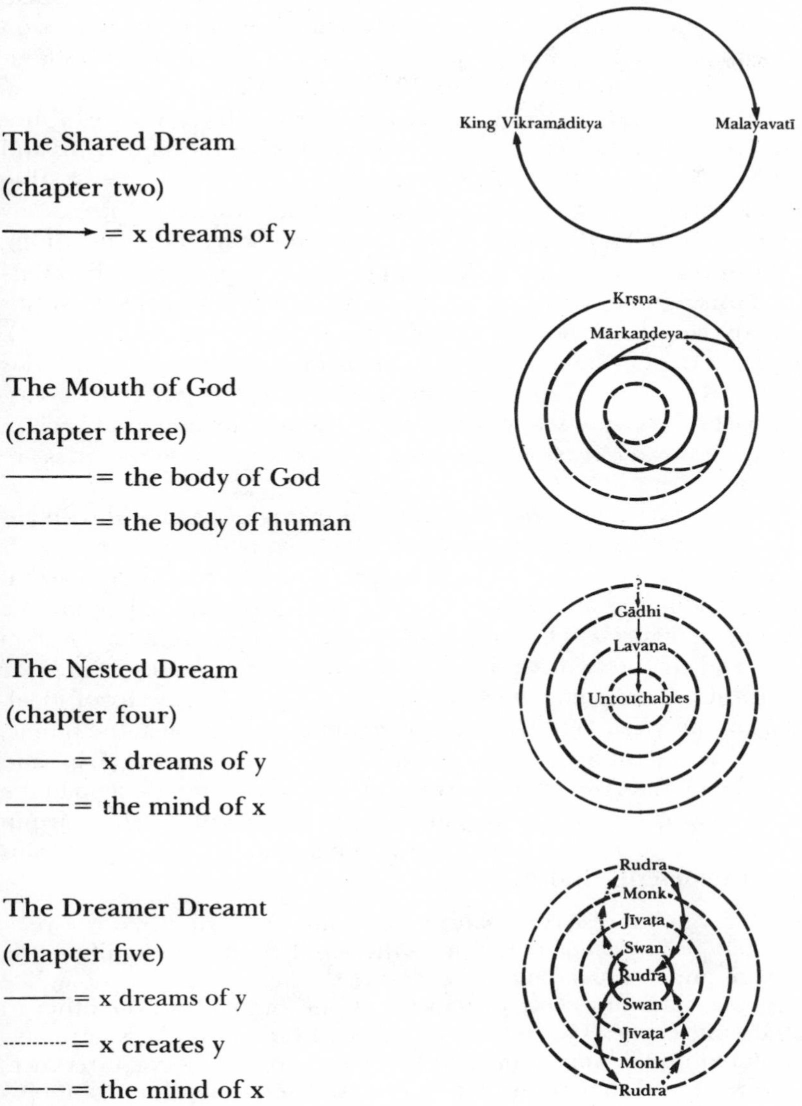

Figure 8. The Shared Dream, the Mouth of God, the Nested Dream, and the Dreamer Dreamt

have used a broken line for God—to indicate that he is only speculatively real—and a solid line for mankind—the solid given of experience. But in India, theology takes the place of anthropology; God is the measure of all things. Similarly, I have used a solid line for mental creation (dreaming) and a dotted line for physical creation (begetting or fashioning); this, too, I think, reflects the Indian priorities.

The theme of mutual dreaming thus draws to itself the theme of mutual creation: Rudra and the monk create each other the way Viṣṇu and Brahmā create each other. This conflation of apparently contrasting modes of being is what ultimately short-circuits Hofstadter's one-way rule. When Viṣṇu and Brahmā argue about who is the father of whom, Śiva proves that *he* is the father of both of them; this is the Indian parallel to Hofstadter's hypothetical situation in which the third author (Śiva) is the author of both of the other authors (Viṣṇu and Brahmā). But the tale of the monk's dream demonstrates that the third author (Śiva, alias Rudra) is part of someone else's story (Vasiṣṭha's), that Vasiṣṭha is part of yet another, and that all of them ultimately fold back in upon the Godhead (*brahman*) that is the Möbius strip whose two sides are matter and spirit.

In the West, the hypothesis that God is thinking of us provides an answer to the terror of solipsism; in India, the hypothesis that God is *made of us* provides a very different sort of answer. And it is this difference that causes the Indian paradox to develop as it does, to continue looping the final frame in on itself. The Indian Möbius strip has the mind of God on one side and the body of God on the other. It encompasses us in a far more profound and complete way than the Tangled Hierarchy of idealism does in the West. Western thought would place the hard, the public, the material, and all the others in that list on one side of the strip, and the soft, the private, the spiritual on the other. By twisting the strip in the Möbius manner, Indian thinkers argue that the two dimensions are in fact one; the inside is the outside. A. K. Ramanujan has used the Möbius metaphor to describe Indian poetics:

> The Swiss linguist Ferdinand de Saussure once said that the relationship of *signifiant* and *signifié*, the signifier and the signified, the forms and the meaning of words, are distinct and inseparable, like the two sides of a piece of paper; cut one and you cut the other in the same curve. This inseparableness, as Indian thinkers have also pointed out, is not peculiar to poetry. . . . But in poetic utterance, the relationship becomes usable for a further dimension: A Möbius band, made up of two-sided paper, is an object that has only one surface. The flowing of the two surfaces into one continuum is made possible by one little twist, the obliquity in the use of language: *vakrokti*, the crooked way of saying it, the bend in language or the oblique is the source of the poetic.[123]

The creative twist is not, indeed, "peculiar to poetry"; it is characteristic of the supreme creative process itself, the process of *māyā*. The bend in the mind turns the symbol for infinity into the symbol of the illusory universe.

The ontological rope (or snake) in India is not twisted in on itself merely once, like a simple square knot; it is a very tricky clove hitch, which catches up not only the characters in the story but the author himself—the one who seems to exist on the inviolate level. This is why Indian Strange Loops are even stranger than Western Strange Loops. Our greatest surprise arises not from the discovery that the hierarchy of dreamers is not fixed, as we thought it was, or that we are not at the top of it, as we thought we were, but from the realization that new hierarchies are constantly being created, by our minds and by those who are thinking about us. In India, not even the drawing hand or the author is safe from the entangling ontological coils. No one, not even God, can escape from *māyā*.

6 The Art of Illusion

Indian literature makes use of two basic devices for depicting the philosophy of illusion. One is narrative—stories in which things happen that must be explained, and are explained, within the texts. The second device is the use of metaphors and similes. Lavaṇa and Gādhi turn out to be metaphors for each other, mutual similes; and the tale of the monk's dream is the acting-out of the simile "The universe is like a dream." The myths of illusion abound in similes and metaphors, for they are trying to show how something can be two things at once, and metaphor and simile are language's way of looking at an object in two ways at once or at two objects in one way.

Metaphor is a typically Indian way of viewing the world. From the time of the *Ṛg Veda*, metaphysical truths were explained in bold metaphors based on a complete equation of microcosm and macrocosm: the sun is not said to be "like" the eye of the sacrificial horse; it *is* the eye of the horse. To understand what a thing is *like* is to understand what it *is*. Everything is connected to everything else as a way of making it familiar, a habit that may betray a cultural anxiety about anything that is strange or inconsistent.[1] As Salman Rushdie remarks, "As a people, we are obsessed with correspondences. Similarities between this and that, between apparently unconnected things, make us clap our hands delightedly when we find them out."[2] Ordering things by categories according to their resemblances is an inherently scientific way of perceiving the world, and analogy (*upamāna*) is therefore one of the basic "ways of knowing."

The *Yogavāsiṣṭha* is a morass of metaphor: almost every verse contains one. It is as if we could not understand anything unless we compared it to something else. Moreover, these metaphors tend to liken various experiences (which are realistic, if not necessarily real) to mythic themes, such as doomsday, which neither the author nor his readers can be assumed to have experienced. This serves not to ground reality in myth; on the contrary, it challenges the primacy of what appears to be real: one's apparently real life can be known only through the unknowable experience of doomsday.

The metaphors and similes of the *Yogavāsiṣṭha* create levels of persuasion through verbal images, drawing us into and through ever widening circles of comprehension. The various orbits of metaphor and simile include the ordinary simile, which is basic to all Sanskrit poetry; the larger philosophical metaphors; the similes implicit in the parallels between the various stories in the text; and, finally, the all-encompassing simile for the universe itself, which is not anything but merely like something.

The *Yogavāsiṣṭha* is explicit about its intentions in using similes (*dṛṣṭānta*), particularly in its judgment of the value of this "way of knowing" (*pramāṇa*) in comparison with other ways of knowing:

> Since *brahman* has no form, how could a simile, which does have a form, fit *brahman*? Similes are merely the expressions of a fool's imagination. But comparing the universe to a dream does not entail the common flaws in the use of similes, such as being an imperfect fit or contradictory. The comparability of the universe and a dream is clear to us from childhood on, and this simile fits precisely with all of our imaginings, meditations, wishes, curses, etc. Finally, the simile of the resemblance between the universe and a dream is found in the Vedas and textbooks. It cannot be explained quickly, but requires a whole chain of arguments.[3]

The chief root metaphor of the *Yogavāsiṣṭha*, the metaphor of the dream, is thus validated by the ultimate authority: the verbal authority of scripture (*śabda*). It is also validated by direct perception (experience "from childhood on"), which is a part (though only a part) of Indian common sense. Metaphor is a basic Indian way of thinking. Despite the inherent inadequacy of similes (or any other form of language) to express what is ultimately ineffable (a fact that is confessed in the Upaniṣads, in the refrain that follows each attempted metaphor for the Godhead, "Not thus, not thus" [*neti, neti*]),[4] it is the only way to approach a definition. Like Zeno's paradox or the expanding circles of the receding frame, the use of metaphor brings us closer and closer to the understanding of the ineffable, but we never quite reach it.

Indian Texts: The Root Metaphors of the *Yogavāsiṣṭha*

The Serpent and the Rope as a Metaphor for a Mistake

The two basic metaphors that we have encountered in Indian discussions of the problem of illusion are the shell that is mistaken for a piece of silver and the rope that is mistaken for a snake. The silver shell is perhaps more popular with the authors of the philosophical texts; it has a cold, mathematical purity about it. The rope/snake is, however, more popular with the author of the *Yogavāsiṣṭha*, perhaps because it encompasses not only the mystery of visual perception but also the mystery of something dead that comes to life. The *Yogavāsiṣṭha* uses the serpent and the rope as the basic metaphor for a mistake (*bhrānti*, *vibhrama*), often in conjunction with the self-evident metaphor of the mirage: "Just as the mistaken idea that a rope is a snake is removed when one looks at it carefully, so the misery of the world of rebirth [*saṃsāra*] is removed when one reads this book. . . . The mistaking of a rope for a serpent is based on the mistaken belief that the word 'serpent' applies to the rope."[5] Tulasī Dās says, "To him who knows not Rāma, the false appears the true, as a rope is mistaken for a snake. To him who knows Rāma, the world is naught, as the illusion of a dream vanishes on waking."[6] The metaphor is a favorite with the *Lankāvatārasūtra*, too, though this Buddhist text uses it to express not a mere mistake but illusion itself, in the extreme Buddhist form of the doctrine: "Like fools who, not recognizing the rope, take it for a snake, people imagine an external world, not recognizing that it is made of their own thought."[7]

Though he criticizes the doctrine of illusion, Sir Roland Penrose draws on (and reverses) the basic Indian metaphor that expresses it:

> A more direct use of illusion which belongs to contemporary art is the use it has made of the enigmatic nature of reality and the uncertainty with which we are able to identify objects. The experience, common to all, of feeling satisfied that a stick lying in our path is insigificant, only to be suddenly disturbed when it moves and is found in reality to be a snake, brings with it a surprise which can make us laugh or cringe.[8]

For Penrose, the snake is wrongly perceived as a rope; for the traditional Indian philosopher, the rope is wrongly perceived as a snake. A far more significant difference, however, lies in Penrose's confidence that, once you see it move, you *know* it is a snake, whereas the Indian philosopher would still think it possible that the snake might turn out to be a rope after all.

A similar reversal (the rope turning into a snake) appears in another non-Indian text, the Hebrew Bible. Indeed, the particular variants in that text suggest some meanings that may well also be hidden in the Indian use of the symbol. In Exodus, God teaches Moses how to turn a rod into a snake (and back again) in order to impress the Jews and to convince the pharaoh that a miracle has occurred. The doubts that Moses himself feels (not about the truth of the miracle but about the chances of convincing the Jews) are eventually assuaged when the rod dutifully turns into a snake and the Jews are duly impressed. When Moses uses this trick to persuade the pharaoh, however, it backfires, because the pharaoh's magicians can do it too, as they immediately demonstrate. In the end, the only way that Moses can convince the pharaoh of his own powers and the powers of his God is not by parlor tricks with serpents but by inflicting great sufferings on the Egyptians, culminating in the slaughter of their firstborn sons.

The metaphor becomes an actual plot device in the Hebrew text: it is an element in the scientific proof of a nonscientific fact. Significantly, it does not work because it functions in the realm of mere mistakes (*bhrama*), making one thing *look like* another. Since it is superficial, other superficial magicians can duplicate it. The existence of a corroborating group, which is used in other texts to prove the public rather than private nature of the trick—and hence its scientific status—is here used to undermine the trick: since everyone can *do* it as well as *see* it, it is devalued.

To move from this false level to the real level of metaphysical proof, it is necessary to raise the stakes. Ironically, the Hebrew God does this with cumulative small annoyances. There is no single blinding earthquake; instead, lots and lots of little things happen that would be quite tolerable if they occurred one at a time, or just a few at a time, as they usually do (one or two gnats or frogs or locusts) but which become intolerable as they mount to the level of a plague. The death of children, even in large numbers, is a tragic but hardly miraculous occurrence; yet this is what finally convinces the pharaoh that divine forces are at work. For this final proof, the death of the sons, is the classic catalyst of theodicy, the universally acknowledged supreme grief,[9] the event that catapults Nārada from one universe to another. To change the rod/rope to a snake is a magic trick, the trick of bringing the dead (or inanimate) to life; this is routinely accomplished by saints. But to change the living to the dead is a far more serious trick, and it more often triggers the breakthrough between worlds. This is something that a god does all the time.

The Son of a Barren Woman as a Metaphor for Impossibility

The *Yogavāsiṣṭha* (like Indian logical tradition) uses the metaphor "the son of a barren woman" to describe a logical impossibility. The idea involved is more complex than the idea that is involved in the serpent/rope metaphor; for where the serpent/rope expresses the concept of *mistaking* something that is there (a rope) for something that is not (a snake), the son of a barren woman *combines* something that is there (a barren woman) with something that is not (a son). Some philosophers, including Śaṅkara, accepted two sorts of unreality: the logical impossibility (the son of a barren woman) and the thing that is never met in experience (the hare's horn). The hare's horn is a less cogent argument and is often simply added on, after the image of the son of a barren woman. In the broader argument about the use of optical illusions to prove the nonreality (as well as the reality) of the universe, Indian opponents of absolute idealism argued that both elements of the mistake and both elements of the impossibility (the rope *and* the snake, the barren woman *and* her son), are real; only the *relation* between them is unreal. One can curse a man (a man who does exist) by saying, "Let your mother be a barren woman [*vandhyā 'thavā bhavatu* (*taj*) *jananī*]," [10] which is roughly equivalent to the Western curse, "You son of a bitch" combined with "I'll make you wish you'd never been born," where the curse cannot come true literally because the object of the curse *was* born. The son of a barren woman appears in the upside-down language of the Indian saints to express the nonsense of the material world but not its nonexistence.

On the simplest level, the *Yogavāsiṣṭha* uses the metaphor of the son of a barren woman to express the formlessness of the Godhead: "It has no form but appears to have a form, as if it were a real thing, like the son of a barren woman." [11] It is used to represent nonsense: Rāma says, "This mountain was made by the son of a barren woman and by the horns of a hare; on it a stone, stretching out its arms, dances a death-dance." [12] And in reply to this, Vasiṣṭha says, "I do not speak in riddles, Rāma; listen and I will explain how it is that 'What is unreal is like the son of a barren woman,' as they say." [13]

But quite often this metaphor is varied in a way that entirely changes its meaning; instead of being an image of impossibility and nonsense, it expresses a poignant emotional reality. The *Yogavāsiṣṭha* says, "Just as a son is born, or has been born, to a barren woman, and is unborn [in reality] even though he is born [in a dream] . . . ." [14] The commentary on this verse interpolates the phrase "in a dream [*svapne*]" simply to make sense of the text, but in the *Lankāvatārasūtra* this phrase appears several times as an integral part of the text: "Is it a dream, or an illusion, or a magic city in the sky? Is it poor eyesight, or a mirage, or a dream that a barren woman gave birth?" "Like a mirage in the sky, appearances have many forms, like the natural child of a barren woman—in a dream [*svapne vandhyauraso yathā*]." "It is like perceiving the rise and disappearance of things in a dream; it is like the birth and death of a barren woman's child." [15] This changes the meaning of the metaphor; for a barren woman, especially in India, is likely to dream constantly of a son. Thus, although the *child* remains unreal, the *dream* of a barren woman—the fact that she dreams about a son—is certainly very real. The latent content is real even if the manifest content is not. The Hebrew Bible tells us of many barren women who had sons—that is, of women who were barren *until* they had sons; but since these women had thought themselves barren forever, they regard the children of their old age as a miracle. Thus the "impossibility" of the son of a barren woman is changed into the "amazing fact" of the son of a barren woman, and the amazement with which this fact is received directly parallels the amazement with which the dream that comes true is received in the Hindu stories.

Both aspects of the metaphor—the impossibility of the actual thing and the certainty of the dream of it—are preserved in a Sanskrit maxim, "The maxim of the request of the aged spinster [*vṛddhakumārīvākyanyāyaḥ*]," [16] which is described as follows:

> Indra said to an old virgin, "Choose a boon." She chose this boon: "Let my sons eat a lot of milk and butter and cakes from a golden bowl." Now, she had no husband, so how could she have sons, or cows, or money? Thus in one wish she encompassed husband, sons, cows, and wealth. (This maxim would be applied to a sentence having a variety of meanings.) [17]

The maxim implies both that such a woman would ask for sons (and the attendant goods of this world) and that she might get them if she were lucky enough and clever enough. Thus there are a number of ways in which dreams do come true, even the dreams of old virgins.

The Crow and the Palm Tree as a Metaphor for Pure Chance

The maxim of the crow and the palm tree connotes pure chance: "A crow alighted on a palmyra tree, and at the same moment some of the fruit fell on its head and killed it. The maxim is therefore used to illustrate a startling and purely accidental occurrence." [18] Its secondary connotation, after the primary connotation of accident, is a bad accident. This secondary meaning, however, is reversed in the folk literature, where the crow-and-palm-tree maxim is used to denote "good fortune or success, which comes, unexpected, to a beneficiary, who himself seems to be the author of that success, but is in reality not so at all." [19] The original tale is lost, but this folk gloss generally refers to a crow who alights on a palm tree just as the tree is falling, so that it appears that the insigificant animal causes the downfall of the enormous tree. In this sense it denotes good fortune of a purely fortuitous nature, a kind of serendipity.

It seems likely that the negative gloss of the maxim is older, and thus closer to the intended spirit of the maxim, than the optimistic folk version. This hypothesis is supported by the evidence of related maxims about pure chance. There are two relevant generalizations that one can make about such maxims: there are a surprising number of them, and most of them connote bad luck, not good luck. Among the "handful" of popular maxims collected by G. A. Jacob in 1900, two are about good luck (though they point out how rare it is), but six (including The Crow and the Palm Tree) are about bad luck—and about how inevitable it is.

"The blind man and the quail." As a certain blind man strikes one hand with the palm of the other hand, a quail lands between his hands. As unlikely as that is, even so difficult is it to be born as a man and to make contact with good people.[20]

"The letter made by the wood-worm." The worm bores holes in wood and in books, and these holes sometimes assume the shape of a letter of the alphabet.[21] [This maxim is roughly equivalent to the metaphor, in Western probability theory, of the monkey who plays with a typewriter and composes the complete works of Shakespeare.]

"The bald-headed man and the wood-apple." A bald man, heated by the rays of the sun on his bare skull, sought some shade and chanced to come to the foot of a wood-apple tree [or, in some variants, a palm tree]. A great fruit fell and broke open his head. For a man who has no luck generally goes straight to a place where disasters occur.[22]

"Dawn by the toll-collector's hut." A man who was anxious to avoid paying toll took a by-road but lost his way in the dark and found himself, at daybreak, right at the tollgate.[23] [A close approximation to this concept is the "Appointment in Samarra" story, cited by John O'Hara in his novel of the same title.]

"The goat and the sword." A nanny goat, rubbing herself on a pillar where a sword is loosely attached, stretches out her neck, and by chance her head is cut off.[24]

"The arrow and the man." An arrow is shot from a bow at the very moment when a man stands up from behind a wall, and the arrow kills him.[25]

"The pebble and the man coming out of the water." Just when someone throws a pebble, a man who has been swimming comes out of the water and is struck by it.[26]

"The crow and the palm tree."

All of these maxims illustrate what Jacob calls "a purely accidental and unforeseen occurrence" or "any surprising event happening altogether by chance" or "a wholly fortuitous occurrence" or "a startling and purely accidental occurrence" or "the occurrence of something quite accidental." Clearly this is an important concept in India, and one with pessimistic overtones.

The crow and the palm tree can also be used, however, to indicate good luck, as in the folk gloss. Thus Viṣṇu tells the king (named "Palm-Tree Banner," Tāladhvaja), who was in love with the sex-changed Nārada in chapter three, "You got her by pure chance [by crow-and-palm-tree], and you lost her by pure chance (since you did not know where she came from or who she was), so do not grieve for her."[27] The *Yogavāsiṣṭha* states that it is by pure chance (by crow-and-palm-tree) that the mind imagines a hard certainty, thinking that what it wishes for is truly existent.[28] In accounting for what happens to Gādhi, the text has recourse to this metaphor to explain the occurrence of a mass hallucination: "Just like the crow and the palm tree, the condition of the Untouchables was an image reflected in the minds of all the Untouchables and Kīras, and in Gādhi's mind, too; by pure chance, a single image may be reflected in many people, for the workings of the mind are complicated."[29] So, too, it is said that by pure chance (crow-and-palm-tree), and by the power of the karmic inclinations of the mind, men of great practicality (*vyavahāra*) in business projects come to agreements with one another.[30] And in the tale of the monk's dream, pure chance accounts not only for the extraordinary events of the story but for much of the process of rebirth that it exemplifies. Pure chance undermines our faith in material reality: "Since the universe arose by chance [crow-and-palm-tree], only a child, and no one else, has confidence in it."[31]

Helmuth von Glasenapp has analyzed the way in which the *Yogavāsiṣṭha* utilizes the metaphor of the crow and the palm tree to express coincidence:

> The *Yogavāsiṣṭha* uses the expression [of the crow and the palm tree] quite often, especially when discussing the coincidence of two events for which there is no explanation. . . . Crow-and-palm-tree is the reason why various people see the same dream-world (5. 49. 7), why dreams sometimes come true and sometimes do not (6. 2. 148. 25). . . . That the *Yogavāsiṣṭha* uses the crow-and-palm-tree metaphor of accidental occurrence so often is surely no accident [!]. For with all its mysticism and its passion for miracles [*Wundersucht*], its author shows a rich measure of skepticism. Despite his high esteem for rationality, our philosopher does not in fact believe that it is granted to human understanding to solve the final riddle of the world. . . . For a man of such prudence, what could interpretation of the world mean, other than a vain attempt to explain why the appearances in a dream or in a *fata morgana* are such that we take them for real in our deluded minds?[32]

The metaphor of pure chance and coincidence, therefore, is a white flag waved at both logic and pure idealism, both skepticism and faith, both common sense and amazement. It states firmly that things simply are as they are and that we cannot hope to know *why* they are as they are.

It is often said that a world-view that uses pure chance (or synchronicity) as an explanatory device is a nonscientific world-view. Einstein characterized the distinction between the scientific and the religious approach in an often misquoted remark he made to Max Born: "You believe in the dice-playing God, and I in the perfect rule of law within a world of some objective reality which I try to catch in a wildly speculative way."[33] Yet the belief that God plays dice may in some cases be a scientific one, as Max Born and Heisenberg show; Stephen Hawking even went so far as to remark (when discussing the problems raised by the fact that there is no way to predict either the position or the speed of the particles emitted by a black hole) that "God not only plays dice but also sometimes throws them where they cannot be seen."[34] On the other hand, the belief that even the dice-playing God may be predictable is also a religious view: the Hindus believe that God (Śiva) plays dice, but they also believe that he cheats,[35] and a game played with loaded dice is no longer an instance of chaos. As a character played by W. C. Fields once said, when asked by a naïve little old lady whether the dice game he was running was a game of chance, "Not the way I play it." Pure chance may operate in the Hindu universe, but its chaos is given order by karma. Karma cheats with the dice of time, and cheats in predictable and visible ways. The palm tree of pure chance gives rise to the seed of karma and is in turn born out of that seed. In the second book of the *Mahābhārata*, Yudhiṣṭhira is invited to play dice against his enemy, who (as Yudhiṣṭhira knows full well) cheats and always wins. Yudhiṣṭhira accepts, gambles everything (including his wife and children, as Hariścandra does), and loses everything. He argues that it is fated that he should play this game and lose. Thus fate (or karma) orders everything, even the chaos that is the *raison d'être* of the metaphor of the game of dice.

The Magic City in the Sky as a Metaphor for Illusion

The term that I have translated by "magic city in the sky" is *gandharva-nagara*, literally, "city of the Gandharvas." It connotes a city in the sky inhabited by magicians and demigods (Gandharvas), benign demons who are masters of illusion and deception. The Gandharvas (probably cognate with Centaurs) preside over fertility and prosperity and are regarded as the consorts of the celestial nymphs (Apsarases) who plague Hindu ascetics. The Gandharvas are great magicians, and one of their best tricks is to construct imaginary cities in the sky. Our texts often imply that the city in the sky is actually built out of clouds, which form apparent shapes and then dissolve, the way all forms in the universe eventually dissolve. Evans-Wentz suggests that the Gandharva cities are "fantastically shaped clouds, which dissolve in rain and vanish."[36] But the images with which these cities are usually grouped are not even as substantial as clouds. For the same reason, our metaphor of sand castles captures only part of the meaning of the Gandharva city, for there *is* sand in a sand castle, but there is really not even water vapor in a magic city in the sky. Yet the way in which a sand castle takes shape and then recedes back into the formlessness of the sand finds a parallel in many Indian metaphors for describing the way that individual souls or forms appear to take shape out of the Godhead. The image of the Gandharva city is used primarily to connote not *bhrama* (a cloud mistaken for a city) but *māyā* (emptiness mistaken for a city). A closer approximation might therefore be found in our "castles in the air" or "castles in Spain," which connote purely mental forms, daydreams. Or, finally, we might speak of a fairytale castle, in the sense that the whole world is the image of a tale told by God.

In India, the city is a metaphor for everything that is unreal, ranging from things that are metaphysically puny, at best, to that which is entirely nonexistent. Indian mythology abounds in stories about great cities that were simply *not there*. Being "not there" was originally expressed as being the creation of demons; demonic cities prevail throughout early Indian mythology. These demons (Asuras) had their architect, Maya, build a triple city, a set of three cities made of gold, silver, and iron. Though the cities were to be invincible and indestructible under almost all conditions, they were destroyed when Śiva pierced them with a single arrow, at the moment when all three cities magically came together in a single line.[37]

What do these cities represent? Eventually, evil, for in the later texts the demons are the archenemies of the gods. But earlier, the cities represented magic (the name of Maya, "The Maker," is an etymological cousin of the word for art, deception, and illusion [*māyā*]). And, at the earliest stage, the three cities represented the triple universe (earth, air, and sky; later, earth, sky, and hell). This triple universe is the illusory phenomenal world that God destroys at the end of each eon, which is a time span divided into three (later, four) ages of decreasing virtue and longevity. These ages are also embodied in the cities, which are explicitly identified with something we foolishly think will be permanent when it is not—namely, time itself. Finally, the cities represent *cities*—the things that men build in false pride and that become the instruments of their final humiliation and destruction.

Indian mythology played this myth in both its major and its minor key. On one level the texts abound in descriptions of the glories of the city of Indra, king of the gods, in heaven; this is the positive, *saṃsāric*, worldly aspect of the image of the magic city in the sky, and it was this aspect that inspired the Khmers to construct one of the great ideal-type cities of the ancient world. As Paul Wheatley remarks, "The Khmers did not hesitate to undertake the colossal expenditure of labour, and to devise the costly solutions to engineering problems, necessary to render their city a worthy likeness of Indra's capital on Mount Meru."[38] The city in heaven becomes a real city—the embodiment, on earth, of the sacred one. Yet the Hindus went on to unravel this myth by setting against it a negative image of itself, an antiworldly, *mokṣic* myth, in which the city in heaven is itself revealed as unreal:

> The architect of the gods, named Viśvakarman ["All-Maker"], was employed by Indra to build a spectacular city. When Indra's pride and impatience and insatiability drove him to make constant demands for architectural improvements, Viśvakarman sought help from the gods. They sent to Indra a young boy, who first complimented Indra on his city and then remarked that none of the other Indras before him had ever had such a wonderful city. When Indra expressed his astonishment and disbelief, the boy—who was Viṣṇu in disguise—dwarfed Indra's achievement with a cosmic description of millions of Indras, like a parade of ants, and millions of palaces, all of them vanished long ago.[39]

If we had assumed that only demons made illusory cities, that there was, at least, something solid in the heaven of the gods, this myth robs us of that easy assumption. Gods, like demons, build illusory cities; for gods, like demons, are proud, jealous, and weakened by their emotional nature.[40]

The two levels of the myth of Indra also reveal two distinct levels—perhaps originally chronologically distinct, but long bonded together in Indian tradition—in the status of the Vedic gods. At first the powerful, life-affirming gods of the Vedas are supreme, and material human values—cattle, progeny, long life, wealth—are accepted as the appropriate goals of religious as well as secular effort. This is the spirit of *saṃsāra* in which the Khmer cities were built. But later, under the influence of *mokṣa*-oriented Hinduism and, even more, Buddhism, the Vedic gods were challenged. Sometimes they were replaced by the metaphysically more subtle Hindu gods; sometimes they were banished altogether by the nontheistic Buddhists.

As a result of this transition, the image of the city of the gods, with its four gates marking the cardinal directions, was satirized by a South Indian Buddhist text that describes a cremation ground, using terms traditionally associated with the ideal city:

> The cremation ground, with its pyres, [has four gates]. . . . The great Mayaṉ [Sanskrit: Maya] created this Cosmos Ground . . . , [which] shows, each in its proper place: Mount Meru standing at the center of the sphere, the seven types of mountain ranges rising around it, the encircling oceans, the four islands described in the tradition, and two thousand small islands, and the other features. . . . Here and there people burn corpses; others just abandon

> them. . . . The flesh-eating hoot-owl screeches, and the Man's-Head Bird, who seizes and devours heads of corpses, sounds his cry. . . . Out in the open, people who dine on corpses serve their guests from pots reeking with human fat.[41]

The Goddess, who narrates this story, calls the place she is describing the Cosmos Ground; everyone else just calls it the Cremation Ground. Whereas the unenlightened (such as the Khmers?) thought it possible to build a Cosmos Ground—a city that was the image of the universe—this text tells us that anything that man builds is nothing more or less than a graveyard. But it goes a step farther: since the cosmos itself is nothing but a graveyard, the graveyard *is* an accurate replica of the cosmos, after all. This is an assertion that we have often encountered in the *Yogavāsiṣṭha*, both in explicit metaphors and implicitly, in the recurrent descriptions of cremation grounds.

The categories of sacred and profane, as these are regarded by traditional Indian religion, become transposed and reversed in their earthly urban manifestations. Something does indeed remain sacred in India, but it is not the sort of thing that can be mapped in a physical city. In later mythology, the holy cities of men—Benares, the city of Śiva, or Dvārakā, the city of Kṛṣṇa—by virtue of their very holiness excite the jealousy of the gods, who empty them of all life by flooding them with water or sand in order to destroy them forever.[42] By definition, in Indian mythology, a city cannot be good, and it cannot last; if it appears to be good, it must be corrupted; if it appears to be immortal, it must be destroyed.

The unreality of earthly cities was often expressed through the metaphor of shadow cities or doublets. Thus the city that we see on earth, Benares or Dvārakā, is the mere shadow of the true city of Śiva or Kṛṣṇa, the city that was destroyed. We have already encountered in chapter three the doublet city of Lankā, inhabited by Mayili-Rāvaṇa. Another illusory Lankā appears in a Buddhist Sanskrit text about the doctrine of illusion. The discourse is set in Lankā at a time that must have been prior to the killing of Rāvaṇa by Rāma and also prior to the abduction of Sītā by Rāvaṇa, though these episodes are never mentioned:

> The Buddha happened to vist Lankā one day, and Rāvaṇa asked him to instruct him. The Buddha mounted Rāvaṇa's renowned flying chariot and came with him to the city of Lankā. Then the Buddha created many mountains, and on the summit of each mountain was the Buddha himself, and Rāvaṇa, and the entire assembly. This Lankā created by the Buddha rivaled Lankā. Then the Buddha vanished, and Rāvaṇa wondered, "What does this mean? What was it that I saw? And who saw it? Where is the city, and where is the Buddha?"[43]

When Rāvaṇa awakens (from his reflections, or from his dream of the Buddha), he realizes that the world is nothing but mind—in this case, his own mind. Though the text goes on to develop at great length the philosophy of idealism, Rāvaṇa is converted at the very start, not by a sermon but by a wordless vision of the shadow of his own city.

The city is also a shadow in another sense: it is the body, and the body is the shadow of the soul. The Upaniṣads refer to the "city of *brahman*," a phrase that Śankara glosses as "the body,"[44] and the metaphor is developed at great length in the Purāṇas. One such story is the tale of King Purañjana, whose name literally means "city-person." This is a pun: Purañjana lives *in* a city, but he also *is* a city: he is the soul who inhabits the city that is the body. This is how his city is described:

> The city had nine gates. One western gate was called Demonic, and through it Purañjana would go to the place of sensuality called Coarse, accompanied by a friend named Crazy. One of the eastern gates was called Mouth, and through it he would go with his friends Knower-of-Taste and Market, to the countries of Much-Giving and Shops. The other western gate was called Destruction [Nirṛti], and through it he would go with his friend Greedy to the land of Butchery.[45]

The commentator glosses the fairly crude symbolism of this metaphorical city: The five doors to the East (i.e., the front) are the two eyes, the two nostrils, and the mouth; those on the North and South are the left and right ears; the first western gate is the penis, and the second is the anus. The city is the bed that the soul sleeps in in its dream of rebirth. The text goes on to describe that dream and that rebirth:

> King Purañjana had a friend named Unknown. He married a woman named Purañjanī and lived with her for many years; he had 1,100 sons and 110 daughters and thousands of grandchildren. One day, Gandharvas attacked the city, but Purañjana was so besotted with his wife that he did not realize the danger until it was too late. Purañjana was killed; as he died, he thought only of his wife, and so he was reborn as a beautiful woman, the daughter of the king of Vidarbha. She married King Malayadhvaja and gave birth to a daughter and seven sons, who begat millions of grandsons. When her husband died, she prepared to mount his funeral pyre; but the Brahmin named Unknown, who had been Purañjana's friend, came to her and said, "You are not the daughter of the king of Vidarbha, nor were you the husband of Purañjana's queen. This is the illusion that I created, that you think you are a man, or a woman, or neither."[46]

This story loudly echoes the tale of Nārada and makes many of the points made by the Nārada cycle. In addition, however, it acts out the metaphor of the body as a city. This city is also a Gandharva city. King Purañjana comes upon the city one day when he is wandering about, as a lost traveler might come upon a mirage, and he finds that it belongs to a woman named Purañjanī, who is, according to later Indian tradition, a female Gandharva.[47] Appropriately, too, the city is destroyed by Gandharvas. In this way the city draws on three different layers of symbolism: it is the dream city in which the hero finds his princess; it is the illusory city of the Gandharvas; and it is the body. This cluster of symbols is further adorned with a group of abstractions personified almost as in a medieval European allegory. Purañjana's friend, Unknown, is the universal soul, who reminds Purañjana that once they were two swans together in the lake of the mind.

One story in the *Yogavāsiṣṭha* is explicitly based on the construction of an imaginary city, insubstantial as a cloud, that is real to a fool:

> There was once a man made by a magic machine [Māyāyantramaya], a stupid idiot. He lived all by himself in an empty place, like a mirage in a desert. Everything else was just a reflection of him, but the fool didn't realize this. As he got old, he thought, "The sky is mine, and I will rule over it," and so he made a house out of air in the sky in order to rule over the air and the sky. But after a while the house faded away. He cried out, "Oh, my house made of space, where have you gone?" and he built another, and another, and another, and all of them dispersed into the air, and he went on lamenting for them.[48]

In commenting on this parable, the *Yogavāsiṣṭha* says that the man is egoism (*ahaṃkāra*) and the houses are the bodies that encase the soul. The man, who is actually acting out the nightmare of solipsism, does not know it; he thinks that his mental creations are real and that his body is real. In this way, the city becomes a metaphor for the illusory body housing the (real) soul.

This is the background of the metaphor of the magic city in the sky. In the *Mahābhārata,* as we have seen, the Gandharva city is regarded as one of the bad omens that one may see;[49] that is, it is unreal, not in the sense of being nonexistent (for it is listed along with comets and naked men, things that undoubtedly do exist), but unreal in the sense of being evil, of having a negative value. The *Lankāvatārasūtra* describes the illusory Lankā as a castle or city of the Gandharvas,[50] a metaphor that is used often in that text to express what is unreal,[51] and the Gandharva city is often grouped together with the dream city to express the unreality of the universe:

> [Our misconceptions about the reality of the universe are] just like the idea of a city that fools conceive about a city of the Gandharvas, which is not a city. The form of a city appears because of their at-

> tachment to the residues of unconscious memories of a city preserved in seed from beginningless time. Thus that city is neither a city nor not a city. . . . It is just like some man who is asleep in bed and dreams of a city with its women, men, elephants, horses, and so forth, . . . and who wakes up just as he enters the inner apartments of the palace. And when he is awake, he remembers that very city with its inner apartments.[52]

The city of dreams (a further metaphor for the city of the Gandharvas, which is itself a metaphor for the illusory universe) is a central image in the myths of shared dreams. The hero dreams of a city and of a beautiful princess in it; he awakens and goes forth to look for her, to make his dream city real. In the folktales, with their worldly, *saṃsāric* orientation, the hero succeeds in finding the dream city; in the *mokṣic* philosophical texts, even the city in which the hero originally falls asleep is proved illusory. In both, he awakens as he approaches the "inner apartments"—the harim where the women sleep (in the worldly tales), but also the still center of the dream of the world (in the philosophical texts).

The *Lankāvatāra* tells us more about the Gandharva city:

> People tend mistakenly to attribute reality to what is in fact as unreal as an illusory man in a Gandharva city. For children might imagine the various people in a Gandharva city, illusory people, going in and going out. They would think, "These are going in and going out," whereas no one there is going in or going out. . . . An illusory man is neither born nor does he die; there is no cause whatsoever of his existence or nonexistence.[53]

The puppet show that fools the children—us—appears here as a negative image, a symbol of ignorance. This same image, of the child looking at the magic city, is transformed by the *Yogavāsiṣtha* into a positive metaphor: "Just as a little boy makes a city in his mind, and plays with it and does not take pleasure or sadness in it because he realizes, 'It is all merely an artificial construction,' even so, one who understands the highest meaning is not defiled."[54] The child sees truly; he frames his game as a game, just as the wise dreamer tells himself, "This is just a dream."

Throughout the *Yogavāsiṣṭha*, the Gandharva city is an image used to conjure up our positive awareness of the trick that God plays on us by creating the entire universe—not merely imaginary cities in the sky. Gādhi thinks that his complex vision of himself as king in the royal city was a magic trick or a magic city in the sky, or an illusion; and even when he returns to the dream city (which does exist) and sees it there, he perceives it as being like a magic city in the sky.[55] The Gandharva city occurs over and over again in this text,[56] where it is linked with other metaphors, such as a mirage, an echo, the *fata morgana*, the reflection of the moon in water, and, above all, a dream, all used as metaphors for the illusory universe. The term is sometimes replaced by a "dream city" or a "city of the future, made in the mind," to emphasize its imaginary character.[57] The metaphor is used to express our larger delusions: "The universe is unreal, as in the simile of the magic city in the sky."[58]

The magic city in the sky appears in the Tibetan *Book of the Dead* in a list of phrases describing the illusory nature of the mental projections that the soul in limbo takes for real and that therefore cause him to be reborn. The dying man becomes an embryo as he witnesses the copulation of his future parents, and he is told to meditate as follows:

> Alas! The father and mother . . . all these apparent phenomena are illusory in their real nature. . . . All these are projections of my mind, and since the mind itself is illusory and nonexistent from the beginning, from where externally do they arise like this? . . . Now they are all like dreams, like illusions, like echoes, like cities of the Gandharvas, like mirages, like images, like optical illusions, like the moon in water; they are not real, even for a moment. Certainly they are not true, but false![59]

If even the mind is unreal—there being no God to establish its reality for the Buddhists—the city of the Gandharvas does not even have the thin substance of the rope/snake, which other Buddhist texts (such as the *Lankāvatārasūtra*) describe as "made of thought."

But, in Buddhist texts, yet another overtone enriched the connotations of unreality associated with the city in the sky. When the Bodhisattva was young, his father the king feared that he would leave the palace and become a holy man. In order to avoid this, the king assigned him a dwelling place in the inner parts of the upper stories of the palace, with no access to the ground; the upper stories of the palace were pale as clouds, like heavenly mansions on earth, like Kailāsa, the holy mountain of Śiva. The Bodhisattva never descended from the top of the palace to earth, just as one would not go down to earth from a heavenly palace.[60] Here is the Indian image of the ivory tower, the place high in the sky where one hopes to be free of suffering. But the whole point of the story is that the Bodhisattva was fated to leave the palace and to find suffering. The palace in the sky was, in Buddhist terms, entirely illusory.

The image of the illusory city is used in Indian philosophy in two different ways. In the first, which we have just now seen, it is used as an idealistic lever to pry us loose from our conviction that the cities we inhabit are real, to make us wonder if we will not someday wake up from our dream of solid cities to find that they are, in fact, nothing but clouds or less than clouds. The second appears in Indian texts of a more realist bent; here the image is used to teach us that we must learn to tell the difference between Gandharva cities and real cities, which *do* exist. In refuting the doctrine called "The Falsity of Everything," the philosopher Gautama objects to the argument that "both the instruments of knowledge and their objects are false like dream objects or like magic or a mirage or the city of the Gandharvas. The answer is that there is no reason to suppose that these phenomena are not aspects of the natural world; dream objects are on the same plane as memories and imagination; the illusory objects disappear when we know the truth, and are therefore shown to have causes like natural objects."[61] The commentary on this passage takes a very hard line indeed:

> In the case of dreams, magic, and the city of the Gandharvas (explained here as a sort of mirage), there is always some real object, which, though misapprehended, nevertheless is the object of a wrong judgment. That there is [such an object] is shown by the fact that in every such case the judgment would not be possible were it not for the existence of an object. Thus in the mirage, where we see a lake in the desert, the object is the sun's rays flickering due to contact with the earth's surface heat; we think we see water because of the similar quality (flickering) between water and the said behavior of the rays. But there would be no such illusions at night, when the sun does not shine.[62]

How very scientific it all is. And yet when we look closer at the magic city in the sky, we see that it is not, in fact, made of refracted light rays; it is made of a cluster of some of the most important mythic and metaphysical cultural assumptions in India.

Now, all these meanings are *mokṣa* meanings, meanings that give a negative evaluation to the illusory nature of the universe. Yet, if we look at the actual metaphor and ask why it should be a city of the Gandharvas rather than of something else (like demons), we discover a powerful *saṃsāric* layer underneath the glimmering surface. The Gandharvas are closely associated with two things: sex and flying. They are the incubi who come to women in the night, as the nymphs (Apsarases) come to men; they are the ones who carry the hero to his secret rendezvous with the woman in the other world. The phrase "Gandharva marriage" (which occurred in the dreams of Malayavatī and Uṣā in chapter two) indicates a marriage that is sanctified by the presence of Gandharvas as the only witnesses to a sexual union (a fanciful equivalent of our less glamorous common-law marriage); it is a marriage in which the danger of the solipsism of lovers is countered by the presence of corroborating eyewitnesses: Gandharvas. They thus represent the positive—and positively real—aspect of the dream adventure. They also share with the dream adventure the theme of magic horses. For Gandharvas (Centaurs) are great horsemen, and the hero Arjuna is said to have gotten lovely frog-eyed horses from a Gandharva city[63]—*real* horses (frog eyes are a sign of great beauty in real horses, particularly those of Arabian stock).[64]

How can you get real horses from an unreal city? One answer to this riddle is provided by the tale of Bellerophon, who got a real bridle from a dream he had of Athena, or by the Vīraśaivas who fall into other peoples' hells, or the people who get real eggs from illusory chickens. But another, perhaps more basic, answer is provided by the background of the Gandharvas themselves. As purveyors of the treasures of the dream adventure—sexual fulfillment and transportation to the world where immortality may be won—the Gandharvas and their cities are a metaphor for the reality of the emotions and the desire for life.

If we cast our eyes over Western myth and history, we find several different sorts of cities. In classical religious texts, we encounter the city as a pivotal image for what is real and most important to our civilization, including, of course, the term civilization itself. The Greeks defined themselves in terms of their city, their *polis*; in the Hebrew Bible, too, cities were the incarnation not just of evil (the Cities of the Plain, Sodom and Gomorrah) but of good; but they were the incarnation of *real* evil or *real* good. In the realms of both myth and history, the ancient Western city is a symbol of religious reality: Jerusalem and Rome are real embodiments of spiritual as well as temporal power.

In another contrast with India, where cities that appeared to be made of matter turned out to be made of spirit, in the West the City of God comes literally down to earth to find its *pied-à-terre*, to be measured out in real furlongs and cubits and built of real gold and gems:

> And I John saw the holy city, new Jerusalem, coming down from God out of heaven, prepared as a bride adorned for her husband. . . . And the city lieth four square, and the length is as large as the breadth; and he measured the city with the reed, twelve thousand furlongs. And he measured the wall thereof, an hundred and forty and four cubits, according to the measure of a man, that is, of the angel. And the building of the wall of it was jasper; and the city was pure gold, like unto clear glass. And the foundations of the wall of the city were garnished with all manner of precious stones. The first foundation was jasper; the second, sapphire; the third, a chalcedony; the fourth, emerald.[65]

The city of God, which descends like the woman from the other world, can be *measured* in the West, as the cosmos is "measured out" (and thus made) in the *Ṛg Veda*. But later Indian philosophy questioned both the solidity of what was measured and the solidity of the measuring stick. Indian theologians, every bit as pedantic and hair-splitting as their Western counterparts, were quite capable of arguing about how many Gandharvas danced on the head of a pin, but this measurement would not have proved, to them at least, the reality of the Gandharvas *or of the pin.*

In keeping with the earlier, *saṃsāric*, view, Indian kings like Vikramāditya dreamed of magic cities and then set out to find them—and *did* find them. But in the *mokṣic* view, kings like Lavaṇa and Gavala (né Gādhi) watched their dream cities disappear and then looked with new eyes upon their waking cities. In the West we have the myth of Troy—the expedition to carry back the woman from the other world—and then we have Schliemann setting out to find Troy, and *finding* it, in waking life. In the West, even mythical cities are built out of real stones.

Schliemann thus supplies us with a parallel to Vikramāditya, who found his city. Are there any Western parallels to Lavaṇa or Gādhi, who lost their cities? Yes and no. Against the classical Western religious view of the city we must set the secular values of Utopia, which challenged the established views of the city to just as great a degree—though in a very different way—as the Gandharva cities challenged the great sacred cities of India.[66] Another, and again entirely different, challenge was provided by Plato in response to his interlocutor:

> "I understand," he [the interlocutor] said; "you are speaking of the city that we have been describing as a place to live in, the one that exists in words; for I think that it cannot be anywhere on earth." "But," I said, "perhaps there is a paradigm of it lying in heaven for the man who wants to see it and for the man who sees it to live in. But it makes no difference if it exists now or ever will exist. For that is the only city whose affairs matter, and no other." "Maybe," he said.[67]

Such complexities in the Western tradition would require a lengthy exploration, taking us far from our course, before we could begin to make a careful comparison between the illusory cities of India and those of the West. For the moment, however, I think it is safe to say that in India the *emphasis* is on the insubstantiality of the city, in the West, on its substantial reality. Plato spoke of the shadows in the cave, shadows of ideal forms like the city, which we mistake for real objects. India, too, knows shadows, and shadow doubles of more-real forms; but both the shadows and the objects that cast them—the cloud cities and the cities of stone—are unreal. They may not be equally unreal, but the question of which is the more unreal is not easily resolved. Western medieval texts described the castle of the shimmering grail, a castle that disappeared whenever a false knight approached but became visible to the true knight. We might see in this a Western parallel to the city of the Gandharvas, with the Brahmins (or enlightened yogins) alone able to see the truth. But the Western authority (the true knight) sees that the city *is* there, while the Indian authority (the enlightened man) sees that it is not.

The metaphor of the serpent and the rope primarily designates a mistake: a real rope is mistaken for an unreal snake; but it can be used to designate an illusion: the image of a snake is seen even when there is no real rope there at all. So, too, the metaphor of the magic city in the sky primarily designates an illusion: the image of a city is seen when there is nothing there at all; but it can be used to designate a mistake: a real mass of water vapor is mistaken for an unreal city. The Indian idealists would use both images to describe pure illusion, and the relative realists would use both to describe mistaken perceptions; for, as we have seen, these two problems of perception are but different steps along the continuum of epistemology, which (like the phenomena to which they refer) is seen differently by people with different ways of seeing.

Indian and Western Arguments
Projection in Art and Reality

The phenomenon of projection—imposing the images of the mind on the world outside, or creating a world outside by projecting images out of the mind—is used by many Indian texts as a clue to the nature of illusion, both in art and in life. We have seen the level of experience known as *pratibhāsika* (a word that may be translated either as "reflected" or as "contradictory") explained as the superimposition of a mental image on a kind of Rohrschach test posed by the phenomenal world. Sir Ernst Gombrich has discussed, in many different publications, the way that we fill in certain vital elements that are merely suggested by paint on canvas. *Māyā*, after all, means artistic creation, and the *Yogavāsiṣṭha* teaches us that the illusion of art is of the same nature as the illusion of life.

When King Lavaṇa was being drawn into the illusion of his life as an Untouchable, his paralysis made him look "like a form in a painting, as if he were merely sketched on a page, as he gazed with unblinking eyes at the horse," and when he heard his mother-in-law's corroborating words, he "became amazed and looked into the faces of his ministers as if he were painted in a picture."[68] When Gādhi had a vision of himself as a corpse, he saw the image "as if it were made out of clay."[69] As we saw in chapter four, the process of projection is used to explain one aspect of Lavaṇa's and Gādhi's experience. The end of chapter five demonstrated the way in which the tale of the monk's dream forces us to hypothesize an Artist creating the dream or story or painting in which we find ourselves.

Metaphors of art occur throughout the *Yogavāsiṣṭha*. "People say of the illusory universe, 'Sand oozes with oil; stone dolls read; clouds in paintings thunder.'"[70] Since clouds are themselves highly charged with illusion (as in the image of the magic city in the sky), *painted* clouds are doubly illusory. Ignorance itself (*avidyā*) is said to be "like a woman in a picture, with breasts and buttocks, who does not act like a woman, nor *is* a woman," and knowledge is projected on our minds as a picture is painted on a wall rather than on the surface of the sky.[71] "All of this, Rāma," says Vasiṣṭha, "arises in ignorance. The quality of a pot appears in pictures of pots, created by mistaking one thing for another, as in dreams."[72] The pot metaphor appears often in this context, as does the painting, often reminiscent of the Existentialist atheist metaphor of the pot made by no potter: "A painting arises in the sky, without any painter and without any paint. And the experience of this world, which has no witness [*adraṣṭakam*], is like a waking dream."[73] But where Sartre used this image to express the Existential boostraps paradox (that we are the only potters making the pots that are ourselves), the *Yogavāsiṣṭha* uses it to express the paradox of *māyā*: there is no potter at all—and no pot. And the painting in the Indian metaphor lacks not only an artist but a viewer, like Bishop Berkeley's tree (or painting) that stands hidden in a forest; without corroborating witnesses, there is only illusory reality. Indeed, we have seen the quandary of the Buddhist idealists, who deny the existence of both the Artist (*brahman*, the Godhead) and the viewer (*ātman*, the self).

Let us glance for a moment at the conventions with which illusions are painted. As compared to depicting things commonly seen, is it harder or easier to depict realistically something no one has ever seen? Sir Ernst Gombrich refers to a Chinese treatise that raises this question: "Everyone is acquainted with dogs and horses since they are seen daily. To reproduce their likeness is very difficult. On the other hand, since demons and spiritual beings have no definite form and since no one has ever seen them they are easy to execute."[74] Now, in the *Yogavāsiṣṭha* (and in India in general), demons are very real indeed, as are gods and other "spiritual beings." It is therefore not surprising to note that these creatures are painted in great and altogether convincing detail in the illustrations to our text. The gods fighting with the demons (plate 16), Viṣṇu in the scene with Gādhi (plate 7), Rudra with Vasiṣṭha (plate 14), the nymphs with Nārada (plate 1), the god of death with Bhṛgu (plate 2)—all are depicted with painstaking realism, as are several male ogres and female ogresses (plates 10 and 11). Even more significant is the fact that illusory scenes—dreams, hallucinations, and projected desires—are depicted in the same realistic way. When Queen Cūḍālā conjures up an image of herself with a lover (in order to test the equanimity of her husband), the scene is painted as if the king were actually looking at Queen Cūḍālā and her lover (plate 9).[75] We have already unknowingly encountered an illustrated illusion that is a verbal rather than a visual falsehood and yet is visually depicted, for the story of Nārada among the nymphs (plate 1) is a lie:

> When Queen Cūḍālā's husband was dwelling away from her, engrossed in meditation, she decided to visit him. She took the form of a young Brahmin boy and went to her husband, and when he asked her who "he" was, she told him this story: "Once upon a time, the sage Nārada saw a bevy of nymphs bathing in a river; he became excited and shed his seed into a crystal pot filled with milk, and the boy born of it was called 'Pot' [Kumbha]. I am that boy." After spending some time with her handsome husband, Cūḍālā began to feel that it was a pity that she could not make love with him, and so she went away (in the form of Kumbha) and returned in her own true form, with yet another story: "The sage Durvāsas cursed me to become a sensuous woman every night." As the moon rose each night, she did indeed become a woman (her original form), and eventually she persuaded her husband the king to marry her.[76]

The image of Nārada among the nymphs is here encased in a complex series of sexual pseudo-transformations. This time, Nārada himself is not transformed; in fact, he does not even appear in the story of Cūḍālā and her husband at all. But the artist depicts Nārada nevertheless, since the *idea* of Nārada among the nymphs is true—true to type (Nārada is often seduced by nymphs) and true to the image that Queen Cūḍālā projects in order to enlighten her husband.

All the illusions experienced by King Lavaṇa and the others are depicted with the same artistic conventions used for the "real" frame of the illusion—the life of Rāma at court, for instance. The scene in which Lavaṇa enters the Untouchable village for the first time (plate 5) and the one in which he returns later with his courtiers (plate 6) are evidently by two different artists, and there are certain interesting differences between them. The first scene is more highly colored than any other illustration in the manuscript; the blood is red, the skins of the Untouchables are dark, and the characters are also more highly emotional than in the other scenes: the girl is adoring and anxious; the mother is greedy and curious, with a child straining hungrily at her breast; the father is ill at ease; and the king evinces repulsion. This is a highly dramatic moment, infused with all the vividness of a dream. By contrast, the second scene is painted in pale colors; here there is no blood or gore, and the Untouchables are not so dark; the mother-in-law is now much older than she was in the first scene (perhaps this reflects the passage of time), and Lavaṇa is emotionless. Reality here is noticeably vaguer and hazier than in the dream scene.

In contrast with the vividness with which the illusory dream experiences are painted, there were different conventions the artist could use to convey things that were *really* illusory (including illusory demons as opposed to real demons). For instance, the artist depicts the personification of the demonic desires that kept the Brahmin Vasiṣṭha's spirit trapped in his home (plate 13). The Brahmin's desires hover over the house where he lived until he experiences (in imagination) his unfulfilled cravings. To show this, the artist uses the conventions of altered perspective and size, a floating cloud (rather like a Gandharva city or the "balloon" of thought in a Western cartoon), and a hazier palette to indicate the different ontological status of this group of demons. In a similar way, Western artists used such devices as halos, exaggerated size, and translucent images to indicate the divine or illusory nature of certain subjects. Sir Ernst Gombrich has remarked on a series of luminous dots that cause us to project a supernatural element into an otherwise largely realistic painting:

> But how else could art suggest what is in fact unrepresentable, the idea of the infinite? In the context of his beautiful painting, the artist leads the willing beholder from the charming angels in the foreground to more and more indistinct shapes and thus makes him project a vision of infinite multitudes of the heavenly host into the sparkling dots that fade into the distance.[77]

This passage would also serve as a description of the infinitely receding frames of the map of the Indian cosmos. But the Indian artist does not use "sparkling dots" to depict the gods or ogresses or dream scenes of the *Yogavāsiṣṭha*. By neglecting to use the available techniques to differentiate between the scenes—the techniques that are used, for example, in the single illustration of the Brahmin's incarnate desires—the artist of the *Yogavāsiṣṭha* manuscript may be making a serious (if perhaps unconscious) statement about the equal validity of the experiences of Lavaṇa in his court, in the Untouchable village, and in his consecration sacrifice and the equal validity of Rāma's conversations with Vasiṣṭha and Queen Cūḍālā's tall tale about Nārada and the nymphs. True, it is always dangerous to argue negatively, and this danger is compounded in the present instance by the fact that the *Yogavāsiṣṭha* manuscript was illustrated by several different artists, all of whom were working within the constraints of conventions inherited from non-Indian painting traditions (there are Persian and even some European influences) that used precisely the same techniques in depicting everyday, waking experiences and divine or magical illusions. It is therefore difficult to conjecture "the artist's" reasons for not doing what he did not do. Nevertheless, it is worth noting that, though he had at his disposal techniques for depicting unreal experiences, he used them only to indicate the embodiment of an abstract concept (an unsatisfied desire) and never to indicate the content of a dream or a story or a mythical confrontation.

Gombrich has said, "I have trailed my coat and proposed the formulation that the world does not look like a picture, but a picture can look like the world."[78] The *Yogavāsiṣṭha*, on the other hand, says that the world *does* look like a picture; that the picture and the world have an equal claim to real existence. Though both Gombrich and the Sanskrit text distinguish carefully between illusion and hallucination (or delusion), they do this in different ways and to make different points. Gombrich asks, "When and how can artifice trigger not only responses of the kind I have discussed at some length [i.e., responses to aesthetic illusion], but something akin to a visual hallucination?"[79]

The distinction between the two experiences is easy enough to spell out if we add a qualification to our working definition of illusion and specify that, when it comes to art, we *can* watch ourselves having an illusion. We can do it by consciously suspending our critical judgment of reality—not abandoning it altogether, but letting it hang in limbo between cynicism and faith. The observer of an illusion (in this modified sense) knows that, in spite of appearances, what seems to be there is not, in fact, there. The observer of a delusion (*moha*, or *bhrama*, mistaking a rope for a snake) believes that what seems to be there is in fact there. In artistic illusion, the observer is aware from the very start that everything is illusory; in divine illusion, even though the observer may *know* that everything is illusory (for every Hindu cuts his teeth on Vedānta in some form), he does not *feel* his life to be illusory. The *Yogavāsiṣṭha* uses artistic illusion to suggest the feeling of divine illusion in life.

Max Black treats the difference between illusion and delusion as a matter of "as if": we see a picture of a poodle "as if" we see a poodle. "Of course, I know all the time that there is no such poodle in the place where I seem to see it; and that is what makes the experience an illusion, but not a delusion."[80] King Lavaṇa loses his sense of "as if" when he hears his story corroborated; the text tells us that there *is* no "as if" in his delusion or, rather, that there is just as much of an "as if" in his life as a king as there is in his life as an Untouchable. But on another level, the text, itself an art form (an "as-if" form for the Hindus, as it is for us), uses illusion in precisely the way that Gombrich suggests that illusion is used both in experience and in art: "Illusions are also tools for discovering processes of perception. . . . We may expect abnormal perceptions (deviations from the truth) to give insights and data for understanding normal (correct) perception."[81] The *Yogavāsiṣṭha* is a rather perverse example of this process, for the true perception that it reveals through illusion *is* the doctrine of illusion, the doctrine that *all* perception "deviates from the truth." In India, as in the West, "'perceptual distortions' . . . reveal new aspects of the world and of ourselves."[82] When we realize that we have lost hold of the "as if" of art, that we have made a mistake, we suspect that we may also have lost hold of the "as if" of life, that we have fallen into the trap of illusion.

Many Indian stories dissolve the "as if" in a painting. In Kālidāsa's play, when King Duṣyanta forgets about Śakuntalā, he later emerges from his curse of forgetfulness and remains in love with a painting of her, to which he responds so passionately that people must keep on reminding him that it is merely a painting; it is more real to him, now, than the real girl was when he abandoned her.[83] So, too, in the myths of the shared dream, the lovers often use a painting to mediate between the softest form of the experience—the dream—and the hardest form—the actual presence of the beloved. The theme of the lifelike image is also woven into the corpus of myths about doubles that we saw in chapter three: the painting of Rāvaṇa comes to life in Sītā's bedroom.

A story about a picture that comes to life also plays on the classical Vedāntic image of the ambiguous snake:

> A young boy . . . was predicted to die of a snakebite when he was sixteen. His parents were orthodox Hindus who took this prediction very seriously. On the day on which it was predicted that he would be bitten, his parents locked him up in a room with no opening through which a snake could creep. They stationed servants as guards near the door and would not permit anyone to enter or leave. The boy, who was somewhat annoyed and amused by all this fuss, spent the day studying. Then, as a private joke, he got up and drew a snake on the wall and said, "So you are supposed to kill me, are you?" With that he jabbed his finger at the snake's fang. A rusty nail happened to be slightly protruding from the wall at that point. It pierced his finger and infected him with tetanus. He died within a few days' time.[84]

This story is a conflation of several traditional Indian folk themes: the Bengali tale of Lakhindar, doomed to be killed on his wedding night by a snake who entered the sealed room through a tiny hole, and the *Mahābhārata* tale of King Parikṣit:

> King Parikṣit was doomed to be killed by snakebite on a certain day. Growing arrogant as the sun was about to set, Parikṣit picked up a tiny worm and said, "The sun is setting; now let the prediction come true: let the worm bite me." And as the king placed the little worm on his throat and laughed, the worm—who was the king of serpents in disguise—coiled around him and gave him a fatal bite.[85]

The tale of the boy and the rusty nail has added to these folk motifs another popular theme: the picture that comes to life. But reality plays an even more important role in this story than may at first appear, for this is in fact the story of a recent event, recorded by an American anthropologist in South India in the 1970s, where it was witnessed by an entire village and therefore, we may assume, *really* happened.

In one sense, we might say that the boy's familiarity with the folk tradition about paintings coming to life caused him to project his own snake onto the nail and therefore to make the nail into a snake. His mental construction of reality turned the nail into a snake, which had a very real effect upon him; this was indeed a self-fulfilling prophecy. The *locus classicus* in South Asia for the use of visual images to construct a reality is Tibetan Buddhism, where the adept carefully and systematically constructs the deity by amassing visual detail, usually with the aid of a highly detailed painting or cosmic diagram (a *yantra*). This elaboration of detail is significant, as we shall soon see. But, for the boy, a rusty nail was a quite sufficient *yantra*, an *objet trouvé* that he used, unwittingly, to construct a work of art that came to life. This, too, is a traditional Indian philosophical image: Śankara argues that dreams are real because they are experienced and have effects in waking life; a man bitten by an imaginary snake can die from the imaginary venom.[86]

Within the text of the *Yogavāsiṣṭha* the illusions that the characters experience reveal to them the true nature of reality. Outside the text, the doctrine of illusion is revealed to the reader through the device of narration, the art of the storyteller. How does art teach us about reality?

> We must always rely on guesses, on the assessment of probabilities, and on subsequent tests, and in this there is an even transition from the reading of symbolic material to our reaction in real life. . . . It is the power of expectation rather than the power of conceptual knowledge that molds what we see in life no less than in art. Were we to voyage in the Mediterranean we would, alas, be unlikely to see the train of Neptune's suite so convincingly conjured up as did the 17th century traveler steeped in the reading of the classics and the experience of mythological painting.[87]

By painting visual pictures (*yantras*) of illusions and verbal pictures (*mantras*) of mistakes, the *Yogavāsiṣṭha* provides its culture with a vocabulary with which to expect and therefore to see and hear illusions when they are encountered in life.

Moreover, art allows us to act out assumptions that cannot be acted out in normal circumstances; here we can extrapolate them to their extreme, and therefore most revealing, implications. Thus art allows us to experience illusion "as if" it were real: "What I can experience in illusion states cannot always be carried out in behaviour. But in the symbolic behaviour of art we might communicate by shared internal illusion."[88] This "shared internal illusion" is the making-public of the private vision, the sharing of the dream, the corroboration that rescues the observer from the dangers of solipsism. The illusion shared by Lavaṇa and the Untouchables is also shared by us, the readers of the text. We experience it as real at least within the "as if" frame of the narrative; but sometimes (as we saw in chapter five) its reality may also spill over into the frame of our own lives.

Detail and Banality in Surrealistic Illusion

Surrealist and cubist art uses illusion to change our perception of reality: "We are, in fact, obliged by the artist to reconsider fundamentally the hypotheses we have formed previously,"[89] just as Lavaṇa had to reevaluate his experience as a king. In particular, visual puns (such as Picasso's famous bull's head made of a bicycle seat and handlebars) "attack our acceptance of the reality of everything in the objective world. Each invention acts as an insult to preconceived ideas."[90] The "Gestalt" switch flickers between two different readings of an image, like the rabbit that can also be seen as a duck, or like "Rubin's Vase," which at one moment appears to be a black vase on a white ground but, if one looks again, appears to be two white profiles facing each other across a negative black space.[91] The drawings of Escher, discussed in chapter five, are a vivid example of this reality-switching. The metaphor of the Gestalt switch was used in a different way to express the mental leap that takes place when a person changes from one paradigm to another or, by grasping both paradigms at once, attempts to break out of the receding frame.

The detailed ambiguities in the visual nature of objects, as well as in representations of them, are the elements of constant retransformation in art. The observer performs a kind of *bricolage* similar to that wrought by the cubists and surrealists. Picasso's "*Baboon and Young* [1951; made of toy cars] is an excellent example of a sculpture composed of discarded objects and junk which have been brought to life again and given new meaning . . . a circumstance which causes us to marvel at the ambiguity of reality."[92] The snake becomes a rope that becomes a snake . . . . Myths can accomplish verbally what pictures (especially surrealist pictures) accomplish visually: they can present the paradoxes and ambiguities of reality. These paradoxes move in both directions, as we have seen: they become entangled until we can no longer tell whether the snake looks like a rope or the rope looks like a snake, whether the king seems to be an Untouchable or the Untouchable seems to be a king, whether the world is like a picture or a picture is like the world. So, too, Picasso's bull's head made out of a bicycle bars and seat does not stop there, for Picasso expressed the hope that "One day a clever mechanic might find it and say, 'This bull's head will make excellent handle bars and a saddle for my bicycle.'"[93]

The paradox arises when one regards the object simultaneously as a bicycle seat and a bull's head. In the world of art this paradox does not involve a contradiction, but in the world of reality it does. Surrealism produces an imaginary world so real that it makes us doubt our previously perceived reality; the myths of illusion set out to do much the same thing. As Paul Eluard put it, "Images . . . were long mistaken for illusions because they were made to undergo the test of reality, an insensitive and dead reality."[94] The *Yogavāsiṣṭha* might be regarded as the first surreal (or Dadaist) piece of literature, an extended verbal pun of the same nature as the visual pun of the bull's head/bicycle seat or the snake/rope.

But the analogy between surrealistic projection and Indian (or Tibetan) projection is flawed:

> This provocative surrealist model, however, gives only a limited analogue for the total collapse of the boundary between the public and private universe. . . . Where the surrealist image is thrust upon a reality already given in experience, the Tibetan yogin sees the complete and absolute interpenetration of the two unitary fields. His image and his object are not superimposed, but rather are primordially one, and this is what makes possible his magical ability to manipulate the universe.[95]

The surrealist technique is based on a mistake (*bhrama*, mistaking an unreal thing for a real thing), whereas the Tibetan yogin is playing with illusion (*māyā*, building one equally real/unreal thing upon another). Yet in surrealism, as in Indian philosophy, the mistake may be the clue to the illusion. As Sir Ernst Gombrich remarks of Salvador Dali, "Dali's way of letting each form represent several things at the same time may focus our attention on the many possible meanings of each colour and form—much in the way in which a successful pun may make us aware of the function of words and their meaning."[96] Though puns can be committed in any language, it is, I think, no accident that the doctrine of illusion arose in a literature composed in Sanskrit,[97] a particularly double-jointed language, in which it is possible to make not only compound words but the component syllables of simple words yield rich ambiguities. (It has been said that every word in Sanskrit denotes itself, its opposite, a term for an elephant, a position in sexual intercourse, and a name of God.) The ambiguity of words is the shadow double of the ambiguity of images. Dreams abound in both verbal and visual puns.

The reification of the people and events in the ambiguous stories, like the reification of the ambiguous objects in a surrealist *trompe l'oeil*, is made possible by the use of detail. We have seen this process at work in dreams, which convince us by their inclusion of matter-of-fact items from waking life (chapter one), and in cosmologies, which curtail our questions by their inclusion of wearying and mind-boggling numbers and circles (chapter four). The painter reifies his images through the use of perspective, texture, shading, and so forth, all of which draw on a knowledge of the way that we structure the visual sense data that we seek and find. The poet reifies his images through the use of a dizzying flood of verbal detail. The descriptions of the Untouchable village convince us that the author—and the king—must have been there:

> The village was littered with cut-up bits of monkeys and birds. Vultures flew into nets made of strings of moist entrails stretched out to dry. Children clutched in their hands balls of flesh crawling with flies. The houses were strewn with splattered brains.[98]

When, however, we later encounter this same gruesome detail in the description of the cremation of Gādhi's corpse, it greatly increases the tension between reality and illusion, for Gādhi *knows* that he is seeing an illusion. Yet how vivid it seems:

> The pyre that was covered with a net of flames gorged on dry wood made a "chatachatachata" sound as it cracked open the pile of bones, and the membranes and blood vessels popped open, as a clump of hollow bamboo sticks cracks open when an elephant steps on them, so that the sap runs out on all sides.[99]

These are nightmare images; often, however, more ordinary detail is more convincing. Herbert Read said of Picasso, "His symbols are banal, like the symbols of Homer, Dante, Cervantes. For it is only when the widest commonplace is inspired with the intensest passion that a great work of art, transcending all schools and categories, is born."[100] The banality of this detail allows us to pull up our illusions by their own bootstraps, never truly grounding them in reality but creating the illusion of such a grounding. In the story of Lavaṇa, we learn many details about his sumptuous life as a king, but it is not until we hear the ghastly details of his wretched life as an Untouchable that we *feel* his reality for the first time and so become more willing to be persuaded—against the dictates of logic—that this was a real experience. Similarly, a most banal argument is used to prove that the magician in Lavaṇa's court must have been a divine messenger: the courtiers point out, "My lord, this was no magician, for he did not try to get money, as magicians always try to do; they do not simply vanish, as he did."[101]

All myths are to a certain extent surreal, for they partake of what Eliade has called "the banality of the sacred." Like dreams and cosmologies, myths sweep infinity under a carpet of obfuscating layers.[102] (This is one of the reasons why the "point" of a myth cannot be summarized, for it sounds idiotic and obvious when it is thus reduced; the detail is what makes the meaning that cannot be explained.) In science, too, the sheer weight of banausic detail is persuasive; we see this in the exhaustive (and exhausting) descriptions of experiments given in early scientific journals (Robert Boyle's accounts provide an extreme case).[103]

Surrealist painters like Magritte and Escher use realistic detail to pin us down in a specific spot before they draw us back to show us the nature of the larger canvas to which we have unwittingly committed ourselves. When we do see the whole canvas, we are taken aback, suddenly aware that we have come farther than we intended—have in fact painted ourselves into a philosophical corner that we had not intended to occupy. Indian art of this type (including the *Yogavāsiṣṭha*) is another sort of bootstraps operation, one that uses words to teach the reader to distrust words even as the surrealist painter teaches us to distrust painting. It is a ladder designed to be climbed up and then kicked out from under us. Science has been characterized as the same sort of self-destroying enterprise, strongly akin to Dadaism.[104]

The Artist as a Magician

The legerdemain that the artist carries off in this way is often likened to the tricks of the magician. This comparison blurs the distinction between illusion (in the special sense of a false appearance that one knows to be false) and delusion (a false appearance that one takes for real), delusion being the achievement of the magician, illusion the achievement of the artist. In India, as we have seen, the same person often fills both roles at once. Citralekhā, who is both a magician (a yoginī) and a painter (her name means "Sketcher of Pictures"), has a pencil that is a magic wand; she actively creates an image only to find that it is the reflection of a dream hero who actually exists. Uṣā passively receives this reflected image in her dream. Citralekhā's painting is thus harder than Uṣā's dream but not so hard as the objects—which had not previously existed—that the Kashmiri yogin could materialize out of his own mental image. The clue to this distinction may lie in the Indian attitude to emotion: the powerful emotion of love somehow carries the image from one mind (or one reality) to another mind—in this instance, from Aniruddha to Uṣā. But since the yogin is the master of emotion, in complete control of his lust and anger, he (or she, as in this instance) can use his (or her) powers actively, whereas we lesser mortals can merely receive them passively. The artist, midway between the yogin and the ordinary person, receives the dream passively but learns to control it actively, to transform it into a material object that all of us can see and touch. Instead of merely telling his dream, he shows his dream, drawing us inside his own experience in a way that nonartists can usually do only when they are in love. In this way, the mere "illusion" of the shared dream becomes a true form of *māyā*, the artistic creation of another reality.

Magicians appear on several levels in the tale of Lavaṇa. The magician who enters Lavaṇa's court and initiates the king has been sent by Indra, the greatest of divine magicians; his magic horse is repeatedly likened to the flying horse of Indra, and his wand to Indra's rainbow; and Lavaṇa says that the magician has come to the court like the very architect of the demons, the deluding Maya himself, rising from the nether world.[105] Yet there is a greater divine power behind the magician, for his wand is said to create mistaken perceptions, just as the *māyā* of the Godhead does, and the courtiers point out that, since he could not have been a real magician (not being sufficiently venal), he must have been a divine instrument.[106] If you believe that the world is created by imagination, the question must arise, by whose imagination? To the Indian, as we have seen, the answer is obvious: God's imagination. The world is a magic trick, and man is the dupe, and God is the magician.

Thus, "The magician acts as a god. He enfolds a creation of his own."[107] The *Yogavāsiṣṭha* employs this as a favorite metaphor: "The universe, which is like a building without walls, or the colors [that one thinks one sees] in the sky, all this is the work of the master magician [*śambareśa*] called Ignorance."[108] Ignorance (*avidyā*) is the instrument by which God clouds our minds, as he clouded Vasiṣṭha's at the beginning of creation. Ignorance is what keeps us from seeing the true nature of the universe, the true power of karma, and the meaning of our own lives. This master magician is often personified as a demon named Śambara, whom we have already encountered (in chapter three) as the abductor of Māyāvatī. The *Yogavāsiṣṭha* refers to the demon Śambara as a magician *sans pareil* who "abandoned this magic of *saṃsāra*." This phrase conflates the demon who causes illusion with the sage who is able to free himself from illusion. Since demons and sages are often grouped together as curators of antinomian wisdom, this is an irony but not a paradox. Yet there is paradox here too:

> There once lived in the subterranean world a ruler of demons named Śambara. He made a demonic palace in the sky, with an artificial sun and moon, and temples to the gods. But whenever he fell asleep, or went somewhere else, the gods would attack. Then by his powers of illusion he created three demons to protect him from the gods. These demons, who had been made artificially and not from living seed, had no karma or karmic memory traces [*vāsanās*], nor any desires; they were like half-asleep children. With no sense of self, they knew and cared nothing of life or death or battle or defeat. They were mercenary soldiers purely by chance [crow-and-palm-tree]. And since they had no wish to stay alive and no desire for victory, they could not be killed or conquered. Their names were Snare, Snake, and Screen [Dāma, Vyāla, Kaṭa]. These three demons routed the gods until Brahmā filled the demons with pride

and egoism, the sense of self [*ahaṃkāra*] and the desire for victory; then the gods were able to overcome them and kill them. The demons went to hell, where they were tortured in the flames of hell, together with their wives and children. After that they were reborn as Untouchable hunters, then as vultures, hogs, and other animals, and finally they became fish in the muddy waters of a lake in Kashmir.

When Śambara realized that his first demons had been overcome by their foolishness and egoism, he created three more demons who were impervious to false illusions and egoism, who understood true reality [*tattva*]. Their names were Formidable, Fair, and Firm [Bhīma, Bhāsa, and Dṛḍha]. These demons could not be conquered. But Viṣṇu came to the aid of the gods and waged a battle with Śambara that was like an untimely doomsday. He killed Śambara and sent him to the city of Viṣṇu. Then Viṣṇu extinguished the three demons, as a wind blows out the flame of a lamp. And since they had no desires or karmic memory traces, they were not reborn. No one knows what became of them.[109]

Paradoxes abound in this story. The demon who wages war on the gods is nevertheless entirely aware of the illusory nature of the universe; he therefore is necessarily aware of the nonreality of the war (and, indeed, of the warriors, including himself). He uses his powers of illusion to produce mental images of demons who are immune because they are illusory; yet they fall prey to those same powers when they begin to believe that they truly exist (that "I" exists). As long as they do not *want* life or victory, they are assured of life and victory; when they want them, they lose them. That same desire for life and victory transforms the first three demons from mere mental images to "real" transmigrating souls; emotion puts flesh on desires. They are burnt in hell, with their wives and children, just as Lavaṇa and Gādhi are burnt, and they are reborn as various animals in a brief recapitulation of the genre that we know from the tale of the monk's dream. Significantly, they end up not only as fish—which symbolize the loss and recovery of memory in rebirth—but as fish in Kashmir, the home of the *Yogavāsiṣṭha* and the spawning ground of Indian shamanism and magic.

When the demon then succeeds in creating (still by illusion) demons who will *not* be susceptible to illusion, they are nevertheless overcome, this time not by the flames of hell but by a battle that is likened to the flames of doomsday. These demons are less substantial than the first; where the first trio was named with nouns redolent of the magician's toolbox, the second trio is named with adjectives that suggest desirable mental qualities. These demons cannot be physically destroyed or mentally seduced; Viṣṇu simply intervenes *ex machina* and kills in single combat the master demon, who is *not* immune to emotion and illusion. And when Viṣṇu smashes the machine that generates the mental power that projects the image of the demons, the demons are extinguished, blown out like a candle (or a Buddhist). Magic not only supplies a metaphor for the illusory nature of reality; it also demonstrates ways in which that illusion may, and may not, be combated.

Magic is a way of testing a philosophy of illusion; it is a kind of unreality-testing. What is at first an attempt to relinquish perceived reality and thus to dissolve the barrier between perceived and imaginary reality—to make imaginary reality become real (as the Tibetan Buddhists do)—may later become manipulative and magical, used to alter conditions in perceived reality (as many Indian yogins do). As a result of these various possible purposes, and also as a result of the combination of divine and demonic sanctions on the practice of magic, the magician is regarded with considerable moral ambiguity. Vasiṣṭha calls Lavaṇa's magician a haughty, shifty rogue and a noxious lizard, and Lavaṇa himself calls the magician a crook.[110]

Much of the ambiguous status of the magician is related to his role as an artist, a creator of illusions. Plato damned both artists and magicians in a single thrust when he called the poets liars. He pointed out that "the same things appear straight to those who view them in water and crooked to those who view them outside of water, and things seem concave to some and convex to others, because of the distortion of vision. . . . And because scene-painting exploits this weakness of our nature it is no better than witchcraft."[111] Sir Ernst Gombrich remarks on this passage: "Plato, it will be remembered, objected to the art of his time because the artist did not create the thing itself but only a counterfeit, a mere dream or illusion. He was like the sophist who conjured up an impression in other people's minds which did not correspond to reality." And in writing of the "phantom perceptions" that artists produce, Gombrich suggests that "there is no class of people better able to bring about such phantom perceptions than conjurers. They set up a train of expectations, a semblance of familiar situations, which makes our imagination run ahead and complete it obligingly without knowing where we have been tricked."[112]

People who can bamboozle our minds in this way make us nervous, and sometimes angry, in the West. Many witches were burnt to death in Europe because *other people dreamt of them*; that is, the witches projected their own seductive images into the innocent minds of priests and married men. Their power to project themselves in this way was an evil power. The *Yogavāsiṣṭha*, by contrast, finally accords its ontological stamp of approval to the dreaming, magic-making, art-creating parts of the person because it identifies them with the dreaming, magic-making, art-creating parts of God, through the identification of the soul and the Godhead.

Magic illusions, like dreams, are often distinguished from harder forms of reality only in retrospect, when they have disappeared; they do not last for a long time, as real objects do. In the West we tend to think of art as more permanent than magic or dreams; our libraries are full of books, our museums full of paintings, and these books and paintings are often the only surviving traces of lost civilizations. But in India neither books nor paintings are assumed to have that sort of permanence. Literature, particularly sacred literature, has traditionally been preserved orally; it is not physically incarnate on pages; it lasts no longer than the mind that knows it. Painting, too, is not always intended to be permanent. The women painters of Mithila use vivid natural colors that soon fade.

> For the artists this impermanence is unimportant—the paintings are not meant to last. The *act* of painting is seen as more important than the form it takes, and elaborately produced marriage sketches may be cast off after use to be eaten by mice or even used to light fires. Frescoes on courtyard walls often fall victim to rain, whitewash, or the playing of children.[113]

Books and paintings, like cities, are thus ephemeral in India, creatures of a day (or perhaps of a night). This is yet another reason why art serves as an apt metaphor for the impermanent universe, whose only *raison d'être* is "the *act* of painting," the process of creation: *māyā*.

God as an Artist

The image of the creator as an artisan can be traced back to the Ṛg Vedic hymns to Viśvakarman, the All-Maker, who is imagined as a sculptor, a smith, a woodcutter, or a carpenter.[114] This image of God appears in the *Yogavāsiṣṭha* story of the girl in the stone, where the creative powers of God carve worlds out of each atom of the stone as a sculptor would carve a single block. This is an underlying assumption of the *Yogavāsiṣṭha*: God is the artist who paints the pictures that we mistake for the world.

An oblique body of scientific support for this view may be seen in the widely discussed phenomenon of natural deception: beetles that look like leaves, grasshoppers like twigs, and so forth. Whoever designed these creatures, it might be argued, knew how to fool the perceiving eye—and was, therefore, an artist. There is, of course, a perfectly good (though still hotly disputed) scientific explanation for all of this, deriving from Darwin. But the relationship between natural and artistic illusion has always intrigued artists and theologians as well as scientists. In our day, Max Ernst and others of his circle were drawn to the mimicry in nature, which "attracted them by its closeness to the metamorphoses and ambiguities that they were fond of."[115] In ancient times, artists were interested both in the way that nature could fool man and in the way that man could fool nature. Man's ability to fool nature was often used as a test of excellence in art: "Sparrows came to pick at the grapes painted by Zeuxis, a stallion attempted to mate with a mare painted by Apelles, the painted picture of a snake silenced birds, and so on."[116] Indeed, it was this aspect of art that was particularly repellent to Plato.

But it was the way that nature fooled man that more often led to metaphysical speculation. A fine example of such an argument is Philostratus's record of a dialogue between Apollonius of Tyana and a man named Damis:

> "Now," said Apollonius, "the things we see in the sky, when the clouds are separated from one another, centaurs and goat-deer, and wolves and horses for that matter—how do you account for them? As the products of imitation, I suppose?" "I suppose so," Damis said. "Then god is an artist, Damis? Does he leave the winged chariot in which he travels, setting the affairs of gods and men to right, and sit on these occasions, drawing these things for fun, like children in sand?" Damis blushed when his argument proved to come to such an absurd conclusion. Apollonius did not embarrass him, for he never pressed his questions, but said, "Surely what you mean, Damis, is that things that pass through the sky are shapeless and haphazard as far as god is concerned, but we, because imitation is our nature, depict and create them?" "Yes," said Damis, "that is the belief we should hold, Apollonius. It is more plausible and sounder."[117]

If poor Damis had been up on his Indian metaphysics, he might not have crumbled so easily and helplessly into the traditional role of Socratic straight man. The concept of god as an artist (though heresy to anyone laboring in the shadow of Plato) is one for which much has been said in India. Apollonius insists that, in the god's-eye view, the clouds are "shapeless and haphazard"; but an Indian would argue that the clouds (and all matter) are not only formless but substanceless and that it is our mental activity that gives them their form and substance. The same artist that made the clouds made the things that they resemble, and that artist *is* God—but God in the form of our minds. Indian idealists would maintain not only that we project onto amorphous clouds images of horses and centaurs (and Gaṇdharva cities) from our minds but even that the horses and centaurs themselves, like the clouds that imitate them, are mere imitations (reflected images). That is why the forms of the clouds coincide with the forms of horses and centaurs: we make them both. The Indian would also argue that God does indeed amuse himself (through his *līlā* or divine sport) by spreading his illusion over us. Perhaps it is therefore no mere accident that, as Philostratus takes pains to tell us, these thoughts occurred to Apollonius when he had arrived in India and was waiting for an audience with an Indian king, a monarch whose name Apollonius does not state,[118] but who might well have been Lavaṇa or Gādhi, for all that we know.

Thus the Greek version of the Indian argument is turned inside out to demonstrate that god is *not* an artist: we are the artists. In recent years, however, the argument for the artistry of god has been resurrected and given a new twist by historians and philosophers of science, who have pointed out the resemblances between scientists and artists[119] and have gone on to explain how it can be that the purely subjective and arbitrary formulations of the artist coincide with the objective and lawful formulations of the scientist. Michael Polanyi spells out the theological implications of this coincidence:

> Our appreciation of originality should make clearer the distinction between the personal and the subjective. A person may have the most peculiar predilections or phobias, yet not be credited with originality . . . . Instead, he will be said to be subject to obsessions and illusions, and may even be certified as insane. Originality may, of course, be mistaken for sheer madness, which has happened to modern painters and writers; and the reverse is also fairly common, namely for people labouring under delusions to believe themselves to be great inventors, discoverers, prophets, etc. But two totally different things may often be mistaken for each other. It is enough to establish here once more the principle which distinguishes them: namely, that commitment is a personal choice, seeking, and eventually accepting, something believed . . . to be impersonally given, while the subjective is altogether in the nature of a condition to which the person in question is subject.[120]

Polanyi begins his argument by taking up the problem of isolation: if a man is truly original, he will, theoretically, say things that no one else thinks are true, and that amounts to throwing down the gauntlet to society and inviting accusations of madness. And Polanyi admits the regressive aspect of one's own belief that one is *not* mad: madness and true originality look alike from the outside. Yet, finally, Polanyi argues that they do not look alike from the *inside*; one somehow "knows," through personal commitment, that one's own truth is "impersonally given." Once again, the Möbius strip of mind, with subjectivity on one side and objectivity on the other, twists around and brings us back up against the problem of faith.

If the scientist is an artist, constructing his world out of mind, how does he "know" that that world is "impersonally given"? Because he knows that God, too, is both a scientist and an artist, constructing the world out of mind. This belief in the congruence of the map-maker and the treasure-seeker explains why it is that the maps agree with one another in detail as well as in structure. When the artist invents the realistic detail that convinces the reader or perceiver, he does not invent it to perpetrate a fraud (*pace* Plato) but rather because he senses it to be true. The detail is there, along with the structure, waiting for us to discover it and to make it for ourselves.

Thus the form of the myth, as well as the content of the myth, provides us with yet another example of the mutual feedback between finding (dreaming of what is already there) and making (dreaming something into existence). Indeed, the form and the content themselves interact in such a cybernetic *rêve à deux*: the artist *is* what he is telling about. He can make only something that is already there; and what is there can be there only because he makes it. Where Polanyi implies that we find what we are looking for because God is looking for it too, dreaming our dreams, Indian philosophy implies that we find it because we *are* it, even as we are God. Since the Indian universe is made of God's body, as well as of God's mind, any act of scientific or artistic creation is literally a self-revelation. In this context, the correlation between making something and finding it is hardly a coincidence; it is just common sense.

Conclusion

Serendipity and Obsession

Serendipity, or "the faculty of making happy and unexpected discoveries by accident," is a term that was coined by Horace Walpole from a fairytale about the three princes of Serendip, the heroes of which "were always making discoveries, by accidents and sagacity, of things they were not in quest of."[1] The name Serendip is probably derived from the Sanskrit *suvarṇa-dvīpa*, or "Golden Island," which designated Śrī Lankā.[2] Lankā, it will be recalled, was the Other World of the *Rāmāyaṇa*, the island to which Rāma flew in order to rescue Sītā. Serendipity is thus a pseudo-Indian word about a magic island in a fairytale; it refers to the physical embodiment of the Gandharva city to which the prince flies to find his princess—whether or not he is looking for her. As for its connotations in English, the closest Indian equivalent term would probably be "crow-and-palm-tree" in the folk version: good luck that comes unexpectedly and rarely.

Serendipity was thus originally the privilege of South Asians—the mythical princes of Serendip. Obsession, on the other hand, is a peculiarly Western gift. The stories in this book, made by ancient Indian thinkers, were found by a Western scholar and then remade for a Western and modern Indian audience. The process of understanding myths has often been called a science;[3] I think it is an art. In any case, like both of these enterprises it proceeds through the alternating phases of finding and making that could be equated with serendipity and obsession. When we select a group of myths to talk or write about, our mind delimits the text and thus creates it. But if we keep finding the stories that we are looking for, it is because *they are there*, like Mount Everest or Mount Meru. The stories in this book are real—as real as the events that happen to us. For, as the *Yogavāsiṣṭha* tells us, "The world is like the impression left by the telling of a story."[4]

This may be the appropriate place to trace the thread of the obsession and the supplementary episodes of serendipity that have resulted in this book. It all began when my mother taught me to read by starting with

Alice in Wonderland. It continued, years later, when I began to study Hinduism at Harvard and found the myths of the mouth of God. I remained obsessed with them enough to write an article about them for *Daedalus* twenty years later.[5] At that time, the main point that I saw in those myths was the blurring of the line between dreaming and waking. One sentence in that article referred to a story about the tale of King Lavaṇa, which I had heard at a conference about karma.[6] One day in Dublin I went to the Chester Beatty Library, and there I saw a magnificent illustrated manuscript of the *Yogavāsiṣṭha*. It was then that I decided to write an article about Lavaṇa. When I was asked to give the Sir George Birdwood Memorial Lecture in London, in May, 1980, I used this manuscript as my theme; and it struck me then that the writings of Sir Ernst Gombrich (who was in the audience) would provide an ideal springboard from which to understand the visualizations of illusion and art.

Then I began to see that in order to understand the story of Lavaṇa one needed a great deal of background, of four basic sorts: one needed to know more stories of the genre (kings and Untouchables); one needed to know more about dreams; one needed to know the rest of the *Yogavāsiṣṭha*; and one needed to know more Indian philosophy than I knew then. This led me into that long process of scholarship (or "normal science") that is powered by obsession and sparked by serendipity. I spent a summer reading Plato and Polanyi and Popper and Potter and Proust. I read through the mythological texts, and I read the *Yogavāsiṣṭha* with my Sanskrit students. As I came up short, again and again, on the question of scientific testing, I recalled my work as a teaching assistant in Leonard Nash's course on the history of science at Harvard in 1963; I wrote another article on Lavaṇa, for *Quadrant*, from this point of view. I gave courses on Indian and Western theories of dreams and on Freud's *Interpretation of Dreams*, on paradigm clashes in science and myth, and on illusion in Indian philosophy. I lectured on all aspects of the project to anyone who would sit still and listen,[7] and they gave me comments, arguments, questions, enthusiasm, offprints, criticisms, and more things to read. I started to put together my ideas about the Indian concept of the shared dream for an issue of *Parabola* devoted to dreams. Other stories from the *Yogavāsiṣṭha* then began to capture my imagination, particularly the tale of the monk's dream; I wrote another article for *Daedalus* about the monk's dream. And all this time I kept finding more stories about illusion and dreams.

One day my son Michael brought me the tale of Shlemiel and Chelm. This started me thinking about the difference between Indian and Western attitudes toward the hypothesis of multiple universes. Then I realized that I had missed the most important point in the myths of the mouth of God, the peculiar Indian twist in the complex tale of the dreamer dreamt: the concept of the universe as the dream of God and the body of God.

The Dream That Wanders in the Daylight

We emerge, appropriately enough, with a paradox. On the one hand, it seems that very few people have ever been able to take seriously, for any length of time, the belief that the entire universe is illusory or that their lives are just part of their own dream or someone else's dream. But many myths have been fueled by just such a belief, and most Indians find it inescapably a part of their perceived world. Why do people tantalize themselves with an idea that is so disturbing?

One answer to this question is that certain aspects of the doctrine of *māyā* are more comforting than disturbing; it might even be said (and it often has been said by Indian philosophers) that *māyā* is disturbing only to those who do not understand it, who are not enlightened. Indian philosophers were well aware of the fact that most people are disturbed by the implications of the theory of illusion; this resistance was one of the main obstacles to enlightenment. To those who had an incorrect view of the self, the implications of the illusory nature of the self may well have been not merely disturbing but terrifying; but to those with the right view of the self, such an implication was not merely comforting but a great relief.

Some people, as we have seen, preferred *saṃsāra* to *mokṣa*, and some chose to abandon *saṃsāra* and seek *mokṣa*. The first of these views seems more natural to most Westerners and needs little justification, but the second has often been misunderstood. There are two different reasons for choosing *mokṣa*, one negative (a turning away from *saṃsāra*) and one positive (a turning toward *mokṣa*). Even the negative reason has a positive as well as a negative aspect: many people distrusted *saṃsāra* not because the world was full of pain but rather because it was so wonderful that one could not bear to be parted from it over and over again at the end of each life, to be torn away from all the people one had come to love. These people feared re-death, not rebirth. But others feared rebirth itself and hated *saṃsāra* more directly; they could not stand the thought that they would die only to be reborn. They anticipated with dread the physical discomfort of the embryo squashed in the womb and smothered in disgusting body fluids; they pictured the embryo as already full of chagrin and remorse in the knowledge that the new life about to begin would bring the same failures, losses, embarrassing mistakes, and ruined opportunities that had plagued the countless lives of the past. And, finally, people might choose *mokṣa* not because they feared re-death or rebirth but simply because they wanted *mokṣa*, which they perceived as a state of eternal and infinite joy. The doctrine of illusion did not imply that, if you left *saṃsāra*, you would go out like a candle; you left it to enter bliss (*ānanda*), variously not-described. Awakening from the dream of *saṃsāra* did not mean entering into a stage entirely devoid of experience.

To those who found *saṃsāra* terrifying, *māyā* provided a way out, for *māyā* could work against *saṃsāra* as well as within it. In the Bengali tradition, for example, *māyā* takes two different forms: to those who do not understand her, she appears as *māyā-śakti*, a negative force that distorts and teases; but to those who do understand, she is *yoga-māyā*, who makes possible the play (*līlā*) of God in the world.[8] And, just as *māyā* could be valued in different ways, it was also quite possible to value both *saṃsāra* and *mokṣa*, though in different ways. On the one hand, you could regard *saṃsāra* as a necessary trial, an experience through which you earned your right to *mokṣa*. Or, if you liked *saṃsāra*, you could postpone your efforts toward the inevitable encompassing goal of *mokṣa*; like Saint Augustine, who prayed to God to give him chastity—but not yet, the Hindu could strive for *mokṣa*—but not yet.

Another answer to our paradox becomes apparent when we turn the question upside down and ask, not why people believe that the universe is just a dream, but why they believe that a dream could be the universe. In this way, the glass is half full, not half empty. Though the idealistic hypothesis does seriously undermine our basic, common-sense, everyday assumption that our lives are real, it offers in place of that jeopardized assumption the suggestion that something else that we instinctively value deeply might in fact be more real than common sense ordinarily allows. As children, we believe that our dreams are real, objectively real; in most societies we are forced to give up that belief, though it lingers in our myths.

Even as adults, however, and even in the *soi-disant* most rational societies, we come to value our dreams as purveyors of another kind of reality, not objectively verifiable but still strangely persuasive: the reality of feelings we normally hide from ourselves, of memories that we have lost or suppressed, and of insights into a nonmaterial world that our everyday activities screen from us. By granting to dreams the status of a kind of reality, we affirm values that we cherish. Yet to retreat entirely into our dreams is to retreat into solipsism or even madness; we long to have company in our private worlds. The myths of dreams that turn out to be real are attempts to bridge this gap, to people our lonely fantasies.

We tend to confuse reality and illusion in both directions. On the one hand, what makes fantasy potent is the possibility that it might become real; that is why we prop up our dreams with the bric-a-brac of everyday life. It *might* happen, we assure ourselves; I might awaken and find my dream lover still beside me. On the other hand, what makes reality beautiful is the possibility that it might become unreal; that is why we pepper our perceptions with flashes of imagination. It *might* happen, we assure ourselves; I might leap into the air and find that I can fly. Many artists and saints have been willing—or perhaps forced—to sacrifice the comfort of the fellowship of the objective world, the confirmation that comes from surrounding ourselves with other people who assure us that we are in fact real, in order to gamble on the unverifiable reality of the world of dreams. Some have tried to hedge their bets, to have the best of both worlds, to speculate about a dream universe that is in fact verifiably real in every sense of the word. From the Western point of view, such people are selling out reality and objectivity, but from the Indian point of view they are enriching objective reality by infusing it with the values of the world of dreams.

We reach out to grasp hold of our dreams at different times and in different ways. When life—*saṃsāra*—becomes too full of suffering, or even too full of happiness, we tell ourselves, "This must be a dream," hoping in this way to transform the all-too-real into what we define as unreality. By contrast, we sometimes find ourselves caught up in a dream that we cannot get enough of, a dream so wonderful that, when we wake, we cry to dream again.[9] Then we pull this moment closer to us, telling ourselves, "This is real life; I am awake," hoping in this way to turn the dream into what we define as reality.

It may seem that these two situations are not true parallels, that these are not two different self-deceptions but the same one. For both of them load the dice in favor of unreality, the first by undermining waking life, the second by preserving sleep. But there is always a voice in us that speaks in defense of reality, defining the dream as (merely) a dream and defining what appears to be waking life as reality. This voice is the nagging whine of common sense. There is, however, a more insidious imbalance implicit in our use of the two phrases ("This is just a dream"/"I am awake"): the first occurs far more often than the second. We often discover that we have been dreaming; we realize this every time we wake up. But we seldom discover—or tell ourselves—that we are awake. We *assume* that waking reality is our fail-safe position, the resting point to which the gravity of our common sense invariably returns us. We do not, therefore, have to keep telling ourselves that we are awake.

The burden of proof then falls upon unreality, and its advocate is myth. If common sense reassures us that we are awake, it remains for myth to remind us that we may be asleep—listening or reading in our sleep, as we know that we sometimes talk in our sleep. Common sense is always on the *qui vive* against the night raids of myth: "It's only a story," it murmurs to us as it feels us slipping away from its stranglehold when we are drawn into the truth of the narrative. But we can, and do, steel ourselves against the comforting, seductive drone of common sense. Something inside us tells us that what we read in the New York *Times* is *not true*, not only in the superficial sense that conscious political distortions, misprints, and poor reporting have intervened between the event and us (i.e., newspapers are full of mistakes, or *bhrama*), but in the deeper sense that no event can ever be truly witnessed or recorded (i.e., words are full of illusion, or *māyā*). And something inside us tells us that *Anna Karenina* is *true*. Though we may read certain kinds of narratives—and not merely escapist or fantasy literature—in order to escape from reality, we also read in order to find reality and to bring it from the page back into our active lives. And I think that when we read this second, deeper kind of narrative we do not find it necessary, or possible, to say, "This is just a story."

I never fail to be moved when I read about the death of Tiny Tim, even though I know that it is "just a story" and that, even in that story, it is not true but serves only as a vision of what might have been; for Dickens goes on explicitly to tell us (as I have read dozens of times) that Tiny Tim did *not* die. The death of the child is a real element in Scrooge's dream (as in so many dreams), and so it moves us to real tears. For one of the things that the *Yogavāsiṣṭha* teaches us is that, from the god's-eye view, *all* stories are true.

To a certain extent, the reality of created characters is a feature of all inspired literature. As Unamuno remarked, Hamlet is more real than Shakespeare: Shakespeare died on a certain date, while Hamlet has continued to transform the subsequent history of European thought. The reality of such characters stems from the fact that they are both found and made. Herodotus felt something of this with regard to the Greek gods: "Whence each of these gods came into existence, or whether they were for ever, and what kind of shape they were, was not known until the day before yesterday, if I may use the expression; for I believe that Homer and Hesiod were four hundred years before my time—and no more than that. It is they who created for the Greeks their theogony, it is they who gave to the gods the names derived from their ancestors and divided among them their honors, their arts, and their shapes."[10] In this remarkable passage, Herodotus seems to be saying that the Greek gods were there before Homer and Hesiod (either there for ever or there once they had come into existence) and also that Homer and Hesiod, a relatively short time ago, made the gods what they were.

Yet it was in India that such concepts had particularly fertile ground in which to develop. For the fact that there is no historical author for most

Indian stories (the *Yogavāsiṣṭha*, for instance, is attributed to the primeval poet Vālmīki and the mythical sage Vasiṣṭha) meant that it was all the easier for the story to blend into nonfictional life. The tale was there to be picked up and found, to be claimed like a piece of uncultivated land, or, rather, to be salvaged as the treasure of anyone who could dive down and haul it up out of the ocean of story. The story was, in any case, believed to exist before it was put into words by a particular author; but the fact that the author was anonymous helped to preserve the independence, the free-standing quality, of the story even after it had been given artistic form.

Stories about dreams ought to be even farther removed from reality than realistic stories about people like Anna Karenina, and *Indian* stories about dreams should be even farther away from our reality than European stories are. When we view the Indian myths about dreams through the triple lenses of sleep, narrative, and another culture, the lenses magnify, rather than shrink, our view of reality. This may be because we have confidence in the power of these frames or lenses to protect us by distancing us; we think that, if the going gets rough, we can always fall back and say, "This is just a story—and, even less, a story about a dream—and an *Indian* story about a dream, to boot!" This confidence allows us to let down our guard and so to take in truths that we would simply look right through were we to encounter them in the course of our waking experiences in the West.

Each lens does this in its own way. Depth psychology has revealed to us the ways in which dreams allow us to express and perceive powerful truths that our inner censors do not allow us to admit, let alone to express, when we are awake; these are fragmented truths that only the master spy, the analyst, can reassemble. So, too, as Claude Lévi-Strauss has demonstrated, myths allow us to formulate paradoxes that in the factual and practical world would seem impossible or immoral; by fragmenting and reassembling the parts of a contradictory truth, the myth is able to express a concept that the culture is unable to take in when it is expressed in blunt, nonnarrative terms.[11] And, finally, the foreignness of India simultaneously mutes and intensifies the shock of recognition by presenting our home truths from an unexpected angle. At this point we fail to use the protection at hand; we do not call upon our consciousness of the triple lens to yank us three times as fast out of the moment of truth, like a trinity of *dei ex machina*. When the story captures for us a moment of reality, however painful, we do not say, "It's only a myth."

Let me hasten to say that India does not give us merely the Indian version of the truths we cannot recognize or face if they are told to us in our own tongue, for India does know things that no one else knows, strange truths that are truly strange. Indeed, it is from India—

from the tale of the king among the Untouchables—that we learn that very truth, the fact that certain essential truths come to us only from Others: from women, demons, and Untouchables. But our home truths, too, come to us more vividly from the Sanskrit texts, not only (as I would argue) because they have been said best in Sanskrit, but because Sanskrit is not our own language. These three filters—the dream, the narrative, and the foreign tongue—are like the three sieves that filter the Soma juice in the ancient Vedic sacrifice:[12] unfiltered, the ambrosia is dangerous for mortals to drink; filtered, it gives a taste of immortality.

What truths are expressed through these three filters, which merge—for us—in the *Yogavāsiṣṭha*? Some are self-referential truths, insights into the nature and interrelationship of dream, myth, and alien cultures. Others are more particular human truths, which expand our vision of what it means to fall in love, to bear children, to see them die, to create a work of art that speaks to others, to test our guesses about the nature of the physical and nonphysical world, to contemplate our own death. And, finally, these tales force us to speculate not only about the relationship between our mental perception of the world and its mental perception of us but about the relationship between our dreams of God and God's dream of us.

The central truth that is particularly Indian—that is not merely the Indian version of archetypal truths—is the insight into the primacy, the solidity, and the power of the world of dreams and illusions. In India, the realm of mental images is not on the defensive. Common sense has a powerful lobby there, as it has with us, but it does not always have everything its own way. Reality has to share the burden of proof with unreality in India, and it is by no means a foregone conclusion that reality will win. Or, rather, from the Indian point of view, *māyā* is what we must always start from and perhaps end with. Some philosophical schools deplore this, while others celebrate it; but it is always there.

Aeschylus used the phrase "a dream that wanders in the daylight" to describe the helplessness and weakness of old men left behind in time of war: "The overold, in the parching of the leafage, walks its three-footed way, no better than a child; it wanders, a dream in the daylight."[13] For Aeschylus, and for much of Western tradition, the dream that helplessly crosses the barrier into waking life is what is unreal—socially unreal (like the old men of Argos), mad (like lunatics who live in their fantasies), or childish. But in India the dream that wanders in the daylight does not fade but instead makes daylight all the more luminous; it shines into the hidden corners of waking life to show us shadows brighter than the light.

1. Nārada sees the water nymphs (CB 34, fol. 268b)

The earliest extant manuscript of the *Yogavāsiṣṭha* was made at the end of the sixteenth century, probably for the Mughal Emperor Akbar. It is now in the Chester Beatty Library in Dublin. All but one of the plates in this book (the exception being plate 15, M. C. Escher's "Drawing Hands") are reproduced from that manuscript, with the kind permission of the Chester Beatty Library. "CB" followed by a number is the number of the illustration in the series of 41 listed in the Chester Beatty catalogue; "fol." followed by a number is the number of the folio in the manuscript itself.

2. Bhṛgu takes his son back from the god of death (CB 15, fol. 107)

3. King Vidūratha and King Sindhu wage war (CB 8, fol. 58b)

4. King Lavaṇa falls from his horse (CB 11, fol. 85b)

5. King Lavaṇa enters the Untouchable village (CB 12, fol. 87b)

6. King Lavaṇa returns to the Untouchable village with his court (CB 14, fol. 101)

7. Viṣṇu appears to the Brahmin Gādhi in the pond (CB 23, fol. 157b)

8. King Lavaṇa performs a sacrifice in his mind (CB 13, fol. 95)

که بچیزی که منشا دوستی و دشمنی و سپه مایه مواهای نفسانی شد
و ربایندهٔ عقل و هوش یو دراجه را پاز ما ینشب مهتاب برکنار جوی راجه
سکهد بوج پسپح مشغول یو دکه پوراله درکنجی که بساخهای در رخت کلپ

فروکرفته و بانواع شکوفها برآموده کویا خانه دیوتهای صحرائی بود خودار
بغفد کلها آراسته برتوشک کلها پرا سته بامردی ا فنین خود دریه منجته

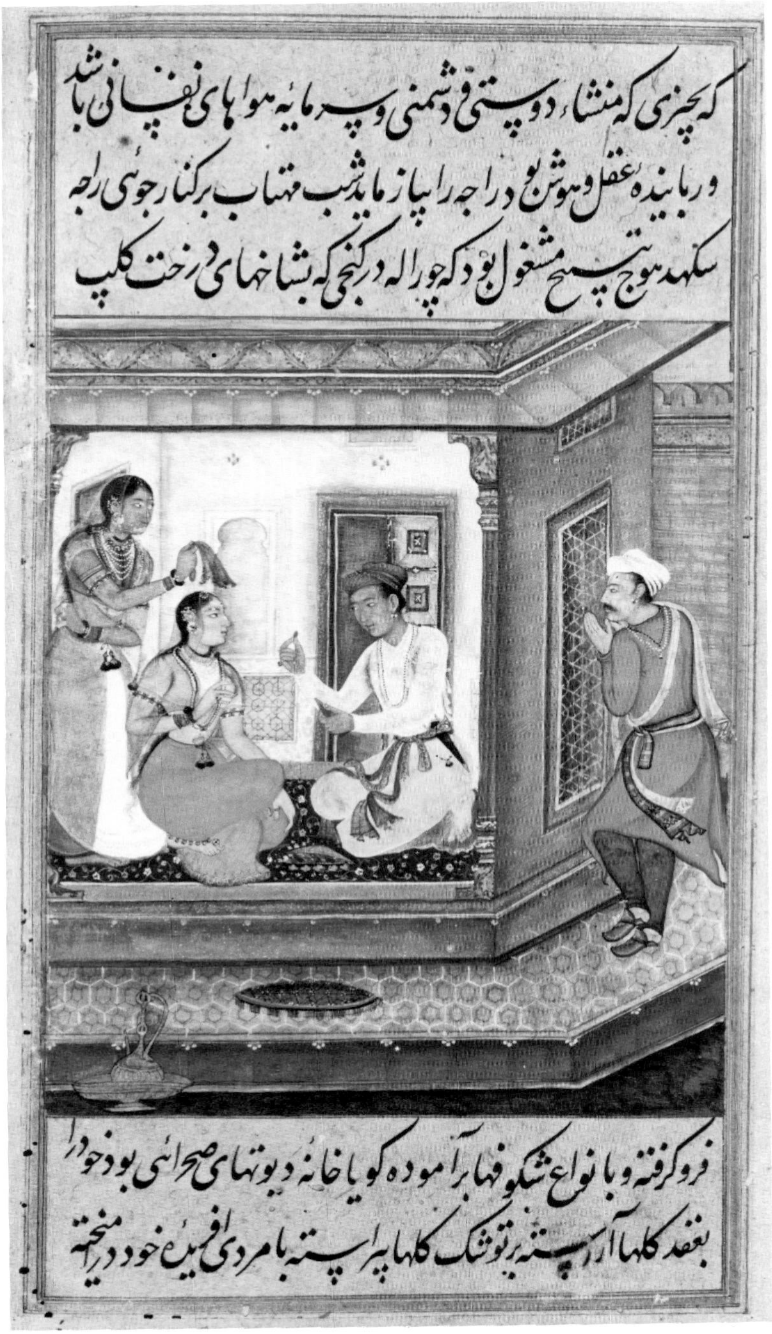

9. Queen Cūḍālā creates an illusion of herself with a lover (CB 38, fol. 293b)

10. The ogress Karkaṭī is instructed by a king (CB 10, fol. 73b)

11. An ogre instructs a king (CB 31, fol. 249)

12. The brothers Puṇya and Pāvana discuss rebirth (CB 20, fol. 139b)

13. The desires of Vasiṣṭha become personified as demons (CB 6, fol. 47)

14. The god Rudra, with his wife, visits Vasiṣṭha (CB 30, fol. 230)

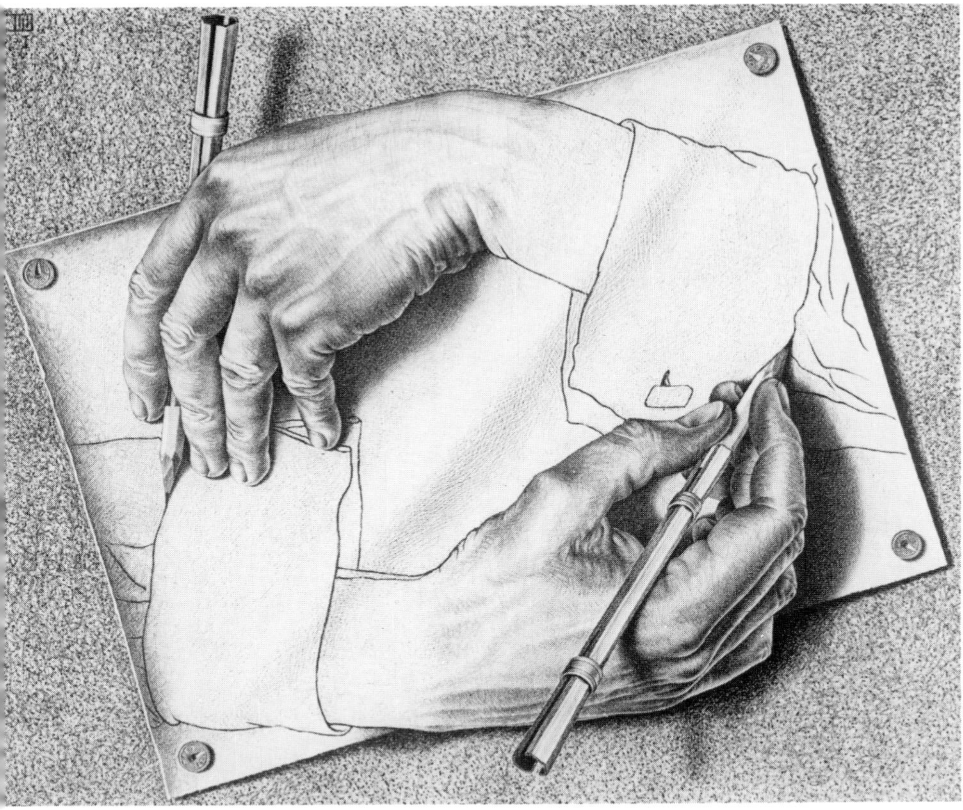

15. M. C. Escher, *Drawing Hands*. Reproduced by permission of Beeldrecht, Amsterdam/VAGA, New York, 1983, Collection Haags Gemeentemuseum—The Hague

16. The gods and demons wage war (CB 17, fol. 114)

Appendixes

1. The Erotic Dream in China

The physical proof of a magical flight to the woman in the other world is described in a Chinese text[1] in which a man dreams that he has had intercourse with a beautiful woman; he wakes up and she is not there. But "on waking, he found that he had had an emission. He was struck by the experience but attributed it to mere coincidence. However, when he had the same dream the following night, and again for three or four nights in succession, he became alarmed and went to bed without extinguishing the candle light, maintaining a state of vigilance." Though he guarded himself against the succubus, she came to him again. This time he awoke "in the midst of disporting himself with her and, opening his eyes, he found the girl, beautiful as a fairy maiden, actually in his arms. . . . 'How violent you are,' the girl protested. 'It is a good thing that I took the precaution of coming to you in your dreams.' . . . Later, when they extinguished the light and went to bed, the young man found her no different from ordinary living humans. There was always a wet spot on the bedclothes afterwards." Eventually he brought her into his waking life; she exhorted him to become a devout Buddhist, and they lived together happily for many years.

What is particularly notable about the story is that the physical proof that convinces the young man that the girl truly exists (a proof that he at first dismisses as "mere coincidence," as if it were indeed a puzzling fact) is his own orgasm.

2. The Dream Adventure in China and Ireland

There is a Chinese story that bears a striking resemblance to the tale of King Lavaṇa. It is the story of King Mu:

> In the time of King Mu of Chou, there came from a country in the far West a magician who could enter fire and water, . . . who rode the empty air without falling. . . . He not only altered the shapes of things, he also changed the thoughts of men. King Mu built himself a mansion seven thousand feet high, called "The Tower in the Middle Sky," filled with beautiful virgins and fine foods. One day, the magician invited the king to come with him to *his* palace in the Middle Sky, above the clouds; in the distance it looked like a congealed cloud. When it seemed to the king that he had lived there twenty or thirty years without thinking of his own country, the magician took him on another excursion, to a place where they could not see the sun and moon above them, and the king became terrified and

> asked the magician to let him go back. The magician gave him a push, and the king fell through space and awoke to find himself sitting as before in his own palace, with his attendants waiting at his side. His wine had not yet cooled, the meats had not yet gone dry. When the king asked where he had been, his courtiers answered: "Your majesty has only been sitting here absorbed in meditation."
>
> From this time King Mu was not himself, and it was three months before he recovered. He again questioned the magician, who answered: "Your Majesty has been with me on a journey of the spirit. Why should your body have moved? Why should the place where you lived be different from your own palace, or the place of our excursion different from your own park? Your Majesty feels at home with the permanent, is suspicious of the sudden and temporary. But can one always measure how far and how fast a scene may alter and turn into something else?"[1]

This story was composed "early in the Christian Era, at a time when Buddhist philosophy and Taoist philosophy were influencing and enriching each other."[2] A. C. Graham has commented as follows on the Taoist adaptation of the Buddhist theme of illusion in *The Book of Lieh Tzu* and, particularly, in this story:

> The doctrine that the world perceived by the senses is an illusion is familiar in mystical philosophies everywhere; we expect it to have the corollary that illumination is an awakening from illusion to the Reality behind it. It is impossible to draw this conclusion within the metaphysical framework of Taoism, which assumes . . . that the visible world is more real than the Tao, the Nothing out of which it emerges. Nevertheless, the idea that life is a dream appears occasionally in early Taoism, not as a metaphysical thesis, but as a fancy exciting the imagination. . . .
>
> In the *Lieh-tzu* this theme occupies a whole chapter. Although its new prominence may well be the result of Buddhist influence, the treatment of the theme remains purely Taoist; there is no implication that it is either possible or desirable for the living to awake from their dream. . . . The first and longest story in this chapter compares the visible world to a magician's illusion; and the dominant feeling throughout is not that life is futile, but that it can assume the marvellous quality of magic and dream.[3]

The Taoist attitude to illusion, therefore, is closer to the folk attitude (that the adventure in the other world is great fun) than it is to the Vedāntic (or Buddhist: that the illusory nature of life makes it sorrowful).

The story of Mu and the magician plays on the glories of magic in an idealistic way; the text seems to say that it is more impressive that the magician can alter soft reality, psychological reality—can change men's thoughts—than that he can manipulate hard, physical reality—"the shapes of things"—as well as pass through fire and water, like any true shaman. The author also juggles the levels of reality: King Mu's palace is *called* "The Tower in the Middle Sky," and it is a real palace; but the magician's palace actually *is* in the Middle Sky—if, indeed, it is a real palace at all. These are Buddhist tricks. Moreover, it appears that the story of Mu ends on a Buddhist note, with the king disenchanted with worldly life; for the text states, "He ceased to care for state affairs, took no pleasure in his ministers and concubines." But the king is not (or not yet) truly disillusioned; he simply wants to go on another journey. The story continues:

> King Mu gave up his thoughts to far journeys. He gave orders to yoke his eight noble horses in two teams. They galloped a thousand miles and . . . then he was the guest of the Western Queen Mother, who gave a banquet for him on Jasper Lake. The Western Queen Mother sang for the king, who sang in answer; but the words of his song were melancholy. He looked westward at Mount Yen, where the sun goes down after its daily journey of ten thousand miles. Then he sighed and said, "Alas! I, who am king, have neglected virtue for pleasure. Will not future generations look back and blame me for my errors?"

Thus, either by resisting the queen's wiles or through weary satiety, the king comes to understand the nature of (Buddhist) virtue and the duties of kingship (Confucian duties, one assumes, rather than the Hindu virtues of the Sanskrit text). The Taoist background of the text interacts with the Buddhist and Confucian values to leave open several of the possible moral implications of the tale; so, too, as we have seen, the Vedic and Vedāntic values underlying the Sanskrit text give both a positive and a negative value to the life that the king experiences in his dream world.

Given the remarkable correspondence between the tale of King Mu and the tale of King Lavaṇa, how can one account for the similarities? Did the tale travel from India to China, from China to India, from somewhere else to both of them, or did it originate independently in the two countries? The answers to these questions depend in part on how one defines "the tale." The story of Lavaṇa, as we have seen, dates from the ninth century A.D. in Kashmir, long after the composition of Lieh-tzu's work; but the Lavaṇa story can be traced back, in most of its themes, to earlier Indian texts that long antedate the book of Lieh-tzu, though they do not antedate all the works that the Chinese work draws upon. Clearly, both the Chinese and the Indian texts owe a great deal to Buddhist philosophies, which migrated from India to China at an early period but then reentered India after acquiring various attributes from their sojourn further east.

The tale of Mu is one of a corpus of dream adventure stories in Chinese literature that are characterized by a vision of grandeur, an illusion of the passing of time, and the use of "a material object to measure the amount of time that actually passes in a dream." For example, "the dream may take the space of time it requires to cook a meal, saddle a horse, or wash one's hands." These stories may be traced in European variants as well, perhaps transmitted from China to Europe through Islamic intermediaries. Attempts have been made to provide an Indian ancestry for the Chinese pillow stories: "Miss P'ei P'o-hsien in her study of the influence of Indian literature on Chinese literature suggests that the pillow story found in *Yu ming lu* and *Sou shen chi* is derived from an Indian source. She cites the story of Sha-lo-na and Katyayana, which existed both in Aśvaghosa's *Sūtrālamkāraśāstra* and the *Samyukta-ratna-pitaka-sūtra*. Both of these works existed in Chinese translation beginning in the early fifth century A.D."[4] David Knechtges is suspicious of this hypothesis, maintaining that the Chinese stories were "native creations," though he admits that "the stories are enough alike that it may yet be possible to trace a definitive connection between them." In light of the shamanistic elements in both sets of stories,[5] it seems entirely possible to imagine a Central Asian origin for the corpus, diffused, via Buddhism—and hence with Buddhist philosophical overlays upon the folk materials—throughout China and India, particularly Kashmir. One might equally well hypothesize, however, that a basically Buddhist story from India was brought to Central Asia, where it underwent certain modifications. This latter hypothesis is supported by the existence of variants of the tale at the other end of the Indo-European spectrum, in Ireland.

Through Indo-European diffusion, or through Buddhist proselytizers, or through the medium of Islam, these stories were carried to Europe. One particularly close variant is attested in a rather late set of Irish texts:

> Oisin, the son of Fionn, one day met a beautiful woman on a white horse; she was Niamh, the daughter of the King of Tir na nOg ["the Land of Youth"]. She asked him to come back with her, to be her husband, and he consented. He mounted behind her and the white horse galloped away swift as the wind, his feet barely touching the ground, leaving no mark on the sands, and he galloped across the ocean, and Oisin disappeared, and Fionn never saw him again.
>
> When Oisin had lived happily with Niamh for three years, he longed to see his father and his people once more. Unwillingly, she let him go back for a visit, though she warned him never to dismount from the white horse, nor let his feet touch the ground. He came to Ireland and found everything changed; as he stooped to help some men lift a stone, his foot touched the ground; his horse vanished, and he turned suddenly into a blind old man. For three hundred years had passed.[6]

J. A. McCulloch remarks of this corpus, "These stories illustrate what is found in all Celtic tales of divine or fairy mistresses—they are the wooers, and mortals tire of them and their divine land sooner than they weary of their lovers."[7] The disjunction in time between this world and the other (though here time passes slower in the other world rather than faster, as in the *Yogavāsiṣṭha*); the gift of immortality, which slips through the hero's fingers; the longing for this world; and, above all, the flying white horse (which is here identified with the magic of immortality; for when the hero leaves the horse and touches the ground, he loses the magic)—these identify this typically Irish tale as one belonging in the same corpus as our Chinese, Indian, and Central Asian tales.

3. Stories from the *Yogavāsiṣṭha* Told (or Cited) in This Book

Titles enclosed in parentheses indicate that tales are merely cited, not told.

Abbreviations

AV	*Atharva Veda*
M	*Mahābhārata*
P	*Purāṇa*
R	*Rāmāyaṇa*
RV	*Ṛg Veda*
U	*Upaniṣad*
YV	*Yogavāsiṣṭha*

Notes

Introduction: Transformation and Contradiction

1. This was James Boon's summary of the book.

2. Clifford Geertz, "Common Sense as a Cultural System."

3. This is the first of a number of thoughtful and relevant formulations—too numerous to acknowledge separately—made by David Brent in response to an earlier draft.

4. One could enlarge on the list of things that we normally place under the headings of hard and soft:

Hard		*Soft*
real	vs.	illusory
historical		mythical
true		false
awake		asleep
public		private
permanent		transient
present		past/future (memory/prediction)
outside		inside
objective		subjective
sane		insane
rational		emotional
male		female
Western		Eastern
scientific		religious
right		left

The last few categories are more obviously arbitrary than the first few, but they make us realize, in retrospect, how arbitrary *all* of them are. From there it is easy to move on to still more arbitrary (i.e., private, false, subjective, emotional . . .) pairs:

clocks	vs.	clouds (from Popper)
speech		thought
brain		mind
body		mind
computer		program
hardware		software
hardcore porn		softcore porn
tough		tender

experience	imagination
concrete	abstract
rock	banana (from Eliade)
Freud	Jung (from Freud)
Popper	Kuhn (from Popper)
cooked	raw (from Lévi-Strauss)
mechanistic	organic
text	footnote

5. This quality of South Asian thinking is well described by Sheryl B. Daniel in "The Tool-Box Approach of the Tamil to the Issues of Moral Responsibility and Human Destiny."

6. Sir Ernst Gombrich, "Illusion and Art," p. 222.

7. *Kauṣītaki Upaniṣad* 1. 2. It was A. L. Basham who brought this passage to my attention (in a lecture at the University of Chicago on April 29, 1983) and pointed out that it is unique in the *śruti* literature.

8. I am grateful to my teacher, Daniel H. H. Ingalls, for reminding me, early in my work on this book, that the presence of *brahman* as a ground of reality must be taken as implicit even in many texts that seem to propose an unmitigated idealism.

CHAPTER 1. THE INTERPRETATION OF DREAMS

1. Roger Caillois, *The Dream Adventure*, p. ix; this passage is repeated in his "Logical and Philosophical Problems," p. 23.
2. *RV* 2. 28. 10 and 10. 164. 5; Wendy O'Flaherty, *The Rig Veda*, pp. 218, 288.
3. *RV* 10. 162. 5–6; Wendy O'Flaherty, *The Rig Veda*, p. 292.
4. *Praśna U* 4. 5.
5. *Māṇḍūkya U* 3–4.
6. *Bṛhadāraṇyaka U* 2. 1. 18.
7. *Māṇḍūkya U* 7 and 11.
8. *Bṛhadāraṇyaka U* 2. 1. 20.
9. Ibid. 4. 3. 9–10.
10. Ibid. 4. 3. 13; 4. 3. 20; *Chāndogya U* 8. 10. 1.
11. *YV* 3. 41. 53.
12. *YV* 3. 117. 18–19.
13. Sudhir Kakar, *Shamans, Mystics, and Doctors*, p. 246.
14. Alex Wayman, "Significance of Dreams," p. 10.
15. *Praśna U* 4. 5.
16. *Chāndogya U* 5. 2. 9.
17. *AV* 68. 1. 13–19, 29–37, 44–47.
18. *AV* 68. 1. 51–52.
19. *AV* 68. 1. 52.
20. *AV* 68. 1. 53a.
21. *AV* 68. 2. 21–22.
22. *AV* 68. 2. 9–20, 23–24, 31–33.
23. Wendy O'Flaherty, *Women*, pp. 299–311.
24. *AV* 68. 5. 1–14.
25. *AV* 68. 2. 51–54; 68. 5. 1–9.

26. *AV* 68. 2. 25–29.
27. *AV* 68. 2. 25.
28. *Mānava Gṛhya Sūtra* 2. 14. 7–12.
29. Ibid. 2. 14. 13.
30. *Suśruta Saṃhitā* 1. 29. 54–64.
31. Ibid. 1. 29. 68.
32. *Garuḍa P*, *Uttara Khaṇḍa* 11. 5–12.
33. *Suśruta Saṃhitā*, cited by A. M. Esnoul, "Les songes," p. 225.
34. *Suśruta Saṃhitā* 1. 29. 67.
35. *Angavijjā*, pp. 186–91.
36. *Caraka Saṃhitā* 5. 5. 42.
37. Karl Potter, *Presuppositions*, p. 112.
38. Karl Potter, *Indian Metaphysics*, pp. 293–94.
39. *Pitṛputrasamāgama-mahāyānasūtra* (Kyoto-Tokyo photographic reprint of the Tibetan canon), XXIII, 201–4, cited by Alex Wayman, "Significance of Dreams," p. 5.
40. Alex Wayman, "Significance of Dreams," p. 11.
41. Vasugupta's *Spandakārikā* 34, cited by A. M. Esnoul, "Les songes," p. 229.
42. *Tantrāloka* 15, cited by A. M. Esnoul, "Les songes," p. 231.
43. *R* 5. 20. 8–9.
44. *R* 5. 24–27.
45. Kampaṉ *Rāmāyaṇa* 5. 368 (3. 3a).
46. *R* 5. 30. 4–8.
47. *R* 5. 32. 14–23.
48. *R* 5. 33. 76–78.
49. *R* 7. 84–87.
50. *R* 2. 63. 1–18.
51. *M* 5. 141. 5–42.
52. *Brahmavaivarta P*, *Gaṇapati Khaṇḍa* 33. 35–43, 58–62.
53. Ibid. 34. 10–14.
54. Ibid. 32. 41–81; 35. 1–46.
55. *Aśokāvadāna*, chapter 27. I am indebted to John Strong for this translation of the Kunāla story (which I have summarized), taken from pp. 105–25 of the Mukhopadhyaya edition of the *Aśokāvadāna*.
56. *Kathāsaritsāgara* 12(72). 93–153.
57. A. M. Esnoul, "Les songes," p. 228.
58. *Lalitavistara* 14, *Anguttaranikāya* 3, and in other Buddhist texts.
59. *Vessantara Jātaka*.
60. As does A. M. Esnoul, in "Les songes," p. 228.
61. Pindar, Thirteenth Olympian, lines 63–92.
62. Heraclitus, Frag. 89, trans. Cleve, p. 90. I owe both the Heraclitean citation and the basic analysis of the philosophy of dreams in the *Republic* to Stephen Gabel's unpublished essay "Dreaming and Waking in Plato's *Republic*: Transformations of a Distinction." To David Grene I owe my understanding of Plato in general.
63. *Māṇḍūkya U* 9.
64. Plato *Theaetetus* 157c–158e.

65. Plato *Republic* 476c–d.
66. Ibid. 520c.
67. Ibid. 534c–d.
68. Ibid. 571c–d.
69. Ibid. 573a–d and 574e–575a. This translation is by David Grene, who pointed out to me its relevance to this discussion.
70. Ibid. 382e.
71. Plato *Timaeus* 29b–d.
72. Plato *Republic* 613–620.
73. The Loeb translator, Paul Shorey, here cites Urwiek, *The Message of Plato*, p. 213: "If Plato knew anything at all of Indian allegory, he must have known that the swan (Hamsa) is in Hinduism the invariable symbol of the immortal Spirit; and to say, as he does, that Orpheus chose the life of a swan, refusing to be born again of a woman, is just an allegorical way of saying that he passed on into the spiritual life." The swan is indeed a recurrent motif in Indian myths of rebirth; we will see in chapter five myths that resemble the tale of Er in so many ways that one is tempted to believe that Plato did, in fact, know something of Indian allegory or, at least, something of the Indian doctrine of rebirth.
74. Indian tradition, roughly contemporaneous with Plato's myth of Er, tells the tale of Naciketas, who journeyed to the house of Death in the underworld, ate no food, learned the secret of immortality, and returned to the land of the living. The story is prefigured in the *Jaiminīya Brāhmaṇa* (1. 42) and expanded in the *Kaṭha Upaniṣad*. See Wendy O'Flaherty, *Tales of Sex and Violence* (forthcoming).
75. Sigmund Freud, *An Outline of Psychoanalysis*, p. 47.
76. Sigmund Freud, *The Interpretation of Dreams* (henceforward, *Dreams*), p. 610.
77. Ibid.
78. Ibid., p. 526.
79. Ibid., pp. 373–74.
80. Ibid., p. 267.
81. William Dement, *Some Must Watch*, p. 77.
82. Charles Dickens, *A Christmas Carol*, Stave I.
83. Freud, *Dreams*, p. 106, citing Stricker.
84. *YV* 3. 3. 17.
85. Ramakrishna, *Tales and Parables*, p. 54.
86. Freud, *Dreams*, p. 106.
87. Ibid., p. 651; p. 497 of the German edition.
88. Ibid., p. 605.
89. Ibid., p. 414.
90. I am grateful to Sudhir Kakar for this observation on Freud.
91. Freud, *Dreams*, pp. 658–59.
92. Ibid., p. 55, n. 2, and p. 221.
93. William Dement, *Some Must Watch*, pp. 85–86.
94. Stephan Beyer, *The Cult of Tara*, p. 82.
95. William Dement, *Some Must Watch*, pp. 85, 87.
96. Freud, *Dreams*, p. 83, citing Strumpell.

97. Sir Ernst Gombrich, "Illusion and Art," p. 217.
98. William Dement, *Some Must Watch*, p. 49.
99. Freud, *Dreams*, p. 93.
100. Ibid., p. 614.
101. Ibid., p. 84.
102. The logical absurdity of the statement "I am asleep" has been analyzed at great length by Norman Malcolm in his book *Dreaming* and in several articles.
103. Wendy O'Flaherty, *Women*, p. 58.
104. David Shulman, letter of September 14, 1981.
105. C. G. Jung, "Synchronicity: An Acausal Connecting Principle."
106. C. G. Jung, "Psychological Commentary on *The Tibetan Book of the Dead*," pp. lxiii and li.
107. Rosemary Dinnage, review of Sudhir Kakar's *Shamans, Mystics, and Doctors*, *New York Review of Books* 30 (February 17, 1983): 16.
108. Michael Polanyi, *Personal Knowledge*, p. 313.
109. Shweder and LeVine, "Dream Concepts."
110. Lawrence Kohlberg, "Stage and Sequence."
111. Shweder and LeVine, "Dream Concepts," p. 211, paraphrasing Kohlberg.
112. Jean Piaget, *The Child's Conception of the World*, p. 32.
113. Shweder and LeVine, "Dream Concepts," p. 213.
114. Ibid., pp. 214–15.
115. This fourth category is also covered by certain people who have recently claimed to be able to photograph dream images on the retina of the dreamer (and to record the sounds in auditory hallucinations).
116. Shweder and LeVine, "Dream Concepts," pp. 217–18.
117. Ibid., p. 225.
118. Ibid., p. 226.
119. Ibid., p. 227.
120. See Thomas Gregor, *Mehinaku: The Drama of Daily Life in a Brazilian Indian Village* (Chicago, 1977).
121. Richard A. Shweder, "On Savages and Other Children," p. 362.
122. Mary Durack, *The Rock and the Sand* (London, 1969), p. 5. I am indebted to Peter Bartlett for telling me about this.
123. This phenomenon is discussed in Robin Horton's work on African thought and in *Rationality*, the collection of essays edited by Bryan Wilson.
124. Wendy O'Flaherty, "Inside and Outside," pp. 119–20.
125. See D. W. Winnicott, *Playing and Reality*. For the relevance of Winnicott to the problem of the objectivity of dreams in India I am indebted to June McDaniel, particularly to her study "The Transitional God: The Projection of the God-Image in Tantra and Christian Mysticism" (Chicago, 1982, ms.).
126. G. M. Carstairs, *The Twice-Born*, p. 122.
127. Here one may recall that Jung once suggested that even the *membrum virile* itself is, "psychologically speaking, . . . an emblem" (*Dreams*, p. 105). If a phallus is a phallic symbol, then castration can surely symbolize castration—"psychologically speaking," though perhaps not logically speaking.
128. Paul Feyerabend, *Against Method*, p. 229.

Chapter 2. Myths about Dreams

1. For other examples of the Swan Maiden, see Wendy O'Flaherty, *Women*, pp. 173–74, 180–82, 211–12.

2. For motifs, see Stith Thompson, *Motif-Index*; for tale types, see Stith Thompson and Jonas Balys, *Oral Tales of India*.

3. Sir Richard Carnac Temple, *Legends of the Punjab*, vol. 2, p. 169.

4. A. J. Carnoy, *Iranian Mythology*, p. 341, citing J. Darmesteter's commentary on book 3 of the *Zend Avesta* in his translation of it (p. lxxxi).

5. *Kathāsaritsāgara* 18. 3. 24–110.

6. *Bhāgavata P* 10. 62. 12–26; 10. 63. 1–53.

7. This physical proof of the magical flight to the woman in the other world is described in a Chinese text. See Appendix 1.

8. *Viṣṇu P* 5. 33. 49.

9. *Harivaṃśa* 107–8; cf. *Kathāsaritsāgara* 6. 5. 11–32; *Viṣṇu P* 5. 32. 11–50.

10. *Harivaṃśa*, verses inserted after 108. 10.

11. *Brahmavaivarta P*, *Kṛṣṇajanmakhaṇḍa* 114. 1–94; 115. 1–10.

12. "The Brushwood Boy," pp. 283–318 in *The Day's Work*, by Rudyard Kipling.

13. Kipling returned to the theme of the shared dream in another story published in the same collection, "The Bridge Builders" (pp. 7–42). Here an Englishman and his Hindu Lascar servant, Peroo, take opium together and dream that the Hindu gods come to them and talk with them. When they speak of this experience later on, the Englishman claims, "There was a fever upon me . . . . It seemed that the island was full of beasts and men talking, but I do not remember." The Hindu remembers, however, what it was that the gods told him: "When Brahm ceases to dream, the Gods die. . . . The dreams come and go, and the nature of the dreams changes, but still Brahm dreams." This is a combination of the theme of the shared dream and the closely related theme of the dream of being dreamt by someone else (we will encounter the latter in chapter five). The fact that the Englishman does not accept the testimony of Peroo as convincing evidence is, I think, sociological rather than epistemological. As Peroo remarks, "Has the Sahib forgotten; or do we black men only see the Gods?"

14. Leo Tolstoy made use of the motif of the shared dream in *Anna Karenina*. Vronsky dreams one night and awakes in horror, recalling his dream:

> "The peasant-beater—a dirty little man with a matted beard—was stooping down doing something, and all of a sudden he began muttering strange words in French. Yes, there was nothing else in the dream," he said to himself. "But why was it so awful?" [*Anna Karenina*, p. 380]

That day, Anna tells him that she knows she will die, because of a dream she had, long ago. It was a dream of a dreadful-looking little peasant with a tangled beard, stooping down, fumbling over a sack. He

> "kept muttering very quickly, in French. . . . And I was so terrified I tried to wake up . . . and I did wake up, but it was still part of the dream. And I began asking myself what it meant. And Korney said to me: 'In childbirth you'll die, in childbirth, ma'am. . . .' And then I woke up." [Pp. 386–87]

This is both a shared dream and a dream within a dream; Anna wakes up first from the inner dream, then from the outer. That it is shared is a function of the intense bond between Anna and Vronsky; "She knew every detail of his existence," Tolstoy remarks, right before she tells the dream (p. 382).

Yet it is also a symbol of a growing distance between them. For Vronsky, the peasant is compounded of "a mental image of Anna and of a peasant who had played an important part as a beater in the bear-hunt" (p. 380). For Anna, he is compounded of a guard who fell under the train the day she first met Vronsky (p. 79) and a peasant who stood beside her on the day she fell in love with Vronsky, also beside a train: "The stooping shadow of a man glided past her feet and she heard the tapping of a hammer upon iron" (p. 117). In Anna's dream, the peasant does not tap upon iron, but he talks about doing it; he mutters, in French, "It must be beaten, the iron" (p. 386). Up to this point, many of the coincidences in the dream might be explained by coincidences in the experience of the dreamers, in memories from real life. But Tolstoy goes on to say far more. For when Anna dies, throwing herself under a train, Tolstoy writes, *after* she has jumped, "A little peasant muttering something was working at the rails" (p. 802).

The striking coincidences between the two dreams reveal the closeness of the minds of the two lovers: both speak of the matted beard, the stooping, and the peculiar fact that a *peasant* was speaking French (from the Russian point of view, this is the one "fantastic" element in the dream, though physically it is perfectly possible). Vronsky is deeply troubled by this coincidence, but, instead of drawing closer to Anna, he pulls away; he had meant to tell her how he had fallen asleep (p. 382) and, presumably, how he had dreamt; but when he hears her dream, he does not speak of his. There is an implicit lie between them at this point; the dream, too, lies on the explicit, manifest level: Anna does not die in childbirth. Yet the rest of the manifest content tells the truth: Anna will indeed die at a place where a peasant is hammering upon iron. These details are in no way archetypal; they are not standard dream images but are either culturally inflected images (the Russian preoccupation with peasants) or very specific personal images (the train in Anna's life).

Finally, the fact that the dream is truly predictive, that the peasant who symbolizes Anna's death *is* going to be part of her death, indicates that what the lovers dreamt of was not merely each other but the truth—the future. Even if they had known that Anna would die under the wheels of a train, they could not have known that the little peasant with the matted beard would be tapping on the rails, "muttering something," at that moment. Something in the intensity of their emotion tore open to them a part of the fabric of the larger world. The power of the bond between their two minds went on to extend beyond them and to tie their minds into yet another mind, the mind that knew all that was going to happen to them.

15. *YV* 3. 27. 4, with Mitra's gloss.

16. Roger Caillois, *The Dream Adventure*, p. xiv; this passage is repeated in his "Logical and Philosophical Problems," p. 34.

17. *YV* 3. 121. 8–28.

18. *YV* 3. 121. 21.

19. *YV* 5. 49. 11–12.
20. R. L. Gregory, *Eye and Brain*, p. 131.
21. Surendranath Dasgupta, *History*, vol. 1, p. 477.
22. Jules Eisenbud, "The Dreams of Two Patients," p. 276.
23. Cf. Edmund R. Leach, "Genesis as Myth."
24. Géza Róheim, "Telepathy in a Dream," p. 154.
25. Ibid. (the italics are Róheim's).
26. Charles Rycroft, *The Innocence of Dreams*, p. 3.
27. Sudhir Kakar, *Shamans, Mystics, and Doctors*, p. 177.
28. I am indebted to Aziz Esmaili for this translation from an Ismaili poet.
29. Dr. Martin Stein told me of this interpretation of the dream of the lost tooth.
30. Géza Róheim, *The Gates of the Dream*, p. 428.
31. Gananath Obeyesekere, *Medusa's Hair*, pp. 14–21, 181–82; Dorothy Eggan, "The Personal Use of Myth in Dreams."
32. Nándar Fódor, "Telepathy in Analysis," p. 295, first citing J. N. Rosen.
33. The importance of making a distinction between a story about an experiment and an actual experiment—a theme to which we will return in chapter four—was pointed out to me by Arnaldo Momigliano in a conversation on October 21, 1980.

Chapter 3. Myths about Illusion

1. Heinrich Zimmer, *Myths and Symbols*, p. 31. Salman Rushdie makes use of this story in his novel *Midnight's Children*. One of the children of the title comes from Kashmir (the home of so many of our myths of magic and illusion); it was "a blue-eyed child of whose original sex I was never certain, since by immersing herself in water he (or she) could alter it as she (or he) pleased. Some of us called this child Narada, others Markandaya, depending on which old fairy story of sexual change we had heard. . . . Up in Kashmir, Narada-Markandaya was falling into the solipsistic dreams of the true narcissist, concerned only with the erotic pleasures of constant sexual alterations. . . . [When the children were all sterilized], because one . . . , whom we called Narada or Markandaya, had the ability of changing sex, he, or she, had to be operated on twice" (pp. 237, 305, 524). Rushdie incorporates into even these brief allusions the implications of a connection between Nārada's transformations and the rather different transformations of Mārkaṇḍeya (whom we will soon encounter), as well as an awareness of the problem of solipsism implicit in the dream double, a problem that we will also soon encounter.
2. *Devībhāgavata P*, 6. 28. 1–54; 6. 29. 1–66.
3. *Śrī Kāśī-mokṣa-nirṇaya*, p. 61. I am indebted to David White for bringing this text to me, and to Sudhir Kakar for translating the Hindi commentary.
4. *Devībhāgavata P* 6. 30. 36.
5. Vettam Mani, *Purāṇic Encyclopedia*, p. 528, citing *Bhāgavata Purāṇa* 7 (not in the printed text of the *Bhāgavata*); see also Teun Goudriaan, *Māyā Divine and Human*, pp. 44–46, 433, n. 73), and Ramakrishna, *Tales and Parables*, pp. 49–51.
6. *Padma P*, *Pātāla Khaṇḍa* 75. 23–51.

7. See Wendy O'Flaherty, *Women*, pp. 87–90, 303–34.
8. *YV* 6. 1. 85–106.
9. For other examples, see Wendy O'Flaherty, *Women*, pp. 299–308.
10. Heinrich Zimmer, *Myths and Symbols*, p. 33, citing Sri Ramakrishna, *The Sayings of Sri Ramakrishna*, bk. 4, chap. 22.
11. *Devībhāgavata P* 6. 30. 1–29.
12. See Wendy O'Flaherty, *Women*, pp. 122–29, on Sītā and the Swan Maiden.
13. *Devībhāgavata P* 6. 30. 38–46.
14. *Śrī-Kāśī-mokṣa-nirṇaya*, p. 64, citing the *Skanda Purāṇa*.
15. Ibid.; this commentary was translated for me by Sudhir Kakar.
16. The still-powerful appeal of this concept has been demonstrated by the great popularity of Raymond Moody's writings about out-of-the-body experiences.
17. *Bardo-Thödol* (*Tibetan Book of the Dead*), trans. Francesca Fremantle and Chögyam Trungpa, pp. 39–40, 74, 76.
18. Ibid., p. 79.
19. *M* 12. 310–20.
20. *YV* 4. 5–16.
21. *R* 6. 103–6. There are two significantly different versions of this episode in the Vālmīki *Rāmāyaṇa*. In the first, Sītā survives the ordeal, through divine intervention. In the second (*R* 7. 42), she disappears forever into the earth, her mother. For further remarks about the relationship between Rāma and Sītā, see Wendy O'Flaherty, *Women*, p. 80.
22. *Kūrma P* 2. 33. 113–41; *Devībhāgavata P* 9. 16. 28–53; *Mahābhāgavata P* 9–11; *Śiva P* 2. 24 ff.: W. D. P. Hill, *The Holy Lake*, D. 23–24, 108–9, and Charlotte Vaudeville, *Etudes*, pp. 191, 259, give variants of this episode.
23. *R* 3. 16–17.
24. David Shulman, "Sītā and Śatakaṇṭharāvaṇa," pp. 12–16.
25. David Shulman, *Tamil Temple Myths*, pp. 324–26, citing *Tiruvarañcaram* 5–7.
26. *Tamil Temple Myths*, p. 326.
27. This tale, a folk variant, appears in both C. R. Sarma, *The Rāmāyaṇa in Telugu and Tamil*, pp. 54–55, and David Shulman, "Sītā and Śatakaṇṭharāvaṇa," p. 22.
28. *R* 4. 6, two verses inserted after 19.
29. *Śiva P* 3. 20. 34.
30. The story is also told in Kṛttivāsa's Bengali version of the *Rāmāyaṇa*, which has now been transformed into the Indian equivalent of a Classic Comic, number 207 of the *Amar Chitra Katha* ("Our Wonderful Story") comic series. In this version, Mahī Rāvaṇa is Rāvaṇa's son, not his brother; Hanuman does not meet his own son, but he is constantly warned not to let even his father (the wind) enter the fort. Mahī Rāvaṇa puts everyone in the fort to sleep, including Rāma and Lakṣmaṇa, who later awaken in the underworld and remain awake. Thus the family relationships that are so dreamlike in the Tamil text are greatly muted and transformed. And though the motif of the dream enchantment is extended to the rest of Rāma's camp, the fact that Rāma and Lakṣmaṇa awaken blurs the point of Rāma's dream of Hanuman's dream adventure.

31. I am indebted to David Shulman for this summary of the Mayilirāvaṇaṉ story and to George Hart for helping me to read portions of the text.

32. *R* 5. 1.

33. *R* 5. 7.

34. *Catakaṇṭarāvaṇaṉ Katai*, cited and analyzed by David Shulman in his "Sītā and Śatakaṇṭharāvaṇa."

35. Robert P. Goldman, in "Rāma Sahalakṣmaṇaḥ," discusses Lakṣmaṇa as Rāma's alter ego.

36. Stephan Beyer, *The Cult of Tara*, p. 81.

37. See Wendy O'Flaherty, *Women*, pp. 121, 236–37, for this split woman.

38. *Devībhāgavata P* 6. 29. 52.

39. In Homer's version of the story, it is Helen herself who is carried off by Paris to Troy and brought back home again by Menelaus. Homer constructs doubles of other people (Apollo makes an image of Aeneas for the Greeks and Trojans to fight over, while Aeneas himself is carried off through the air [*Iliad* 5. 443–53]) but not of Helen. Herodotus reported the Egyptian version of the story: Paris stole Helen away but landed in Egypt, not in Troy; Proteus, king of Egypt, took Helen from Paris and kept her safe for Menelaus, who (not knowing that Helen was in Egypt) went to Troy, took the city, discovered that Helen was in Egypt, went there, and took her home (Herodotus 2. 112–20). Euripides combined these two versions and (perhaps inspired by the figure of Proteus in the Herodotean story) added the theme of the double of Helen (a theme which had already been briefly alluded to by Hesiod and Stesichorus). This is how Helen tells her tale:

> Hera . . . made void the love that might have been for Paris and me
> and gave him, not me, but in my likeness fashioning
> a breathing image out of the sky's air, bestowed
> this on King Priam's son, who thinks he holds me now
> but holds a vanity which is not I.
> . . . .
> I myself was caught up by Hermes, sheathed away
> in films of air, for Zeus had not forgotten me,
> and set me down by him where you see me, in the house
> of Proteus, chosen because, most temperate of men,
> he could guard my honor safe for Menelaus.
> . . . .
> I yet shall make my home
> in the famous plain of Sparta with my lord, and he
> shall know I never went to Ilium, had no thought
> of bed with any man.
> . . . .
> Thus, though I wear the name of guilt in Greece, yet here
> I keep my body uncontaminated by disgrace.
> [Euripides *Helen* 31–67, trans. Lattimore]

As Lattimore remarks of Euripides' reworking of the myth, "Although he used the Herodotean variant, he contrived, through the old idol-story, to remove that stain of dishonor which the Egyptian version had reattached to Helen. And he exploited fully the factor common to both legends: the tragic futility of that utterly unnecessary Trojan War" (Lattimore and Grene, eds., *Complete Greek Tragedies*, vol. 3, p. 484). Helen symbolized to the Greeks the same qualities of sexuality and danger that Rati symbolized to the Indians; both of them are exonerated of the "stain of dishonor" by the construction of stand-ins at the critical moment. Yet the second concern of Euripides—to emphasize the futility of the war—appears in India in a rather different key. The double in these Indian myths points out the emptiness and insubstantiality not (as in the tale of Helen) of one particular incident in an otherwise full and meaningful life—a war whose tragedy inheres in the very fact that it deprives so many of the good life they would otherwise have lived for many years—but of the entire structure of life in general, the existential basis of the normal life that one hopes to live.

40. See Wendy O'Flaherty, *Women*, pp. 190–96, 273–75, on the rape of the Brahmin woman.

41. *Viṣṇu P* 5. 27. 1–31; cf. *Bhāgavata P* 10. 55. 1–12.

42. *Harivaṃśa* 99. 1–49; *Brahmavaivarta P*, *Kṛṣṇajanmakhaṇḍa* 112. 7–32.

43. *Harivaṃśa*, passage inserted after 99. 7.

44. *Brahmavaivarta P*, *Kṛṣṇajanmakhaṇḍa* 112. 7–32.

45. *Skanda P* 1. 1. 21. 106–25.

46. *Brahmavaivarta P*, *Kṛṣṇajanmakhaṇḍa* 115. 76–80. Cf. *Tiruccĕṅkoṭṭumāṉmiyam* 200–204, cited by David Shulman, *Tamil Temple Myths*, pp. 294–95.

47. *YV* 3. 16–59, esp. 3. 44–59.

48. *R* 1. 56–59.

49. *Skanda P* 6. 7. 16.

50. *Skanda P* 6. 7. 1–16.

51. *Śrībhāṣya* of Rāmānuja 1. 1. 1.

52. David Shulman, "On Kings and Clowns," p. 27.

53. *Devībhāgavata P* 7. 10. 1–58; 7. 11. 1–53; 7. 12. 1–64; 7. 13. 1–62; 7. 14. 1–23. Cf. *Harivaṃśa* 9–10 and *Viṣṇu P* 4. 3. 14.

54. *Devībhāgavata P* 7. 10. 53.

55. Sir Monier Monier-Williams, *Sanskrit-English Dictionary*, s.v. Viśvāmitra.

56. I am indebted to Philip Lutgendorf for telling me this story and supplying me with his translation, which I have somewhat condensed. The tale is "Camatkārī Haṇḍā (The Amazing Pot)," from Sāvtrīdevī Varmā's *Uttara Pradeśa kī loka kathāem* (Delhi: Rajpal & Sons, 1978), p. 23.

57. *Bhāgavata P* 10. 8. 21–45. Cf. Wendy O'Flaherty, *Hindu Myths*, pp. 218–21, and O'Flaherty, "Inside and Outside the Mouth of God," passim.

58. *Bhagavad Gītā* 11. 7–30, 41–44.

59. *Bhagavad Gītā* 11. 51: *sacetāḥ prakṛtiṃ gataḥ.*

60. *Matsya P* 167–68.

61. Géza Róheim, *The Gates of the Dream*, p. 428.

62. I am indebted to David Haberman for these insights into Bengali devotionalism.

63. Stephan Beyer, *The Cult of Tara*, p. 91, citing Nāgārjuna 7. 34.

64. Stephan Beyer, *The Cult of Tara*, p. 92.

65. Surendranath Dasgupta, *A History of Indian Philosophy*, vol. 1, p. 425.

66. Ibid., pp. 424, 437. See also Daniel H. H. Ingalls, "Śankara on the Question: Whose is *Avidyā*?"

67. David Shulman, "On Kings and Clowns," p. 86.

68. A dramatic example of this phenomenon is recorded in the film *Kataragama: A God for All Seasons*, made under the supervision of Gananath Obeyesekere.

69. Surendranath Dasgupta, *A History of Indian Philosophy*, vol. 1, p. 380.

70. V. Narayana Rao, "*Bhakti* in Opposition to *Karma*," p. 17.

71. It was Frits Staal who pointed this out to me.

72. For these formulations, and for general enlightenment on the subject of illusion, I am grateful to David Shulman.

73. Jan Gonda, *Four Studies in the Language of the Veda*, p. 168.

74. Thomas Burrow, "Sanskrit *mā*."

75. *RV* 1. 154.

76. Jan Gonda, *Four Studies*, p. 126.

77. *RV* 7. 104. 24; 10. 54. 2.

78. Thomas Burrow, "Sanskrit *mā*," pp. 319, 312.

79. A. A. Macdonell, *Vedic Mythology*, p. 24.

80. *Concise Oxford English Dictionary*, s.v. solipsism.

81. Much of this formulation is based on a statement made by David Shulman in a letter to me, September, 1981.

82. David Shulman, "Tĕnāli Rāma," pp. 30–31.

83. B. L. Atreya, *The Yogavāsiṣṭha and Its Philosophy*, pp. 104–5.

84. V. Narayana Rao, "Bhakti in Opposition to Karma," pp. 8–9. Cf. Salman Rushdie's comment, "Hell is other peoples' fantasies" (*Midnight Children*, p. 541).

85. Isaac Bashevis Singer, *When Shlemiel Went to Warsaw*, pp. 99–116. I am indebted to my son, Michael Lester O'Flaherty, for bringing the tales of Chelm to me.

86. Peter de Vries, *Sauce for the Goose*, p. 231.

87. Roland Penrose, "In Praise of Illusion," p. 45.

88. Sir Karl Popper, *Objective Knowledge*, p. 37.

89. *Brahmavaivarta P* 1. 8.

90. Karl Potter, *Presuppositions*, p. 223.

91. Śankara's commentary on the *Vedānta Sūtras* 2. 2. 29 and 3. 2. 3.

92. Ibid., on 2. 1. 14.

93. The suggestion of several ways to express the range of Indian realities came from David Shulman in a letter of January 5, 1982.

Chapter 4. Epistemology in Narrative

1. Many of the insights in this introduction arose out of conversations with David Grene.

2. This was a personal communication from Sudhir Kakar, in a letter of October 21, 1982.

3. Plato, *Timaeus* 29c–d and *Phaedo* 114d.

4. *Bṛhadāraṇyaka U* 2. 4. 12.

5. The clarifications in this discussion of narratives and audiences came out of a panel discussion organized by Norman Cutler at the meeting of the Association of Asian Studies in Chicago on April 4, 1982. This first point was made on that occasion by A. K. Ramanujan.

6. This formulation was made by V. Narayana Rao at the April 4, 1982, panel.
7. It was A. K. Ramanujan who said this, on another occasion.
8. *R* 6. 84–86.
9. *Adhyātmarāmāyaṇa* 2. 4. 77–78.
10. This point was made by V. Narayana Rao on April 4, 1982.
11. This phrase was coined by Gail Hinich, in conversation.
12. For discussions of the date and place of the text, see the works of B. L. Atreya, Sivaprasad Bhattacharya, Prahlad C. Divanji, T. G. Mainkar, and V. Raghavan, cited in the bibliography.
13. Cf. C. R. Sarma, *The Rāmāyaṇa in Telugu and Tamil*. A variant of Knowles's Kashmir version of the story of Gādhi was told to me in Mysore in August, 1980, by Mrs. Lalita Handoo, who had heard it from her great-aunt in Kashmir.
14. India does have a kind of Classic Comics (the Amar Chitra Katha series). As far as I know, none of the *Yogavāsiṣṭha* tales has appeared in this form, though the tales of Mahī Rāvaṇa, Aniruddha, and Pradyumna have. However, a recent issue of the popular Hindi quarterly devoted to mythology, *Kalyāṇa* (vol. 35, no. 1, January, 1961) was devoted entirely to a retelling of the *Yogavāsiṣṭha*. Even this abbreviated version occupied 700 pages of small print; it tells the tales of Padma and Līlā, and Śikhidhvaja and Cūḍālā, at great length and with many illustrations (both black and white and in color), but it does not so much as mention Lavaṇa, Gādhi, the monk's dream, or the girl inside the stone.
15. For a list of stories from the *Yogavāsiṣṭha* that I have used in this book, see Appendix 3.
16. The passages that I have translated and summarized come from book 3 of the *Yogavāsiṣṭha*, sections 104. 1–49; 105. 1–28; 106. 1–72; 107. 1–48; 108. 1–30; 109. 1–31; 120. 1–30; and 121. 1–7.
17. *YV*, book 5, secs. 44. 1–40; 45. 1–48; 46. 1–47; 47. 1–66; 48. 1–70; 49. 1–43.
18. Helmuth von Glasenapp, *Zwei philosophische Rāmāyaṇas*, p. 477.
19. *YV* 3. 121. 14.
20. *YV*, book 5, secs. 44. 23–25; 45. 16–18, 21–23; 47. 59; 46. 22; 47. 50.
21. Sir Ernst Gombrich, *Art and Illusion*, pp. 5–6.
22. This paragraph is based on a suggestion from James Boon.
23. *Bṛhadāraṇyaka U* 2. 1. 18.
24. *YV* 1. 10–11.
25. *YV* 2. 1. 11.
26. *Bhagavad Gītā* 2. 37; 3. 8; 3. 19; 3. 35; and 18. 47 correspond closely to the lines spoken by Viṣṇu to Gādhi at *Yogavāsiṣṭha* 5. 48. 69 and 5. 49. 18. So, too, the dialogue between Arjuna and Kṛṣṇa at *Yogavāsiṣṭha* 6. 1. 52–58 is strongly reminiscent of the *Gītā* as a whole.
27. *YV* 3. 115. 25–36; 3. 116. 1–7.
28. Allen Thrasher, "Magical Journeys."
29. *Aitareya Brāhmaṇa* 7. 13–18.
30. *Mārkaṇḍeya P* 7. 1–69; 8. 1–270.
31. Gombrich, in Richard F. Gombrich and Margaret Cone, *The Perfect Generosity*, pp. xxv–xxvi.

32. *Vessantara Jātaka*, number 547.

33. Brian K. Smith has discussed this pattern in "The Domestication of the Vedic Sacrifice" (Ph.D. dissertation, University of Chicago, 1984).

34. *Kathāsaritsāgara* 16. 3 (133).

35. *YV* 2. 10. 13–38.

36. *Anguttara Nikāya* 1. 145; cf. *Majjhima Nikāya* 1. 163. I am grateful to Frank Reynolds for hunting down this series of texts for me and for helping me to sort them all out.

37. André Bareau, *Bouddha*, pp. 81–83, citing a Mahicasaka text.

38. W. Woodville Rockhill, *The Life of the Buddha*, p. 22.

39. Introduction to the *Jātaka*, 1. 58.

40. *Buddhacarita* 3. 26–29; 5. 16–20.

41. *Lalitavistara*, chapter 14, opening prose.

42. *Anguttara Nikāya* 3. 240.

43. *Lalitavistara*, chapter 14. 42–47.

44. Ibid. 14. 22–39.

45. David Shulman, "On Kings and Clowns," p. 44.

46. I am grateful to David Haberman for pointing out the element of freedom that results from the journey and is imported back into the original world.

47. Some scholars believe that Buddhism challenged certain inequities of the ancient Hindu social system; others believe that it dismissed such problems as irrelevant to the central concerns of a religion of salvation. I do not wish to enter into that argument at this time; my own inclination is toward the second view, that Buddhism largely ignored social problems in favor of soteriological problems.

48. I owe the ideas in this paragraph to Bruce Lincoln, who suggested them to me in a letter on September 29, 1981.

49. These formulations were made by Mary Douglas, in response to an early draft of this chapter, in a letter of November 14, 1982.

50. *YV* 6. 77–110.

51. *YV*, Mitra translation, vol. 2, p. 97 n.

52. Teun Goudriaan, Māyā, p. 101.

53. Ibid., p. 103, citing the *Mañjuśrīmūlakalpa*.

54. Ibid.

55. Charlotte Vaudeville, trans., *Kabir*, 31. 8a (p. 301).

56. *YV* 3. 77–82.

57. For other instances, see Wendy O'Flaherty, *The Origins of Evil*, pp. 75–78, 164–65.

58. *YV* 6. 1. 70–73.

59. *Kathāsaritsāgara* 75–99.

60. See Wendy O'Flaherty, *The Origins of Evil*, pp. 97–104.

61. Demons, who are often magicians, have the skepticism of magicians. As Salman Rushdie remarks, "The ghetto of magicians disbelieved, with the absolute certainty of illusionists-by-trade, in the possibility of magic. . . . The magicians were people whose hold on reality was absolute; they gripped it so powerfully that they could bend it every which way in the service of their arts, but they never forgot what it was" (*Midnight's Children*, pp. 462, 275–76).

62. *YV* 3. 106. 46, 50.
63. *YV* 3. 107. 31, 33.
64. *YV* 5. 46. 27.
65. *YV* 2. 3. 12.
66. *YV* 3. 106, 56, 71; 3. 107. 25, 40; 3. 109. 9.
67. *YV* 5. 47. 42.
68. *YV* 3. 106. 4, 6–7, 9–10, 36, 65; 3. 108. 3; 3. 109. 1; 3. 108. 29.
69. *YV* 5. 44. 38; 5. 46. 40–42; 5. 48. 2–4.
70. *YV* 3. 105. 8; 3. 106. 20, 27–28.
71. *M* 1. 165. 1–5; 13. 4. 46; 5. 117. 4–6; 5. 104–21; *R* 1. 34. 1–5; *Harivaṃśa* 23. 84–88.
72. *M* 12. 139. 13–92. See also Wendy O'Flaherty, *The Origins of Evil*, p. 31.
73. See Wendy O'Flaherty, *The Origins of Evil*, pp. 290–93.
74. See Wendy O'Flaherty, *Women*, pp. 40–42.
75. This "upside-down language" is characteristic of Kabir, in particular. See the article by Linda Hess, "The Cow Is Sucking at the Calf's Teat."
76. Cf. the story of Bhṛgu in the *Jaiminīya Brāhmaṇa* (1. 42–44), translated and analyzed in Wendy O'Flaherty, *Tales of Sex and Violence* (forthcoming).
77. Kabir, *śabda* 62, cited by Linda Hess, "The Cow Is Sucking," p. 314.
78. James Hinton Knowles, *Folktales of Kashmir*, pp. 16–19.
79. R. K. Narayan, *Gods, Demons, and Others*, p. 23.
80. Maurice Bloomfield, "On the Art of Entering Another's Body."
81. *Śrī-kāśī-mokṣa-nirṇaya*, pp. 60–67, text and Hindi commentary, courtesy of David White and Sudhir Kakar.
82. The first half of the story of King Lavaṇa is an example of a theme that is found outside India, too, but within a literary corpus closely related to India through the Buddhist connection. There is a Chinese text, dating from some time before the third century A.D. and perhaps as early as the third century B.C., that tells this tale. See Appendix 2.
83. I am grateful to V. Narayana Rao for giving me a detailed translation of the Telugu tale, which I have somewhat abridged and paraphrased.
84. *Yavana* is the Sanskrit transcription of "Ionian." Originally it designated any Greek; later it came to mean any foreigner but, more particularly, a foreign soldier or ruler who entered India as a conqueror. The British were called Yavanas by Sanskrit-speaking Brahmins.
85. *YV* 2. 1. 11.
86. *YV* 3. 116. 1–4.
87. Karl Potter, *Presuppositions*, pp. 57–92.
88. Ibid., p. 57.
89. Ibid., p. 58.
90. Ibid., pp. 59, 186–235. Dreams are a form of authority in the folk tradition (and in many other traditions) but not in the classical Indian philosophical tradition. In Satyajit Ray's film *Devi* (1960) the hero's father dreams that the hero's wife is an incarnation of Devi, the Goddess. The hero confronts him and asks, "What proof [*pramāṇa*] do you have?" At first, the old man counters by saying, "I have read all the scriptures; do you doubt my word?" But when he goes on to say, "I had a dream [*svapna*] that she was Devi," the hero becomes angry

and says, "Do you mean that all of this uproar is just because of a dream? Are you out of your mind?" At that moment, word comes that the girl had revived a child thought to be dying. "There," says the old man triumphantly, "there is my proof." Eventually, however, the girl fails to save the life of a child she loves, and she goes mad—awakened from the illusion of her divinity by the traditional catalyst, the death of a child. (Ironically, since the Goddess often kills children, the death of the boy could have been proof that the girl *was* an incarnation, that she was not mad or dreaming.)

91. This point is made by Prahlad C. Divanji in his "*Yogavāsiṣṭha* on the Means of Proof," pp. 105–6.

92. *YV* 2. 19. 16, 133.

93. Divanji, "*Yogavāsiṣṭha* on the Means of Proof," p. 111.

94. Ibid., p. 112.

95. Hilaire Belloc pointed this out long ago in his paean to the microbe, which concludes (after a long, fantastic description of the creature):

> his eyebrows, of a tender green,
> All this has never yet been seen.
> But scientists, who ought to know,
> Assure us that this must be so.
> Oh! Let us never, never doubt
> What nobody is sure about!
> (Belloc, *More Beasts for Worse Children*, pp. 95–96).

96. *YV* 4. 1. 4.

97. Karl Potter, *Presuppositions*, pp. 223–24.

98. Rāmānuja, *Śrībhāṣya* 1. 1. 1 (pp. 18 and 23).

99. Karl Potter, *Presuppositions*, p. 94.

100. Ibid., p. 224.

101. *YV* 5. 47. 35.

102. *YV* 5. 47. 37–38.

103. Leon Festinger, *A Theory of Cognitive Dissonance*, passim.

104. I am grateful to Bimal Matilal for telling me about Jayaśrī.

105. *Bhāgavata P* 10. 39. 40–43; 10. 41. 1–3.

106. This development was discussed at some length by William K. Mahony in his doctoral dissertation, "Flying Priests, Yogins and Shamans in Early Hinduism and Buddhism" (University of Chicago, 1982).

107. *YV* 3. 18. 6, 15, 16–17; 3. 20. 7.

108. *YV* 3. 57. 38–40.

109. *YV* 6. 1. 69. 4.

110. *YV* 6. 1. 63. 6.

111. This suggestion was made by David Shulman.

112. *YV* 3. 121. 8–28.

113. *YV* 3. 120. 1–3.

114. *YV* 5. 48. 31–70; 5. 49. 1–43.

115. Freud uses a variant of this anecdote (the man who borrowed a leaky pot) to characterize multiple defenses and overdetermination in dream work (*Dreams*, p. 153).

116. Surendranath Dasgupta, *History*, vol. 1, pp. 454–55, 487.

117. I am grateful to James Boon for his response to an early draft (January 25, 1983), in which he made me aware of the need to point out the complexity of the Western literature on dreams.

118. As an example of the twists that the Western tradition puts on the theme of the dream adventure, let us consider a Jewish story that strikes a sobering, if not satirical, note, as the tale of Shlemiel in Chelm does for the tales of double universes. This is a sixteenth-century story from the Hebrew *Eretz ha-Hayim*:

> There was once a wicked king who pressed the Jews of his kingdom with harsh decrees. Rabbi Adam saw their plight and cast a deep slumber on the king and caused him to dream. In the dream the king awoke and found himself in a deep pit. He suffered various tortures there for six months, during which his nails were clipped regularly and the clippings kept in a snuffbox. At last, Rabbi Adam appeared and set him free, after he had made the king sign a decree renouncing his harsh measures against the Jews. He told the king to lie down on the bed, and the king awoke in his palace chamber.
>
> The king could not understand why his servants did not seem surprised to see him, when he had been held captive for half a year. Then one of the servants said, "Surely the king must have had a dream, for the king's bodyguards stood guard at his door all night." The king saw the snuffbox, opened it, and found that it was half full of nail clippings; this confirmed the events he had experienced. Then the Rabbi came to him and explained that both he and the servants were correct. The king had been sentenced to death, the Rabbi said, and during the night his soul had departed from his body and was handed over to the evil spirits to be punished; and then it returned to him at dawn. "The snuffbox half full of nail clippings is a sign of the truth of this experience," Rabbi Adam continued. "And now, the king surely remembers this decree, which he signed." He took it out, with the king's signature and seal affixed to it, and when the king saw it, he understood the meaning of his dream, and had it announced that the decrees against the Jews had been abolished.

The king's soul travels in a time span outside the time span of the body, as in the tale of Gādhi. But here the physical proof of the reality of the dream, the equivalent of Bellerophon's bridle, takes two forms: the first, the nail clippings, is, like Rip Van Winkle's beard, a natural measure of time (and one that is, incidentally, highly polluting to Hindus and could never be part of an Indian myth). The second, the new point of the whole story, is the decree that the king sealed, apparently during his dream (as Aśoka sealed Tiṣyarakṣitā's decree with his teeth). If the king accepts the nails as proof—and he clearly wants desperately to do so—then he must also accept the reality of the decree. Yet, all the same, the story does assume that material things can be salvaged from dreams.

This story is told by Howard Schwartz in *Elijah's Violin*, pp. 197–202, drawing on collections by Hayim Libersohn (Przemyśl, Poland, 1926) and Shlomo Meinsterl (from the *Shivhei ha-Ari*, published in Jerusalem in 1905). I am grateful to Mircea Eliade not only for the citation but for the actual gift of the book.

119. Roger Caillois, "Logical and Philosophical Problems," p. 46.

120. Sir Karl Popper, *Objective Knowledge*, p. 41.

121. Michael Polanyi, *Personal Knowledge*, pp. 313, 316.

122. Leon Festinger et al., *When Prophecy Fails*, p. 4.
123. Ibid., p. 28.
124. Michael Polanyi, *Personal Knowledge*, p. 313.
125. Sir Karl Popper, *Objective Knowledge*, p. 5, citing Russell, on Hume, in *A History of Western Philosophy*.
126. Heisenberg once characterized the difference between science and art by suggesting that, if he had never lived, someone else would have discovered the principle of indeterminacy, but that, if Beethoven had never lived, no one else would have written his symphonies. By this criterion, it seems to me, myths are more scientific than artistic in their outlines but more artistic than scientific in their details.
127. Thomas Kuhn, *The Structure of Scientific Revolutions*, p. 17.
128. Ibid., p. 168.
129. Paul Feyerabend, *Against Method*, p. 126 n.
130. Sir Karl Popper, *Objective Knowledge*, p. 360.
131. R. L. Gregory, "The Confounded Eye," p. 61.
132. Roger Caillois, *The Dream Adventure*, p. xiii.
133. J. S. Bruner and Leo Postman, "On the Perception of Incongruity," p. 22.
134. Sir Ernst Gombrich, *Art, Perception, and Reality*, p. 17.
135. Thomas Kuhn, *The Structure of Scientific Revolutions*, p. 151.
136. Ibid., pp. 89–90, 122.
137. See Wendy O'Flaherty, "Inside and Outside," pp. 102–4.
138. Arthur Koestler, *The Sleepwalkers*, p. 20. Johannis Kepler, who first published one of his major scientific discoveries in the form of a fictional account that he called "The Dream," spoke of his early discoveries as "a dream of the truth . . . inspired by a friendly God" (Koestler, *The Sleepwalkers*, p. 264). Nor was this a simple dream; it was a *rêve à deux* dreamt by Kepler and Plutarch. Kepler mused: "I wonder greatly how it happened that our dreams, or rather our fictions, were in such close agreement" (Johannis Kepler, *Somnium*, pp. 87–88). Arthur Koestler, in commenting on this phenomenon, remarks, "If the 'harmony of the world' was a fantastic dream, its symbols had been shared by a whole dreaming culture. If it was an *idée fixe*, it was derived from a collective obsession" (Koestler, *The Sleepwalkers*, p. 396).
139. Roger Caillois, *The Dream Adventure*, p. xiii.
140. Sigmund Freud, *The Interpretation of Dreams*, pp. 185–86.
141. Ibid., p. 191.
142. The problem of pinning down the receding frame was delightfully demonstrated to me when I lectured on this topic in New York, at the American Museum of Natural History. A young man in the audience asked two questions, after remarking that he had had the haunting sensation of having heard me give that lecture before, in that very auditorium: (*a*) Did my lecture have anything to do with *déjà vu*? and (*b*) Had he ever asked me that question before?
143. Sir Karl Popper, *Objective Knowledge*, pp. 38–41, 64.
144. Ibid., pp. 42, 124.
145. Idem, "Normal Science and Its Dangers," p. 56.
146. Ibid.
147. Idem, *Objective Knowledge*, p. 148.

148. Thomas Kuhn, *The Structure*, pp. 78, 94.
149. Paul Feyerabend, *Against Method*, p. 32.
150. Sir Ernst Gombrich, *Art and Illusion*, p. 6.
151. Douglas Hofstadter, *Gödel, Escher, Bach*, p. 478.
152. William Dement, *Some Must Watch*, p. 52.
153. *Bṛhadāraṇyaka U* 3. 9. 1.
154. Ibid., 3. 6.
155. A good example of this technique of pulling up short in the quest for the infinite is the anecdote, variously attributed, of the professor lecturing on Indian cosmology. One variant of this story has found its way into the local lore of Swift Hall, home of the University of Chicago Divinity School, whose dean, Franklin I. Gamwell, tells it like this:

> It seems a small boy once asked his father what holds up the world, and the father, pleased with his spontaneous mythology, replied that the world rests upon the back of a very large turtle. The answer sufficed for a day or two, but presently the son returned to ask what holds up the turtle. The turtle, said the father, rests upon the back of a very large tiger. When, with time, the boy wanted to know what holds up the tiger, the father, now committed to this line of thought and beginning to panic, said that the tiger rests upon the back of a very large elephant. Inevitably, the question arose: What holds up the elephant? The father, thoroughly exasperated and not a little annoyed, said: "Son, it's elephants all the way down!" ["Religious Civility in Hyde Park," a speech presented to the Council of Hyde Park Churches and Synagogues, June 17, 1982, pp. 1–2]

Clifford Geertz tells the story (on pp. 28–29 of *The Interpretation of Cultures*), as a conversation between an English ethnographer and an Indian, and it ends, "Ah, Sahib, after that it is turtles all the way down."
156. James Joyce, *A Portrait of the Artist as a Young Man* (New York, 1964), pp. 131–32.
157. Cited by R. F. Gombrich, "Ancient Indian Cosmology," p. 110.
158. Diana Eck made these points in a paper presented at a panel at the annual meeting of the American Academy of Religion in New York on December 21, 1983.
159. This was pointed out by Alex Wayman at the December 21, 1983, panel.
160. Don Handelman made this formulation in response to El Guindi and Read's *Mathematics in Structural Theory*, in *Current Anthropology* 20 (1979): 777.

Chapter 5. Ontology in Narrative

1. *YV* 6. 1. 62. 1–31; 6. 1. 63. 1–75; 6. 1. 64. 1–8.
2. Stith Thompson, *Index*, vol. 2, p. 308. The concept of the dream that begins in the head of one person and then gets into the heads of a number of other people appears as a leitmotif in Salman Rushdie's *Midnight's Children*. A mother eavesdrops on the dreams of her daughter (p. 60), but then the dreams become far more public. India itself is "a mythical land, a country which would never exist except by the efforts of a phenomenal collective will—except in a dream we all agreed to dream" (pp. 129–30). The hero discovers that he has the uncanny ability to tune in, like a radio, on the dreams of all the children born on the day

of his birth; but, more than that, he transmits his own image and then his voice to each of them, and eventually they are all able to communicate with one another through him (pp. 197, 262). He functions like Rudra in our myth; and, indeed, his own violent alter ego is Shiva, another name for Rudra. Moreover, he is a radio in the classical sense, a "Sky-Voice" (Akashvani), the Sanskrit word used for "radio" in India; in ancient texts the Sky-Voice was the voice of the god, the *deus ex machina*, the impersonal divine force that spoke up at crucial moments in the myth. When the children begin to communicate in their dreams, however, "Brahmins began to feel uneasy at permitting even their thoughts to touch the thoughts of untouchables" (p. 306), and they discover that their magic powers are ranked hierarchically: one can fly, and another says, "Today, I went to visit tomorrow" (p. 272). The themes and structures of the ancient myth are preserved in this modern exploration of the theme. A very different treatment of it may be seen in James Joyce's *Ulysses*, where one man's dream keeps on getting into other peoples' heads during the long night of "Nighttown."

3. *YV* 5. 20. 9–30.
4. *Karpūramañjarī* of Rājaśekhara.
5. *YV* 6. 1. 64. 6–13; 6. 1. 65. 6–8.
6. *YV* 6. 1. 69. 1–6.
7. *YV* 6. 1. 66. 29–34.
8. *YV* 6. 1. 64. 21.
9. *YV* 6. 1. 69. 4.
10. *YV* 6. 1. 63. 4.
11. *YV* 6. 1. 63. 21.
12. The Sanskrit term *haṃsa* denotes both a goose and a swan and is probably more accurately translated as "goose." I have used the term "goose" to distinguish the penultimate bird in the story (the *haṃsa*) from the ultimate bird (the *rājahaṃsa*, royal goose or swan). "Swan" also captures some of the spiritual overtones that this bird has in English and that the goose, by explicit contrast, lacks.
13. Kālidāsa's *Kumārasambhava* 1. 30.
14. *Bhāgavata P* 4. 28. 51–64.
15. *YV* 6. 1. 63. 1–3.
16. *YV* 6. 1. 62. 7.
17. *YV* 6. 1. 63. 19; 6. 1. 62. 20–21.
18. *YV* 6. 1. 62. 22–26.
19. *YV* 6. 1. 66. 22–24.
20. *YV*, commentary introducing verse 6. 1. 62. 1.
21. Surendranath Dasgupta, *History of Indian Philosophy*, vol. 1, p. 30.
22. Sir Monier Monier-Williams, *Sanskrit-English Dictionary*, p. 947.
23. *YV* 6. 1. 62. 32.
24. *YV* 6. 1. 63. 17.
25. Sean Dwan told me about this wonderful word.
26. For a discussion of the shock of recognition, see Wendy O'Flaherty, "Inside and Outside," pp. 117–19.
27. Kālidāsa, *Śakuntalā*, act 6.
28. *Bṛhadāraṇyaka U* 4. 3. 18.

29. I am grateful to A. K. Ramanujan for permission to cite this passage from his unpublished poem.

30. Stith Thompson, *Index*, N 211.1. Herodotus tells the tale of Polycrates (3. 40–44), which has rather a different moral from the Indian story: the ring is a curse that the king tries, in vain, to lose, not a treasure that he longs to have back again.

31. Wendy O'Flaherty, *Hindu Myths*, pp. 100–102.

32. I am grateful to Gail Hinich for permission to cite this passage from her unpublished essay "Manu and the Fish: Three Versions of the Flood Legend in Indian Mythology" (May, 1982).

33. See Gananath Obeyesekere, "Theodicy, Sin and Salvation."

34. See Charles Keyes and E. Valentine Daniel, *Karma*, introduction.

35. See McKim Marriott, "Hindu Transactions."

36. See Wendy O'Flaherty, "Emotion and Karma."

37. Salman Rushdie, *Midnight's Children*, pp. 457–58.

38. See Wendy O'Flaherty, *Karma and Rebirth*.

39. I am indebted to both David Shulman (private communications) and A. K. Ramanujan (remarks at the 1982 Association of Asian Studies panel on narrative) for the formulations in this paragraph.

40. *YV* 1. 10. 20; 1. 14. 21; 1. 17. 12, 20.

41. *YV* 5. 45. 8–15; 5. 48. 6.

42. *YV* 3. 89–90.

43. For this story, see Wendy O'Flaherty, *Asceticism and Eroticism*, pp. 85–89; *Hindu Myths*, pp. 94–96.

44. Sir Ernst Gombrich, "Illusion and Art," p. 216.

45. *Māṇḍūkya U* 5.

46. *YV* 3. 108. 14, 17, 25–26.

47. *R* 1. 44. 5.

48. Śankara's commentary on *Vedānta Sūtras* 3. 2. 3.

49. *M* 5. 118–20.

50. *Padma P* 2. 64–83; Wendy O'Flaherty, *The Origins of Evil*, pp. 236–43.

51. Lewis Carroll, *Through the Looking Glass*, "Wool and Water."

52. Salman Rushdie, *Midnight's Children*, p. 123.

53. James Boon reminds me that, long ago, Claude Lévi-Strauss pointed out (in *The Raw and the Cooked*) the bond between myths and loops and music.

54. *YV* 4. 43. 44.

55. *YV* 6. 1. 63. 9; 6. 1. 62. 7.

56. *YV* 6. 1. 62. 6; 6. 1. 63. 10–11, 36.

57. *YV*, commentary on 6. 1. 62. 6.

58. *YV* 6. 1. 63. 13; 6. 1. 62. 2; 6. 1. 63. 10; commentary on 6. 1. 62. 2.

59. *YV* 6. 1. 65. 12.

60. *YV*, commentary on 6. 1. 67. 1.

61. *YV* 6. 1. 67. 6.

62. *YV* 6. 1. 64. 28.

63. *YV* 6. 1. 65. 10–20; 6. 1. 66. 1–28; 6. 1. 67. 1–6.

64. *YV* 6. 1. 66. 6.

65. *YV*, commentary on 6. 1. 65. 13.

66. *YV* 6. 2. 56–94.

67. A similar attempt to construct, mentally, a place in which to construct, mentally, a place . . . appears (perhaps under Indian influence) in the practices of certain European groups of meditators. Together they would concentrate on building a palace; the strong meditators would make the foundations, the weaker the chairs and tables. Then the group would transport themselves, mentally, to that place *en masse*, sit in it, and together concentrate on building another palace . . . .

68. *YV* 6. 2. 86. 46.

69. See Wendy O'Flaherty, *Asceticism and Eroticism*, pp. 52–64.

70. *YV* 3. 19.

71. See Webster's *Third International Dictionary*, s.v. Möbius.

72. See George Gamow, *Mr. Tomkins in Wonderland*, pp. 25–29, and Martin Gardner, "The World of the Möbius Strip."

73. Willibald Kirfel, *Die Kosmographie der Inder*, p. 93.

74. C. S. Lewis, *The Last Battle*, pp. 118, 162, 165.

75. Wendy O'Flaherty, "The Interaction between Nirguṇa and Saguṇa."

76. Patrick Hughes, *Vicious Circles*, notes on his plates 1, 11, and 12. His plate 12, entitled "Endless Snake," is a painted ceramic sculpture that he created.

77. Alan Dundes pointed out to me the distinction between cumulative tales and nested tales, not only in the story of the monk's dream but in folklore in general.

78. James Boon was the one who realized that I had left out this final link in the earlier version of the diagram. This note is my dotted line to him. (Audiences over the past few years have frequently made uneasy jokes about the possibility that they—*or I*—could have been dreaming that I was lecturing to them.)

79. Jorge Luis Borges, "The Circular Ruins," "Avatars of the Tortoise," and "Partial Magic in the Quixote," *Labyrinths*, pp. 72–77. See also Borges' "The Secret Miracle" and "Tlön, Uqbar, Orbis Tertius," both from *Ficciones*, translated by Anthony Kerrigan (New York, 1962). Roger Caillois has translated Borges into French.

80. Aeschylus, *The Libation Bearers* 527–34, 548–50, 928.

81. Ibid. 1048–61.

82. Aeschylus, *Eumenides* 47, 68.

83. Ibid. 130–33.

84. Ibid. 94.

85. Homer, *Iliad* 23. 68.

86. Aeschylus, *Eumenides* 116.

87. George Devereux, *Dreams in Greek Tragedy*, p. 155. The italics are Devereux's.

88. As Devereux also maintains, ibid., p. 151.

89. Ibid., p. 152.

90. Ibid., p. 156.

91. Saint Augustine, *The City of God*, bk. 18, chap. 18 (Penguin ed., p. 783).

92. This line of thought infuriated most realists and even drove one of them, Ronald Arbuthnott Knox, to commit a limerick, entitled "Idealism," to which someone else offered "A Reply":

There once was a man who said, "God
Must think it exceedingly odd
If he finds that this tree
Continues to be
When there's no one about in the quad."

Dear Sir,
Your astonishment's odd.
I am always about in the quad.
And that's why the tree
Will continue to be
Since observed by
Yours faithfully,
God.

(Bishop Knox's limericks are reprinted in Harold Monroe's *The Weekend Book.*) A similar brace of limericks, whose author shall remain anonymous, first mocks the Indian theory of illusion and then offers a reply.

"The Indian sage," said the Pope,
"Is a theological dope.
For the world, so it seems,
Is just one of God's dreams,
And He can't tell a snake from a rope."

The yogins and naths and hakkims
Tell their pupils, "It's not as it seems.
Though you think that your mind
Thought up God, you may find
You're a figment of one of His dreams."

93. Lewis Carroll, *Through the Looking Glass*, "Tweedledum and Tweedledee."
94. Martin Gardner, *The Annotated Alice*, p. 238.
95. Lewis Carroll, *Through the Looking Glass*, "Which Dreamed It?"
96. Unamuno, in a letter to Walter Starkie, October, 1921. Cited by Starkie in his introduction to Miguel de Unamuno, *Our Lord Don Quixote* (Princeton, 1967), p. xxxiv. David Shulman found this and gave it to me.
97. Chuang Tsu, "The Equality of Things and Opinions," 2. 1. 2. 11.
98. Woody Allen, *Without Feathers*, pp. 192–93.
99. George Devereux, *Dreams in Greek Tragedy*, p. 156, n. 31.
100. Russell Hoban, *The Mouse and His Child*, pp. 34–35, 67–80 (where "The Last Visible Dog" is a play that satirizes Beckett), 120–26 (where the mouse child uses the image of the infinitely receding dog as a yantra for meditating on nothing and infinity), and 190–200 (where this image is used as a symbol for the final resting place). Cf. Wendy O'Flaherty, "Inside and Outside," pp. 119–20.
101. The concept of the shared dream is twisted in a rather cynical way by Arthur Schnitzler in his story of Redegonda's diary (in *Die erzählenden Schriften* [Frankfurt, 1961]).
102. Douglas Hofstadter, *Gödel, Escher, Bach*, p. 127.
103. Ibid., p. 184.

104. Ibid., p. 15.
105. Bruno Ernst, *The Magic Mirror of M. C. Escher*, p. 14.
106. The legerdemain involved in this drawing, which involves a Riemann surface and an empty center, is analyzed by Ernst, ibid., pp. 31–33.
107. Kabir, *śabda* 16, cited by Linda Hess, "The Cow Is Sucking," p. 314.
108. Douglas Hofstadter, *Gödel, Escher, Bach*, p. 692.
109. Ibid., p. 689.
110. Ibid.
111. Ibid., p. 691.
112. Ibid., p. 185.
113. *RV* 10. 90. 5. Wendy O'Flaherty, *The Rig Veda*, p. 30.
114. *RV* 10. 72. 4. Wendy O'Flaherty, *The Rig Veda*, pp. 38–39.
115. Yāska, *Nirukta* 11. 23.
116. *Aitareya Brāhmaṇa* 7. 13; *Mānavadharmaśāstra* 9. 8.
117. *Kūrma P* 1. 9. 6–87.
118. *Śiva P* 3. 8–9.
119. *Skanda P* 5. 1. 2. 1–65.
120. See Wendy O'Flaherty, *Asceticism and Eroticism*, pp. 124–25, 353.
121. The theme persists in Salman Rushdie's *Midnight's Children* (pp. 309–10): "He had accepted that he, too, was one of that endless series of parents to whom I alone had the power of giving birth."
122. *Bhagavad Gītā* 4. 1–6.
123. A. K. Ramanujan, "Indian Poetics," pp. 115–16.

Chapter 6. The Art of Illusion

1. Personal communication from Sudhir Kakar.
2. Salman Rushdie, *Midnight's Children*, p. 359.
3. *YV* 2. 18. 55–61.
4. *Bṛhadāraṇyaka U* 2. 3. 6; 3. 9. 26; etc.
5. *YV* 2. 17. 9; 3. 21. 13.
6. Tulasī Dās, *Rāmacaritamānasa*, C. 112; trans. W. D. P. Hill, *The Holy Lake of the Acts of Rāma*, p. 56.
7. *Lankāvatārasūtra* 10. 498.
8. Sir Roland Penrose, "In Praise of Illusion," p. 27.
9. See Wendy O'Flaherty, *The Origins of Evil*, pp. 212–14.
10. *Bālagopālastuti* 349.
11. *YV* 3. 2. 20, 56.
12. *YV* 3. 4. 71.
13. *YV* 3. 4. 75.
14. *YV* 6. 2. 105. 12.
15. *Lankāvatārasūtra* 1. 39–40; 2. 158; 3. 43.
16. G. A. Jacob, *Popular Maxims*, p. 34.
17. Patañjali, *Mahābhāṣya* 8. 2. 3.
18. G. A. Jacob, *Popular Maxims*, p. 11, citing the *Kāśikāvṛtti* on Pāṇini 5. 3. 106.
19. Maurice Bloomfield, "The Fable of the Crow and the Palm Tree," p. 12.
20. G. A. Jacob, *Popular Maxims*, p. 2, citing *Yaśastilaka* 2. 153 and *Śrīśrutasāgara*.

21. G. A. Jacob, *Popular Maxims*, p. 19.
22. Ibid., p. 15.
23. Ibid., p. 18.
24. Ibid., p. 1.
25. Ibid., p. 18.
26. Ibid.
27. *Devībhāgavata P* 6. 30. 18.
28. *YV* 3. 96. 22.
29. *YV* 5. 49. 7, 10.
30. *YV* 3. 121. 21.
31. *YV* 4. 56. 8.
32. Helmuth von Glasenapp, *Zwei philosophische Rāmāyaṇas*, pp. 490–92.
33. Max Born, *Natural Philosophy of Cause and Chance* (1949), p. 122.
34. Michael Harwood, "The Universe and Dr. Hawking," *New York Times Magazine*, January 23, 1983, p. 56.
35. Wendy O'Flaherty, *Asceticism and Eroticism*, p. 223.
36. W. Y. Evans-Wentz, *The Tibetan Book of the Dead*, p. 181 n.
37. *Aitareya Brāhmaṇa* 1. 23; *Śatapatha Brāhmaṇa* 3. 4. 4. 3–27; *M* 8. 24.
38. Paul Wheatley, *The City as Symbol*, p. 10.
39. *Brahmavaivarta P*, *Kṛṣṇa Janma Khaṇḍa* 47. 80–81.
40. See Wendy O'Flaherty, *The Origins of Evil*, pp. 57–93.
41. *Maṇimēkalai* 6. 23–206. I am indebted to Paula Richman for introducing me to this text and for providing the translation, which is a part of her Ph.D. dissertation, "Religious Rhetoric in the Tamil Buddhist Text, *Maṇimēkalai*" (University of Chicago, 1982).
42. See Wendy O'Flaherty, *The Origins of Evil*, pp. 189–204, 260–71.
43. *Lankāvatārasūtra* 1. 1–38.
44. *Chāndogya U* 8. 1. 1.
45. *Bhāgavata P* 4. 25. 45–53.
46. Ibid. 4. 25–28.
47. Ibid. 4. 27; Vettam Mani says that the woman in the city is a female Gandharva (*Puranic Encyclopedia*, p. 616).
48. *YV* 6. 1. 112. 16–35.
49. *M* 5. 141. 21.
50. *Lankāvatārasūtra* 2. 19. 52.
51. Ibid. 10. 173, 297, 533, 875, etc.
52. Ibid. 2. 146.
53. Ibid. 3. 85.
54. *YV* 4. 38. 17.
55. *YV* 5. 47. 8, 14, 41.
56. *YV* 2. 19. 52; 3. 3. 30; 6. 2. 56. 26; etc.
57. *YV* 3. 4. 76; 3. 13. 16; 4. 1. 14.
58. *YV* 6. 2. 147. 12.
59. *Bardo-Thödol*, trans. Francesca Fremantle, p. 86.
60. *Buddhacarita* 2. 28–32; see also *Anguttara Nikāya* 1. 145.
61. Gautama's *Nyāyasūtras* 4. 2. 31–37, cited by Karl Potter, *Indian Metaphysics*, p. 237.

62. Karl Potter, *Indian Metaphysics*, p. 268.
63. *M* 2. 25. 6.
64. See Wendy O'Flaherty, "Contributions to an Equine Lexicology."
65. Revelation 21. 2, 16–19.
66. I am indebted to James Boon and David Toolan (of *Commonweal*) for pointing out to me the complexity of the range of Western attitudes to the city.
67. Plato, *Republic*, 592b. See also 499 and 540.
68. *YV* 3. 104. 14; 3. 121. 4.
69. *YV* 5. 44. 31.
70. *YV* 3. 4. 72.
71. *YV* 3. 113. 32 and 5. 35. 64.
72. *YV* 3. 120. 12.
73. *YV* 4. 1. 3.
74. Sir Ernst Gombrich, *Art and Illusion*, p. 269.
75. *YV* 6. 1. 108.
76. *YV* 6. 1. 85–106.
77. Sir Ernst Gombrich, *Art and Illusion*, p. 219.
78. Sir Ernst Gombrich, "Illusion and Art," p. 206.
79. Sir Ernst Gombrich, "The Evidence of Images," p. 60.
80. Max Black, "How Do Pictures Represent?," p. 114.
81. Sir Ernst Gombrich, *Illusion in Nature and Art*, p. 7.
82. Ibid.
83. Kālidāsa, *The Recognition of Śakuntalā*, act 6.
84. Sheryl B. Daniel, "The Tool-Box Approach," p. 23.
85. Edward C. Dimock, *The Thief of Love*, pp. 252–55; *M* 1. 39.
86. Śankara's commentary on *Vedānta Sūtras* 2. 1. 14.
87. Sir Ernst Gombrich, *Art and Illusion*, p. 225.
88. R. L. Gregory, "The Confounded Eye," p. 91.
89. Sir Roland Penrose, "In Praise of Illusion," p. 273.
90. Ibid., p. 274.
91. Sir Ernst Gombrich, "Illusion and Art," p. 239.
92. Sir Roland Penrose, "In Praise of Illusion," p. 274.
93. Ibid.
94. Stephan Beyer, *The Cult of Tara*, p. 87, citing Paul Eluard.
95. Ibid., p. 88.
96. Sir Ernst Gombrich, *The Story of Art*, p. 443.
97. It was Richard Gombrich who pointed out to me, at the Royal Society of Arts lecture in May, 1980, the relevance of this characteristic of Sanskrit.
98. *YV* 3. 106. 61–65.
99. *YV* 5. 44. 39–40.
100. Sir Roland Penrose, "In Praise of Illusion," p. 273, quoting Herbert Read.
101. *YV* 3. 109. 28–29.
102. Madness, too, grounds its reality in everyday detail. Milton Rokeach tells of a schizophrenic who claimed to be both the governor of Illinois and God; he justified the former role by pointing out, "I have to earn my living, you know," and the latter by walking into a Social Services office and announcing, "I am

God. I would like to apply for Social Security" (Rokeach, *The Three Christs of Ypsilanti*, pp. 76–77, 269).

103. I am grateful to Leonard Nash for this observation.
104. Paul Feyerabend, *Against Method*, p. 189.
105. *YV* 3. 104. 32; 3. 106. 4; 3. 106. 3.
106. *YV* 3. 104. 31; 3. 109. 23–29.
107. Teun Goudriaan, *Māyā*, p. 248.
108. *YV* 6. 2. 146. 10.
109. *YV* 4. 25–34.
110. *YV* 3. 104. 26, 29; 3. 105. 20, 21.
111. Plato, *Republic* 602c–d.
112. Sir Ernst Gombrich, *Art and Illusion*, pp. 191, 205–6.
113. Yves Véquaud, "The Colors of Devotion," pp. 62–63.
114. *RV* 10. 81–82; Wendy O'Flaherty, *The Rig Veda*, pp. 34–37.
115. Sir Roland Penrose, "In Praise of Illusion," p. 274.
116. Sir Ernst Gombrich, "Illusion and Art," p. 194.
117. Philostratus, *Life of Apollonius*, p. 59.
118. The king was probably Gondophares (Philostratus, *Life of Apollonius*, p. 57, n. 3).
119. Paul Feyerabend, *Against Method*, pp. 52–53.
120. Michael Polanyi, *Personal Knowledge*, p. 302.

Conclusion

1. *Oxford English Dictionary*, s.v. Serendipity.
2. Leo A. Goodman, "Notes on the Etymology of Serendipity," p. 456.
3. By F. Max Müller and Claude Lévi-Strauss, among others.
4. *YV* 2. 3. 12.
5. Wendy O'Flaherty, "Inside and Outside the Mouth of God."
6. Allen Thrasher told me the story at a meeting (sponsored by the Social Science Research Council and the American Council of Learned Societies Joint Committee on South Asia) at Lake Wilderness, near Seattle, in October, 1976.
7. See Acknowledgments.
8. David Haberman pointed out to me the significance of these two Bengali goddesses of illusion.
9. *The Tempest*, act 3, scene 2, line 148.
10. Herodotus, *History* 2. 53; translated by David Grene.
11. Claude Lévi-Strauss, *Structural Anthropology*, p. 229; and *The Savage Mind*, p. 22.
12. See R. Gordon Wasson, *Soma*, pp. 51–58.
13. Aeschylus, *Agamemnon*, line 82; translated by David Grene in "Aeschylus: Myth, Religion, and Poetry."

Appendix 1

1. The text is the story of Wu Chi'iu-Yueh, in the *Liao Chai Chich I*, composed by P'u Sung-ling (1640–1715). The translation into English, by Chi-Chen Wang, appears in Roger Caillois, *The Dream Adventure*, pp. 42–46. I have summarized that translation here.

Appendix 2

1. A. C. Graham, *The Book of Lieh Tsu*, pp. 61–63 (*Lieh Tzu* 3. 1a–3a). I have based my summary on Graham's translation but have supplemented it with a few details that appear in other texts: Lionel Giles, *Taoist Teachings*, pp. 58–61; Roger Caillois, *The Dream Adventure*, pp. 4–6; Herlee Creel, *What Is Taoism?*, pp. 20–21; and Michael Loewe, *Ways to Paradise*, p. 93.
2. Herlee Creel, *What Is Taoism?*, p. 21.
3. A. C. Graham, *The Book of Lieh Tsu*, pp. 58–60.
4. David Knechtges, "Dream Adventure Stories," pp. 114–15.
5. Allen Thrasher, "Magical Journeys."
6. John Arnott McCulloch, *Celtic Mythology*, p. 181.
7. Ibid., p. 182.

Bibliography

Sanskrit, Pali, Tamil, and Tibetan Texts

Adhyātma-Rāmāyaṇa. Calcutta, 1884.

Aitareya Brāhmaṇa. With the commentary of Sāyaṇa. Calcutta, 1896.

Angavijjā. Benaras, 1957.

Anguttara Nikāya. 6 vols. London, 1885–1910.

Atharva Veda, The Pariśiṣṭas of the. Vol. 1, text and critical apparatus, pt. 2. Edited by George Melville Bolling and Julius von Negelein. Leipzig, 1910.

Bālagopālastuti. Manuscript reconstructed by Elinor Gadon as part of her 1983 University of Chicago Ph.D. dissertation.

Bardo-Thödol (Tibetan Book of the Dead). Translated by Francesca Fremantle and Chögyam Trungpa. Berkeley, 1975. *See also* Evans-Wentz.

Bhagavad Gītā. Book 6, chapters 23–40, of the *Mahābhārata*, q.v.

Bhāgavata Purāṇa. With the commentary of Śrīdhara. Bombay, 1832.

Brahmavaivarta Purāṇa. Poona, 1935.

Buddhacarita, or Acts of the Buddha, by Aśvaghoṣa. Edited and translated by E. H. Johnson. Delhi, 1936.

Caraka Saṃhitā. Delhi, 1963.

Devī Purāṇa. Calcutta, 1896.

Devībhāgavata Purāṇa. Benares, 1960.

Garuḍa Purāṇa. Benares, 1969.

Harivaṃśa. Poona, 1969.

Jaiminīya (Talavakara) Brāhmaṇa. Nagpur, 1954.

Karpūramañjarī of Rājaśekhara. Edited and translated by Charles Lanman. Harvard Oriental Series. Cambridge, Mass., 1901.

Kathāsaritsāgara of Somadeva. Bombay, 1930.

Kūrma Purāṇa. Varanasi, 1972.

Lalitavistara. Edited by S. Lefmann. 2 vols. Halle a. S., 1902–8.

Lankāvatārasūtra. See *Saddharmalankāvatārasūtra*.

Linga Purāṇa. Calcutta, 1812.

Mahābhāgavata Purāṇa. Calcutta, 1812.

Mahābhārata. 21 vols. Poona, 1933–60.

Mahābhāṣya of Patañjali. Edited by K. V. Abhyankar and J. M. Shukla. Poona, 1969.

Mānava-Dharma-Śāstra. Edited by J. Jolly. London, 1887.

Mānava-Gṛhya-Sūtra. Groningen, 1941.

Mārkaṇḍeya Purāṇa. Bombay, 1890.

Matsya Purāṇa. Poona, 1907.

Mayili Rāvaṇaṉ Katai. Maturai, 1922.
Mūlamādhyamakakārikā of Nāgārjuna. Edited and translated by Kenneth K. Inada. Tokyo, 1970.
Padma Purāṇa. Poona, 1893.
Rāmāyaṇa of Kampaṉ. *Irāmāvatāram* of Kampaṉ. 7 vols. 5th ed. Madras, 1953–55.
Rāmāyaṇa of Vālmīki. 7 vols. Baroda, 1960–75.
Ṛg Veda. With the commentary of Sāyaṇa. 4 vols. London, 1890–92.
Saddharmalankāvatārasūtra. Edited by P. L. Vaidya. Darbhanga, 1963.
Śiva Purāṇa. Benares, 1964.
Skanda Purāṇa. Bombay, 1867.
Śrībhāṣya of Rāmānuja. 2 vols. Bombay, 1914–16.
Śrī-kāśī-mokṣa-nirṇaya. With Hindi commentary of Ambikadatta Upādhyaya Śāstri. Gorakhpur, 1931.
Suśruta Saṃhitā. Delhi, 1968.
Svapnavāsavadatta of Bhāsa. Trivandrum, 1912.
Upaniṣads (*One Hundred and Eight Upaniṣads*). Bombay, 1913.
Vedānta Sūtras of Bādarāyaṇa. With the commentary of Śankara. Bombay, 1917.
Vessantara Jātaka. No. 547 in vol. 6 of *Jātakas*, edited by V. Fausbøll. 6 vols. London, 1877–96.
Yogavāsiṣṭha-Mahā-Rāmāyaṇa of Vālmīki. With the commentary Vāsiṣṭha-Mahā-*Rāmāyaṇa-Tātparyaprakāśa*. Edited by W. L. S. Pansikar. 2 vols. Bombay, 1918.

Texts in Non-Indian Languages and Secondary Sources

Allen, Woody. *Without Feathers*. New York, 1976.
Arnold, Sir Thomas W. *A Catalogue of the Indian Miniatures in the Library of A. Chester Beatty*. Edited and revised by J. V. S. Wilkinson. Oxford, 1936.
Atreya, B. L. *The Philosophy of the "Yoga-Vāsiṣṭha*." Adyar, 1936.
———. "A Probable Date of Composition of the *Yogavāsiṣṭha*." In *Proceedings and Transactions of the Seventh All-India Oriental Conference, Baroda, December, 1935*, pp. 55–59. Baroda, 1935.
———. *The "Yogavāsiṣṭha" and Its Philosophy*. Moradabad, 1966.
Augustine, Saint. *The City of God*. Translated by David Knowles. Harmondsworth, Eng., 1972.
Bareau, André. *Bouddha: Présentation, choix de texte, bibliographie*. Paris, 1962.
Bastide, Roger. "The Sociology of the Dream." Pp. 199–211 in Von Grunebaum and Caillois, eds., *The Dream in Human Societies*.
Belloc, Hilaire. *More Beasts for Worse Children*. 1898. Reprint, New York, 1961.
Beyer, Stephan. *The Cult of Tara: Magic and Ritual in Tibet*. Berkeley and Los Angeles, 1973.
Bhattacharya, Sivaprasad. "The Cardinal Tenets of the *Yogavāsiṣṭha* and Their Relation to the Trika System of Knowledge." *Annals of the Bhandarkar Oriental Research Institute* 32 (1952): 130–45.
———. "The *Yogavāsiṣṭha Rāmāyaṇa*: Its Probable Date and Place of Inception." In *Proceedings of the Third All-India Oriental Conference, Madras, 1924*, pp. 545–53. Madras, 1925.
Black, Max. "How Do Pictures Represent?" Pp. 95–129 in E. H. Gombrich et al., eds., *Art, Perception, and Reality*.

Bloomfield, Maurice. "The Fable of the Crow and the Palm-Tree: A Psychic Motif in Hindu Fiction." *American Journal of Philology* 40 (1919): 1–36.

———. "On the Art of Entering Another's Body: A Hindu Fiction Motif." *Proceedings of the American Philosophical Society* 41 (1917): 1–43.

Borges, Jorge Luis. *Labyrinths*. Harmondsworth, Eng., 1970.

Borges, Jorge Luis, with Margarita Guerrero. *The Book of Imaginary Beings*. Harmondsworth, Eng., 1969.

Born, Max. *Natural Philosophy of Cause and Chance*. New York, 1949.

Bruner, J. S., and Postman, Leo. "On the Perception of Incongruity: A Paradigm." *Journal of Personality* 18 (1949): 204–23.

Burrow, Thomas. "Sanskrit *mā*, 'to make, produce, create.'" *Bulletin of the School of Oriental and African Studies* 43 (1980): 311–28; 44 (1981): 85.

Caillois, Roger. *The Dream Adventure*. New York, 1963.

———. "Logical and Philosophical Problems of the Dream." Pp. 23–52 in Von Grunebaum and Caillois, eds., *The Dream and Human Societies*.

Carnoy, Albert J. *Iranian Mythology*. Vol. 6, pt. 2, of *The Mythology of All Races*, edited by L. H. Grey. Boston, 1917.

Carroll, Lewis. *Alice in Wonderland*. London, 1865.

———. *Through the Looking Glass*. London, 1872.

Carstairs, G. M. *The Twice-Born*. London, 1958.

Coomaraswamy, Ananda K. "Early Indian Architecture. I. Cities and City-Gates." *Eastern Art* 2 (1930): 208–23.

Creel, Herrlee G. *What Is Taoism? and Other Studies in Chinese Cultural History*. Chicago, 1970.

Daniel, Sheryl B. "The Tool-Box Approach of the Tamil to the Issues of Moral Responsibility and Human Destiny." Pp. 27–62 in Keyes and Daniel, eds., *Karma: An Anthropological Inquiry*.

Dasgupta, Surendranath. *A History of Indian Philosophy*. Vol. 1. Cambridge, Eng., 1922.

Dement, William C. *Some Must Watch, While Some Must Sleep*. Stanford, 1972.

Devereux, George. *Dreams in Greek Tragedy*. Berkeley, 1976.

———, ed. *Psychoanalysis and the Occult*. New York, 1970.

de Vries, Peter. *Sauce for the Goose*. Boston, 1981.

Dimock, Edward C. *The Thief of Love: Bengali Tales from Court and Village*. Chicago, 1963.

Divanji, Prahlad C. "The Date and Place of Origin of the *Yogavāsiṣṭha*." In *Proceedings and Transactions of the Seventh All-India Oriental Conference, Baroda, December, 1933*, pp. 14–30. Baroda, 1935.

———. "Further Light on the Date of the *Yogavāsiṣṭha*." *Poona Orientalist* 3 (1938): 29–44.

———. "*Yogavāsiṣṭha* on the Means of Proof." In *A Volume of Indian and Iranian Studies Presented to Sir E. Denison Ross*, pp. 102–12. Bombay, 1939.

Dubs, Homer H. "An Ancient Chinese Mystery Cult." *Harvard Theological Review* 25 (1942): 221–40.

Eggan, Dorothy. "The Personal Use of Myth in Dreams." In *Myth: A Symposium*, edited by Thomas A. Sebeok, pp. 67–75. Bloomington, Ind., 1958.

Eisenbud, Jule. "The Dreams of Two Patients in Analysis as a Telepathic *Rêve à Deux*." Pp. 262–76 in Devereux, ed., *Psychoanalysis and the Occult*. (Originally published in *The Psychoanalytic Quarterly* 16 [1947]: 39–60.)

Ernst, Bruno. *The Magic Mirror of M. C. Escher*. New York, 1976.

Esnoul, A. M. "Les songes et leur interprétation dans l'Inde." In A. M. Esnoul et al., eds., *Les songes et leur interprétation: Sources Orientales*, vol. 2, pp. 208–47. Paris, 1959.

Evans-Wentz, W. Y., trans. *The Tibetan Book of the Dead*. Oxford, 1960.

Festinger, Leon. *A Theory of Cognitive Dissonance*. New York, 1957.

Festinger, Leon; Riecken, Henry W.; and Schachter, Stanley. *When Prophecy Fails: An Account of a Modern Group That Predicted the Destruction of the World*. Minneapolis, 1956.

Feyerabend, Paul. *Against Method*. London, 1978.

Fremantle, Francesca, and Trungpa, Chögyam. See *Bardo-Thödol*.

Fódor, Nándor. "Telepathy in Analysis." Pp. 283–96 in Devereux, ed., *Psychoanalysis and the Occult*. (First published in *The Psychiatric Quarterly* 21 [1947]: 171–89.)

Freud, Sigmund. *Die Traumdeutung*. Frankfurt, 1942. (Reprint of the 6th edition of 1921.)

———. *The Interpretation of Dreams*. Translated by James Strachey. Vols. 4 and 5 of the *Standard Edition*. New York, 1965.

———. *An Outline of Psychoanalysis*. Translated by James Strachey. Vol. 23 of the *Standard Edition*. New York, 1949.

Gamow, George. *Mr. Tomkins in Wonderland*. Cambridge, Eng., 1965. Rev. ed., *Mr. Tomkins in Paperback*. Cambridge, 1979.

Gardner, Martin. *The Annotated Alice*. Harmondsworth, Eng., 1970.

———. "The World of the Möbius Strip: Endless, Edgeless, and One-Sided." *Scientific American* (December, 1968): 112–15.

Geertz, Clifford. "Common Sense as a Cultural System." *Antioch Review* 33 (1975): 5–26.

———. *The Interpretation of Cultures*. New York, 1973.

Giles, Lionel. *Taoist Teachings from the Book of Lieh Tsu*. London, 1925.

Goldman, R. P. "Rāmaḥ Sahalakṣmaṇaḥ: Psychological and Literary Aspects of the Composite Hero of Vālmīki's *Rāmāyaṇa*." *Journal of Indian Philosophy* 8 (1980): 149–89.

Gombrich, Sir Ernst H. *Art and Illusion*. New York, 1961.

———. "The Evidence of Images." In *Interpretation, Theory, and Practice*, edited by Charles S. Singleton. Baltimore, 1969.

———. "Illusion and Art." Pp. 193–243 in Gombrich and Gregory, eds., *Illusion in Nature and Art*.

———. *The Image and the Eye*. New York, 1982.

———. "The Mask and the Face: The Perception of Physiognomic Likeness in Life and Art." Pp. 1–46 in Gombrich et al., eds., *Art, Perception, and Reality*.

———. *The Story of Art*. New York, 1950.

———. "The 'What' and the 'How': Perspective Representation and the Phenomenal World." In *Logic and Art: Essays in Honor of Nelson Goodman*, edited by Richard Rudner and Israel Scheffler, pp. 129–49. Indianapolis and New York, 1972.

Gombrich, Sir Ernst H., and Gregory, R. L., eds. *Illusion in Nature and Art*. London, 1973.

Gombrich, Sir Ernst H.; Hochberg, Julian; and Black, Max, eds. *Art, Perception, and Reality*. Baltimore, 1972.
Gombrich, Richard F., and Cone, Margaret. *The Perfect Generosity of Prince Vessantara*. Oxford, 1977.
Gonda, Jan. *Four Studies in the Language of the Veda*. The Hague, 1959.
Goodman, Leo A. "Notes on the Etymology of *Serendipity* and Some Related Philological Observations." *Modern Language Notes* 76 (1961): 454–57.
Goudriaan, Teun. *Māyā Divine and Human*. Delhi, 1978.
Graham, Angus Charles, trans. *The Book of Lieh Tzu*. London, 1960.
Gregor, Thomas. *Mehinaku: The Drama of Daily Life in a Brazilian Indian Village*. Chicago, 1977.
Gregory, R. L. "The Confounded Eye." Pp. 46–96 in Gombrich and Gregory, eds., *Illusion in Nature and Art*.
———. *Eye and Brain: The Psychology of Seeing*. London, 1966.
Grene, David. "Aeschylus: Myth, Religion, and Poetry." *History of Religions* 23 (1983): 1–17.
———. *Greek Political Thought*. Chicago, 1950. (Originally published as *Man in His Pride*.)
———. *Herodotus: The History and Its Presentation*. Evanston, 1982.
Grene, David, and Lattimore, Richmond, eds. *The Complete Greek Tragedies*. Chicago, 1959.
Hallowell, A. Irving. "The Role of Dreams in Ojibwa Culture." Pp. 267–89 in Von Grunebaum and Caillois, eds., *The Dream and Human Societies*.
Hess, Linda. "The Cow Is Sucking at the Calf's Teat: Kabir's Upside-Down Language." *History of Religions* 22 (1983): 313–37.
Hill, W. D. P. *The Holy Lake of the Acts of Rāma*. A translation of Tulasī Dās's *Rāmacaritamānasa*. London, 1952.
Hinton, H. E. "Natural Deception." Pp. 97–159 in Gombrich and Gregory, eds., *Illusion in Nature and Art*.
Hoban, Russell. *The Mouse and His Child*. London, 1969.
Hofstadter, Douglas R. *Gödel, Escher, Bach: An Eternal Golden Braid*. New York, 1980.
Hughes, Patrick, and Brecht, George. *Vicious Circles and Infinity: An Anthology of Paradoxes*. Harmondsworth, Eng., 1975.
Ingalls, Daniel H. H. "Śankara on the Question: Whose is *Avidyā*?" *Philosophy East and West* 3 (1953): 69–72.
Jung, C. G. *Dreams*. Translated by R. F. C. Hull. Extracted from vols. 4, 8, 12, and 16 of *The Collected Works of C. G. Jung*. Bollingen Series 20. Princeton, 1974.
———. "Psychological Commentary on *The Tibetan Book of the Dead*." Pp. xxxv–lii in Evans-Wentz, trans., *The Tibetan Book of the Dead*.
———. "Synchronicity: An Acausal Connecting Principle." Translated by R. F. C. Hull. In *The Structure and Dynamics of the Psyche*, vol. 8 of *The Collected Works of C. G. Jung*. 2d ed. Princeton, 1969.
Kakar, Sudhir. *Shamans, Mystics, and Doctors*. New York, 1982.
Karmarkar, R. D. "Mutual Relation of the *Yogavāsiṣṭha*, the *Lankāvatārasūtra*, and the *Gauḍapāda-kārikās*." *Annals of the Bhandarkar Oriental Research Institute* 36 (1955): 298–305.

Kepler, Johannis. *Kepler's Dream.* Includes full text and notes of *Somnium, sive astronomia lunaris.* Edited by John Lear. Translated by Patricia Frueh Kirkwood. Berkeley and Los Angeles, 1965.

Keyes, Charles F., and Daniel, E. Valentine, eds. *Karma: An Anthropological Inquiry.* Berkeley and Los Angeles, 1983.

Kipling, Rudyard. "The Brushwood Boy" and "The Bridge-Builders." In *The Day's Work.* 1889. Reprint, New York, 1964.

Kirfel, Willibald. *Die Kosmographie der Inder.* Bonn and Leipzig, 1920.

Knechtges, David. "Dream Adventure Stories in Europe and T'ang China." *Tamkang Review* 4 (1973): 101–19.

Knowles, John Hinton. *Folktales of Kashmir.* London, 1883.

Koestler, Arthur. *The Sleepwalkers.* New York, 1959. Reprint, 1968.

Kohlberg, Lawrence. "Stage and Sequence: The Cognitive-Developmental Approach to Socialization." In *Handbook of Socialization Theory and Research,* edited by David A. Goslin, pp. 346–480. New York, 1969.

Kuhn, Thomas. *The Structure of Scientific Revolutions.* 2d ed. Chicago, 1970.

Lattimore, Richmond, and Grene, David, eds. *The Complete Greek Tragedies.* Chicago, 1959.

Leach, Edmund R. "Genesis as Myth." *Discovery* 23 (1962): 15–30. Reprinted in *Genesis as Myth and Other Essays,* pp. 7–23. London, 1969.

Lewis, C. S. *The Last Battle.* Harmondsworth, Eng., 1964.

Lincoln, Jackson Stewart. *The Dream in Primitive Cultures.* Baltimore, 1935.

Loewe, Michael. *Ways to Paradise: The Chinese Quest for Immortality.* London, 1979.

Macdonell, Arthur A. *Vedic Mythology.* 1897. Reprint, Delhi, 1963.

Mainkar, T. G. *The Vāsiṣṭha Rāmāyaṇa: A Study.* New Delhi, 1977.

Malcolm, Norman. *Dreaming.* 3d ed. London, 1964.

Mani, Vettam. *Purāṇic Encyclopedia.* Delhi, 1975.

Marriott, McKim. "Hindu Transactions: Diversity without Dualism." In *Transaction and Meaning: Directions in the Anthropology of Exchange and Symbolic Behavior,* edited by Bruce Kapferer, pp. 109–42. Philadelphia, 1977.

McCulloch, John Arnott. *Celtic Mythology.* New York, 1918.

Mitra, Vihrī Lāla, trans. *The Yogavāsiṣṭha.* Delhi, 1891–94. Reprint, 1976.

Monier-Williams, Sir Monier. *Sanskrit-English Dictionary.* Oxford, 1899.

Moody, Raymond. *Reflections on Life after Death.* Harrisburg, Pa., 1977.

Narayan, R. K. *Gods, Demons and Others.* New York, 1964.

Narayana Rao, Velcheru. "*Bhakti* in Opposition to *Karma,* in the Telugu *Basava-Purāṇa.*" Paper presented at the Social Sciences Research Council and American Council of Learned Societies Joint Council on South Asia Conference on Karma, Philadelphia, 1981.

Nayak, G. C. "The Doctrine of Karma and the Criterion of Falsifiability: A Critical Evaluation." *Calcutta Review* 180 (1966): 117–20.

Obeyesekere, Gananath. *Medusa's Hair: An Essay on Personal Symbols and Religious Experience.* Chicago, 1981.

———. "Theodicy, Sin, and Salvation in a Sociology of Buddhism." In *Dialectic in Practical Religion,* edited by Edmund R. Leach, pp. 7–40. Cambridge, Eng., 1968.

O'Flaherty, Wendy Doniger. *Asceticism and Eroticism in the Mythology of Śiva.* Oxford, 1973. (Reissued, 1980, under the title *Śiva: The Erotic Ascetic.*)

———. "Contributions to an Equine Lexicology, with Special Reference to Frogs." *Journal of the American Oriental Society* 98 (1978): 474–78.

———. "The Dream Narrative and the Indian Doctrine of Illusion." *Daedalus* 111:3 (Summer, 1982): 93–113.

———. "Emotion and Karma in Max Weber's Theodicy." In *Max Weber's Writings on India*, edited by Wolfgang Schluchter. Forthcoming.

———. *Hindu Myths: A Sourcebook, Translated from the Sanskrit*. Harmondsworth, Eng., 1975.

———. "Inside and Outside the Mouth of God: The Boundary between Myth and Reality." *Daedalus* 109:2 (Spring, 1980): 93–125.

———. "The Interaction of Saguṇa and Nirguṇa Images of Deity." In *The Sant Tradition of India*, edited by Karine Schomer and Hew McLeod. Berkeley and Los Angeles, forthcoming.

———, ed. *Karma and Rebirth in Classical Indian Tradition*. Berkeley and Los Angeles, 1980.

———. *The Origins of Evil in Hindu Mythology*. Berkeley and Los Angeles, 1976.

———, trans. *The Rig Veda: An Anthology*. Harmondsworth, Eng., 1981.

———. *Tales of Sex and Violence: Folklore, Sacrifice, and Danger in the "Jaiminīya Brāhmaṇa."* Chicago, forthcoming.

———. *Women, Androgynes, and Other Mythical Beasts*. Chicago, 1980.

Penrose, Roland. "In Praise of Illusion." Pp. 245–84 in Gombrich and Gregory, eds., *Illusion in Nature and Art*.

Philostratus. *Life of Apollonius*. Translated by C. P. Jones. Harmondsworth, Eng., 1970.

Piaget, Jean. *The Child's Conception of the World*. New York, 1929.

Polanyi, Michael. *Personal Knowledge*. Chicago, 1958.

Popper, Sir Karl. "Normal Science and Its Dangers." In *Criticism and the Growth of Knowledge*, edited by Imre Lakotosh et al., pp. 51–58. Cambridge, Eng., 1970.

———. *Objective Knowledge: An Evolutionary Approach*. Rev. ed. Oxford, 1979.

Potter, Karl H. *Indian Metaphysics and Epistemology: The Tradition of Nyāya-Vaiśesika up to Gangeśa*. Princeton, 1977.

———. *Presuppositions of India's Philosophies*. Boston, 1963.

Raghavan, V. "The Date of the *Yogavāsiṣṭha*." *Journal of Oriental Research* 13 (1939): 110–28; 17 (1947–48): 228–31.

———. "The *Yogavāsiṣṭha* and the *Bhagavadgītā* and the Place of Origin of the *Yogavāsiṣṭha*." *Journal of Oriental Research* 13 (1939): 73–85.

Ramakrishna, Sri. *The Sayings of Sri Ramakrishna*. Mylapore, 1938.

———. *Tales and Parables of Sri Ramakrishna*. 2d ed. Mylapore, 1947.

Ramanujan, A. K. "Indian Poetics." In *The Literature of India: An Introduction*, edited by Edward C. Dimock et al., pp. 115–43. Chicago, 1974.

Rockhill, W. Woodville. *The Life of the Buddha*. London, 1884.

Róheim, Géza. *The Gates of the Dream*. New York, 1969.

———. "Telepathy in a Dream." Pp. 147–57 in Devereux, ed., *Psychoanalysis and the Occult*. (First published in *The Psychoanalytic Quarterly* 1 [1932]: 227–91.)

Rokeach, Milton. *The Three Christs of Ypsilanti: A Narrative Study of Three Lost Men*. New York, 1964.

Rushdie, Salman. *Midnight's Children*. New York, 1980.

Rycroft, Charles. *The Innocence of Dreams*. New York, 1979.

Sarma, C. R. *The Rāmāyaṇa in Telugu and Tamil.* Madras, 1973.
Schwartz, Howard. *Elijah's Violin and Other Jewish Fairy Tales*. New York, 1983.
Servadio, Emilio. "The Dynamics of So-called Paranormal Dreams." Pp. 109–16 in Von Grunebaum and Caillois, eds., *The Dream in Human Societies*.
Shulman, David. "On Kings and Clowns: Indra, Triśanku, and the Killekyāṭa." Paper presented at the Indo-American Conference on Folklore, Mysore, India, August 22–26, 1980.
———. "The Mythology of the Tamil Śaiva Tālapurāṇam." D.Phil. dissertation, University of London, School of Oriental and African Studies, 1976.
———. "Sītā and Śatakaṇṭharāvaṇa in a Tamil Folk Narrative." *Journal of Indian Folkloristics* 2 (1979): 1–26.
———. *Tamil Temple Myths*. Princeton, 1980.
———. "Tĕnāli-Rāma: The Obliquity of the Real." Manuscript, 1983.
Shweder, Richard A. "On Savages and Other Children: A Review of *The Foundations of Primitive Thought*, by C. R. Hallpike." *American Anthropologist* 84 (1982): 354–66.
Shweder, Richard A., and LeVine, Robert A. "Dream Concepts of Hausa Children: A Critique of the 'Doctrine of Invariant Sequence.'" *Ethos* 3 (1975): 209–30.
Singer, Isaac Bashevis. *When Shlemiel Went to Warsaw and Other Stories*. New York, 1968.
Smith, Brian K. "The Domestication of the Vedic Sacrifice." Ph.D. dissertation, University of Chicago, 1984.
Stevenson, Ian. *Twenty Cases Suggestive of Reincarnation*. New York, 1967.
Suzuki, Daiseta Teitaro, trans. *The Lankāvatāra Sūtra*. London, 1932.
Temple, Sir Richard Carnac. *Legends of the Punjab*. 3 vols. Bombay, 1884–1900.
Thompson, Stith. *Motif-Index of Folk Literature*. 6 vols. Bloomington, Ind., 1955–58.
Thompson, Stith, and Balys, Jonas. *Oral Tales of India*. Bloomington, Ind., 1951.
Thrasher, Allen. "Magical Journeys in Classical Sanskrit Literature." Manuscript, 1977.
Tolstoy, Leo N. *Anna Karenina*. Translated by Rosemary Edmonds. Harmondsworth, Eng., 1954.
Vaudeville, Charlotte. *Etudes sur les sources et la composition du Rāmāyaṇa de Tulasī Dās*. Paris, 1955.
———. *Kabir*. Oxford, 1974.
Venkatesananda, Swami. *The Concise Yoga Vāsiṣṭha*. Albany, 1984.
Véquaud, Yves. "The Colors of Devotion." *Portfolio* (February–March, 1980): 60–67.
Wasson, R. Gordon. *Soma: Divine Mushroom of Immortality*. New York, 1968.
Wayman, Alex. "Significance of Dreams in India and Tibet." *History of Religions* 7 (1967): 1–12.
Wheatley, Paul. *The City as Symbol*. London, 1969.
Winnicott, David Woods. *Playing and Reality*. New York, 1971.
Wilson, Bryan R., ed. *Rationality*. Evanston, 1971.
Zimmer, Heinrich. *Myths and Symbols in Indian Art and Civilization*. Princeton, 1946.

Index of Names and Terms

Subject Index

(Consult the preceding index for cross-references to names and Sanskrit terms.)

adultery, 105–8, 226–27, 245, 280, 316–17, 320–21
amazement, 41, 67, 108–9, 133–35, 168, 170, 181–87, 208–11, 213, 225, 230–31, 233–36, 264–65, 267, 279
analogy. See *upamāna*; metaphor; simile
animals, 19–23, 25, 32–33, 40–41, 85, 89, 147, 153–54, 207, 209–10, 215–16, 236, 291, 316. *See also* ant; bee; bird; cat; centaur; chicken; cow; crow; deer/doe; dog; donkey; elephant; fish; goose; horse; monkey; snake; swan; tiger; turtle/tortoise
ant, 91, 209, 232, 270
archetype, 21, 73–75, 184–86, 219, 221, 227, 238, 242, 304, 317
art, 4, 8, 62, 79, 101–2, 118, 195, 213, 233, 260–62, 279–96, 302, 304, 328. See also *māyā*
audience, 113–14, 127–31, 154, 180, 183–87, 200, 206, 229, 332
author. *See* narrative
authority, 9, 88, 140, 167, 172–77, 180, 192, 261, 278, 325

baldness, 21–22, 27–28, 34, 103, 154, 266
banality, 44, 48–49, 72, 167, 251, 263, 287–89
barren woman. *See* son: of barren woman
bee, 207–9, 216, 218, 220
beheading, 17, 19, 21, 34, 59, 78, 203, 221, 250, 256, 266, 271
bird, 19, 21, 33, 35, 66, 76, 89, 138, 203, 209, 226, 230, 250, 288, 294. *See also* crow; goose; swan
blindness, 34, 59, 78, 193, 266, 308. *See also* eyes
blood, 18–20, 32–34, 66–68, 133, 224, 226, 245–47
body, 15, 28–29, 55, 66, 88, 91, 103–6, 129, 139–40, 168, 172, 209, 226, 230, 272–73, 311 (*see also* dreams: somatic; mind); of God, 110–14, 120, 124, 212, 214, 251, 256, 296, 299
bootstraps, 88, 90, 195, 201, 280, 288–89. *See also* chicken-and-egg; circle; mutuality
Brahmin, 82, 91, 99, 106, 120, 134–40, 144, 146, 156–59, 165–67, 175, 192, 207, 209, 217, 231, 252, 272, 277, 330. *See also* Untouchable
bricolage, 16, 48, 212, 285–86
bridle, 38–39, 61, 194, 277, 327

cannibalism, 33, 40, 162, 164–65, 168, 228, 271. *See also* flesh-eating
cat, 147, 178, 189, 192, 239
centaur, 268, 276, 294
chance, 75, 165–66, 180, 207, 216, 218–19, 230, 234, 265–68, 290. *See also* coincidence; crow-and-palm-tree
chariot, 16, 19, 27, 31, 69, 93, 150–52, 181–82, 216, 271, 294
chicken-and-egg, 79, 121–22, 192, 252–53, 277. *See also* mutuality
children, 8, 11–12, 15, 53–60, 75, 109–14, 157, 163–65, 195–96, 205, 248, 251–52, 255, 261, 267, 274, 290, 293–94, 304
Christianity, 9, 12, 183, 189, 242
circle, 10, 58–59, 139, 192, 201, 203–5, 229, 241–44, 246–49, 261, 287. *See also* Möbius strip; mutuality
city, 19, 32, 39, 63, 65, 71, 115, 134–35, 150–52, 207, 213, 264, 268–79, 294
clock, 58, 311. *See also* time
cloud, 76–77, 153, 165, 210, 268–69, 275, 278–80, 294, 305, 311

Addenda to the Second Printing

Since this book first went to press, I have continued to think about dreams and to learn from responses to the book. These afterthoughts did not seem to me to call for a genuine revision of the book at this stage, but they may prove of interest to the readers of this printing. I have listed them below according to the pages to which they pertain.

p. 16 Several Upaniṣads refer to a "person inside the eye," an image that suggests that the soul or godhead is the dreamer who sees and is seen within the organ of our own sight.

p. 22 McKim Marriott has discussed "coded substance" in several works, one of which is listed in the bibliography.

p. 26–7 The ancient Indian textbooks on dreams tell you how to make sure that you will have an auspicious dream (that is, one that will have a good result) and how to fall asleep at the time of night when the right dream awaits you; but they do *not* tell you how to act directly to have the desired result; they do not tackle reality head-on.

p. 77 Sudhir Kakar has pointed out that while the *shared* dream is what interests Indian metaphysicians, the *sharing* of the dream is what is of primary interest to Western psychologists: "It is not only the sharing of the dream with the analyst in the therapeutic situation where the dream narrative is actually sought to be constructed and understood by their shared labors, but also in other situations. For instance, husbands and wives often tell each other their dreams in order to convey information about themselves or their relationship which they cannot do otherwise" (paper presented at the annual meeting of the American Academy of Religion in Chicago, a panel devoted to this book, December 1984).

p. 79 Sudhir Kakar sees this distinction between myth and dream as a factor that requires us to use some word other than "dream" to define the dream-stories in metaphysical texts such as the *Yogavāsiṣṭha*: "These dreams are not even invented dreams one is familiar with from literature and which stand midway between real dreams and imaginative creations. Invented dreams in literature can indeed be interpreted by paying very close attention to their context, to the dreamer's feelings and thoughts at waking and to the associations of the audience or the analyst (in place of the missing associations of the dreamer, as in analytical practice). All these techniques which succeed in interpreting dreams in literature, at least to the analyst's satisfaction, simply do not succeed with the Indian dreams. From the psychological viewpoint, they are not dreams but imaginative creations, conceits in the service of the metaphysical narrative, . . . in spite of their formal similarities to what we today call dreams" (*ibid.*).

p. 108 One modern retelling of the story of Viśvāmitra's double universe states that the buffalo that Viśvāmitra created in place of the cow gave better and more milk than the cow, and that all the other creatures in that second heaven were better, too; people from the original heaven left it to go to the new duplicate heaven, which so frightened the gods that they allowed Triśanku to enter the original heaven and cancelled the duplicate one (whose inhabitants were sent to the first heaven or, in the case of animals, to earth). (Recorded by Carmel Berkson at Ellora in 1984.)

p. 122 Borges lists the double among his imaginary beasts, and cites examples from Plato, Rossetti, Dostoyevski, Egyptian and Jewish mythology, Wilde (Dorian Gray), and Yeats, among others. The myth of Tristan and Isolde, particularly in the detailed version told by Gottfried von Strassburg, gives Isolde two sexual doubles, one of whom (the maid Brangene) masquerades as Isolde in the dark and sacrifices her own maidenhead, while the other (Isolde of the White Hands) unknowingly serves Tristan merely as the ghost of the true Isolde and fails to move Tristan to take her maidenhead.

p. 203 Borges cites a Moslem tradition about an imaginary beast named the Bahamut (Behemoth): "God made the earth, but the earth had no base and so under the earth he made an angel. But the angel had no base and so under the angel's feet he made a crag of ruby. But the crag had no base and so under the crag he made a bull endowed with four thousand eyes, ears, nostrils, mouths, tongues and feet. But the bull had no base and so under the bull he made a fish named Bahamut, and under the fish he put water, and under the water he put darkness, and beyond this men's knowledge does not reach" (*The Book of Imaginary Beasts*, p. 25). As Borges remarks, "The idea of the crag resting on the bull, and the bull on Bahamut, and Bahamut on anything else, seems to be an illustration of the cosmological proof of the existence of God. This proof argues that every cause requires a prior cause, and so, in order to avoid proceeding into infinity, a first cause is necessary" (*ibid.*, p. 26). As we shall see in chapter 5, a related proof of the existence of God results when the imaginary beast bites its own tail. Another instance of this mechanism appears in Thornton Wilder's *Our Town*, when Emily imagines that her address is Grover's Corners, Vermont, . . . the Solar System, the Universe, the Mind of God.

p. 240 The ambivalence of the dreamer within his dream, the author within his narrative, is often perceived as a conflict between omnipotence and impotence. The dreamer is all the personae, the time and space, the one who designs and controls all the action and gives the actors their lines. This apparent omnipotence makes the dreamer feel like a god and may be one of the sources of the belief that God is a dreamer or the mystic's assertion that only when dreaming do you recognize your oneness with God. But sometimes the actors take over and do not say the lines that the dreamer has written for them; the dreamer loses control inside the dream and may indeed experience the nightmare of complete helplessness (he tries to run but his legs will not move). In fact, only after the dreamer awakens does he realize that he was omnipotent throughout the dream, that, in fact, he was the only one there; for during the dream he thought that there were other people there. If we translate this pattern into the metaphysical terms of the Indian texts, only after waking up (enlightenment) does the individual realize that all the people in his life were no one but God, or that he himself created his life and told himself the story of all the people in it. This is why the author/dreamer/god becomes helplessly entangled in his own projected images.

p. 244 As for the role of God as audience, as well as narrator, Swami Muktananda aptly remarks, "Most of the scriptures were narrated by God to His devotees, but the *Yoga Vāsiṣṭha* was narrated to God Himself. It is the teaching of the sage Vasiṣṭha imparted to Lord Rāma" (Preface to the Swami Venkatesan translation of the *Yoga Vāsiṣṭha*).

p. 245 Clytemnestra and Orestes do not share precisely the same dream of the suckling serpent, for she dreams that *he* is a serpent (which he confirms), but he refers to *her* as a deadly viper who threatens the lives of the eagle's children, himself and his sister (*Libation Bearers* 247 and 994–96). Moreover, Clytemnestra's dream that she gave birth to and suckled her serpent child is contradicted first by the testimony of the nurse, who says that *she* nursed Orestes (who, instead of drawing blood from her, peed on her; *Libation Bearers* 750–59), and then by the testimony of Apollo, who argues that the woman does not, in fact, give birth to the child, but merely harbors the father's seed and then nurses the child (*Eumenides* 658–67). Thus Clytemnestra did not give birth to or suckle the serpent, but the predictive aspect of the dream is true: the serpent son does kill her.

p. 262 A basic Indian myth of a serpent that is transformed into a rope is the myth of the churning of the ocean of milk, in which the serpent Vāsuki serves as the rope of the churn, while the inverted mountain Mandara serves as the churning stick. In this cosmic image, the ouroboros encircles the upside-down mountain that is both the center and the periphery, and the ouroboros becomes a rope. (*M* 1.15–17; O'Flaherty, *Hindu Myths*, pp. 273–80)

p. 263 It is worth noting that when Aaron's rod becomes a serpent, it then swallows up the serpents made from the rods of Pharaoh's magicians. Here is another example of the receding frames of reference and of the ouroboros, one serpent swallowing another.

pp. 294–95 The foolishness of people who mistake clouds for other things is a persistent theme in Shakespeare's plays. Antony says,

> Sometimes we see a cloud that's dragonish;
> A vapour sometime like a bear or lion,
> A tower'd citadel, a pendant rock,
> A forked mountain, or blue promontory
> With trees upon 't. . . (*Antony and Cleopatra* (IV.14.)

And Hamlet teases Polonius:

> *Ham.* Do you see yonder cloud that's almost in shape of a camel?
> *Pol.* By the mass, and 'tis like a camel, indeed.
> *Ham.* Methinks it is like a weasel.
> *Pol.* It is backed like a weasel.
> *Ham.* Or like a whale?
> *Pol.* Very like a whale. (*Hamlet* III.2.)

Alexander Pope mocks this theme in his "Hymn to Man":

> Lo the poor Indian, whose untutored mind
> Sees God in the clouds, and hears him in the wind.

p. 340 Only now have I come across two fine articles by A. Syrkin on the symbolism of dreams in ancient India, one in *Semiotics Unfolding*, vol. 1 (Berlin, 1984), pp. 625–29, and one in *Semantische Hefte IV* (Heidelberg, 1979–80), pp. 167–96. He cites a rich bibliography in both Sanskrit and European languages, among which the more recent items are E. Abegg, "Indische Traumtheorie und Traumdeutung," *Asiatische Studien* 12 (1959): 5–34, and J. Filliozat, "Le sommeil et les rêves selon les médecins indiens et les physiologues grecs," in *Laghu Prabandhāh* (Leiden, 1974), pp. 212–32. He also calls attention to the theme of the dream within the dream in M. Lermontov's "Dream" (which V. S. Soloviev called "a dream in cube").